Once They Heard the Cheers

Books by W. C. Heinz

Once They Heard the Cheers
Emergency
Run to Daylight!
(WITH VINCE LOMBARDI)
The Surgeon
The Fireside Book of Boxing
(EDITOR)
The Professional

Once They Heard the Cheers

W. C. HEINZ

DOUBLEDAY & COMPANY, INC.
GARDEN CITY, NEW YORK
1979

ISBN: 0-385-12609-3
Library of Congress Catalog Card Number 78–20076

To
those who did the living and the telling

An Acknowledgment

In sports the scene changes quickly, about once every ten years. As each new generation shoulders its way in, occasioning its own clamor and claims to greatness, a writer experiences a hesitancy to attempt to intrude with his own memories of the people who moved him and stay with him still from a time now gone.

Certainly it had never occurred to this one to do so until a day three years ago when Dr. H. Richard Hornberger, known as Richard Hooker to readers of his novel *MASH* and, as they say in medicine, its *sequelae,* made the suggestion to Sam Vaughan, publisher at Doubleday. Thus, in addition to the debt I owe to those about whom I have written and to whom this effort is dedicated, my appreciation goes to Dick Hornberger and Sam Vaughan as starters, to Jim Owers for early assistance, and especially to Hugh O'Neill who, with the energy and enthusiasm of youth, weighed every move in the manuscript and, more often than I like to admit, caught me punching off the wrong foot. It also goes to my wife for whom, over the years, many of these have been more than twice-told tales but who, having to live with them again during the building of this book, did so with characteristic understanding and patience.

Contents

Let us, while waiting for new monuments, preserve the ancient monuments.

Victor Hugo, *Notre Dame de Paris*.

Once They
Heard the Cheers

Transition
(Autumn 1945)

Those were the good years, right after the war. I mean that if you got out of it alive and all in one piece, and if you did not lose anyone close to you, and if you had done honest work during that time, no matter what it was or where it was, you knew that the next years, after all that had happened, had to be the good ones, as long as your luck held out.

It was early in the fall after the war ended, and I was standing in the sports department by Wilbur Wood's desk. Wilbur Wood was the sports editor of the paper, and before that he had been its boxing writer. He was rather large-boned and balding, and because at some time his nose had been hit he looked tough, but he was a soft and sentimental man. During the war he used to write me V-mail letters, giving me the gossip of the office and recounting something that he had found memorable or amusing in sports. Once he described a block that Doc Blanchard, the Army fullback, had thrown in the Yankee Stadium on Tree Adams, a 6-foot, 7-inch Notre Dame tackle. I can still see it the way Wilbur described it in the letter—which I got after we had crossed the border into Germany—with Adams going up in the air and turning a somersault and landing on his head. In all his letters Wilbur said he liked what I was writing, and several times he added that he guessed now he would never be able to get me into sports.

I had been wanting to get into sports since I had been in high school, and trying, with time out for the war, for the eight years I had been on the paper. In high school I weighed 118 pounds, and my heroes were the football players, the ones who 10,000 came out to see in a big game, filling the concrete stands and, across the field, the wooden bleachers, and lining the sidelines. Several of them were six feet tall, or more, and must have weighed 180 or 190 pounds, and I felt that I was fortunate when I was in the same class with one or another of them.

I would sit near the back of the room, so that I could watch them in their letter sweaters lolling behind the desks, their legs out into the aisle. They made their desks seem small, and the books seemed small in their hands, and at the end of the class, when we all stood up and walked out, they towered not only above the rest of us but above the teacher. They seemed to me to be men, and as we all walked out of the class I felt that they could walk right out of the school and be men out there in the world too.

Many years later, when I came to live in training camp and travel with the New York Football Giants and then the Green Bay Packers in their great years, they still seemed big to me, those heroes of my youth. Remembering them, in a Giant or a Packer dressing room, I still had to tell myself that Tommy Mallon and Eddie Williams and Ernie Jansen had been only teen-agers, really, and that they were never such superb football players as Andy Robustelli or Alex Webster or Frank Gifford, with the Giants, or Bart Starr, Paul Hornung, Jimmy Taylor, Forrest Gregg, Jerry Kramer, or Willie Davis of the Packers.

That was how bad I had it in high school, when I was too frail for football and afraid of a baseball thrown near the head and had been a reluctant starter and worse finisher in street fights. Once, when we were both eight years old, they put the shoemaker's son and me together in the school playground with gloves on us, and he punched me around for three one-minute rounds.

"You know," I said, a long time after that, to Sugar Ray Robinson, the greatest fighter I ever saw, "you and I fought the same guy. When we were little kids he punched my head off in a playground fight."

"Who was that?" Robinson said.

"Vic Troisi," I said.

"Vic Troisi?" Robinson said. "Did I fight him?"

"Yes," I said, "you fought him in the Eastern Parkway, and knocked him out in the first round."

"Is that so?" Robinson said.

It was the same with Frank Boucher, another hero of my youth, when he centered a great forward line of the New York Rangers, with the Cook brothers, Bill at right wing and Bun on the left, and they won the Stanley Cup twice. The year after the war ended, Boucher was coaching the Rangers, and he and I got on the subway at the Garden to ride out to Brooklyn, where the team was to practice, and I told him about a remembered youthful embarrassment that I still carried with me after thirteen years.

"In high school," I said, as we sat together on the subway, "I played on the hockey team. We were a terrible team. We won one game and tied one in two years, and one night we played between the periods of a Bronx Tigers game in the Bronx Coliseum. You were refereeing, and in one scramble after a face-off I knocked you down."

Turned toward him, I was watching Boucher's face. I was waiting for some sign of recollection to invade it, to start with a quickening in the eyes and then around them, but nothing was happening.

"When I knocked you down," I said, "the crowd roared, and I wanted to melt into the ice, because I was so ashamed that I had knocked Frank Boucher down, and people were laughing. Do you remember me knocking you down?"

"No," Boucher said, smiling now but shaking his head. "In fact, I don't even remember refereeing that game."

There was no way I could ever be one of them—first the football heroes of high school and then, as I projected myself into manhood, those paragons of the professional sports. When I read the sports pages, though, I discovered that the sportswriters rode on the same trains and lived in the same hotels with the ballplayers and visited the training camps of the prize fighters and knew them man to man. Now the sportswriters acquired an eminence of their own by association with those whom, if my mother had known anything about sports, she would have referred to as "the higher ups." If you were a German-American family that had survived World War I in this country, when they called sauerkraut "Liberty Cabbage" and changed the name of Wittenberg Place in the Bronx to Bradley Avenue, and if you were not of that arrogant type that had always made trouble for themselves and the world, then you were so humble that all you hoped for your offspring was that he would get a steady job on which he would come to know those who hired and fired.

"He has a very good job," my mother said once, after I had started on the paper and she was telling me about one of my former high school classmates. "He works for the telephone company."

"What does he do?" I asked, wondering if he climbed poles or sat in an office half the size of a gymnasium with half a hundred others, all of them at desks, all of them poring over open ledgers.

"I don't know," she said, "but he's getting to know the higher-ups."

They do not run newspapers the way they run ball clubs, though, because there is a paternalism that contravenes their professionalism. There is no place to trade off old baseball writers who can no longer go into the hole or get the bat around in time to meet the fast ball, and so they go on beyond their best days, while their replacements wait in vain to get into the lineup. For two years after college I ran copy, and when I was twenty-four they were still calling me "Boy." For the next four years, before they sent me to report the war, I covered and wrote almost everything from push-cart fires on the Lower East Side to political campaigns, but when I came back from the war I figured I finally had the leverage to get into sports.

We were in Weimar, the birthplace of the Republic that had failed, and it must have been about seven o'clock when I was awakened that morning by a rooster crowing. They had us in two small hotels, and the sun was coming into the room, bright on the flowered rug, and I lay in bed and looked out the open window into the May morning. I could see tree tops, the new leaves yellow-green and clean, and through them house tops. I could hear Germans talking and working in the yard below, and I lay in the soft bed between the clean sheets and for the first time in a long time I was empty of fear. On the morning that peace came again to Europe I lay in that bed and it came to me that all of the rest of my life, for however long it would go on, would derive from this morning.

Some years later I asked the oldest son of a Massachusetts shoe worker what it had been like for him when he had awakened in that hotel room in Philadelphia on what must have been his own great and beginning morning. The night before, in the thirteenth round of one of the most vicious of heavyweight title fights, Rocky Marciano had knocked out Jersey Joe Walcott with a single right hand.

"You know how it is when you wake up in a strange place and you don't know where you are?" Marciano said. "I thought to myself, 'Something nice happened to me.' Then I remembered, 'That's right. Last night I won the heavyweight championship of the world.'"

We had the best duty in the war, those of us who by the accidents of age and occupation were picked to report it. The Army provided our transportation and our keep, and we who otherwise might have been carrying rifles and sleeping in foxholes, carried typewriters and slept under roofs even as we pursued our profession. We saluted no one physically, and figuratively only those we felt deserved it. We never had that responsibility that came down from generals to noncoms of sending others where they knew some of them would be killed and others maimed, and so we would never have to live with that for the rest of our lives. Our only responsibility was to order ourselves to go where we could see it, and then to try to tell it as it really was, as those who were being killed and maimed would have wanted to tell it if they could, and not as some of the big-name writers wrote it, or told it on lecture tours, after they came back from junkets on which they were briefed at any Army headquarters or maybe even at some Division command post.

"It was a marvelous speech," Harry Markson was telling me some months after I came back. "You should have heard it."

We had had lunch at Lindy's and were walking west on 50th Street back to Madison Square Garden. Harry was doing publicity then for Mike Jacobs when Jacobs was running boxing in this country, and later Harry would run the boxing at the Garden.

"You know he was a big Roosevelt man," Harry was saying, talking about the writer, "and this was at a Democratic fund-raising luncheon at the Waldorf. I'll never forget it because at one point he said, 'And when your son, your brother, or your husband lands on that foreign beach under fire, and when he finally finds a moment of respite from the shelling and the horror and opens his K-ration, do you know what he finds therein? Among the other things, he finds four cigarettes. Now someone must have thought of those cigarettes. Could it have been F.D.R.?' "

What I said I don't want in this book, and then I said, "If he'd ever landed on a beach or made an attack and opened a K-ration during his moment of respite, he'd have found that the cigarettes were Avalons or Wings, and he wouldn't have mentioned them."

You see, if they didn't get the cigarettes right they weren't going to get any of it really right for the sons and the brothers and the husbands, and for all those who also served by waiting. We despised them while they were doing it, and there was one of us, who tended to be irascible anyway, who became absolutely irate one night when he read in a letter from his wife that she had spent $3.00 to listen to a lecture by one of them who had been with us for five days, and that she had found what he had said fascinating. After it was over though, and I was introduced to the cigarette shill, he was so impressed by a magazine piece I had written about Rocky Graziano and so humble and obviously ashamed of all his own work that, reasoning that it was too late to do any good, anyway, I found that I didn't have the heart to level on him.

So we knew what the cigarettes were in the same breakfast issue with the insipid port-and-egg-yolk, and we learned the mechanics of how war was made on the ground, how attacks were mounted, and how men behaved under stress and great danger—and what they did and how they did it and why. We learned early, of course, the rules of self-preservation, how to analyze a situation map in order to decide where to go and where not to go, and our ears became attuned to the sounds of shelling, the difference between the incoming and the outgoing, so that we were not constantly cowering. When, in late afternoon we would come back from the front on a day when we had really been out, and not just covering something from the perimeter around regiment or battalion, we would be joyous in the jeep, sometimes even singing, so exalted were we to be still alive.

"What's the matter with you?" John Groth said to me one evening. He had come into my room where I had been trying for more than an hour to write my piece about what I had seen that day. He was doing his drawing and his water colors then for the Marshall Field publications, and two years later I would take him into Stillman's Gym for the first time and then introduce him to the baseball and thoroughbred-racing people, and he would do those fine things he did on sports.

"The matter?" I said.

"You look terrible," he said. "What's going on?"

"I'm coming apart," I said.

It was late September, and we were inside Germany now. That day several of us had gone up to the Ninth Infantry Division, and a captain named Lindsey Nelson had taken us up to a battalion command post in the Huertgen Forest. Nineteen years later I was driving north out of Manhattan one night, and when I got on the Major Deegan Expressway in the Bronx, I could see, across the Harlem River, the lights of the Polo Grounds. That was after the Giants had gone to San Francisco and the Mets had moved in, and I turned on the car radio and I heard Lindsey doing the game.

There were two hundred square miles of it in the Huertgen, the fir trees sixty feet tall and planted ten feet apart in absolutely straight rows. It was a picture forest, and there in the cool, soft, and shaded dampness, in a place that had once known the cathedral quiet that is a forest's own, they were dying between the trees and among the ferns.

"I don't think I can do it any more," I said to John.

"You have to," he said.

"Day after day," I said, "I see those kids going out and sacrificing themselves. They haven't even had a chance to live yet. They're eighteen and nineteen and twenty, and they're giving their lives, and what am I doing for them? They deserve the best writers we have, and except for Hemingway, they're not here."

John had just come back from living for several days with Hemingway in a house he had taken over in the Siegfried Line.

They had become friends, and later John would illustrate the Living Library edition of *Men Without Women*.

"I try," I said, "but it isn't any good."

"You can't write *War and Peace* every night," John said. "Nobody can."

"I'm not trying to," I said. "I'm just trying to get it right, but I can get so little of it in."

"Just do the best you can for today," John said, "and tomorrow try again."

"And then every afternoon," I said, "we wave them a hearty farewell, and we leave them up there. We run around with our little notebooks and pencils making a living, and then come back here and leave them to die up there."

"Gee," John said, "you've got it bad. I don't know."

"I don't know, either," I said. "The whole thing is wrong."

"I mean I don't know about you," John said. "You'd better pull yourself together. You know what's going to happen to you if you don't pull yourself together?"

"Who knows?" I said.

"I know," John said. "They'll come around and wrap you up and send you home."

"I'm no psycho," I said.

"You will be if you don't pull yourself together," John said. "You want to be sent home? Then you better stop this. You better just write your piece for today and say to yourself, 'That's that for today and there's another day tomorrow.'"

"There isn't for a lot of them," I said.

"You've got to do that," John said. "You really have to do that."

We talked for another half hour or so, and then John left, telling me again to just take it one day at a time, and I finished my piece, such as it was. It was about how the Germans had all the main roads, and all the crossroads in the forest zeroed in for their artillery, and about how they had the pillboxes hidden among the trees and about the land mines that would explode at knee height and take a man's legs and his masculinity and about the almost invisible trip wires they had strung from tree to tree so that, when they were touched, they would set off a whole chain of explosives.

When I finished I took the piece across the street to where the censors were set up, and I handed it to one of them and I came back and went to bed. I was fortunate that night because there was no way I could have known then that it would take more than three months to get the Germans out of what remained of that forest, and that five infantry divisions and parts of four others would be chewed up and we would suffer 33,000 casualties in there. I was fortunate, too, that I had John Groth for a friend and that he scared me about being sent home, and I lay in bed that night thinking about that and about how odd it was that he should be fathering me because we were always fathering John.

John was the most impressionable of all of us, and he saw everything through the wide, unspoiled eyes of a child. He knew little about the martial art, about troop dispositions or unit actions, and when, now and then, the others of us would get into an argument about where we were going, John would never put in but just come along.

"Wherever you guys are going," he'd say, "it's all right with me."

When we got up to where we were going, and the rest of us were trying to cover our ignorance with professional poses, the way insecure outsiders do when they want to seem to belong, John would ask the simple civilian questions that were the best, but that gave the impression that he had no idea of what was going on.

"But I don't understand," John would ask some major or captain who was filling us in. "Why are you fellows going to do that?"

It was the same two years later, when I took him to Stillman's gym the first time. After I introduced him to Lou Stillman, I left him standing behind the two rings on the main floor while I went back to the dressing rooms to interview some fighter, probably one who would be fighting in the Garden that Friday night. When I came back out a half hour or so later, John was still standing there and sketching, with the fighters shadow boxing around him and sparring in the raised rings above him.

"How are you doing?" I said.

"I don't know," he said, showing me his notebook and riffling through the pages.

"Hold it a second," I said. "Go back a couple of pages. There. That's Rocky Graziano's right leg, isn't it?"

Graziano toed in with his right foot, and his right leg was slightly bowed. I always figured that that was one of the reasons he was such a great right-hand puncher, and now, with a few quickly scrawled lines on a notebook page, John had captured with absolute definition the one leg that was distinctively different from all the other legs in that gym.

"Who's Graziano?" John said.

"He's the leading contender for the middleweight title," I said. "He's the hottest fighter in years."

"Gee," John. "He is?"

"Yes," I said, "and he's the reason most of this crowd is here in those chairs and up in the balcony."

"Oh," John said, and then pointing, "it's that fella over there."

"Right," I said. "That's Rocky Graziano."

The next week, when I stopped off at the gym again, Lou Stillman spotted me as I came in. He hollered at me and motioned for me to come over to where he was sitting on the high stool under the time clock and from where he ran the traffic in and out of the two rings.

"Listen," he said, growling at me in what someone once described in print as that ash-can voice, which Lou resented. "You know that beard you brought in here last week?"

"John Groth?" I said.

"Yeah," Lou said. "You know what he done? Two days later he come in here with a whole gang of beards."

"He teaches at the Art Students' League," I said.

"Up on my balcony there's a whole gang of beards, all of them drawin'," Lou said. "What are they tryin' to turn this place into, anyway?"

"I don't know," I said. "Ask them."

"You ask them," Lou said. "I ain't got time to bother with them."

The next time I saw John, I told him what Stillman had said. I told him that Stillman had all the fighters cowed, which was the way he kept order in the gym full of them, and I said that some of that carried over to the way he talked to everyone.

"Oh, we get along fine," John said. "You know what Stillman

does at home on Sundays? He paints in oil, and we talk about that."

"There are some fighters I know," I said, "who won't believe it."

Lying in that bed, though, that night after John had fathered me, I remembered the time he showed up without his bedroll and slept in my trenchcoat. I remembered the time I had found him in a barn behind a chateau in France, drawing in ink with a goose quill. The dampness had affected his drawing paper, so that he couldn't get the lines he wanted with his pens, and he had run down a goose and plucked a couple of quills and sharpened them with a penknife.

"Now I can draw thin lines, thick lines, any kind of lines I want," he said, "but with everything that's going on over here, I don't get enough chance to draw the lines."

There was the time, too, when he was worried that he was going to lose his accreditation because he was supposed to be back at Army Group instead of up with us. Then I remembered the day he was so obviously depressed that I asked him what was wrong, and he showed me the letter he had just received from a friend back home in New York.

"I play volleyball for the Grand Central 'Y,'" John said, "and this guy is on the team, too. He writes here, see, that they got into the semifinals of the Nationals at Kansas City, and look at this."

With his index finger he pointed out the sentence ending one paragraph: "Al Burwinkle says that if you had been with us we would have won the national championship."

"He's got to be kidding," I said.

"No he's not," John said. "Al Burwinkle is our captain, and if he says we could have won it if I was there, we could have won it."

"Those guys must be on another planet," I said. "They're playing volleyball in Kansas City and you're covering a war in Germany, and they're blaming you because they lost?"

"That's what Al Burwinkle said," John said, and he walked away still depressed.

So each day after the night John scared me about being sent home, I would tell myself that I would just try to do the best I could for that day, and then hope I could get more of it in, and right, the next day. I always lived, though, as most of us did, with that suppressed guilt about the way it was at the front and the way we had it, and with that growing personal fear. Man is born with the illusion that he is immortal, and as every good writer who has gone into man's reactions in war has written, he goes under fire the first time shielded by that illusion and believing that others will be killed but that it will not happen to him. Then it happens, not to him, but so close to him that it could have been to him, and that is the beginning of the fear.

"A good soldier does not worry," Hemingway wrote in his introduction to *Men at War,* the anthology he edited. "He knows that nothing happens until it actually happens, and you live your life up until then. Danger only exists at the moment of danger. To live properly in war, the individual eliminates all such things as potential danger. Then a thing is only bad when it is bad. It is neither bad before nor after. Cowardice, as distinguished from panic, is almost always simply a lack of ability to suspend the functioning of the imagination. Learning to suspend your imagination and live completely in the very second of the present minute with no before and no after is the greatest gift a soldier can acquire. It, naturally, is the opposite of all those gifts a writer should have."

That was the problem we had, we who were not soldiers but writers, we who were not ordered by others but had to order ourselves. Each day, two or three to a jeep and with a G.I. driver from the motor pool, we would go up toward the front and stop off at Corps to be briefed on what the divisions were doing, and then we would split up by jeeps and go to one division or another. At Division they would fill us in about what the regiments were doing, and at Regiment what the battalions were doing. Then we would go up to a battalion and sometimes to a company or a platoon until we got what we thought were our stories.

At first, and functioning behind that illusion of immortality, we all bore ourselves as if we were brave, but then, depending upon what happened around us, and to us, and upon our separate abilities to suspend our imaginations, we all came to live in fear. Then it became more difficult to go beyond battalion, and we went less often, and there wasn't a one of us who lived through it who could honestly say to himself that he had covered the war the way he should have. Two I knew, who had been in it too long and whose pieces had become irrational, were called home, and I heard later that, months after it was over, one of them was still walking around New York in uniform and carrying his musette bag. Then, when the Germans broke through during The Bulge, scattering our troops and us in panic, several of us, including the one who had been so irate about his wife buying that lecture by the Five Day Wonder, took off for Paris and London, and the rest understood. When their replacements arrived, we watched them sally forth behind the shields of their own illusions, as we once had, and then always that thing happened, whatever it was, near them and thus to them, and they too became, like us, cautious in their fear.

The soldier fights the enemy and his fear, and exercises that fear, if it is not so big that he can't handle it, against the person of the enemy. For the writer, implanted weaponless in war, his two personal enemies are his guilt and his fear, and after a while it was only our guilt that sent us out against our fear. We did whatever we did because, knowing what those we left at the front were doing, we were ashamed not to, and if we were honest with ourselves, we knew that all we were doing was trying not just to go on living, but to go on living with ourselves.

If ever there is a time to die in a war, it is not after the issue has been decided. That time came after the bridge across the Rhine was captured at Remagen, and we broke out of the bridgehead on the east bank, and one day, five years later, I was sitting in the Yankee dugout at the Stadium watching batting practice, and talking with Ralph Houk. This was when Houk was a second-string catcher with the Yankees and, of course, before he managed them and later the Detroit Tigers, and I knew what he had done in the war. Among other things, during the Bulge he had taken a night patrol in to Bastogne while the Germans had it surrounded, and he had brought out the plans for the defense of the town. During the last week of the 1949 baseball season, though, with the Yankees and the Red Sox wrestling for the pennant in a game at the Stadium, Johnny Pesky had slid home under Houk's tag with the winning run. The next day, all of the New York newspapers, and I suppose the Boston papers as well, carried a photo sequence of the play intended to let the reader make up his own mind as to whether Pesky had been safe or out, and now a lot of people finally knew Houk's name because an umpire had said he had missed a tag in a game.

"You remember Remagen?" Houk was saying in the dugout. We had been talking about the war that had just started in Korea, and Houk had said that he couldn't tell much about it from what he read in the paper, and that got him onto our war.

"Remagen?" I said. "Sure I remember it."

"You remember," Houk said, "how, in the town, there was one road that turned right along the river?"

"I know where you mean," I said. "One day I came back across the river and I was driving along our side, and somebody was working south along the other side. You know the river's nowhere near as wide there as the Hudson, and I could see and hear a fire-fight going on over there in the trees just south of the bridge."

"You saw that?" Houk said, looking right at me.

"Yes."

"That was me," Houk said. "We had a hell of a fire-fight there. I'll be damned."

"So will I," I said, sitting there and watching Joe DiMaggio, Yogi Berra, Phil Rizzuto, Hank Bauer, and the others taking their batting practice.

Once they broke out of that bridgehead, though, and the tanks started east, the infantry rode on the tanks or in trucks for miles before they had to dismount, cursing, to clear out the scattered pockets of resistance. Now it was obvious that the Germans were finally beaten, and now the dying seemed sadder than ever. In the residential suburbs of Halle, the birthplace of Handel, they fell among the fallen petals of magnolias, when there was no longer any reason for it. Now the fear, supressed for so long, of not surviving swept the troops themselves, whole units, and we were all of us one as the time wore down slowly to that new morning.

As I lay in that bed now, on that morning, free again at last, I heard the voices of the Germans in the yard below rising and, although I had no idea what they were saying, I could tell that they were arguing, women's voices among men's. Then the voices of two men began to dominate, as if they had singled out each other, and I thought that maybe this would turn into a fist fight, and I would enjoy seeing Germans fighting among themselves. When I got up and looked down, though, I couldn't see them through the leaves and branches of the trees, and even as I tried to make them out, the intervals between the verbal exchanges became longer and the two voices less assertive, so I went across the hall and washed and shaved. When I came back there were no sounds at all in the yard below, and I dressed and went downstairs and walked, in the cool, clear morning, around the corner to the other hotel where they fed us. We sat there, eating and then smoking with our coffee, and we were all of us loose and lazy and dull, like men who have slept themselves out for the first time in a long while.

Several of us walked back to our hotel together. We got a jeep and a driver from the motor pool, and we drove out of Weimar into the Thuringian countryside. The lilacs were blooming in the farmyards, and under the yellow of the morning sun the apple trees were white and pink along the sides of the roads. In the rich brown fields the Germans were walking along the furrows, sowing their grain, and we went out to get a story of V-E Day in Germany because it would be the last story and it was a way to end a job.

We drove for almost an hour, following our map and looking for the Third Armored Division, until we saw the tanks in a field on the left. There were four or five divisions that we had come to know well and for whom we had the highest admiration. The Third Armored was one, and so we had decided that we would end the war with them—or what was left of them.

There were seventeen of the tanks parked in the field on the left and along the partial cover of a long gray barn. Across the road on the right the land rose, and on the flat of the rise and forming a quadrangle there were some low, brown wooden barracks of what had been a Nazi youth camp. We could see the tankers walking about and lolling in the sun on the plot of winter-browned grass in the middle of the quadrangle, so we drove up the rise and into the quadrangle.

The lieutenant was the eighth commanding officer the company had had in ten months of fighting, which will give you an idea of what they had been through, and he had the Silver Star and the

Bronze Star and the Purple Heart with cluster. His name was Thomas Cooper and he was from Henderson, Kentucky, and we asked him how I Company of the First Battalion of the Thirty-third Regiment of the Third Amored Division had heard the news of the German surrender.

"I got a telephone call from Battalion headquarters at 9:10 last night," he said. "I told the first sergeant. He had an old nickle-plated horn from a Kraut car, and he went to the door and blew the horn a couple of times. Then he hollered, 'The war is over. The war is over, you guys. It's official now.' "

"Then what happened?" one of us said.

"Nothing much," the lieutenant said. "We knew for a long time it was gonna be over."

Some of the kids from the company were standing around us as we talked with the lieutenant. Out of the eighty-five who had started out with the I Company in Normandy, there were only six originals left on the day that peace came, and one of the best was a staff sergeant named Juan Haines from Gatesville, Texas.

"This tank of yours," I said to Haines. "What's its name?"

At the beginning, almost all of them gave their tanks names. I wanted to find out if the soldier who went through the war with a tank had any affection for it, if he felt anything about his tank on the day the war ended.

"I don't rightly know," Haines said. "This is the fourth tank we had. We lost three."

"When did your tank fire its last shot?" another of us asked, trying to establish when the war in Europe had really ended for the sergeant and the others in his tank.

"I'll have to think," Haines said.

He was tall and thin and with reddish hair. He stood looking at the ground at his feet.

"It was on the outskirts of Dessau a week or so ago," he said.

"It was April 22," one of the other kids, listening said. "We were firing on a pillbox."

"Was the pillbox built against a building," I asked him, "or was it out in the open?"

"It was out in the open," the kid said, "covering a field."

"Did you get the pillbox?"

"Hell, we got 'em all," one of the other kids said.

We turned back to the lieutenant. He had been standing and listening, a little bored by our questions.

"What will you people do now?" I said. "After all, it's V-E Day, and are you going to do anything special?"

"Well," the lieutenant said, "at noon we're going to drink a toast to General Eisenhower. He sent the division champagne after we crossed the Rhine, and there's enough for one glass for each man."

"Then what?"

"We have a ball game on this afternoon," the lieutenant said, "and there's some German museum near here, and one of the platoons will visit that."

We walked around with the lieutenant for a while, looking in at the kids in the barracks. Most of them were lying on their bunks in the barracks, brown uniforms on the brown Army blankets, reading or writing letters, and when we stopped to talk with them they wanted to know if we knew where they were going next, and if they could get home soon. It was strange, having them ask us the questions, and there was one who wanted me to put his lieutenant's name in the paper. He said his lieutenant's name was Loren Cantrell and that the lieutenant came from Springfield, Illinois, and that the kids under him wanted to get him a citation.

We got back into the jeep, and as we started to drive out of the quadrangle we could hear a guitar being played, and we could hear the voice of a G.I. singing. The G.I. was singing that song they retitled, "Those Eighty-eights Are Breaking up that Old Gang of Mine."

They had been a great outfit, the Third Armored, and suddenly in one day they weren't anything that was important any more. Riding along, I thought about how great they had been at Mons where, with the First Infantry Division, "The Big Red One" that had been in it since Africa, they cut off the Germans trying to get back to the Siegfried Line and killed nobody knew how many and took 8,000 prisoners, including three generals. On the day we crossed the German border with them and they took Roetgen, they were the first to capture a German town since Napoleon, and when they breached the Siegfried Line and were pinned down by the shelling on a hillside outside of Stolberg, their general came up, erect, immaculate and handsome, and got them out of their holes and up the hill.

I remembered them, with their tanks painted white, in the snow and fog of the Ardennes, and then driving across the brown-gray Cologne plain in the mist and the rain and then taking the city, fighting around the cathedral and knocking out a German tank at the cathedral steps. After they broke out of the bridgehead across the Rhine, I was with them the day they went more than ninety miles behind the German lines. It was the longest single combat advance in the world's military history, and the next evening, in the dusk and on a dirt road outside of Paderborn, their general was killed.

"It can't be him," the young lieutenant said. "I'm sure it ain't him."

"They've identified the body," the major said.

"I sure hope it ain't him," the lieutenant said.

We had spent the night where they had coiled the tanks and halftracks in a field next to a woods. It was eight o'clock in the morning, and I was standing, talking with some tankers around a fire, when the major called me over and the colonel told us that they had found the general's body. We got our typewriters out of the jeeps and we walked over to a fieldstone farmhouse and we wrote our pieces. I wrote about what the young lieutenant said, and why at first he couldn't believe it, and about the risks the general had always taken and how, two nights before, he had called us over to his CP to tell us that at six o'clock the next morning we would be starting that drive to the north that took us that more than ninety miles.

"This thing is almost over now," one of us had said. "When it is, what are you going to do?"

"I have a son," the general had said. "He's four years old now, and I don't know him. We're going to get acquainted, and that's going to take a lot of time."

Now, in the stone farmhouse, we finished our pieces about the death of the general, and they gave us an armed jeep to escort us back around the pockets of Germans who were still holding out. In places on the way back we left the roads and drove across fields and over low hills, following the tracks the tanks and the halftracks had made, and when we got to Marburg we found the press camp set up in a big private mansion on a hill. We turned our pieces in to the censors, and then gave the rest of them the word that Major General Maurice Rose was dead.

"He was a Jew, wasn't he?" one of them asked me.

"A Jew?" I said. "How would I know? All I know is that he was a great general, and he's dead."

We learned later that he was the son of a Denver rabbi, and that a congressman from Colorado—so far from it all—had stood up in the House of Representatives and made an impassioned speech calling for a Congressional investigation into the general's death. To me he was a great general, as two years later, when Jackie Robinson came up to the major leagues, he was a great ballplayer. It should have been as simple as that, and after the general was killed, the Third Armored linked up with the Second Armored, coming down from the north, and they sealed off the Ruhr pocket with 374,000 German prisoners inside.

So we left them now to have their one drink of warm champagne in their tin cups and to their ball game and the visit to the museum, and we drove back between the same brown fields, with the Germans still working in them, and through the same little towns we had passed through coming out. In all of the towns there were duck ponds, and there were white ducks and geese and small yellow goslings paddling around in them. There were young German women wheeling their babies in the sun, and there were other women and children waiting patiently near the doorsteps of their small stone and stuccoed houses. They were waiting for the American trucks to come through, loaded with the German soldiers on the way back to the prison cages.

In one town we stopped to let the trucks go by. The American trucks came through the town quickly, fast and high and with the dust rising around them and behind them, and with the grinding of their gearing and the noise of their exhaust loud in the tight aisle of the road lined by the small closely packed houses. Ahead of the convoy the women and children had spread, jumping into their doorways as the trucks passed through at high speed, each truck, after the first, fifteen feet behind the one ahead.

In the open trucks the prisoners stood tightly, seventy packed into each half-ton truck. They stood facing the rear, their gray-green uniforms dirty and dust-covered, all of them rocking together with the motion of the trucks, the rush of air from the forward motion blowing at the backs of their heads.

From some of the doorways the women and children threw bread. Some of the men in the trucks managed to catch some of the hard half-loaves, but more often the bread bounced off their hands or bodies or hit the sides of the trucks and then rolled in the dust under the trucks that followed. The women and children who threw no bread just stood, their heads turning back and forth in the doorways, as they tried to recognize in a second in the seas of faces on the trucks someone of whom they had not heard for many months, because they wanted to know if he was still alive now that peace had come to Europe again.

When we got back to the hotel we went into the pressroom and wrote our last stories. We wrote them quickly, just telling what it was like where we were on V-E Day in Germany and not trying to tell everything that we wished we could tell. For the last time we turned our stories over to the censors, and then we had lunch. After lunch I went back into the pressroom, and I wrote a cable to Edmond Bartnett, who was my boss on the *Sun*. The cable said: "Hopefully request permission start homeward shortly." That night I got the answer back: "Gladly grant permission for homeward trip. Bartnett."

We had written so hard every day for so long that it was a strange feeling. We did not know how to kill time. We just sat around a lot and talked some about the best moments, but mostly about our homes and our families and about what we might do now. I said that I had wanted to write sports ever since I had been in high school, and the irate one, who had taken off for London during The Bulge but had joined us again for the easier going after the Rhine crossing, said that he had already done that. He said that he had had enough of games and, as he put it, "the spoiled brats who play them." Then one night the word came.

The next morning we walked across the street under the trees with our blankets and our helmets and our canteens and our mess gear, and we turned them in to a lieutenant behind a table set up just inside the doorway of a small one-family house. He gave us our slips of paper for them, and they put us in a weapons carrier, and we rode out to the small airfield on the top of the raised ground.

While we waited for the C-47 to come in, we stood in the shade under the wing of another plane. There was a major there, and he had with him a young pilot in a leather jacket and dark green dress trousers.

"This man has a hell of a story," the major said to me. "You should write it."

The young pilot told me his story, standing in the shade under the wing of the plane. He said he had been shot down over the outskirts of Berlin, and when he parachuted down he landed in the walled garden of a large estate. As he came down in the garden, the S.S. guards grabbed him and took him into the big stone mansion.

"I was standing in the living room," he said. "It was a great big room with a lot of rich furnishings and oil paintings, when the door opens and the big shot walks in. Who the hell is it but Herman Goering, himself. I recognized him right away from his pictures—a big fat guy with medals."

The young flier said that Goering treated him very well. He said Goering knew a lot about American planes, and then he told me how he was liberated by the Russians, and I told him it was a good story.

"Are you going to write it?" he said. "What paper will it be in?"

"No," I said. "I'm sorry. The war is over. Two months ago it would have been a real good story, and two weeks ago it would still have been a good story. Now I think it's still a good story, but the war here is over, and the day it ended the people stopped wanting to read these stories from here. My own head is filled with good stories, but no one would print them now. I'm sorry about it."

I don't think the young pilot quite understood why I would not write his story. He flew back in the plane to Paris with us, and I noticed that he was watching Victor Bernstein, who was sitting across from him and who had his typewriter on his lap, trying to write a story.

Victor Bernstein came over late, not really to write about the fighting but to write about post-war Europe. He wrote some of the fighting, but now he was doing what he was meant to do, and I realized this as I watched him typing on his knees until the motion of the plane and his concentration on the lines of his typing became too much for him. Then he put the typewriter down and went to the back of the plane and was sick on the floor, and that meant that, for the moment, now even he could not do any writing.

It took us four hours to get back to Paris by plane, and it had taken us eight months when we were going the other way. We sat in the plane trying to look out of the small windows at the country below, trying to recognize something when we flew over beaten towns, realizing now how rapidly we were putting it all behind us, all of the ground that had been taken so slowly and at that great cost.

"Do you remember," I said to Gordon Fraser, "when we said we would go back the way we came?"

Fraser worked for the Blue Network, and we called him "The Little Colonel." I think he could have taken over a regiment, he knew so much about it, and one day during The Bulge when I went up to a company we had all been with some days before, the captain asked me about him.

"How's that little radio fella who was here with you that time?" he said.

"Gordon Fraser?" I said. "He's fine."

"The day after you two were here," the captain said, "he came up alone, and he made the attack with us. The kid carrying the ammo for the machine gun got hit, so your friend picked up the ammo cases and carried them up to the gun. He's a hell of a guy."

If I hadn't known it before, I knew it then, because Fraser had never mentioned it. Years later, when I used to drop in to see him at NBC in New York, where he was working on "Monitor," I knew the rest of them in that office didn't know what he was or what he had done in the war.

"What we said we were going to do," I said to him, as we looked down out of that plane flying back, "was follow every side road and stop and walk in particular fields and examine hillsides we remember. We'd go into houses and cellars we slept in, and go over all of it again so we might understand it better and never forget it."

"I know," Fraser said, "but now let's just get home."

There were ten of us in the room on the ship in officer country, but down in the holds they were stacked in bunks four tiers high.

There were 7,000 on what, when the Italians had her and called her the *Conte Grande,* had carried 1,000 passengers in luxury. Among the 7,000 there were 3,000 of what the Army called RAMPS, for Recovered American Military Personnel. They had been shot down over Berlin or captured at Kasserine or in the Ardennes, and they had survived the prison camps at Sagan and Barth and Hammelburg, and they had bad stomachs. They were supposed to be careful about what they ate, but they stood in the chow lines for hours like everyone else, and they ate everything and were sick.

In that room we were just as we had been back in Weimar. We read and slept and played cards for eleven days. We didn't talk about any of it any more, until the last night out when somebody broke out a bottle we didn't know he had been saving and put it on the table—and we heard some truth.

There was one I had traveled with a lot in the jeep because we wanted to see the same things and because he laughed a lot and relaxed me. If we were behind a wall and had to make a run for it, or if we had to go down a stretch of road, he always said the thing that got us out from behind the wall or down the road.

He was a very good mimic, and at night he was our best entertainment. He turned the things that had happened to us during the day into comedy bits, and we spent much time laughing with him. We knew he had been in the Pacific before he joined us in Europe, and now he was sitting with us around the bottle and his voice was rising and cracking.

"For Tarawa we drew lots," he said, "and I got it. I got it, but then I was afraid to go and they got slaughtered, and because I was afraid to go they sent me home."

We did not know what to say. I had had no idea of what he had been carrying, behind those walls and facing those roads, when he got me out. I tried to say something and somebody else said something but it didn't do any good, and so we just let him try to cry it out in our room on the ship coming home.

The next morning when we came through the Narrows, there was a fog over the Lower Bay, and they were lined four deep along the rails. On the starboard side in the last row there were three kids with First Armored patches on their shoulders, and they were looking over toward where you could just make out the parachute jump at Coney Island, and they said they were trying to see the Statue of Liberty. They said they had been captured at Faid Pass in Africa in February of 1943, and that one of the German guards at Fuerstenberg had told them they would never see the Statue of Liberty again, and I told him that the statue would show up off the other side.

"Look, sir," the Marine guard who was standing there said. "I know they want to see the Statue of Liberty. There are seven thousand guys on this ship who want to see the Statue of Liberty, and if I let them all go on that side, this damn thing will tip over."

"But these guys have been prisoners for more than two years," I said.

"We got three thousand of them that were prisoners," the Marine guard said. "What am I supposed to do?"

"Look the other way," I said.

I led them over to the port side, the big ship listing that way now, and all along the rows at the rail you could hear, "Where? Where?" I could just make it out, just a shadow in the fog, and I tried to point it out to the three kids.

"I think I can see it," the one from Illinois said to the other two. "If you'd ever seen it before, I think you could make it out. You see that something a little dark and kind of sticking up in the gray?"

"Yeah, I think I can see it," the one from North Dakota said. "I'm sure I can."

"I'm sure I can, too," the one from Kentucky said. "That's got to be it there."

"That Kraut has got to be dead now," the one from Illinois said.

"Yeah, and we made a liar out of him, too," the one from North Dakota said.

It was eleven days on the end of a long time, and when I reached out to push the bell in the apartment entrance, my finger shook so that I had to breathe deeply and steady it. When the buzzer sounded I kicked the door open and I held it with my body and moved my old black bag and my barracks bag and my typewriter into the lobby.

I stood at the foot of the stairs and I was shaking. I swung the barrack's bag onto my back and took the typewriter in one hand

and I left the old black bag and I climbed the three flights of stairs. I climbed the stairs as hard as I could to keep from crying, and my wife stood in the doorway. She looked small and frail, and I could not begin to tell her, no less write it. There was so much that had finally ended.

"We're giving you three months vacation," Keats Speed was saying. I was sitting in his office off the City Room on the day after we came up the Bay and you could barely make out the Statue of Liberty if you had seen it before and knew it was there. "We're also giving you a $1,000 bonus."

He was the managing editor, and from all I had heard about him and read about him in one or two memoirs, I knew he had once been a great newspaper man. Like the once great paper, though, and it was now 112 years old five years before its death, Speed was also getting old.

"I thank you," I said. "I didn't expect this."

"You've earned it," he said.

"About the bonus," I said. "A couple of months ago Mr. Bartnett cabled me $600 for additional expense money, and I still have about $300 of that left."

"If I were you," he said, "I'd just keep that, and forget about it."

"I thank you again."

"But I've saved the best for last," he said. "Phelps Adams has asked to have you as the second man under him in the Washington office, and I've approved."

How do you tell them? They have put on the party and raised the toasts and now, with the music rising and everyone standing and applauding they bring it in, all decorated and with the candles on it all ablaze. How do you tell them that they must have been thinking of someone else, because that's not your name on it and it's not your cake?

"I don't know how to say this," I said, "because I appreciate everything you're doing and the Washington offer. The trouble with me is that, since I was a kid, I've always wanted to be around athletes and write sports. Covering the war, where the material was so dramatic, I think I started to learn how to write. I want to continue to learn, and writing sports, where men are in contest, if not in conflict, and where you can come to know them, one can grow as a writer better than anywhere else on the paper."

"But we don't want you to write the hard news in Washington," he said. "We want you to do features."

"I'm sorry," I said, "but for me it just wouldn't be like being in sports."

"There are no openings in the sports department," he said.

"I was afraid of that," I said. "I guess I'll just have to wait and hope."

"When you come back from vacation in September," he said, "report to Mr. Bartnett again in the City Room."

He was no longer looking at me. That handsome, aristocratic head, the gray hair smoothed precisely back, was lowered and he was looking at some papers on his desk.

"Yes, sir," I said, "and thank you again for everything."

All that summer, while my wife and I bicycled from New York City to twenty-five miles from the Canadian border, and lived in a cabin on the east shore of Lake Champlain where only the lightning storms that sounded like artillery landing in a town bothered me, I wondered and worried about how I could do it again in the City Room. I didn't see how I could stand it, covering the routine court cases and fund-raising luncheons and doing rewrite on fires and holdups and updating wait-order obits and meeting the Twentieth Century Limited with some Midwestern politician or musical conductor or Hollywood star on it. I would never really get to know any of them or any of it, or get to grow as a writer.

I fully expected that on that first day back in the City Room I would find at my desk, as a starter, a sheaf of publicity notices to be ground down, each one, into a B-head, which is what we called a one-paragraph item. There was nothing on my desk, however, and for more than an hour I just sat there, reading the morning papers while around me the others rewrote the publicity or took the phone calls from the leg-men covering the districts or suddenly got up, folding copy paper into a pad as they started for the door.

It occurred to me, sitting there and reading in the morning papers, news that really didn't interest me but that I had to prep myself on in case I should be assigned to the story, that perhaps Ed Bartnett was hesitating to send me out, or to have me take the first phone call, on the first routine story. He was, and still is I am sure, a reserved but kind man, and I wondered if, because I had covered D-Day and then, after the liberation of Paris, all of it on the drive east into Germany and the fighting and the Huertgen and The Bulge and then, finally, the meeting with the Russians on the Elbe, he was embarrassed and reluctant to reassign me to the prosaic. When, finally, he called me over, he said he wanted me to do a piece on the control tower at LaGuardia airport, so I called there and made an appointment for one o'clock that afternoon. I had just hung up, and I was assuring myself that it could be worse, when I felt a hand on my shoulder and it was Wilbur Wood.

"Get out of here," he said. "I've just talked to Speed again, and he's letting me have you. You're now in sports."

"You're not kidding?" I said.

"Follow me," he said. "I'm your new boss."

"In a minute," I said.

I walked over to the City Desk and told Ed Bartnett. He said that he'd just heard it and that he was sorry to lose me but that he knew that was what I wanted. I told him about the one o'clock appointment at LaGuardia, and he told me to give that to Millie Faulk, who had the desk next to mine. When I did she said something, kidding, about the cushy jobs in sports. I took my automatic address finder, with the phone numbers of the American Dental Association and the District Attorney's office and the Bronx Zoo that I wouldn't need any more, out of my desk and walked out of the City Room and down the hall and into sports.

"You had better go up and see Lou Little," Wilbur Wood was saying now at his desk. "We need some football in the paper, and if you're going to write sports in this town he's one guy you should get to know well."

"That's fine with me," I said. "Whatever you say."

"You won't have any trouble," Wilbur said. "He's a very nice guy."

"From what I've read about him," I said, "I expect so."

I went over to a phone and called Lou Little at Columbia. He said I should come up to see him at the field at three o'clock, and although he was being friendly I could tell that he had never heard of me. While we were writing the war, I guess we all thought that everyone should be reading everything we wrote because we had never had such material and we had never written so well. In New

York alone, though, there were nine papers then, and we should have remembered that.

At two o'clock I took the subway and it is a long ride to Baker Field where the Columbia football team practices and where it plays its home games. The subway comes out into the open and goes down into the ground again. You ride to the end of the Eighth Avenue Line, and after I became bored with reading the paper I realized that I was nervous about meeting Lou Little.

After all, he was a famous football coach, and I was just starting to write sports. I did not know the things I should know about him, but I could remember that New Year's Day of 1934, when I was just out of high school and wanting to be a sportswriter, and I sat by the radio in a corner of the living room listening to the Rose Bowl game.

It had said in the newspapers that the California sports writers had been referring to Columbia as "Pomona High School in light blue jerseys," and when Columbia beat Stanford, 7–0, it became one of the great upsets in football history and, of course, a major professional accomplishment for Lou Little. Almost twelve years later, they were still referring to it, and to KF-79, the naked reverse with which Columbia scored its touchdown.

At the end of the subway I followed the directions they had given me at the office. The afternoon was warm, even for early September, and I walked along the sidewalk with the hilly park on the left. In the park, the leaves were turning yellow and the grass drying, and I walked by the small narrow stores and the used car lot and the gas station and turned left up the hill where, across the street and on the right, the chain-link fence runs around the field.

I crossed the street and looked for a gate in the fence until I saw one that was open and walked in past some green wooden barracks. I walked around the end of the barracks and along one side under some elms. There were two college kids with books under their arms walking ahead of me and they went through a doorway into the barracks, and when I came to the doorway I followed them.

There were metal lockers around the walls of the room and there were about a dozen kids undressing in front of them. They were talking in loud voices and kidding back and forth, and I walked around the room and down a hall and looked into a smaller room with white walls and with a rubbing table in the middle and a long wooden bench along one wall.

A couple of kids were sitting naked on the bench and there was another sitting on the rubbing table. There were two men working on the kid on the table, each bandaging an ankle. One of the men was thin, with an Irish face and wearing a white linen cap like Ben Hogan used to wear. The other was rather stout and with white bushy hair and a rather florid face. There was some talk going on in the room.

"You're an athlete?" the large man with the white hair was saying to the kid on the table. "You're an athlete, my elbow. A man of my years and experience and the great athletes I've handled, and at this stage of my life they send me children. You're no athlete."

The kid sitting on the rubbing table was grinning and winking at the kids sitting on the bench along the wall. I waited for the talk to quiet.

"Excuse me," I said, "but is Lou Little around?"

"He hasn't come in yet."

It was the large man with the white hair who answered. He had stopped bandaging, and he had turned his head and was looking at me out of the tops of his eyes. I told him who I was and he said he was Doc Barrett, and I recognized from his name that he was the head trainer. He introduced me to the other whose name was Jimmy Judge.

"How's Will Wedge?" Barrett said.

"He's all right," I said. "He's covering the Yankees."

"Don't you think I know he's covering the Yankees?" Barrett said. He was looking at me again out of the tops of his eyes. "Don't you think I read your paper every night?"

"I'm glad you do."

"How long you been writing sports?"

"I've just started."

"You want to know something?"

"Yes."

"Read Will Wedge," Barrett said. "You'll be all right if you write like Will Wedge. He's a good writer."

"Yes, he is."

Transition

"He could write a book. He's a learned man. He's a gentleman. He comes up here a lot. He wrote a good story about me once."

"I'm sure he did."

He looked at me again in that same way, studying me.

"Will Wedge is not a knocker," he said. "He doesn't knock people. There's too many sportswriters knocking people. What do they think they are? You don't have to tell me. I know them. Their noses still run. They come up here and sit around and yes people. They're such timid little men. They ask you for favors, and they can't even wipe their own noses, and you're nice to them and then they go back and knock you."

He tried to show disgust in his face.

"I'd like to punch them in the nose," he said. "If I wasn't associated with a fine and respectable institution, I'd punch them in the nose. Who do they think they are anyway?"

"I don't know," I said.

They had finished with the boy on the table, and he got up and another boy climbed up and lay down. It was quiet in the room for the moment.

"What kind of a team are you going to have this year?" I said.

"How would I know?" Barrett said, looking at me again. "We don't know anything in here. You can come in here if you want, but you won't learn anything. If there's anything you want to know, you'll have to ask Lou Little. Lou Little does the talking around this club."

"That's all right with me," I said.

There was a man standing in the doorway, and I presumed he had been listening. He seemed to be in his mid-forties, but he was well built and only starting to get soft. He had on a dark blue suit and a blue shirt and a dark blue tie.

"Excuse me," he said. "Is Lou Little around?"

"He's not in yet," Barrett said, looking up from his work and at the man.

"I played fullback here in 1921," the man said. He had walked into the room and he was standing in front of Barrett and he put out his hand. "My name's Charley Appleton."

"Don't you think I know?" Barrett said, stopping his work and shaking hands. "I don't forget a face. How are you?"

He introduced the man named Appleton to Jimmy Judge. He

went back to his work, and I walked outside and back into the locker room and I waited around there. After a while Appleton came out and stood there until Lou Little came in.

I recognized Lou Little, with his large nose, from all the pictures and cartoons I had seen of him. He had two boys with him, and he led them down the hall to where there was a Dutch door with the top half open, and I could hear him talking in a husky voice to someone in the room beyond the door while the two boys stood in back of him.

"Fit these gentlemen out with uniforms," he was saying. "These gentlemen are going to play a little football for us."

When he walked back toward us Appleton walked up to him. He stuck out his hand and Little took it.

"Can I have a uniform too, coach?" Appleton said.

"Sure," Little said, looking at him, "but you're a little heavy, aren't you?"

"That's right. My name's Charley Appleton, and I played fullback here in 1921. You weren't here then."

"Sure," Little said.

"Next year is our twenty-fifth anniversary," Appleton said. "What I want to know is if I can borrow a jersey to be photographed for a little book we're getting out."

"Sure," Little said. "One of the boys here will fit you with a jersey, and take a helmet too. Want a helmet?"

"Yes. A helmet would be fine too. The photographer is right out here."

"That's all right," Little said.

He started to walk through the locker room, and I stopped him and introduced myself and we shook hands. I could tell that he still thought that maybe he should know me.

"I'm glad to see you," he said. "Come up any time."

I followed him into the small room where several other coaches were getting out of their clothes, and he introduced me to Buff Donelli and Tad Wieman and Ralph Furey and a couple of others. Then he started to undress in front of his locker, and I was impressed by his flawless taste in clothes. Everything was a shade of tan, trousers, sports jacket, shirt, suspenders, tie, shoes, and socks.

"What can I tell you?" he said after a while, looking at me.

I was sitting on a stool near his locker.

"I'm not sure," I said. "I just thought I would come up and write a story telling what a practice is like. I think it might tell some people something they don't know."

"That will be all right."

"You know," I said, "coming up here I was remembering something. I was remembering when I was just out of high school and sitting by the radio in our living room and listening to you beat Stanford in the Rose Bowl. I can still see that radio in the corner. That was a big thrill, and I'll never forget that game."

"I'll never forget it either," he said.

He was pulling on a pair of baseball pants and then a sweat-shirt, and I was still ill at ease, because he was Lou Little and I was still new at this. I wanted him to accept me, and I did not want him to be aware of my ignorance, and finally I asked him about his team and he named off some names which I wrote down.

"My line isn't much," he said. "I've got two or three good backs who can run, though, and I like some of the boys I'm getting from our Naval R.O.T.C. They're bigger and better football players than our V-12 boys. Our V-12 boys were all right, but they were mostly pre-med and pre-engineers, which means they were smart enough, but they weren't always football material, if you know what I mean."

"Yes," I said, "I know what you mean."

"Some of our backs are out there now," Buff Donelli said.

He was coaching the Columbia backs then. He was wearing a pair of black shorts and a white T-shirt, football shoes and white woolen sweat socks, and he was standing by the open door that looked out onto the practice field.

"I guess they're ready," Lou Little said. "We might as well go."

He turned to me.

"Come out on the field," he said. "Watch us work as long as you want, and if there's anything else you want to know, you can ask me when we come in."

They left the dressing room, and I followed them out under the elms and onto the field. The sun was starting to get well down now and it was beginning to cool a little. On the field the kids in the light blue jerseys were kicking and passing footballs back and forth. There was the sound of the footballs against shoes and the sound of their shouting, and when Lou Little blew a whistle they stopped what they were doing and ran to him and formed a semicircle in front of him.

Lou Little talked to them for a while in that husky voice, and he kept it low. I did not stand close enough to hear what he was telling them, but after a while they turned from him and joined into groups and spread around the field. I walked to the far end of the field and watched and listened while Little and Donelli worked with the backs.

"Look, look," Little was saying to one of them who had just thrown the ball. "Don't just stand there. When you're not ready to throw it, don't just stand there. Keep moving around. Move around. Move around."

The player was just a kid. He couldn't have been more than 5'9" or have weighed more than 165 pounds. He had his helmet off, and he had dark curly hair and dark eyes. As Little talked to him he listened carefully, nodding his head, and a few minutes later Donelli was shouting at him.

"Hey!" Donelli was shouting, running up to him, when the play had stopped. "What's the reason you're always bumping into him? You've got no reason to be bumping into him. You're supposed to take two steps and then drop back. You're not supposed to be anywhere near him, but you're bumping into him all the time."

After I had watched for a while longer I walked over to the bench at the side line near midfield, where Doc Barrett and Jimmy Judge were sitting. Doc Barrett introduced me to Dr. Stephen Hudack, the team physician, and I sat down near them. I was listening to their talk when one of the student managers came running across the field.

"Jimmy!" he was calling, "Mr. Little wants to see you, Jimmy!"

Jimmy Judge got up and ran out onto the field. When he came back he had one of the players with him. It was not the little kid with the dark wavy hair and the dark eyes, but an older one, husky and with his black hair starting to thin in the front.

"He's sick," Jimmy Judge said to Dr. Hudack, motioning with his head toward the player.

"You're sick?" the doctor said, standing up and looking at the player. "What's the matter, son?"

"I don't know," the player said. "I get all congested and spit up cotton, and then I start to feel sick to my stomach."

He was standing in front of the bench in his soiled uniform, his face pale and the drops of perspiration on it and on his neck. He had his helmet in his hands.

"Have you been sick lately, or have you had a cold?" the doctor said.

"No," the player said, shaking his head.

"Do you have any idea what it might be?"

"Well," the player said, "I think I may have T.B."

"You think you may have T.B.?" the doctor said. "T.B.? What makes you think you may have T.B.? Is there any T.B. in your family?"

"No, sir, there isn't," the player said.

"Then what makes you think you have T.B.?"

"Well, sir," the player said, "I drank some raw milk."

"You drank some raw milk?" the doctor said, looking right at the player. "Don't you know better than to drink raw milk? Don't you know that you should boil raw milk before you drink it?"

"Yes, sir."

"Then why didn't you boil it? Why didn't you boil the milk?"

"You see, sir," the player said, slowly, "I was in a German prison camp for fifteen months. Once all we had was raw milk."

We were all looking at the player. Then I looked at the doctor.

"Oh," the doctor said, and I could see and hear him soften. "Oh. Is that so?"

"Yes, sir," the player said.

"Were you sick in the camp?"

"Sometimes. I lost forty-one pounds, but I got it all back."

"So," the doctor said. "Well now, you're going to be all right. I think maybe you're just pressing too hard. I think you're just trying to do too much. Too much exercise isn't too good for you. I'll tell you what we'll do, You come in to see me tomorrow morning, and I don't think you should do any more today."

"Yes, sir," the player said. "Thank you."

He started back toward the barracks, but I stopped him and introduced myself and I talked with him for three or four minutes. He said he had been a gunner on a Flying Fortress and that he had been shot down over Northern Italy.

"You'll be all right," I said.

"I hope so," he said.

"You'll be fine," I said.

He walked back to the barracks and I walked out onto the field and I found Lou Little. I told him I thought I had better get back to the office, and then it came to me that he might wonder what I would write about. I didn't want him to think that I was lazy or careless, leaving so early during the practice.

"One of your players was just sick," I said. "I mean the one you sent back with Jimmy Judge, and it turns out he was in German prison camp for fifteen months."

"He was?" Lou Little said. "Is that so?"

"Yes," I said, "and I think I'll write something about that."

"Fine," Lou Little said. "Good. Come up any time."

"Thank you," I said.

"Any time," he said.

Riding back downtown on the subway I started to put together in my mind the piece I would write describing the practice. I would have to work the contrast between the little kid with the curly hair and brown eyes listening so carefully while Little and Donelli lectured him, and the older one coming off the field and, when the doctor asked him what he thought his trouble was, saying he might have T.B. I would have to show somehow without saying it that, at first, the doctor had been a bit patronizing, and then even incredulous when he heard about the raw milk, before he learned that the player had been a prisoner of the Germans, because that should be the way it should come to the reader, too, if I could get that dialogue—the pauses and the emphasis—just right.

The name of the little kid was Gene Rossides, and the older one was Vince Pesature. Rossides was still some weeks away from being eighteen, and during the next four years he became one of the best of all Columbia backs. In his first game he ran eighty yards for one of the three touchdowns he scored, and on a number of Saturday afternoons I sat in press boxes and watched him pull games out. One October afternoon two years later I watched his passes and Bill Swiacki's catches end by 21–20 Army's string of thirty-two games without defeat, and this was almost as important to Columbia and Lou Little as their Rose Bowl game.

Vince Pesature was never much of a football player, and I saw him play only once, late in a one-sided game. What he did in that game I don't remember, but I remember that once he was in a German prison camp and a year later I saw him at Baker Field. He was trying to make the Columbia football team, and he was standing on the side lines, coughing up a little cotton and saying that sometimes he felt a little sick and that he thought he might have T.B. from drinking raw milk.

And I was writing sports. About a month later I was on the field at the Polo Grounds, where John McGraw, Christy Mathewson, Babe Ruth, Ty Cobb, Honus Wagner, Frankie Frisch, Red Grange, Bronco Nagurski and dozens of the other heroes of my youth had performed. I was watching the New York Football Giants practice, as I would do every Tuesday morning during the football season. I would be at the Polo Grounds at ten o'clock, and I would stand around there, watching Steve Owen coach the team. I looked forward to those Tuesday mornings because Steve Owen was a big, open, and honest man, and I was trying to appreciate his problems and the problems of his players. After practice I would go into the locker room and talk with him and with his players, and sometimes I would go to lunch with him. We would sit in a darkened pseudo-Spanish restaurant on Forty-third Street between Fifth and Sixth avenues, with its decorative wall tiles and archways and wrought-iron railings, and he would tell stories about the early days of professional football. After lunch I would walk back with him to Forty-second Street, where he would go up to the Giants's office to work out his problems, and I would take the subway downtown to work on mine.

On this morning it was cold, but the air was clear and the sun was shining. The Giants were running through passing plays in deep right field near the outfield wall with the signs, painted on the dark green, advertising razor blades and hot dogs and ice cream. Steve Owen was standing with his hands in his hip pockets talking to several of us and watching Arnie Herber throw the ball.

Herber threw a pass to an end named Hubert Barker. It was deep and Barker ran for it, but when he was about to run into the wall where the sign advertised Gem blades, he slowed and the pass went over his outstretched hands.

"What are you scared of Barker?" Owen said, shouting at him. "What are you scared of?"

"He's scared of the five o'clock shadow," Bert Gumpert, who wrote sports for The *Bronx Home News,* said.

Owen turned to Bill Abbott. Abbott was the publicity man for the Giants, and Owen asked him for a copy of the team roster. When Abbott gave it to him Owen ran a finger down the list of players.

"Take this McNamara off the list," Owen said to Abbott, and he was talking about Edmund McNamara, a tackle from Holy Cross. "I just sold him to Pittsburgh."

"In other words," Gumpert said, "McNamara's banned."

"He's a pretty nice kid," Owen said, "He has the Silver Star, and they needed tackles more than we do, and I like to give those war kids jobs."

That was how Abbott got to explaining about Marion Pugh. Marion Pugh was one of Owen's good backs, and before that he had been a star at Texas A. & M. I could remember hearing another broadcast of another game, and Ted Husing was doing the game and he talked a lot about Pugh. He kept calling him Dukey Pugh, and Husing had a resonant voice and afterwards the name kept running around in my mind . . . Dukey Pugh . . . Dukey Pugh . . . Dukey Pugh.

"A year ago he was fighting in Europe," Abbott said. "He had a company of tank destroyers. He was wounded twice and got the Bronze Star."

"You should talk to him," Owen said to me. "You might get a story."

After the players had finished running through their plays he had them run up and down the field a couple of times, and then he sent them to the showers. When Pugh came down the old, worn wooden steps from the shower room he was still drying himself, and he walked across the room to his locker. As he started to dress I walked over and introduced myself and stood talking with him.

"They tell me you were in Europe?" I said.

"That's right," he said.

"Where were you?" I said.

"Oh, from France all the way into Germany."

"What outfit were you attached to?"

"The Second Division and the Fourth."

"Is that right? I was with both of them."

"Also the Twenty-eighth."

"Were you with the Twenty-eighth when they were in the Huertgen Forest?" I said. "I mean that time they were chewed up at Schmidt and Kommerscheidt?"

Marion Pugh was not large for a professional football player. He was rather slim, but nicely muscled. He had started to pull on a pair of slacks, but he stopped and straightened up.

"You know something?" he said, looking at me. "You're the first guy I've met who has even heard of those places."

We stood in the locker room of the Polo Grounds and talked about one of the bad beatings the Americans took in the war. Schmidt and Kommerscheidt were two small towns in a break in the Huertgen, and the German attack there was a prelude, a first step by which they positioned themselves for their breakthrough later in The Bulge.

"I lost eleven of my twelve T.D.'s in that," Pugh said, and it is what tank destroyers are called. "We were cut off for six days."

"I remember one thing about it in particular," I said. "There were some wounded Americans cut off in a forester's cabin in the woods, and we were trying to get to them. I wrote a story about it, and I also remember that that was the day we had our first snow."

"I was in that cabin," Pugh said, looking at me again. "That's an odd thing. I was in that cabin."

We had been, with Germans between us, not much more than the length of a football field apart, and now he stuck out a finger. He showed me the scar on it.

"They ambushed my jeep," he said, "and we jumped out and hid in some bushes in the dark. A German was probing through the bushes with his bayonet, and it went right through my finger."

"I'd say you're lucky," I said.

"You're telling me?" he said.

"That was just about a year ago, too," I said. "I think it was right about now."

"No," Pugh said. "It was November fifth. I'll never forget that."

Around us the other players had finished dressing and Steve

Owen was calling them together. They were preparing to play Boston on the following Sunday, and Owen was going to show them the movies of the Boston game of the previous year.

The players pulled the wooden folding chairs up in front of a small movie screen set up in the middle of the old locker room. Somebody turned out the lights, and when the film started and the titles came on the screen, there was the date. Marion Pugh and I sat side by side in the darkness in the locker room in the Polo Grounds, and we read on the screen that the game had been played the previous year on November 5.

"I'll be damned," Marion Pugh said.

Five weeks later the Giants played the Eagles in the mist and rain in Philadelphia. The Eagles won easily, 38–17, and after the game the Giants, hurting and sullen and silent, had crowded into the bus. Now the bus was moving, halting and then moving again through the honking traffic of a Sunday evening and over the wet streets between Shibe Park and the North Philadelphia station.

"Kilroy," somebody said. "Kilroy is the guy who did it."

"How bad is it?" somebody else said. "Is it broken?"

"They don't know," one of the players who had been the last to crowd into the bus said. "They're trying to get a cast on it so they can carry him home."

They were talking about Marion Pugh. Near the end of the game he had just completed a pass and Frank Kilroy, the 240-pound Eagle tackle, had hit him. When they had gone down, Pugh had folded forward in a peculiar position so that he was half on top of Kilroy.

Four players had had to carry Pugh off the muddy field. He had been half lying and half sitting in their arms, and from the press box and through my field glasses I had been able to see his face and he had been grimacing with the pain.

When they had brought Pugh into the dressing room they had placed him on one of the rubbing tables, and then they had looked at his leg and had tried to take off his uniform. Every time they had moved him the muscles of his face had tightened and he had shut his eyes, but finally they had got him out of his uniform and dressed him in his street clothes. He had been sitting there with his leg stretched out on the rubbing table when he had looked up and seen me.

"Hey!" he said, "How are you?"

"That's not the question," I had said. "How are you?"

"The way they were coming at me out there," he had said, "I thought I was back at Kommerscheidt."

Behind me now in the crowded bus George Franck was talking. He had been an All-American halfback at Minnesota and he had flown for the Marines in the Pacific, and he was talking to Mel Hein, the All-Pro center.

"When I was shot down over Wotje," Franck was saying, "I was going to kill myself."

"You were going to *kill* yourself?" Hein said.

"Rather than let those bastards get their hands on me," Franck said, "I was going to put a slug through my own head."

"Good God!" Hein said.

I wasn't seeking them, but when I found them I could not ignore them. They were a part of America and of a world in transition, and one Friday night about three weeks later I was walking down the hallway under the main arena seats on the Fiftieth Street side of Madison Square Garden. It was about eight o'clock, with the crowd starting to come in, and Bob Mele, a fight manager from New Haven, was standing outside one of the dressing rooms they used for preliminary fighters. He was smoking a cigarette and he said he had two fighters in the four-round bouts that night, two brothers named Joe and Jimmy Rogers.

"They were on the *Juneau* when she was sunk," he said.

The *Juneau* was a light cruiser, and when it had gone down in the Pacific it had taken the five Sullivan brothers with it, and that had become a part of the history of the war. Mele was saying now that there had been four Rogers brothers on it, too, and that Pat and Louie had been lost and Joe and Jimmy had had to swim for it, and now they were waiting to fight in the Garden.

"It's a good thing for them," he said. "All the time after they came back they kept talking about Pat and Louie. Pat and Louie were better fighters than these two, and they thought about them all the time. Now they've got their minds on this, and it's a good thing."

"Do you mind if I go in and talk to them?" I said.

"No," he said. "They're a little nervous, you know, about being in the Garden, and it'll probably help them relax a little."

There were several other fighters and their handlers in the room. The Rogers brothers, in their ring trunks and blue satin robes, were sitting together on one of the benches and Mele introduced me. I did not want to ask them about the *Juneau,* but if I were going to write about them I would have to, and so I told them I was sorry about their loss and I asked them how the four brothers happened to be on the same ship.

"We enlisted together right after Pearl Harbor," the one named Joe said. "When the war started we said let's get into it together and take care of one another. We didn't know a damn thing about war. How are you gonna take care of one another on a ship like that?"

I was hoping very much that they would turn out to be good fighters, at least good enough to win their bouts. Joe went on first, just before the main event, and when they called him, Jimmy walked out with him and then stood at the top of the aisle, trying to see over the heads. It was a slow fight, with the crowd, impatient for the main event to come on, booing, and when Joe lost the decision and came back up the aisle, Jimmy threw an arm around Joe's shoulders.

"You did all right," he said. "You did okay."

"You do it," Joe said. "I couldn't get my hands up in there, but you do it."

Jimmy went on in the walk-out bout after the main event, with the Garden emptying now. For whatever reason, the few who stayed got to rooting for Jimmy's opponent, and when Jimmy lost the decision and came up the aisle where Joe was waiting, there was a loudmouth hollering at him.

"Go back to New Haven," he was hollering. "You're a bum!"

I walked back to the dressing room with them and said I was sorry that they hadn't won, and I wished them luck. They thanked me and we shook hands and I walked out of the dressing room and out of the war again. Some of what I walked into, some of what I came to know about those I came to know, is what follows in the rest of this book.

1

The Shy One

Floyd is a kind of a stranger.
Cus D'Amato, 1954

On the telephone two nights before, he had told me to turn off the New York Thruway at the New Paltz exit and then left on Route 299. He has said that I should follow that through the town, across a railroad track and over a bridge and then take the first road on the right.

"What's the name of the road?" I had asked.

"Springtown Road," he had said. "You go half a mile to a fork and then take the right. Two-tenths of a mile after that it's the first house on the left."

"And what time do you want me to show up?"

"Three o'clock," he had said. "I'm looking at my schedule. I may have an appointment, something to do, for a half hour at 3:30, but 3 o'clock is all right."

It was just after two when I turned off the Thruway. There was a motel off to the left, but I decided to drive into the town and, perhaps, find one that would be closer and more a part of the town.

The terrain there, west of the Hudson and just south of the Catskill Mountains, is hilly, and the town, with Route 299 as its main street, spreads down over the western slope of a ridge. The stores, restaurants, and other places of business are close-packed on both sides of the steeply slanting street that was congested now with traffic, and off to the south and on the crest of the ridge there is a multistoried highrise, an architectural aberration erected without regard for the still rural nature of the countryside. Seeing it towering alone there on the ridge like the beginning in New Paltz of a new Bronx, I surmised that it would turn out to be a part of the college, a branch of the State University of New York.

Coming down off the ridge, the road crosses the railroad tracks with the old wooden station on the right, and there was a sign on the station offering it for rent. Beyond the tracks I drove over the bridge and out onto the flat of a valley with farming lands on both sides of the blacktop road. Ahead I could see another blacktop to the right, and when I reached it and saw the Springtown Road sign I backed around and drove the way I had come and back up the hill through the town.

There was a small motel on the left, and when I got to the top of the hill I pulled off and into a gas station. The attendant came out, a young man with red hair and wiping his hands on a rag.

"Fill it up?" he said.

"Please," I said, "and maybe you can tell me something. Do you know where Floyd Patterson lives?"

I wanted to get an idea of how well a former heavyweight champion of the world, this former heavyweight champion of the world, might be known in his adopted town. He had always run from renown, and even as champion had sought seclusion. The fame that came with his title seemed to embarrass him, as if he could never forget that he was a refugee from the black ghetto of the Bedford-Stuyvesant section of Brooklyn. As a child, he had been so shy that he could never look others in the eye and so maladjusted that only special schooling saved him. I liked him very much because, although he was always so serious—even appearing troubled—that I never heard him laugh, his observations were perceptive and reflected a supreme sensitivity, and his answers were honest. He always seemed to me, though, to be the most miscast of fighters, for while he had the physical attributes to be a great fighter—always excepting his inability to absorb a heavyweight's big punch—he also had the compassion of a priest, and I never knew anyone else in sports whose antennae were so attuned to the suffering of others.

"Are you bothered by the sight of blood?" I asked him once.

"How do you mean?" Patterson said.

"Have you ever been scared, as a child or since, when you've been cut?"

I asked this question because a fighter must regard lightly the changes his profession makes upon his physical person. He must also be relatively unaffected by the hurt he inflicts upon others.

"No," he said. "I've seen my blood flow from me when I was younger. One time I got a nail stuck in my foot, and I kept it there for three hours, until my mother came home from work. You see, there was this lady baby-sitting for us, and I was scared to tell her about the nail because she was very mean and she would beat you. So when I got this nail in my foot I kept it there and stayed in the front room for three hours until my mother came home and I told her about it."

"What about seeing blood on others?" I said.

"On somebody else?" he said. "Well, this hasn't happened lately, but in the wintertime, when it's cold and my nose feels cold, I'd sometimes see two people fighting in the street. I'd actually see a guy with a big fist hit another guy square on the nose or face. You know?"

"Yes."

"Well," he had said, "when I'd see that, I'd feel it myself. It really seemed that I could actually feel it, and I would rather be fighting the one guy and taking the punishment than to see the other guy taking it, because I could just imagine how it feels to get hit when you're cold like that."

He was that way in the ring, staying away from a cut when he opened one on an opponent. The day of his second fight with Ingemar Johansson they weighed in at noon at the Commodore Hotel. The big room was crowded with sportswriters and photographers and members of the fight mob, and I was talking with Johnny Attell, who had been matchmaker around New York for many years, when Billy Conn, who had been one of the best of the all-time light-heavyweights and enough of a heavyweight to give Joe Louis one of his toughest fights, walked over.

"Who do you like tonight, Bill?" Attell said to him.

"Me?" Conn said. "I like the Swede for his punch."

"I don't know," Attell said, shrugging. "Patterson's got the equipment to take him if he fights him right."

"You hear what somebody had Patterson say?" Conn said.

"What?" Attell said.

"Patterson said that when he gets a guy cut he lays off the eye and hits him in the belly," Conn said. "You know somebody told him to say that, because he'd pour salt in a cut if he could."

"No he wouldn't," Attell said.

"Are you kidding?" Conn said.

"No," Attell said. "This guy Patterson is really that way."

"Then he's got no business being a fighter," Conn said.

But he was a fighter, an Olympic champion, and then the youngest ever to win the heavyweight championship of the world and the first even to regain it. I hadn't seen him to talk to since 1963, before the second of his two fights with Sonny Liston in which he never got by the first round. Liston, I knew beforehand, would out-body and bully him, and I had given Patterson no chance, and then on television I had watched Muhammad Ali humiliate him twice. Howard Cosell, who knew him well and had seen much of him while Patterson's career was running down, had written in his own autobiography that Patterson had come to live off martyrization and sympathy. Then I had heard that he had been appointed to the New York State Athletic Commission and was living in New Paltz, and I wondered how he was totalling the wins and losses of his life.

"Floyd Patterson?" the attendant said now. "Sure."

"You know where he lives?"

"Sure," he said, pointing. "You go down through town here and across the steel bridge and you take the first right. That's Springtown Road. At the fork you take a right, and I think it's the second house on the left."

I was thinking that no, Floyd said it was the first house on the left, and the young man's earnestness and sincerity made me a little ashamed of my deceit.

"Fine," I said, "and tell me something else. Is that motel beyond the top of the hill the best around here?"

"Right," he said. "That's a good one."

I checked into the "good one" that would have been better if someone had washed the woodwork in recent time. When I turned the thermostat on the air conditioner-heater the sound that came from behind the bent vanes of the grill low on the wall was of a spin-dry washer gurging a load of nuts, bolts and aluminum pie pans. The bathroom had been scrubbed clean, however, and over all, it was an improvement over some of the places where I had known Patterson while he was a fighter.

First there was the Gramercy Gym, on East Fourteenth Street in Manhattan, with the two flights of stairs that groaned and gave underfoot and led up between the mustard-colored walls that were dusty with soot and stained with grime. At the top of the stairs, and low in the door into the gym, there was a jagged hole covered with heavy wire mesh, and behind the door and snarling through the mesh there was a German shepherd that Patterson or Cus D'Amato, who managed him, would chain in a back room before they would let a visitor in. D'Amato reasoned that this approach would weed out the faint-hearted who just thought they might like to be fighters.

Then there was La Ronda, in the woods outside of Newtown, Connecticut, where Patterson lived and where he trained almost as a recluse most of the time, for nine months through the autumn of 1959 and the following winter and spring, to get his title back from Ingemar Johansson. It was an otherwise abandoned roadhouse that was owned and had been operated by Enrique Madriguera, who had finished second to Xavier Cugat in the battle of the big Latin dance bands. Set into the wall beneath the stairway to the second floor there was a cracked ornamental tile of a young boy playing a violin, and that had been Madriguera when he had been a child prodigy, and once, scattered amid the debris in the back yard, I had found pages of sheet music, blowing in the wind. The place was infested with rats that Patterson shot with a .22. While Johansson lived in a private cottage at Grossinger's, the luxury resort in the Catskills, and had his meals served in style, Patterson and Dan Florio, his trainer, cooked for themselves and the sparring partners in the vast kitchen and on the big ranges and in the oversized pots and pans that had been intended to hold the Iberian edibles for the multitudes of music lovers and conga dancers who never came.

When I turned onto Springtown Road now for the second time, I went to the fork and took the road to the right. I watched the odometer, and after two-tenths of a mile, as Patterson had said, on the left on a rise beyond a field of golden-brown stubble, I saw the two-storied, white-shingled house. The blacktop driveway rises for almost a hundred yards between tall pines, and as I drove up it I saw the two gray metal boxes, one on either side of the driveway amid the trees. At the top I turned left and parked by a stone wall in front of the garage doors under the house, and got out. There was an off-white dog of good size and indefinite breeding confronting me and barking at me as I got out of the car, and I could hear a male voice calling.

"Cotton! Cotton! C'mere, Cotton!"

It was Patterson's voice, and as the dog turned from me and started up the steps toward the back of the house, I followed it. Patterson was holding an aluminum combination storm and screen door open, and when the dog disappeared inside, he came out and we shook hands. He was wearing freshly laundered blue jeans and an immaculate white T-shirt, and he didn't look much heavier at age forty-one than he had at age twenty-five when, that night in the Polo Grounds, he landed that wide left hook on Johansson's jaw and became the first fighter ever to regain the heavyweight title.

"Nobody can sneak up on you here," I said.

"That's right," he said.

"I mean with the dog and those boxes down on the driveway. Is that a warning device?"

"It rings a bell in our bedroom," he said. "It's mostly for at night."

He was the third oldest of eleven children, born into poverty and an overcrowded world that he found frightening and from which, from his earliest years on, he tried to escape. Once he told me that when he was six he used to hide all day in the basement of P.S. 25, the school he was supposed to be attending. As he became older, and when he had the eighteen cents for admission, he hid in the Regent and Apollo and Banko movie theaters, and some nights he slept in Prospect Park and others in subway stations.

"You have a lovely home here," I said.

He had led me through the kitchen and the dining room and, off the entry hall, into a family room. There was a twenty-foot fieldstone, mahogany-topped bar curving in front of the far wall, the mounted heads of two mountain goats above it, the windows behind it looking out onto the driveway. Across the entry hall I could see the living room, with a baby grand piano, and I was impressed by the orderliness of everything, the furniture precisely placed and none of the incidental leavings of daily living lying about.

"It's nice," he said.

"How many rooms are there?" I said.

"Well," he said, "there's four bedrooms, one play room, the living room, the kitchen, the dining room, the bar room and four baths."

"Does your wife have help?"

"Help?" he said.

"Someone who comes in to clean?" I said, and his own mother, whom I remember as a serene, soft-spoken and sensitive woman, had been a domestic before she found a job in a Brooklyn bottling factory.

"Nope," Patterson said. "I help her."

"How much land do you have?"

"Forty acres," he said, and he walked to a window and pointed down at the field between the house and the road, the grass stubble in it that golden brown in the sunlight. "You see that field? I did it with a hand scythe and with a hand saw, all summer long."

"That's good," I said, "but what's that monstrosity over there on the ridge?"

"The what?" he said.

"That tower," I said.

"Oh, that's the college."

"That figures," I said. "We're trying to teach people to live with the environment and not abuse it, and a college does that."

A yellow school bus had stopped at the foot of the driveway. Two small girls had got out and were starting to walk up the drive.

"That's my daughters," he said. "They go to the Duzine school. That's the public school, what they call the Duzine school, but next year they'll go to the Catholic school in Rosendale, and I'll have to drive them over."

"You don't like the public school?"

We had walked back from the window. He was sitting on one of the bar stools, and I was sitting on another.

"The public school's all right here," he said, "but New Paltz was number two in the nation for drugs. Los Angeles was number one."

"Can that be correct?" I said.

"That's right," he said. "Three or four years ago I read it in the *Daily News*. That's why I started my boxing club. The Huguenot Boxing Club."

I had read somewhere that he was training young amateur fighters. As a fighter himself he was prone to errors, as the naturally gifted in anything often are. In most of his fights, however, his great hand speed and mobility covered his mistakes and let him get away with them although, of course, they were still there.

"There's this Father Daniel O'Hare," he said, "and he's the founder. It's called AMEN—Americans Mobilized to End Narcotics—and he founded it. He used to be in the rectory here, and about three years ago I got to know him. He's now in the rectory in Newburgh, and he's a very down-to-earth priest. I've gotten to know him so close that sometimes I say a word you don't say to a priest."

"I know what you mean."

"I joined up two years ago, and he takes care of the educational parts, and I take the physical."

"About this drug problem," I said. "I keep reading that it's been with us always. Were there drugs around when you were growing up?"

"No," he said, "the only thing was cigarettes."

"Not even in Bedford-Stuyvesant?"

"Nope," he said. "There were no drugs around in the fifties, but I remember as a youngster I was always getting in trouble, stealing fruit, and from the five-and-ten small stuff. Who knows what I'd be now if it wasn't for boxing."

"You're not the only one," I said.

"So I opened the boxing club," he said. "If you give a youngster something to do that he enjoys, he won't hang around on corners."

"That's right."

"About a year and a half ago," he said, "I opened the gym in this building right out here. It was a barn and a chicken hatchery, and I took young and old. Then I said I was going to close it because they were abusing the equipment, but my wife told me things I didn't know."

In 1956 Patterson had married Sandra Hicks, when he was twenty-one and she was eighteen, and they had three children. I had heard that they had been divorced, and that Patterson had married a white woman, and that they had two daughters, the two girls I had seen starting up the driveway.

"My wife is very personable," he was saying now. "She talks to all, and they tell her things they wouldn't tell me. She told me about this Thruway attendant who had a couple of kids, and every night he used to stop at a bar on the way home. Since he got into the boxing here, he hadn't done that, and I kept the gym open."

"How old are these fighters?"

"The one I told you about is twenty-one. He was about nineteen then, and I have several fifteen-year-olds. I have one—Andrew Schott—who feels as I did. It's like a religion. The kid is here every day. He has had twenty-five fights, and he can recall every fight he's had. There's no chance of him ever getting involved in drugs."

"How many of them," I said, "do you take to tournaments and get fights for?"

"There are fifteen actual fighters," he said. "Then there are two firemen from Poughkeepsie and a councilman from Rosendale that work out and spar to keep in shape. The councilman lost forty-five pounds, and he's been coming here a year and a half, and the gym is open seven days a week, except when we have fights."

"I would think that the town would appreciate what you're doing," I said.

"I like the town," he said, "and I like the people. I have no trouble whatsoever with the people in general, the old as well as the young, as long as I keep away from politics."

"You have a right to be interested in politics," I said.

"It would cause a lot of flak," he said. "Everybody knows me as just plain Floyd. I'm liked by most people, but not by all. No one has done anything to harm me, but I know, given the opportunity, the ones who don't like me would hurt me. I don't know how to say it, and I don't want to say it."

"But you went down to Alabama with Jackie Robinson at the time of all the trouble in Birmingham and Selma," I said.

"Jackie asked me," he said. "A lot of name people went, and I remember landing at the airport and for the first time in my life I saw different rest rooms for blacks and whites. I took movie pictures of the signs—actually there was no film in the camera—so the people would know it was unusual to me, and I was taking it back."

His two daughters were standing in the doorway, and he called them in and introduced them—Janene, who was nine, and Jennifer, seven. We shook hands, the older one looking right at me, and the younger, her head down, examining me out of the tops of her eyes.

"How is school?" I said.

"Fine," the older one said.

"Excuse us a minute," Patterson said. "I have to ask my wife something."

He left, with the girls following him, and I walked around the room, looking at his two championship belts, the plaques and trophies he had been awarded, and the framed photographs. There were pictures of him with Eartha Kitt, Jimmy Durante, Harry Bellafonte, Jack Palance, Bob Hope, Jackie Gleason, Lauren Bacall, one with James Cagney and Roland Winters, that I remembered being taken at Newtown, and another, taken in the White House, with Patterson, his wife and their two girls standing with Richard Nixon. There was, also framed, the gate-fold I had put together for *The Fireside Book of Boxing* in 1961 of pictures of all the heavyweight champions in succession from John L. Sullivan through Patterson. I had discovered three photographs that, when placed together, showed the crowd of 80,000 crammed into Boyle's Thirty Acres in Jersey City on July 2, 1921, for the Dempsey-Carpentier fight, the first million-dollar gate. I needed something for the other side of the fold, and lined up photographs of all the twenty champions in their fighting poses, Patterson twice and on either side of Johansson.

On a shelf at the right of the bar were record albums of Percy Faith, Johnny Mathis, Roger Williams, Jackie Gleason, André

Kostelanetz, Hank Williams, and Jo Stafford, the music I remember Patterson listening to in his training camps. Behind the bar the glasses were neatly aligned, the only bottles being two fifths of Seagram's Crown Royal, the tax seals on them unbroken.

"Do you do much business at this bar," I asked, when Patterson came back.

"It was here when we bought the house," he said. "Like those animal heads up there. My wife takes a drink now and then, but I can't stand the smell of the stuff."

"Don't fight it," I said.

"I was going to have an appointment, like at 3:30," he said, "but the man didn't come. He's the piano teacher, and I told him, 'I'll call you if I'm not going to be here today.' I just called him now to see where he was, and he assumed I would call if I wanted him to come."

"Who's taking the lessons?"

"My daughters and I. I take them because Jennifer is a perfectionist, and she hates to make a mistake and she won't play in front of the teacher. She has taken one lesson and Janene has taken three and I've taken three, and Jennifer plays better than both of us. She's the only one who doesn't have to look at the keys, so I reasoned I should take lessons with her and maybe that would help her.

"She's a natural athlete, too," he said. "She has tremendous coordination, but she hates to be the center of attraction. I remember when she was small and her birthday came and we got her a cake. My wife and I and my older daughter started to sing and she was crying, 'Don't! Don't!'

"In the school she'll play all the games with team participation, but when it comes to her doing it alone, she won't do it. She took ballet. The teacher, he told me she was fantastic, the best of all, and he had about fifty between the ages of six and twelve, but we took her out because she wouldn't do it alone in front of the others."

"I think I can understand that," I said.

"It's understandable to a certain degree," he said.

"I mean," I said, "that I remember a fella who was very shy."

"Yes," he said. "I know."

It was only three weeks after he had knocked out Archie Moore to win the heavyweight championship and it was just before Christmas, but he was back in training at the Long Pond Inn at Greenwood Lake, New York. The inn burned to the ground some years ago, but there used to be a bar and restaurant on the first floor with the living quarters and the gymnasium over it. When I checked with Ollie Cromwell, who was one of the owners and tended bar, he said that Patterson was up in his room, and I went up there where he was lying on the bed and listening to that music, and we shook hands.

"What time is it?" he said.

"One o'clock," I said.

"I'll be down in the dining room in a half hour," he said.

I waited in the dining room for three and a half hours. As I sat there, the place came alive with teen-agers who had been ice skating on the lake, and who had come in to play the juke box and dance. Finally, at 4:30, one of Patterson's sparring partners came in and walked over to the table where I was sitting.

"Floyd says he'll meet you in the gym in five minutes," the sparring partner said. "He apologizes."

"That's fine," I said, annoyed. "Where has he been?"

"Up in the room," the sparring partner said. "He came down a couple of times, but when he saw all these kids here, he went back. He was embarrassed to come in."

I said nothing about it when I met him in the gym, but two nights later we were standing and talking by the pool table beyond the bar. A couple of sparring partners were shooting pool, and I was working Patterson around slowly when I mentioned it, trying to get him to elaborate on the feelings he had had when he saw the dining room jumping with those kids.

"You're heavyweight champion of the world now," I said. "Doesn't that give you the security to walk through a room of teen-agers?"

"No," he said. "I still don't like to be stared at."

I thought of John L. Sullivan, this country's first sports hero, who used to stride into saloons and announce, "I can lick any man in the world!" The next morning we were standing in front of the Long Pond Inn, waiting for one of the sparring partners who had been sent to town to buy the morning newspapers, when I came back to it.

"But you're going to be stared at a lot," I said.

"I know," Patterson said.

"When did you first realize that this was going to be a problem?"

"The day after I won the title," he said. "Just before the fight my wife gave birth to our daughter, so right after the fight, these friends and I, we got in the car to drive back from Chicago. The next day we stopped at one of those roadside restaurants and went in. By then the fight was all over the pages of the newspapers, pictures and all, and I could see the people around the place recognizing me and starting to whisper. I figured we better get out of there quick, so we didn't even finish our meal."

Just before he won the title, Patterson had bought a ten-room house in Mount Vernon, New York, for his mother and the eight youngest of her eleven children. After Patterson beat Moore, the mayor of the city, who was an ex-fighter, staged a torch-light parade for him, and I asked Patterson what that was like.

"I was ashamed," he said.

"Why?" I said.

"Me sitting in an open car and waving to people," he said. "Those are things you only see kings and Presidents doing."

A heavyweight champion has to spend some of his time banquet-hopping, and Cus D'Amato made Patterson buy a tuxedo. He said it embarrassed him to wear it because, in his view, formal clothes were for those who had been born and raised to them, and he was not. When he was not in camp he lived with his wife and daughter in St. Albans, on Long Island, and he would do roadwork in a park there a couple of days a week.

"What time do you run?" I asked him once.

"I get up at 5:30, so I finish before the people start to work and see me," he said.

"Doesn't anybody ever see you?" I said.

"Usually I run on Saturday and Sunday when everybody don't get up so early," he said, "but one day I ran during the week. It was a Thursday, and after I finished in the park the fella who was supposed to pick me up was late. About an hour passed before he came, and there I was sitting on the park bench with my heavy clothes on and all sweaty and a towel around my neck. All these people were going to work by then, and they were looking at me like I was crazy."

"Didn't anyone recognize you?" I said.

"No," he said. "I was the champion, so I hid my face."

"Shyness is so deeply ingrained in you," I said to him another night at the Long Pond, "that I suppose one of your earliest memories is of being embarrassed in public."

"I guess that's right," he said. "I remember when I was just a little kid. I used to have long hair and my father would comb it. Then he'd send me around the corner for cigarettes, and I remember one day a lady stopping me and running her fingers through my hair. I was so embarrassed that I wanted to cry, and I ran."

He thought about it. It was after dinner and we were still sitting at the table.

"I had to be just a tiny kid for a lady to do that," he said, "but I never forgot it."

So all of that was twenty years before, and now he was supplying a gym and running a boxing club to provide a port for the young of the area who need it. At forty-one he was starting to take piano lessons to help a daughter in whom he saw himself.

"I hope she can come out of it by herself," he said now. "The first time somebody asked me for my autograph there were like twenty people waiting, and the guy gave me the piece of paper and I forgot how to spell my own name. I got a mental block."

"I remember you saying how long it took you to be able to look people in the eye."

"It took years," he said, "and I don't want her to have to go through what I went through. When I came back from the Olympics—and I won the Olypmics when I was seventeen—I went to a dinner and they handed me a microphone. I panicked. Fortunately the gentleman before me had said something, and I stopped to think about that and I commented. Thousands of microphones have been handed to me since then, and it's easier, but it's never easy."

"I recall," I said, "how you used to say that some day you wanted to own a place in the country and have horses. Do you own horses?"

"No," he said. "We've got three dogs and a cat and we travel. I take the family wherever I go, to England, to Sweden, to Portugal, to Spain, and to get somebody to take care of horses, too, would be too difficult. Even for me it would be difficult, because I devote so much time to my family. I get up with the kids, and I put them to bed at night. I try to do as much with them as I can, because in my first marriage that was lacking. I was in camp all the time."

"How are your other children?"

"My son spent three weeks with me this summer, and he's thirteen now. The two daughters I see occasionally, but they live in Springfield, Massachusetts, and I don't see them as much as I'd like."

"How did you meet your present wife?" I asked.

"Janet?" he said. "It's strange how I met her. After I had rewon the title—not right then but in 1962—the secretary I had got married. I used to get thousands of letters, and I needed someone to answer the mail. I have this friend, Mickey Allen . . ."

"I remember him. He wanted to be a singer, and once you arranged for him to sing the National Anthem at one of your fights."

I remember how pleased and excited about it Allen was. He reasoned that the exposure on national television would launch him on his vocal career.

"That's right," Patterson said. "He owns a discothèque and a catering service now, and he said, 'My wife's sister can type. She was secretary to the vice-president of the New York Stock Exchange.' So she worked for me once a week, and that's how I met her. She was born in Rosedale, New York, but her parents moved to Greenwood Lake. I have a house right here for her parents when they come here, and they may stay a week or a month."

"I'd like to meet your wife," I said, "and I'm wondering if I might take you both to dinner tonight?"

"That would be nice," he said, "but I'm not sure. There's this seventy-five-year-old woman my wife got to know, and she just lost her husband. She's lonely, and I know it's on the calendar that we're supposed to visit her tonight. Maybe she can change it to tomorrow night, and I'll ask her."

He went out and I walked around the room again reading the inscriptions on the plaques, and there was a framed hand-lettered quotation from Vince Lombardi that had been presented to Patterson by the 501st Replacement Detachment of the First Armored Division. It was about making winning a habit, even as losing can be, and about doing things right not once in a while but all of the time.

"I'm sorry," Patterson said when he came back. "My wife says the lady is expecting us, and she's very lonely and she doesn't want to disappoint her. She's sorry."

"I understand," I said.

"It's time I went over to the gym," he said. "You want to come along?"

"Yes, indeed," I said.

We walked out through the entry hall and the dining room and into the kitchen. The two girls were in the kitchen.

"I'm going over to the gym now," Patterson said to them, "and you lock the storm door after us. All right?"

Outside he turned and waited while one of them locked the door. We walked across the parking area at the top of the driveway to the white-painted two-story barn. The ring is on the first floor, with stairs leading up to the loft, like a balcony, overhanging the first floor. In the loft were a couple of heavy punching bags and one light bag and two full-length mirrors. At the back of the loft is the dressing room with steel lockers, and there was a hand-printed notice on the wall:

> TO ALL CLUB MEMBERS
> Do Not Invite Anyone To The Gym Without
> First Telling Me—I Do Not Want Strangers
> Wandering Around My House—Casing the Place
> —Should Anyone Violate This I Will Have
> To Ask Them To Leave.

There were four young fighters, who seemed to be in their teens, undressing in front of the lockers and getting into their ring trunks and boxing shoes. It had been chilly all day and it was cold in the locker room and, after he had stripped, Patterson put on thermal underwear and a sweat suit.

"You see," he was saying, sitting and lacing one of his ring shoes and looking up at one of the young fighters, "if anybody quits, they can't came back. I take the time. I take the punches, so they can't come back."

"I know," the fighter was saying, nodding. "I know."

Two more young fighters came in, and when Patterson finished lacing his shoes and got up, the ones who were ready followed him down the stairs to the gym. It was 5:15, and it was 7:15 when Patterson called it quits. Others came in, the two firemen from Poughkeepsie among them, and Patterson took them on one after the other, moving around on the worn canvas patched with green plastic tape, blocking and picking off their punches, occasionally countering and the sweat beading on his neck and face so that between rounds he had to towel. For two unbroken hours there was the thwack sound of gloves against gloves and the thup sound of gloves landing to the body, the shuffle sound of the shoes on canvas, the rhythmic sound of heavy breathing, and over it, Patterson's comments.

"You're not bringing your second jab back. Bring it all the way back," he was telling one. To another, "The moment you get close you tend to rear back. Keep your distance. That's it, but don't pull your shoulder back. Keep it relaxed, and when you throw the right hand, throw it from there. If you hold the shoulder up you force the right hand down." To another, "When are you gonna get your hair cut? Every time you lower your head your hair covers your eyes and you have to raise your head." To another, "Why move in? You're smothering your own punches. You have to keep your distance, and you know why you're missing so much? I know what punches you're gonna throw before you throw them. You have to mix them up." To another, "Keep your head down. Every now and then touch your chin to your shoulder." To another, "Throw the right. No good. You're just putting it there. Throw it. That's better. Again. Good."

When we judge professional performers we tend to take for granted, and forget, some of the things that they do well. During the years when I had watched Patterson fight I had fastened on his flaws, and I was impressed now by his boxing knowledge and his ability to spot the errors of the others, even though they were just beginners.

"You see," he was saying to one of them, after I had followed him and the others back upstairs, "as much as I know about boxing, if I was going to fight again I'd need a trainer, because I can't see what I'm doing wrong. I don't know. That's why I tell you these things, because I can see."

He started to undress, then, to take his shower, and I told him that I thought the boxing lessons had gone very well. I said I wanted to see him again the next morning.

"That's all right," he said. "How about 10:30?"

"Fine," I said.

At 10:30 the next morning, when I drove into the parking area at the top of the driveway, Patterson was washing a car. It was a golden-tan Lincoln Continental with the New York license plate FP 1, and Patterson was in the jeans and T-shirt. He turned off the hose and we shook hands.

"Here's something that might interest you," I said.

I had brought along a copy of the February 28, 1959, issue of *The Saturday Evening Post*. In those days the magazine ran long interview pieces they called "visits" with celebrities, and they used to give me the fighters. I did Patterson and Johansson and Jack Dempsey, always with Jacob Lofman photographing it and with my friend Jim Cleary taping it because, although I had been taking accurate notes for twenty years by then, the magazine insisted that everything be recorded and then transcribed onto some sixty pages of typescript from which I had to work.

The Patterson piece led the issue, and on the opening page there was a picture of him in the ring after he had knocked out Hurricane Jackson. At the bottom of the page, was a shot of the two of us sitting and talking by the ring in the Gramercy Gym. Patterson, gesticulating, was wearing a sand-colored, medium-weight cardigan.

"You haven't changed much," I said, showing him the picture, "but I have."

"Look at the sweater," Patterson said. "I still have that sweater."

"I remember it as a particularly fine one."

"Is it all right if I show this to my wife?" he said. "My wife would be interested to read it."

"Of course," I said.

He took the magazine, and I followed him around the front of the house and into the entry hall. He motioned me into the bar room and then excused himself and disappeared with the magazine.

"I'm always interested," I said when he came back, "in the relationships, years later, between fighters who fought each other. In your travels do you ever see Johansson?"

"I've been to Sweden a few times," he said, "but I and Johansson never showed any friendship until lately. He said so many derogatory things. In 1964, when I beat Eddie Machen in Stockholm, he said that Machen would knock me out and that Floyd was over the hill. It was an afternoon fight, and just as I walked out to get in the ring, Ingemar was in the first row. Our eyes met and I went over and shook hands and everybody booed. I don't know why."

"Probably," I said, "because he'd taken himself and his money to Switzerland."

"Then in 1974, after I hadn't fought in two years, I was in a restaurant in Stockholm, and who walked over but Ingemar Johansson. He was very nice then, and I've seen him a few times since."

"What about some of the other fighters you fought?"

"There were some of the guys, coming up in my career, like Hurricane Jackson and Jimmy Slade who were in the same camp until we fought. In camp, Jimmy Slade and I would play cards, and he'd get angry when I won. He'd throw the cards in my face, and in camp he'd be in charge.

"Then one day Cus asked me would I fight Jimmy Slade. I said, 'Of course not. We're friends.' Cus said, 'There comes a time in a fighter's career when he has to forget friendship.' I said, 'Ask Jimmy.' Jimmy said, 'Sure.' I was hurt, it came so easy to him.

"The guys I fought I don't dislike," he said, "and I'd like to stay in communication with them. I tried to call Jimmy Slade for days and days after I beat him, but I never got an answer. Dick Wagner, though, my first fight with him was difficult, and in the second I stopped him, but I made it known to the press that I respected him. He's out in Portland, Oregon, where he works on the railroad, and he's married to a school teacher. I had dinner at his house and his family met my family and I sent him cards from Sweden.

"A lot of guys I fought, though, have nothing but derogatory things to say. I saw Roy Harris when Joe Frazier fought Bob Foster. I met him in the lobby of the hotel and we talked a while, and the following day there was an article in the press where he said some derogatory things. Brian London said derogatory things. Why do they do this?"

"I guess they're still trying to win fights they lost to you years ago."

"It tends to bring them down," Patterson said. "They should carry themselves like Joe Louis."

When Patterson was small Louis was his idol. He kept scrap books filled with clippings and pictures of Joe, and after Patterson won the title the two met for the first time at a dinner.

"What was it like finally meeting him?" I asked Patterson, shortly after that.

"Well," Patterson had said, "I said to myself, 'Is this really Joe Louis? Am I finally meeting the man who is my idol?' I almost couldn't believe it."

"But you were the heavyweight champion of the world," I had said. "You have his old title."

"It seemed to me," Patterson had said, "like Joe Louis was still the champion, and I wasn't."

"Do you ever see Joe?" I asked him now.

"I see Joe often," he said, "and I'll still flash back to when I was nine, ten, and eleven and how I admired him, the way he carried himself. Here it is thirty years later, and I try to carry myself so that they might say the same thing about me."

"You picked a good model," I said.

"I know who I am," he said, "and what I believe in, but today you must be militant—down with Whitey—to be accepted. If that's what it takes, then I'll be the white man's black man, because I won't accept it the other way. I'd leave the country first. In my gym there are whites and colored and Puerto Ricans. I believe in an equal society. I see no colors. Everybody is the same like in my gym—but the militants don't like me."

"You know that?"

"I go over to the college here," he said. "This black group—the black something—asked me to give a speech. I knew they'd harass me. This one guy said, 'How come you call him Cassius Clay. Why not Muhammad Ali?' I said, 'First of all, I think Cassius is a beautiful name, and I can't pronounce Muhammad. My tongue won't pronounce it. Then you give him rights you don't give me. I believe Clay believes in a separate society. You believe the same, or you wouldn't be all blacks here. He called Liston 'The Ugly Bear.' He called George Forman 'The Mummy.' He called me 'The Rabbit.' You must give me the right to call him 'Clay.'"

"But what did you say in your speech?" I said.

"I'll get it," he said. "I'll be right back."

What I had really wanted to say was that he should be done with the name-calling, that the beauty he ascribes to the name Cassius and his problem in pronouncing Muhammad are pretexts and have nothing to do with it. Louis would have pronounced it as best he could. When he came back now he handed me the typewritten speech and I read:

"To all you young people, I would like to see you go out in the world and have all your dreams come true, and they can if you work hard at your God-given talents. Our people have come a long way, and we have had to struggle to get where we are today.

"You young people are our hopes and pride. It is you who must continue to struggle. This world is not all black, and we can't make it so. We must live with all people. The sooner we realize that, the happier we'll be. You're young and you're beautiful and have a whole lifetime of living to do. Be conscious of your dreams and pride. Leave color at the end of the list—not the beginning.

"Black power is not a true power. White power is not a true power. What I ask you to look for is the power of right, not the power of might. My career has shaped my life, and I have learned much. I have met people from all over the world, the highest to the most humble. The finest of these people accept a man for what he is. Be men, and other men will know you at a glance. Remember Jesus said; 'Love.' Racists say: 'Hate.' One of most renowned Americans who died for what he believed preached love. He was a black man. Some of our people did not agree with him, but in the annals of history his name will be at the top. I speak of Martin Luther King."

At the age of ten Patterson was unable to read, and he refused to talk. His family had moved seven times, and he had attended irregularly seven schools before they sent him to Wiltwyck, a school for emotionally disturbed boys, at Esopus, New York, and later to P.S. 614, one of New York City's five schools for maladjusted children.

"That's a good speech," I said now.

"My wife helped me with it," he said. "She helps me with all my speeches."

"What kind of a reception did it get? Did they applaud?"

"Yes," he said. "About two thirds did. One third, I guess they couldn't be broke. If I reach one, though, I think it's fine."

"If I may say so," I said, "you should shut your mind to Ali. To begin with, you were in no shape to fight him the first time, and . . ."

"I had a slipped disc," Patterson said. "It started in 1956, before the fight with Archie Moore, and I took three or four days off. Before the fight with Clay it went out. I took some days off, and it was all right. Then in the first round it went out, and there was a knot in my back as big as a fist. The pain was so bad that it was the first time in a fight I was begging to be knocked out."

Between rounds, as I had watched on television, Al Silvani, who trained Patterson for the fight, would stand behind Patterson and put his arms around him, under the armpits and across the chest. He would lift Patterson, Patterson's feet dangling above the canvas as Silvani tried to slip the disc back in. Then, during the rounds, until they stopped it in the twelfth, Ali would taunt and torture him.

"In the eighth and ninth rounds," Patterson was saying now, "I was saying to myself, 'The first good punch he catches me with I'm going to go down.' He hit me good punches. I was down. I was dizzy, but when I opened my eyes I was up again. I could not take a dive."

"I believe that," I said, "and you should be proud of it."

"There are things I like about myself," he said. "I could not stay down. In boxing you learn about yourself. The feeling of shame I will never lose, because I let people down, but I will never again feel ashamed of being ashamed."

"And you shouldn't," I said.

"It's me," he said. "I can't change it."

"I was impressed yesterday," I said, "watching you teach those kids. When it was over you were telling one of them that, if you were to fight again, you'd need a trainer because you wouldn't be able to see what you were doing wrong."

"That's right," he said.

"I know," I said, "and I remember something you used to do wrong, and I begged you not to do it against Johansson in that second fight."

"You did?" he said.

In their first fight, Johansson, firing the big right hand, had had him down seven times in the third round before they had stopped it. Before the second fight, Alvin Boretz, the television writer, and I wrote a half-hour special that was to be aired on the ABC network the night before the fight. With Manny Spiro, the producer, and a camera crew, I had gone to both camps, first to interview Johansson late one afternoon in the octagonal ski hut at Grossinger's, and then Patterson early the next afternoon in the main dining room of the dilapidated roadhouse in Newton.

We shot them both the same way, from the waist up and full face to the camera and, off camera myself, I asked both of them the same questions, about how they started as fighters, about their previous fights, in particular about what feelings they had had about the men they had fought, before and after those fights. Johansson was excellent, confident and even haughty—the way, if you are handling a fighter, you want him to be.

"After you had knocked Patterson down seven times and were now heavyweight champion of the world," I said, "did you have any feeling, looking across the ring at him, of sympathy for him?"

"No," Johansson said, "I did not. He'd gladly like to have me in the same situation."

"How about in the days after the fight when you thought about him?"

"I know my sister," he said, "she walk over when Patterson went from ring. My sister walked to him and raised her hand, and did like this on his chin. She feel sorry for him. But not me."

"This guy was great," Leonard Anderson, the director, said, as we walked back to the main building at Grossinger's.

"Terrific," Manny Spiro said, and he was obviously excited. "Just terrific, but what is poor Patterson going to do compared to that?"

"Just wait," I said.

The next morning we drove down to Newtown and, coming right out of Grossinger's, the others were appalled by the place. When Patterson came out to greet us he was in his road clothes, and he shook hands humbly, in that small-boy manner, and then he went back inside while they set up.

"This is unbelievable," Leonard Anderson said. "Looking at the two camps and the two fighters, I can't give this guy a chance."

"I feel sorry for him," Manny Spiro said, and then to me, "After Johansson, what can this poor nebbish say?"

"Relax," I said. "In fact, I'll guarantee you one thing right now. I don't know how he'll do in the fight, but I'll bet you he boxes rings around Johansson and flattens him in the interview segment."

I went inside then, and I found Patterson. I explained to him how we were going to film him, just sitting on a stool and facing the camera.

"But I don't know what you want me to say," he said.

"It's going to be easy," I said. "I'll just ask you questions I've asked you before, about your first fight on the street, and about your feelings for other fighters. I'll ask you about how you felt about Archie Moore after you won the title, and then I'll ask you about how you went into seclusion after the Johansson fight, and then about the little girl in the hospital in Atlantic City. All you have to do is tell me what you've told me before."

"All right," he said.

Sitting there on that stool and looking right at the camera, he told it as he had told it to me before, the voice low level and neither rising nor falling, but the answers direct and explicit. He told about knocking out Moore, and then looking across the ring and, realizing that Moore had wanted the heavyweight championship as much as he and was now so old that he would never get another chance, feeling sorry for him. Then I asked him about the month he had spent in seclusion at home after Johansson had knocked him out, and he explained how he had felt that he had let all of his friends and the United States down, and that late one night he was sitting in the game room in the basement, still feeling sorry for himself.

"I was just sitting there, thinking," he said. "You know, when your mind just wanders. I was thinking about some things that had happened in some of the places that I had been to, and I thought about being in Atlantic City one time and going through a hospital for leukemia and blood diseases and cancer, and I specifically remember a girl in the hospital.

"She had leukemia," he said, and he gave a pause that you would celebrate a professional actor for timing. "Cancer. The doctor was showing me through the wards, and he brought me into this little girl's room and she had a tube running through her arms and whatnot, and said she was about four and she was small for a four-year-old girl and you'd think she was just born. She was just nothing but bones, and as I walked out of the room and upon viewing this, I remember the doctor saying to me it would be a miracle if she should live past tonight or tomorrow.

"So," he said, "after thinking about this, I thought, 'Who am I to feel sorry for myself?' I should get down on my knees and thank God for the things I do have, and actually all I did was lose a fight, and I got paid for the fight and I have a beautiful home, and all the things the average man would want and even more. So, why should I feel sorry for myself?' I began to come out of it then, and I started going out the very next day, and that night was the first night that I think I got a good night's sleep."

"Cut!" Leonard Anderson said. "Great!"

"Thank you, Floyd," I said.

"You're welcome," he said.

"Floyd, you were terrific," Manny Spiro was saying. "That was absolutely terrific."

The whole thing had taken no more than fifteen minutes, but I was spent. I walked out into the sunlight and onto the terrace, with the weeds starting to grow between the cracked and uneven slates. Bill Mason, the sound engineer, had set up his recording equipment out there, with the cord to the microphone running through an open window, and he was still sitting there in front of his gear on a wooden folding chair.

"Wow!" he said. "What an interview!"

"It was all right," I said.

"All right?" he said. "Let me tell you something. I've been in this business for twenty years, and I've recorded everybody, including Presidents in the White House. I never recorded anything like that."

"That's Patterson," I said.

"When he told that story about the little girl dying in the hospital," Mason said, "I couldn't see him, but just sitting here with the headset on and listening—I'm telling you—the tears were running down my cheeks."

They had signed up James Cagney to host the program, and I could remember him dying on the church steps in *The Roaring Twenties,* his body riddled with the sub-machine gun bullets that had spewed out of the black limousine as it came around the corner, sliding and careening across the screen, while I sat, a teen-ager, in the Proctor's theater, gripped and hollow-sad. I could remember him, dead and bound like a mummy and propped against his mother's front door, falling forward onto the floor in *Public Enemy,* and now the teen-ager still in me found it almost absurd that he should be reading lines I had written.

"Patterson's great in the interview," he had said, after we had shown him and Robert Montgomery in a screening room on Broadway the rushes of what we had shot in the camps, "but can he lick the other guy?"

Between reels, while we waited for the projectionist to change over, we had talked about fights and fighters he remembered, and I had found that he has what I call the ability to read fights. It is like the ability to read writing, when the writing is worthy of it—not just what a writer says, but what he doesn't say and what he implies. Reading fights is not just reading the punches, which are obvious, but it is reading between the punches, the styles and the thinking, or what each fighter should be thinking, to set up what he has to say while silencing the other.

"He can lick him if he fights him right," I had said. "All he has to worry about is that one punch, the right hand."

"It's some right hand," Cagney had said, "and the way Patterson comes up out of his crouch he bobs right up into it."

Alvin Boretz had shown me how, filming Cagney in the studio, we could interpolate him into the interviews, and then I had had to convince Jack Dempsey to give Patterson a chance. For the last segment of the program I had wanted Dempsey and Joe Louis, the dream match, with Dempsey picking Johansson and Louis explaining how Patterson could beat him. Someone at the advertising agency, or perhaps the sponsor, had discovered, however, that Louis was associated with an advertising firm that represented an account in Castro's Cuba, and so they had turned down Joe, who had defended his title without pay for Army and Navy relief and is one of the noblest of men any of us has known in sports, and they picked Gene Tunney.

"I like Johansson," Dempsey had said, when I had gone to see him in his Broadway restaurant about the segment on the show. We were sitting in one of the booths.

"I know," I said, "but Tunney picks Johansson. Let me tell you what I'd like you to say."

. It was another absurdity. A small boy, his hair freshly shampooed and his mother insisting that he not go to bed before it had thoroughly dried, would come down the stairs to listen on the radio to "The Cliquot Club Eskimos," "The A & P Gypsies," or Billy Jones and Ernie Hare, who called themselves "The Happiness Boys" when they broadcast from the Happiness Restaurant in New York, and later "The Interwoven Pair" when they advertised men's hose. The small boy, out-punched in the playground and scared in the street scrambles, would be wearing a heavy flannel bathrobe with an Indian blanket design on it, as he walked into the living room.

"Here he comes now!" his father would inevitably announce, and the boy would inevitably cringe inside. "Jack Dempsey!"

So I told Dempsey how I thought Patterson should fight it. If he worked inside Johansson's left jab, which in the first fight had set him up for Johansson's right, and if he kept firing left hooks while he turned it into a street fight and backed Johansson up, he could win it.

"That's right," Dempsey said. "If he does that, he could lick the Swede. I can say that."

After we had filmed Cagney in the studio, leading into the interviews and then with Dempsey and Tunney, someone had asked him to visit the two camps for some publicity still photos with the fighters. The next day, he and his friend Roland Winters drove into Patterson's camp where a half dozen of us were waiting.

"You have a picture over there on the wall," I said to Patterson now, sixteen years later, "of you with James Cagney and Roland Winters. That was taken for that TV program before the second Johansson fight when I interviewed you and Ingemar."

"That's right," he said. "I remember."

"After the picture-taking," I said, "the rest of us went to lunch at the inn in Newtown. You weren't having your meal then, but you came along and sat with us. You were at the end of the table, with Cagney on your right and me on your left. We talked awhile, and you were about to leave to work out, and that's when I asked you not to make the same mistake again."

"You did?" Patterson said.

"Sure," I said, thinking that he should remember this. "I said, 'Floyd, do yourself and me a favor. This guy has only one punch, the right hand. His jab isn't much, but it's just heavy enough to keep you in range for the right, so you've got to slip the jab, work on the inside, back him up and turn it into a street fight. None of these fellas from Europe, who have that stand-up continental style, can handle it when it's a street fight.'

"Then," I was saying now, and I was up and demonstrating again as I had in that dining room at the inn, "I told you to finish every one of your combinations, every sequence of punches, with the left hook. I said, 'This is the most important point of all. When you finish with a right hand, and if you hurt him with it or back him up, it still leaves you over here on your left, and in line for his right. You've got to finish with the hook, every time, and I don't care if you don't even hit him with it. Even if you miss it, it will carry you over to your right and out of line of his right.' "

"That's correct," Patterson said now, sitting there and nodding. "That's right."

"So you said, 'But I'm not sure I can learn that, to always finish with the left.' I said, 'Of course you can. When you're shadowboxing, when you're sparring in the ring, finish with the hook. When you're running on the road, throw half-punches and finish with the hook. Keep telling yourself, 'Left hook. Left hook.' You've got to do that, because you'll be taking away his only punch and throwing your best one. You can learn it.' Then you said, 'I'll try.' "

He had shaken hands with us then, to go back to camp. I didn't tell him now what Cagney had said as soon as he had left.

"Tell me something," Cagney said to me. "Who's been teaching this guy?"

"I remember," Patterson said now, "somebody telling me that about the left hook, but I forgot that it was you. Then I remember I also got a letter from a man—I don't know who he was—and he told me to always double-jab."

"That was good advice," I said, "because Johansson liked to throw the right hand over your single jab. That was very good advice."

"And that was some hook I hit him with," Patterson said, a small smile of satisfaction crossing his face.

That night at the Polo Grounds, left hooks and the only anger he ever carried into a ring won the fight for Patterson. He had backed Johansson up from the start, working inside the jab, but he had been in and out of trouble a half dozen times when he had forgotten to finish his combinations with a hook. Only Johansson's inability to spot this and time him had saved Patterson, and then in the fifth round, with Johansson backing up again, he had let go a wide hook, that was more a leaping swing. Johansson's back was to his own corner, and when he went down he landed on his rump and then his head hit the canvas and he lay there, his right leg twitching and the blood coming out of his mouth, for what seemed like ten minutes, while I feared for him, and before they dared move him back to his corner and prop him up on the stool.

When I next saw Patterson he was going into training for the third Johansson fight the following March in Miami. I asked him how he had felt after he had won the title back.

"When I left the Polo Grounds," he said, "the promoters had a car and chauffeur waiting for me. I was sitting in the back seat alone, and when we drove through Harlen and I saw all the people celebrating in the streets, I felt good."

"You should have," I said. "There'd been nothing like it since Louis knocked out Billy Conn."

I meant there had been nothing like it for the Negro race in this country, and this will show you how far we have come. In the summer of 1936 I worked with a mixed gang on the railroad tracks that run through the Bronx and into Manhattan, and the day after Max Schmeling knocked out Joe Louis, Joe's people, so expectant and exuberant the day before, worked all day in saddened silence. Then, after Louis had knocked out Schmeling in 2 minutes and 4 seconds in their second fight, I had read about the all-night celebration in Harlem, and I had seen some of it after the second Conn fight and after Patterson had knocked out Johansson, and we have all come so far that there has been nothing like it since.

"Then I thought about Johansson," Patterson had said, describing that ride through Harlem. "I thought how he would have to drive through here, too, and then he would have to go through what I went through after the first fight. I thought that he would be even more ashamed than I was, because he'd knocked me out the first time. Then I felt sorry for him."

"Do you think," I had asked him, "that you can call up the same kind of anger and viciousness the next time you fight Johansson?"

"Why should I?" he had said. "In all my other fights I was never vicious, and I won out in almost all of them."

"But you had to be vicious against this guy," I had said. "You had to turn a boxing contest into a kind of street fight to destroy this guy's classic style. When you did that, he came apart. This was your greatest fight, because for the first time you expressed emotion. A fight, a piece of writing, a painting, or a passage of music is nothing without emotion."

"I just hope," Patterson had said, "that I'll never be as vicious again."

He never was, in his third fight with Johansson, when he was on the floor himself before he knocked Johansson out, or in the two each with Liston and Ali, when anger translated into viciousness might have given him the only chance he had. In what is the most totally expressive of the arts, for it permits man to vent and divest himself of his hatred and his anger, deplorable though they may be, he had delivered his finest performance when he held himself to be out of character, or at least the character he has tried always to assume.

"You earned a good deal of money," I said now. "Did you get good advice as to how to handle it? Did you have good investment help?"

"I helped myself," he said, "after experiencing losing tremendous amounts of money through people who were handling my finances. I supposedly made $9,000,000 in the ring. I don't know who got most of it, Uncle Sam or the persons handling it. All the money went to the office. Like $100,000 at one time would go to the office, and I would call and say, 'Send me $1,000 to run the camp.' Then I would go back and look at the account and there would be $12,000 in it. I'd say, 'Where's the rest?' "

"But you'd had no training in investments," I said.

"I started learning about various things," he said. "I had some stocks that were very successful. With stocks, if it was not too much of a gamble, I would chance it."

"So you won't ever have to work again?"

"I hope not," he said. "I sure hope not. When you retire and leave the limelight, you do what you really want to do. The days go slower. It's healthier, and you live longer. I think all the time. I do most of my thinking while I'm working, and before I realize it, it will be four or five hours later. It's the same thing when I go to sleep. I think a lot."

"And what are the thoughts that go through your mind?"

"I think about life now, as opposed to the way it used to be, and about my peace of mind."

"And the life you have now," I said, "is it what you wanted, and hoped that someday it might be?"

"Let me put it this way," he said. "Being raised in Brooklyn and coming up through the slums, life is very different. I don't think anyone knows what they want in life. They know what they don't want. It's a process of elimination. I knew what I didn't want. I didn't want the slums.

"Living here," he said, "married, with a couple of kids—I didn't know I wanted this, but I am perfectly contented. I have to remember, though, and that makes me appreciate more what I have today. I wouldn't change one thing in the past because it helped me to this."

"That's the proper way to look at it," I said. "If we could all look at our lives that way, realizing that there's nothing we can do about the past, we'd all be the better for it. I'm happy for you."

"Thank you," he said.

We talked for a few minutes more, about other fighters I would be seeing for the book and about the decline of boxing. Then I stood up to leave.

"If your wife has read that piece," I said, "I'd like the magazine back. It's the only copy I have."

"Oh, yes," he said, and then, after he had come back with the magazine, "My wife enjoyed it."

"I'm glad," I said.

He walked me out to the car and we shook hands. I backed out and drove out to Route 299 and back up the hill through the center of the town. I had checked out of the motel, so I turned onto the Thruway, and I was sorry that, for whatever reasons, I had not met his wife. Perhaps, if they had gone to dinner with me, and if she had trusted me, I could have led them to tell me what it is like, a mixed marriage, an island in the sea of our still social segregation. Perhaps they would have told me, if they had known that I have believed for a long time that fifty or a hundred years from now, if this planet survives that long, it will be accepted that the ultimate and only rational solution will be miscegenation.

2

The Opponent

For me it always typified one thing: the dash of
ingenuity the readiness at the first opportunity that
characterizes the American soldier.

Dwight D. Eisenhower, March 7, 1955

"There's a Bill Heinz calling Norman Rubio," I heard the woman
at the other end of the phone saying, and then I heard the phone
strike against a hard surface, perhaps a table top, and I waited.

"Hello?" he said.

"Norman," I said, "this is Bill Heinz. John Maguire called you
about me, and I wrote you a letter a week or so ago."

"Yeah," he said.

John Maguire writes a column now for the *Albany Times-
Union,* and we have been friends for a dozen years. When Norman Rubio was fighting out of Albany, John knew him, and I had
asked him to find where Rubio was living and to telephone him to
explain what I wanted to do.

"I'd like to come and see you," I said now. "Some week night?
Or on a weekend?"

"Whenever you say," he said.

"Well," I said, "that's up to you."

"Look," he said. "I don't know how far you have to come, and
I don't want to put you out."

"Believe me," I said, "you're not putting me out. How about
Sunday, about eleven in the morning?"

"I'll be here," he said, "but I mean, why should you come a

long distance to see me? I was never a champion. What have I got to say that anybody cares?"

"I care," I said.

I had seen him only once in my life, thirty years before, and we had never met, in the formal sense, and yet he had stayed with me over all this time. It was a Friday night in the Garden, and they were introducing a nineteen-year-old welterweight out of New Orleans named Bernie Docusen. The word that had preceded him was that he was "the new Ray Robinson," and then four days before the fight the other fighter, whoever he was and for whatever reason, had pulled out, and they had substituted Norman Rubio, who three months before had gone ten rounds with Robinson. He was what they call in the fight game "the opponent."

It hurt me to watch. They came out of New Orleans—Bernie Docusen, his brother Maxie, a lightweight; Ralph Dupas, another lightweight, and Willie Pastrano, who went on to the light-heavyweight title—and as boxing is an art form, even as jazz, they were all exponents of what I came to call the New Orleans Style. They were rapier artists, feinting you, sticking you, hooking or crossing you when they got you to stand still, but seldom still long enough themselves to mount the punching power of a Robinson.

If, after the first couple of rounds, anyone in the Garden that night thought Rubio could win, it must have been he, because that was the way he fought. Stocky and muscled and gnarled, he kept carrying the fight to Docusen, who had the height and reach and the hand and foot speed and the youth on him, taking three or four punches or more to get one into the body as Docusen moved away to spear him and then bounce the combinations off him again. On the most generous scorecard he won only one round, and in the papers the next day he was described as "the perfect foil."

What I remembered more clearly than the fight, however, and after all those years, was the scene in the dressing room later. It was hot and humid in the room and Norman Rubio, still in his boxing trunks and his hands still taped and resting on a towel in his lap, was sitting on a stool and leaning back against one of his handlers while the other held an ice bag to his face. We formed a semicircle around him—Lester Bromberg of the *World Telegram,*

Lewis Burton of the *Journal American,* Al Buck of the *New York Post,* and Barney Nagler of the *Bronx Home News,* and I—folded copy paper and pencils in our hands, and we wanted to know only one thing.

"Norman," somebody said, "how good is this kid?"

"He's good," Rubio said, talking from under the ice bag and lying back. "Don't think he can't fight."

"Well, what makes him a good fighter?" somebody else said. "Can you tell us?"

Rubio sat up. As he did the handler pulled the ice bag away and you could see the sweat and the red welts, and over Rubio's left eye, the swelling.

"Well, he moves real good," Rubio said, and now he brought his taped hands up from the towel in his lap. "He's hard to reach and he can use either hand. You can't tie him up."

"How about his hitting?" somebody said. "Does he hit hard?"

"I'll tell you," Rubio said. "He's not what I call a heavy hitter, if you know what I mean. I mean he doesn't hurt you as much as he stings you, but don't get me wrong. He can hit."

"How would he do with Ray Robinson?" That was why we were there.

"Oh," Rubio said, thinking, and now the handler had put the ice bag back on his face. "I would say that he's not ready yet. Robinson hits harder, and he's too strong for him. This is just a kid."

"How would he be with Willie Joyce?"

"Good."

"What about Tippy Larkin?"

"That would be a good fight. You know what I mean? When this kid learns a little more he'll go a long way. He can fight."

"Thanks," somebody said, and then we left.

We left him sitting there with that ice bag on his swollen face, but I guess you could say that I never left. In the memory center of my mind, and many times, I went back to that dressing room and Norman Rubio. For every champion there were the hundreds who never made it, and yet those who fought the champions helped to make the champions, for it was on them that the champions learned. In non-title bouts, Rubio lost twice to Robinson. He had also split with Fritzie Zivic and won one of three with

Freddie "Red" Cochrane, both of whom won the welterweight title. On that night in the Garden he also made experts out of those of us at ringside who had never thrown a punch or taken one inside the ropes and who, when we wanted an opinion, went to Norman Rubio because we knew that this was the opinion of a professional who had won title to it through the pains and the ice bags of many nights. That was why I wanted to see him again.

"Norman Rubio," John Maguire had written, "lives in a place called High Bridge, which is near Chatham in Columbia County, New York, but which is apparently just a neighborhood; it isn't listed in the post offices of the state. He says to drive out of Chatham on Route 203 and turn off onto White Mills Road just before you come on Oliver Chevrolet. His place is on White Mills Road, but apparently doesn't have any street address."

The Hudson River valley there east of the river is rolling farming country still in the process of a half century of change. Farms, a few of them in the families for a hundred years or more, still exist, but others were lost to the lure of the cities or to the antiquated and inequitable methods of local taxation that throughout our nation are based on the erroneous presumption that the ownership of real estate is the sole indicator of one's ability and responsibility to pay. Now what were once in season unbroken undulating fields of hay or pasture land are invaded by scrub growth, saplings, burdock, thistle, goldenrod, mullen and milkweed, those once open spaces now ignored by the retired exurbanites, small plant employees, and commuters by car to Albany and elsewhere to whom the farmer has given way.

"Do you know where White Mills Road is?" I said.

At the crossroads in the center of Chatham the light had gone red, and as there was no route sign showing I had jumped out of the car to ask the driver of the dark green pickup truck that had pulled up behind me. He was middle aged and wearing a red baseball cap, and he shook his head.

"How about Oliver Chevrolet?" I said. "Do you know where Oliver Chevrolet is?"

"Of course," he said, motioning. "Straight ahead."

Just before Oliver Chevrolet another blacktop goes off to the right, and I followed that for a mile or more, seeing no names on the mail boxes, until I came to a Y in the road. On the right, at the end of a short driveway next to a cottage, a rather tall, thin young man in shorts and a sports shirt was on his knees digging with a trowel in a small flower bed, and I turned in there.

"May I help you?" he said, walking over to the car.

"I hope so," I said. "Do you know where Norman Rubio lives?"

"I'm sorry," he said, "but I don't. Do you know what road he lives on?"

"White Mills Road," I said.

"Good," he said. "It's the one to the left there at the Y."

I started checking mailboxes again, most of them nameless, in front of houses close to the road and of independent and non-traditional designs. I pulled over to let a car behind me pass, and after about another quarter of a mile the car stopped in the middle of the road and a woman, slim and dark-haired and wearing white pants and a long-sleeved shirt with a large floral pattern, got out of the driver's side and came hurrying back.

"Are you Mr. Heinz?" she said.

"Yes," I said.

"I'm Mrs. Rubio," she said, smiling. "I noticed your out-of-state license plate."

"I'm glad to see you," I said.

I followed her for another mile or more until she turned right into the front yard of a large, two-story square white house no more than twenty-five feet off the road. I parked just beyond the house, and when I walked back she was getting out of the car with a bag of groceries, and Norman Rubio, short, stocky, but no excess weight showing, was coming down the steps from the porch. He was wearing tan slacks and a short-sleeved tan checkered sports shirt.

"You met my wife, Dorothy?" he said, after we had shaken hands.

He had a full head of dark, wavy hair, gray-streaked now, and a trimmed moustache. He was wearing glasses, and his face was without visible scars, except for a small vertical path through his left eyebrow.

"Yes," his wife said, "we met on the road."

"Or I wouldn't be here now," I said.

"So where you want to talk?" he said. "Outside? Inside?"

"Wherever you say."

"That's up to you," he said.

"So let's go inside," I said.

"I don't know what you want to know," he said, leading me up the porch steps. "I mean, I don't know what I can tell you."

Inside he led me to the left into a large low-ceilinged room, perhaps thirty by twenty-five feet, with the dining area on the right, the living room furniture—heavy chairs and a sofa, end tables and a coffee table—to the left. There was a fieldstone fireplace, and on the hearth stood a telescope mounted on a tripod.

"Sit wherever you like," he said. "You want something? A beer? We got everything."

"Coffee?" his wife said, coming out of the kitchen.

"That would be fine," I said.

"I don't know what I can tell you," he said, as we sat down. "It's a long time ago, and I don't know what I remember."

"Don't worry about it," I said. "Just tell me how you keep in such good shape."

"You hear that? He says I'm in good shape," he said, smiling, and calling it to his wife, and then to me, "They're always kidding me about it, keeping in shape."

"You must live right," I said. "What do you do for a living?"

"I worked for Canada Dry in Hudson," he said, and his voice is rather high and husky. "I used to run machines, a filler operator, but now they've moving and a new outfit—International Soft Drink Company—is coming in, and we're renovating the building and putting up pipes, and like that."

"What did you do when you stopped fighting?"

"I was in the toy business in New York," he said. "My manager was in the business, and I was like a foreman. I was there four or five years, but I didn't like it. I couldn't take the city no more."

"He's a family man," his wife said, coming in with the coffee.

Their youngest daughter, Denise, who is a high school student, had followed her mother in and we were introduced. They have two sons, Norman, Jr., who is a sales supervisor for Canada Dry, and married; Gary, who had just come out of the Army, and another daughter, Diane, who is married.

"We go out on Saturday night," he said, smiling and looking over at his wife. She and their daughter had sat down. "You know, you said the right thing for me here when you said I'm in shape. I mean, with the kidding I get from these two."

"So what did you do when you left the toy business?" I asked.

"I came back here," he said. "I first came here in 1933 with my folks, so I had this farm. I was in the chicken business. I had about 5,000 layers, and I raised broilers and cows, and I tried to raise beef for around ten years, but it was all work and no money, you know?"

I had had a photocopy made of his career record in *The Ring Record Book* for 1948. It lists eighty-three fights, of which he won fifty-one, eight by knockout; drew in eight; and lost twenty-four, three by KO. I took the page out of my pocket.

"I have your record here," I said. "It says you were born in 1919."

"It was 1916," he said.

They were fighters, but they were entertainers. If you started late and were not making it in a hurry, you wanted to be known as a coming young welterweight, or whatever, like a rising young singer or a promising young comic.

"Your record starts here in 1940," I said, "but it says your previous record was unavailable."

"That's right," he said. "I was on the bootleg circuit."

It was during the Depression, and the circuit flourished in New York State, north of New York City, and throughout Massachusetts and Connecticut. They fought, ostensibly as amateurs, in lofts and armories and in fair grounds and ball parks, using one name one night and another the next. The promoters avoided the restrictions and expenses of a professional production, and they paid off sometimes in cash but, more often and to maintain the appearance of amateurism, in watches. There was a $50 watch for the winners and a $25 one for the losers, but they never left their plush-lined boxes. The fighters immediately sold the watches back to the promoters, and I recall one fighter—I no longer remember his name—telling me that one night he insisted for a while that he didn't want the money but preferred to keep the watch, and almost folded the operation.

"Those were hard days," Rubio was saying now. "You didn't know who you were fighting, lightweights, welterweights, middleweights. Then I went into the CCC."

The Civilian Conservation Corps was the brain child of Franklin D. Roosevelt, who had proposed in his acceptance speech at the 1932 Democratic National Convention that the nation put a million unemployed to work in its forests. Enlistment was limited to single men between the ages of eighteen and twenty-five from families that were on relief, and from 1933 through 1941 some 2,750,000 of them came out of the big cities and the small towns, off the rails and the roads to plant trees, dig diversion ditches, build reservoirs and ponds, erect bridges, restore Revolutionary and Civil War battlefields, and clear camp grounds and beaches. It was an army of the young restoring not only their own country but their own respectability.

"I left school," Rubio was saying. "A whole group was leaving. We chopped wood and all that through Idaho and out that way. You got $30 a month and $35 if you were like a leader and up to $45. I used to run through those Idaho mountains in the nice fresh air, and so clear. You know? I spent five years in different camps, and in all those little towns I'd fight. I'd make $100 a week, and I used to save everything. No vices—you know?—and I used to send the folks the money to help out."

"Was that," I said, "when you decided that you wanted to make a living as a fighter?"

"Oh, no," he said. "I always wanted to be a fighter. When I was just a kid I met Jack Dempsey. I was caddying, and he stopped at this golf club in Albany. He was gonna fight Jack Sharkey, and he said, 'I'm gonna knock him out in the sixth round.' I still remember that."

Once, while Dempsey still had the restaurant on Broadway near Fiftieth, I asked him about that fight. In the seventh round he had landed a punch that Sharkey and a number of ringsiders thought was low, and as Sharkey had turned to protest to the referee, Dempsey had landed a left hook to the jaw and knocked Sharkey out.

"In the early rounds he knocked the hell out of me," Dempsey said, "but in the seventh round I hit him on the belt line and he turned and complained to the referee. What was I supposed to do? Write him a letter? I hit him and knocked him out. He said I hit him low, and I said, 'The ref didn't think so, and he's the boss.'"

"So when you decided to become a fighter," I said to Rubio now, "did you think that some day you might be a champ?"

"No," he said. "When I fought I just fought to make money. It was Depression days, and I thought if I could be champ, all right. But I really did it for a dollar."

"As I wrote you," I said, "I've never forgotten you in that dressing room in the Garden after the Docusen fight, and how you sat there in pain and disappointment and still showed so much professional class."

"I don't remember that," he said, "but I remember the fight. I wasn't booked for that fight."

"I know."

"I should have licked the guy," he said. "I mean, somebody who was supposed to fight him got hurt, and I just fought a guy the week before."

"Larry Cisneros," I said.

"A tough fight," he said. "Then I was too light, and a doctor said I should drink Ballantine's ale. I didn't drink, which I thought was dissipating, but I did for three or four days, drinking this ale. Then I had only three days to train, but I had a 147-pound contract and I spent the whole time in a steam room. You know? I really should have licked the guy."

"How about Robinson?"

"A good fighter," he said.

"The best I ever saw."

"Yeah," he said, "but you know something? Everybody, the referee and judges and everybody, always looked at what he did, and they always leaned his way. You know?"

"You went ten rounds with him," I said, "but in the first fight he knocked you out in the seventh?"

"They stopped the fight on a cut," he said. "Always cuts."

"You were never counted out?"

"Never," he said, shaking his head. "Always cuts."

"They don't show today," I said.

"I had the scar tissue removed," he said.

"When you fought Robinson," I said, "did you go in really thinking you could beat him?"

"You see," he said, "you're in the ring every day. It's like you eat food every day, and the guy you're fighting is just another person. You say, 'Tonight's pay night.' I didn't know if I could beat anybody until I was in the ring."

"Did it bother you?" I said, turning to his wife, "that he was a fighter?"

"I didn't like it," she said. "I wanted him to quit."

"I didn't want to quit," he said. "It was all I knew."

"Money isn't everything," she said.

"It was to me," he said.

"He quit just before our first child," she said. "That was the agreement."

"Did you go to his fights?"

"I never saw him fight," she said, shaking her head, "ever. I'd wait for him someplace, in some hotel. I used to tune in on the radio at the end of each round to see if he was all right, and then I'd turn it off again."

"It says here," I said, looking at his record again, "that you were in the Army for three years."

"That's right," he said.

"Where were you?"

"I was in the Ninth Armored," he said. "Company A, 27th Armored Infantry."

"The Ninth Armored?" I said. "I was a war correspondent, and I was with you people."

"We captured the bridge at Remagen," he said.

"I know," I said. "I was there."

It was an accident, the most fortuitous of the whole campaign in Europe. We never expected to find a bridge still intact across the Rhine, and when those first Americans ran across it under fire— that thousand feet of stone-buttressed steel span wired with explosives—not knowing when it might blow up under them and scatter them to the skies, they sealed the fate of the German armies in the west and of Adolf Hitler and the Third Reich.

"How about that?" Rubio was saying, turning to his wife and daughter. "He was there."

"Not the first day," I said.

From the briefings they gave us each evening at the press camp we used to try to handicap the units the way you handicap race horses, trying to figure out where the best story would be the next day. For almost a week we had all been covering the Third Armored Division spearheading the drive across the Cologne Plain, and we were all in the city when, to the south, the Ninth Armored took the bridge at Remagen.

"I was on the point," he was saying, "and we come on the bridge. We were looking down and we said, 'Look at that place, that village down there. Look at that bridge.' For three hours they wouldn't let us cross."

"It took that long," I said, "to get confirmation from Division and Corps and Army. It was a big risk, because if they put you people across and the bridge went out behind you and the Germans counterattacked, everybody would have been lost."

"We kept looking down at that bridge," he said, "and saying, 'Why don't they let us go? We can grab that bridge.'"

"What were you in, a half-track?"

"Yeah, I was on a half-track," he said, "and when they let us go and we got down in there I grabbed a machine gun. You know, when you pile out of a half-track you grab anything, and I happened to grab a machine gun, and guys were goin' nuts. Later planes were comin' down, and we were firing on everything. We even fired on frog men."

The Germans tried with everything they had to knock out the bridge before, ten days after its capture, it finally collapsed into the river. They laid on all the artillery they could move up and sent in planes, and finally at night, six Navy frog men carrying pliable plastic explosives. Our people dropped depth charges and turned searchlights on them and fired on them and captured all six. I remember the one I saw in the jail in the town across the river, lying there, sullen, in his black rubber suit on that cot in that cell.

"My name is in a book," Rubio said, and he got up and walked to the book shelves at the end of the room and he came back. "They sent it to me. I didn't buy it."

He handed me the book. It was *The Bridge at Remagen,* by Ken Hechler, a paperback published by Ballantine Books in 1957.

"I have a copy at home," I said. "It's a good book."

"I've never read it," he said, and he took the book back and turned some pages, yellowing now like those in my copy, and then showed it to me again. "But my name is here. See?"

On pages 236 and 237 of the Appendix, in agate type, are listed the names, three columns on a page, of the members of the leading units that crossed the bridge. At the top of the left-hand column on page 237 is the name Norman Rubio.

"That's good," I said. "I'm glad you're in there."

"It just came in the mail once," he said. "I didn't ask for it or anything."

When the news of the bridge got back to Washington, the members of the House of Representatives and of the Senate stopped their deliberations to stand up and cheer. Its capture was not only to shorten the war in Europe by months but to save no one knows how many thousands of casualties.

"I was in the Bulge, too," Rubio said now. He had taken the book back to the book shelves and had sat down again.

"I probably covered you people then, too," I said, "but everything was so disorganized that I can't recall it now."

As long as the Americans were on the offensive we could handicap our units, but when the Germans broke through we were never sure where anybody was. They chased us out of one press camp and bombed us out of another, but as always, we still had it so much better, of course, than the infantry and the tankers in the lines.

"You know what they told us?" he said now. "They said, 'Go out there. A small skirmish of Germans broke through.' A small skirmish? It was the whole German Army. We had to sleep in that snow and ice-cold water. I figured when I came out I wouldn't be able to do anything.

"They sent up these new kids. They didn't even know how to put a clip in. This one kid wasn't even eighteen. I put his clip in and he said, 'What do I do now?' I said, 'Just shoot at anything you see out there.' He stood up and—bam!—right through the head. Dead.

"One time in a cellar, a shell came in on me and this fella. It threw us back and the blood came out of my nose and ears, and I thought I was dead."

And that night in the Garden, I was thinking now, when you were taking that licking from that Docusen kid, I had no idea that less than two years before you had been through all of that.

"Then we were firing on the Russians," he said. "What was the name of that river?"

"The Elbe."

That was another time when all our handicapping came up wrong. It was a time of just mopping up small pockets of Germans, with the tanks rolling and the infantry riding on them in the half-tracks and trucks, and we were trying to figure what division would get the honor of pushing to the river to meet the Russians. We reasoned that it would go to one of the old outfits that had slugged it out all the way from the Normandy beaches, maybe the First Infantry or the Fourth Infantry or the Ninth, or maybe the Third Armored that had led the breakthroughs. Then the Sixty-ninth Infantry, which was new to the theater, pushed a patrol out and made the first contact, and we all rushed up there and crossed the river in the racing shells of the Torgau Rowing Club to meet the Russians who were friendly, to a point, but whose crudities made our G.I.s seem like babies.

"We were firing on those Russians, and then we saw this white flag," he said, and then he shrugged and said, "but it don't mean nothing. I have a son was in Viet Nam."

He got up and brought over to me two framed color photographs. The one was of their older son and his wife and their small son, the other a wedding picture of their older daughter and her husband.

"I got four kids, all in good health," he said. "If not for money, I have a perfect life."

"That's good," I said.

"I got no complaints," he said.

"Did you ever want your boys to be fighters?" I said.

"No," he said, "I wouldn't want it. You're like a race horse, on a continuous training schedule, from the time you get up in the morning until you go to bed. You're on special food all the time. You ain't supposed to have a girl friend. So what kind of life is that? It's inhuman.

"You see this?" he said, and got up again and walked over to the telescope on its tripod in front of the fireplace. "Gary went to college and studied astronomy. Now he's got us all lookin' at the moon, and things like that. Star gazing. It's nice."

"When you think back to the old days," I said, when he had sat down again, "do you ever wish you were young once more?"

"Yeah," he said, "them were the good days. I loved being in condition. To me it was fun training with all the other guys."

"Yes," I said, "and there was a camaraderie. Fighters together were like guys together in the war."

"Yeah," he said, "we were all friends. When you fought a guy you didn't want to hurt him or kill him, but at the same time you wanted to win, and it didn't matter if he was black or white. You know what's the trouble with fighters? I'll tell you. Fighters lose their money, and they're afraid to take the little jobs. They say, 'I can't do that.'

"They should stay away from those bar rooms. Everybody pats them on the back and says, 'You're the greatest.' They're ashamed to work. Guys say to them, 'You doin' that kind of work? You're crazy.'"

We talked awhile, about some of the fighters we had both known and about Ray Arcel, who worked with seventeen world champions and had trained Rubio for a number of his fights. When I got up to leave, and had shaken hands with his wife and daughter, he walked me out and we stood for a moment on the porch.

"You should read that book," I said.

"The stuff they write," he said, "I don't read it. I was lucky to come out good."

"But that's an honest book," I said. "It really tells the truth of it. If you read it, you'll see what I mean."

"People don't understand," he said. "I've seen generals, captains—officers—decorated for somethin' they never done. A guy hit the dirt got a medal. A lot of my buddies were left there. They never came back. They never mention the poor guys who died. The heroes come back, and the guys who don't are just dead, so I just hate to pick up the book."

"I understand," I said.

"It was nice they sent it to me, though," he said. "I mean I didn't have to pay for it or anything."

The price is printed on the back cover of the book: $.50. Some weeks later I read in *Newsweek* that they had made a motion picture about another bridge, the one at Arnhem, from Connie Ryan's book, *A Bridge Too Far*. The story said that they were paying Robert Redford "a rumored $2 million," and James Caan "at least $500,000 for twelve days' work," just to make believe.

3

The Man Who Belongs in Blue Jeans

Levi Strauss ended last year looking robust as ever, with sales up 20 percent to $1.2 billion and profits up 62 percent to $105 million.

Newsweek, July 5, 1977

The Interstate highways in this country are a monument to the surveyor's calling, the engineer's profession, and the cement and asphalt industries, but traveling them is like reading those summer novels the critics suggest you pack along with your bathing apparel, the tennis gear, the suntan lotion, and the Maalox. Surviving them, you have the feeling that you haven't seen anything, come to know anyone, or been anywhere.

This country comes alive between the highways and not on them, and we had driven halfway across it to the mid-line of America. Medora, North Dakota, dates back only to 1883 and has a year-round population of only 129, but in 1962 they started restoring it, and it has its history. In 1876, George Armstrong Custer, on his way to his unannounced retirement at Little Big Horn, camped with his Seventh Cavalry just five miles south of where the town was shortly to be built. After the Sioux were chased out and the Northern Pacific pushed past on its way west, the town grew up as a railhead and terminus for the cattle drives that started 1,200 miles south on the Oklahoma-Texas border. Cattlemen fattened their stock in the grasslands bordering the town and in the Badlands to the north. From 1883 until 1898,

Theodore Roosevelt owned two ranches here, one five miles south of the town and another thirty miles to the north, and there is a National Memorial Park, in three units, named for him. Medora, itself and in season, sells Teddy to the tourists with a board-sided Rough Riders Hotel and a museum, an amphitheater, a trout pond, gift shops, and a zoo offering "all animals native to North Dakota in Teddy Roosevelt's time."

It was mid-September and the tourists were gone, leaving what were left of the trout, I presumed, to their peaceful pursuits and zoo animals to their privacy. The hotel was closed, but at the smaller of the two motels—the one that had answered my wife, Betty's, postal enquiry addressed to "Chamber of Commerce"— the middle-aged, motherly woman who runs it with her husband had pointed us, the first evening, to the Little Missouri Saloon and Dining Room for dinner, and the next morning, to Bud's Coffee and Gift Shop for breakfast. Now she brought out a large-scale map of the land sections, and spread it on the counter in the motel office.

"You'll have to go down here and onto the Interstate," she said. "Then it's about fourteen miles to Sentinel Butte."

"Good," I said. "I spent a night there in '64."

"Then the road goes north, right here."

"I remember that," I said, "and I think it's right about on this bend of the Little Missouri."

"I wouldn't know for sure," she said, "but I know it's out there somewhere."

"At Bud's they said the road would probably be all right."

"I would think so," she said. "We haven't had much rain."

"Do you know where I might get a map like this?"

"You can have this one."

"Thank you," I said.

"That's all right," she said. "I hope you find it."

At Sentinel Butte the road that leads off the Interstate curves down a gentle hill into the town. The population of Sentinel Butte is 125, and at the corner there is a white-stuccoed general store with two gas pumps under the overhang in front.

"Do you have any high test?" I said.

"No," he said, middle-aged, tanned, and looking healthy, as you're supposed to look if you live in Sentinel Butte.

He put in ten gallons of the regular, and when I handed him the $10 bill and he went inside to make change, I followed him.

"I want to go out to Jim Tescher's ranch," I said. "Do you know how I can get there?"

"Jim Tescher's?" he said. "Sure."

"Wait till I call my wife in," I said. "She's the navigator."

I introduced Betty, and myself, and he said his name was Ward Cook. He marked the route on the map for us, and then, on the back of a letter I was carrying, he drew the route with the landmarks on it.

"You go across I-94," he said, "and take a left with Camel's Hump Butte on the right. You follow the main road for ten or twelve miles to some old run-down farm buildings here on the left. You go straight about eight or nine miles to a deserted school house here on the right, and about a half mile past that you turn off left across a cattle guard. You follow that, and after maybe about twelve miles or so there'll be some signs of Jim's, I'm sure."

"How far is it?"

"About 36 miles," he said. "I haven't been all the way out there in twenty years."

"You think that car of mine will make it? It's kind of low-slung."

"You can make it at this time of year," he said. "You know Jim Tescher?"

"Yes. I met him twelve years ago in Phoenix, while he was riding saddle broncs."

"Jim and his brother Tom were great riders," he said, "but nobody knows it."

"They knew it once in rodeo," I said.

When Betty and our daughter and I had got off the plane in Phoenix on that day in '64, Skipper Lofting had come walking with that slow rolling gate down the ramp to meet us. He used to write short stories for *The Saturday Evening Post* and the other magazines that ran fiction in those days. He had ridden some in rodeo, and his father wrote the first book that captured me. In the first grade, each day after lunch, Miss Kessler, in a black dress and her black hair done up with a bun in the back, would stand up in front of the class and read us another chapter of Hugh Lofting's *The Voyages of Doctor Doolittle,* and each day I could hardly wait to hear what the doctor who talked with the animals, and the duck and the monkey were going to do next.

"I'll tell you what we'd better do," Skipper had said that first night, sitting in the bar of the motel. "I'd sure hate to steer you wrong, hang you up on somebody who just wouldn't be right for everything you want. Maybe we should go up and see Stiffy."

It was early March, and the rodeo was on for four days. The bar was filled with big hats and broad shoulders, western shirts and big belt buckles, and jeans that tapered down into the boots with the slanted heels and pointed toes. Stiffy, after a western cartoon character, is what Skipper calls Gene Pruett. For twenty-one years Gene Pruett rode saddle broncs. In 1948 he won the world title, and he quit in 1955 and now he was editing *Rodeo Sports News,* the bi-weekly published by the Rodeo Cowboys Association.

"What I want to do, or try to do," I said, after Skipper had telephoned and we had gone up to Pruett's room, "is write the definitive magazine piece about rodeo through the life of one cowboy who still ranches. I want a bronc rider or a bull rider, because they put their bodies and sometimes their lives on the line. I want him to be able to tell me how he got into rodeo and why he's in it, and I want to follow him around and into the chutes and find out not only what he does but how he does it."

"That'd be right fine," Pruett said. He goes to well over six feet and he's thin and bony, and he was sitting sprawled, his back to the desk, with his legs stretched out and his feet on the bed. "I'd admire that."

"But I need the right man," I said. "He doesn't have to be a champion—I don't care about that—but he does have to be the cowboy the others look up to, so that when the piece runs and they read it, they'll say, 'Yeah. That's it.'"

"Well," Pruett said, "I'm thinkin', and there's several, but I've been thinkin' about Jim Tescher. How about Tescher, Skip?"

"Well," Skipper said, "I've thought of Jim Tescher. Everybody respects him, and he sure can ride and he ranches, but I'm not sure how much he'll talk."

"He's not big on the brag," Pruett said, "but I'll tell you something. It'd be real hard to pick out even two guys who can ride as good as Jim Tescher—maybe not even one—because he's just about as good a bronc rider as there is today. If Jim and his brother Tom had just rodeoed and rodeoed they'd a been champions."

"That's what Casey Tibbs said," Skipper said, and Casey Tibbs was a nine-time world champion. "Casey said, 'There's no tellin' how far those Teschers could go, if they weren't plagued with common sense.'"

"I like that," I said.

"That's the truth," Pruett said. "Tescher has that ranch he owns north of Medora, North Dakota, and he just doesn't get to enough rodeos."

In rodeo the champion in each event is the one who has earned the most prize money during the year, and the world champion is the one who has earned the most in two or more events. That is like giving the Nobel Prize for medicine to some Park Avenue specialist, and I wanted a cowboy off a ranch and not one of the new school, living in a condominium somewhere, flying his own Cessna, 182 or 206 and making two and sometimes three rodeos a day.

I wanted that, because rodeo is a reminder of a way of life that is almost gone now forever, and there is no other sport that is as indigenous to this country alone. It goes back as far as the Spanish land grants in California and to those early cattle drives when American cowboys would meet on the trail and at shipping points, and the bragging—"we got a guy can ride anything"—and the betting would start. Sometimes those outfits would bet the works, and we have no other sport that grew as naturally out of a way of life.

"Heck," Skipper Lofting said, "I think Jim will talk."

Skipper introduced us the next morning, and Tescher and I walked across the street to the Pancake House, where we ate and talked. He had driven in the night before with his wife, Loretta, and their then four-year old son, Barry—the third of their then four children—in the two-year-old red Chevrolet. The pillow and blankets were in the back seat, and his saddle was in the trunk along with the soiled laundry stuffed into a pair of his blue jeans.

He had managed to get away from the ranch for the five weeks they had been on the road, and at Fort Worth and San Antonio, Houston and Baton Rouge he had won $5,753—about $5,000 riding saddle broncs and the rest of it wrestling steers.

He was thirty-five years old then, and had been riding horses since he was four. When he was ten he rode his first steer for $1.00 in a Fourth of July rodeo in Medora. Although he had never made enough rodeos to win enough to be the world champion in the saddle-bronc riding, he had won the event at the National Finals rodeo, where only the fifteen top contestants in each event compete, in 1959 and 1963.

"Besides," Gene Pruett had said, talking about him, "the National Finals are the real test as far as I'm concerned."

He is five feet, eight and a half inches, and while he was riding he weighed 187 pounds but had a 30-inch waist. It was all up in his chest and shoulders and arms and down in his thighs and calves. His build was like that of a middleweight fighter, but on a larger frame. He talked easily, although not expansively, and I followed him around for the four days, climbing up onto the back of the chute when he mounted to ride, watching how he measured the length of rein he would give the horse and how he took his hold on the resined rope before he nodded for them to swing the gate open. Being with him I had the same comfortable, secure feeling I used to have being around one of those quiet, competent front-line lieutenants and captains who never raised their voices and whose kids were always telling me they wished they could get them a medal.

In rodeo the riding events are not only a contest between the man and the animal but also a partnership. The judges give points for how well the animal bucks as well as for how well the contestant rides, and Tescher drew poor horses and finished out of the money. He had put up the $35 entry fee twice, had the travel expenses for himself, his wife, and their son, and now they would be driving the 1,600 miles back to the ranch where, he had told me, they were living in a basement—the upper story of the house to be built when he had earned the money.

"I'd like to see how you live and ranch," I had said to him.

"You'd be welcome to come any time," he had said.

"Is there a motel near there?"

"Not really," he had said. "We live quite a way out, but we've got room, and you're welcome to stay with us."

So I had given him a day-and-a-half's head start and, after my wife and our daughter had taken the plane back East, I had flown up to Billings and from there to Miles City and then to Glendive, Montana, where Tescher's brother-in-law, Roy Kittelson, had met me at about ten o'clock at night. In a pickup he had driven me the thirty miles east across the state line to Sentinel Butte.

"A lot of people thought Jim wouldn't make it out in the Badlands," Kittelson said, driving through the night. "In the wheat lands they say the topsoil is from six to eight feet deep, and out on those buttes there's no more than six to eight inches, but Jim mined his own coal, smoked Bull Durham, and saved every penny he could."

In Sentinel Butte he drove me up to Jim's father's house. Matt Tescher had once raised cattle and wheat on 1,500 acres outside of Sentinel Butte, and had fathered fifteen children. When Jim was in the fifth grade, the house had burned down, so Matt Tescher had moved the rest of the family into town, while Jim and his brother Alvin, who was eight years older, stayed on the ranch. For six years they lived together in the two-room bunk house while Jim went through the eighth grade as one of seven pupils in the one-room school, and then started making a living breaking horses and hiring out to ranchers.

The house, as we got out of the pickup, seemed completely darkened, but Kittelson led me up a lighted back stairway to the third floor finished attic where there was a double bed and where, he said, rodeo cowboys on their way through regularly slept. The next morning, after breakfast and after I had talked with Matt Tescher about Jim, asking him every question I could think of, Kittelson had picked me up again and driven me out to the ranch on the road we were now trying to find once more.

"In 1964," I was saying now in the general store, "I spent a night in Jim's father's house, but I have no idea where it was."

"Jim's father just passed away," Ward Cook said.

"I'm sorry to hear that."

"The house is right up here," he said. "You passed it on your way in. When you go out and start up the curve to the left, it's the last house on the left."

We drove back on the blacktop leading out of town, with the square, three-story gray-painted clapboard house the last one on the left, and across the Interstate. We turned left onto the dirt and gravel road, with Camel's Hump Butte like a fortress on the right, and we drove north through the grasslands, some of it mowed, some with white-faced Hereford's grazing on it, all of it dry and golden-yellow in the morning sun.

We followed the road for more than an hour, the grasslands giving way to the Badlands, the road narrower now, rising and falling and curving around the mustard-sided, stratified, flat-topped buttes. A coyote, like a small gray-white collie, streaked across the road about fifty feet ahead of us, and a chicken hawk on its hunting glide was low enough to pass through the windows of the car.

This is land that waters flowing eastward from the Rocky Mountains laid down some 60 million years ago. Many centuries of warm rains that followed turned it into a jungle, and new layers of sediment compressed the swamp vegetation into layers of lignite, a soft coal. Clouds of ash from the volcanoes that formed the mountains of the West drifted down and decomposed into strata of blue betonite clay. After the plains had developed, the streams that drained this land started the erosion that still goes on, cutting down through the soft strata and sculpting the Badlands into the buttes, the plateaus, and between them the valleys and gorges.

When you drive through here you drive through eons, the horizontal strata on the sides of the buttes the visible evidence of what were the horizons of their time. Once, off to the left and coming down off a tableland, we saw a black-hatted horseman riding after a stray Hereford. Once a jeep, red and with the dust rising after it, passed us going the other way, and once, unable to find the landmarks—the deserted farm buildings and the vacant one-room school—I drove into the only ranch we saw along the road. My wife got out with the section map in her hand.

"I guess they were startled to see me drop in out of nowhere," she said when she came back. "There were two men working on some machinery, and I said, 'Are we on the right road for Jim

Tescher's?' One of them said, 'That's right.' Then the other one, kind of laughing, said, 'But do you know the way the rest of the way?' "

"Did they say how much farther it is?"

"I didn't ask," she said. "We're on the right road."

We drove, slowly and with the car nodding up and down, over cattle guards—a dozen or so four-inch pipes set six inches apart between the wire fencing—and at some of them the cattle, unable to cross the guards, lay in the road and, protesting with their mooing, moved only when I advanced on them sounding the horn. Beyond the landmarks, and after turn-offs to other ranches, the road in places was no more than wheel tracks and then, where it widened again and climbed up onto a plateau, we saw the first of the signs—Tescher's name among four others, and then another pointing to the right and finally, with the letters cut into a plank supported on two posts: "Tescher Ranch." Between the words was the brand, the inverted V with the single rocker through it, and below, in smaller letters: "Quarter Horses. Herefords."

In the dozen years that had passed so quickly I had wanted many times to return here, just to be reassured that America can still make it. When a national poll reveals that more than half of all workers are dissatisfied with their jobs, and the products they turn out and the services they perform prove it, when exaggerated advertising creates artificial appetites for those products and our economy is based on the waste of the natural resources we should be preserving for generations to come, when the founders' dreams of equality for all go up in ghetto flames and are dissipated in looting, and when, among our highest elective officials and their appointees, integrity becomes for so many, no more than a word, one should have some place to go to find that a man and his family, not afraid of the hard way and rejecting the superficialities and the deceits of our society, can still more than survive.

"Yes, we are still ranching," Loretta Tescher had written some four months before, "although cattle prices aren't anything to brag about. We built our new home and also have a modern bunkhouse that you and Mrs. Heinz are very welcome to stay in instead of Medora, if you wish.

"Our family is growing up. Gary is rodeoing and is setting

twelfth in the standings. He rides broncs and bulls. Bonnie, our youngest, is eight and she is nursing a collarbone she broke while riding horseback. Here's hoping to see you this fall."

The top of the plateau was planted in alfalfa, the road across it straight between the ankle-high deep green. Off to the right, and below, we could see the almost dry bed of the Little Missouri, cottonwoods clumped along its banks, and as we started down the curve toward the river we could see, amid the trees, some buildings.

"That must be it down there," my wife said.

"It has to be," I said. "There's no one else out here."

Where the road flattened just above the river bed we came around a curve, and we drove into the ranchyard and up to the house of stained-cedar siding now standing atop the cement-block foundation and basement where they had been living and I had stayed that night twelve years before. I walked up the three steps and opened the door into the boot room and walked in.

"Hello?" I said. "Anybody here?"

"You made it," his wife said, coming out of the kitchen and shaking hands. She is slim and dark-haired and was wearing slacks and a blouse. "You look just the same."

"I doubt that," I said.

She had grown up on a ranch at the edge of the Badlands. After she was graduated from high school at sixteen, she had taken summer courses at North Dakota State Teachers College at Dickenson and for five years had taught in a one-room school.

"You have any trouble finding it again?" she said.

"A little," I said. "My wife had to ask at one ranch, and we had our doubts a half dozen times."

"Bring your wife in," she said. "Jim's on the phone, but he'll be off in a minute, and Gary's here. He has to be in Abilene tomorrow night, but he said he wouldn't leave till you got here and he saw you again."

He was not quite thirteen then, and he had been a part of my story. In December of 1963 Jim Tescher had won the saddle-bronc riding at the National Finals at Los Angeles, and three months later, during the night I spent with them in that basement, he had told me about coming upon the boy admiring the gold-and-silver belt buckle set with diamonds.

"He said to me," Jim had said, " 'But how come you've never been World Champion?' I tried to explain it to him, that I feel it's more important for me to be with the family and build up the ranch than to be going halfway across the United States to some little rodeo just to win $100 and build up my standing. I told him, though, what I might do this year. I said, 'If you'd really like me to be World Champion, I might give it a try. If I start out winning pretty good and everything's all right here, I might just stay with it more.' I'll have to see how it goes."

Jim and Loretta had moved out of their bedroom that night and into the other room with the three smaller children. Gary and I had shared the double bed, and it seemed to me that most of the night he was riding broncs or bulls. The next morning, when he started for school, I had followed him out into the damp, gray chill of mid-March and across the yard to the bank above the river. Fastened to two posts in the ground was a three-quarter-inch cable that ran the 320 feet across the river to a cottonwood tree on the far bank. Tied to the forward post, and suspended from two pulleys that rode the cable, was a weathered wood platform, about five feet long and half as wide and with eight-inch sides.

The boy had his lunch in a Karo syrup pail. He put that on the platform and then he climbed on. Kneeling, he loosened the tie and he pushed off, the platform sliding down the sag of the cable to the mid-point about eight feet above the water that would be ice during the winter. Then the boy grabbed the cable over his head, and he pulled the platform across the river over to the cottonwood tree where he climbed down the seven slats nailed to the trunk of the tree. He got into the Jeep, which he had left there the afternoon before, and he drove the four-and-a-half miles to the one-room school he attended with seven others.

In 1964 it would go well for Jim Tescher. Going into the National Finals he had won $20,041, and he was second to Marty Wood by $1,206. With Loretta and the boy watching that week in Los Angeles, he won $1,516, gaining $635 on Marty Wood, but with $21,557 for the year he finished second. He was short by

$571, and someone told me later that, sitting in the stands that last night, the boy had cried.

"And you're built like your dad," I said to Gary now. "How are you doing?"

He was twenty-five, and although slimmer than his father, he too had it up in the chest and shoulders and arms. He was wearing jeans and a dark green shirt, and he had greeted us in the kitchen and I had introduced my wife. His father was sitting just inside the living room, the phone cord running from the kitchen, and he had waved to us, with some papers in his hand, as we walked by.

"I guess I'm not doin' too good," Gary said. "I'm not in the top twenty. I was $1,000 out of the top fifteen, I saw in the *Billings Gazette.*"

"Are you making a lot of rodeos?"

"I'm trying to," he said, "but I got hurt in August. A horse threw me down over its head, and stepped on my arm. It didn't break nothing, but it laid me up."

I remember his father's hurts. When he was fourteen, he was hunting deer and riding down off one of those buttes into a draw when the horse turned a somersault and his right arm was broken. When he was sixteen his left ankle was broken while he was rodeoing in Dickinson, North Dakota, and a bareback horse ran away with him. For a week he didn't bother to go to a doctor, and then, with a cast on, he rode bareback at Glendive, Montana, for the $3.00 mount money. When he was twenty he had three vertebrae broken in the small of his back in a car wreck coming away from a rodeo in Forsyth, Montana. At Spencer, Iowa, one year he broke his left thigh bone when the horse reared in the chute, but they poured a couple of drinks of whisky into him and he got back on the horse. In 1959 his collarbone was broken when he was thrown in Madison Square Garden, and two years later he broke two vertebrae in his neck at Beach, North Dakota, just playing around after the rodeo with Alvin Nelson—using each other's saddles and betting on riding—and he was in a brace for two months. His left ankle was broken in the chute at Grand Forks, North Dakota, where he remounted and won money anyway, and he had had calcium deposits removed from his left shin bone. Wrestling steers, he had horns tear the left side of his nose loose and rip his upper lip. And Jerry Izenberg said it well.

"The cowboys," Jerry wrote once in the *Newark Star Ledger,* "represent the last frontier of pure unpampered athletes in an age when basketball players put Ace bandages on acne."

"But don't you ever have any pain from any of this?" I had asked Jim Tescher that night, sitting in the living room in the basement. Just before dusk I had ridden in the pickup with Roy Kittelson driving among the cottonwoods while Tescher, standing in the back, had thrown the seventy-five pound hay bales to the cattle.

"Most all the time," he said. "I can feel it now, sittin' here, and it bothers me lyin' in bed. It doesn't bother me when I work, though, or when I ride—just afterwards. When it gets real bad I know those vertebrae in my back have slipped, so I get Benny Reynolds to put 'em back in place."

Benny Reynolds was a six-foot three-inch, 195-pound, easy-going, four-event cowboy out of Melrose, Montana. In 1961 he won the All-Around World Championship.

"Benny remembers what twist to give 'em," Tescher said, "so why pay one of them fellas $3.00?"

Now, twelve years later, he came off the phone and walked in to where we were sitting at the dining room table and we shook hands. He was wearing blue jeans and a checkered shirt, and he appeared the same, perhaps just a little heavier.

"I'm sorry to hear that your dad just passed away," I said. "Ward Cook told us in Sentinel Butte."

"Thank you," he said. "You met Ward?"

"I stopped there for gas and directions," I said. "He also told me that you and Tom were great riders, but nobody knows it."

"Ward said that?" Tescher said, smiling. "Well, I went to high school with him. That is, I guess I shouldn't say that because I only went two days."

"Coming out here again," I said, as we three sat down, "I've naturally been remembering when Gary and I slept together, and he seemed to be rodeoing all night. Then, of course, I remember how much he wanted you to win the world championship."

"Sometimes now," Tescher said, "I wish I had had sense

enough to go to a few more rodeos, not for me but for my friends and family. I stayed home for harvest, and at Denver I judged, where Marty won, but I was just so darned tickled to finish second."

"I was the one that hurt," Gary said. "I remember that night I was in tears, and I promised myself I was gonna win it. When things are goin' tough, I guess that keeps me going, because I think that if a guy just rides hard enough, he can win it."

Loretta and Betty were starting to set the table for the noon meal that, where the work is still around the home and the workday starts at 5:30 A.M., is still called dinner, and we moved into the living room. When I asked him about his schooling, Gary said that after he finished high school in Beach, which is forty-four miles to the south, he had a rodeo scholarship for one year at Jasper Junior College, in Wyoming, and then he went for one semester to North Dakota State Teachers College in Dickinson, and for another to North Dakota State in Fargo.

"I was having to sell my cows to go to college," he said, "and I wasn't gettin' any rodeos. Then one year I didn't go anywhere. I got a job in Beach in a cheese plant. I wanted to see what it was like, and to prove to myself that I wouldn't like it."

"And other than rodeo," I said, "what do you hope to do?"

"I've been workin' on a loan to buy a ranch up here," he said. "It's about thirty miles northwest, and Dad owns it. It's a 200-head place, with five sections of land on it, seven miles from Trotters."

"What's Trotters?"

"There's a general store and gas station and a post office and a church."

"We built this basement here in 1960," Tescher said, "and we lived in it for six years. Now the FHA wants you to have the best, the biggest tractor, the biggest house that a young fella don't need. They won't let Gary live in a basement, and it's tough on the young."

"What about the others you went to school with around here?" I said to Gary. "Back East a lot of the younger generation haven't known what to aspire to, and they're lost."

"It's like that here."

"Really?"

"A lot of the guys I went to grade school and high school with were straight and clean cut, but now some of them have sure strayed. They're long-hair, pot-smoking guys, and some have been alcoholics already."

"A lot aren't willing to work," Tescher said. "They think they need big modern equipment, and to hire other guys."

"Why do you think this has happened to your age group," I said to Gary, "where it didn't happen to your dad's?"

"People get exposed more now," he said. "They see a life that looks easier to them."

"You mean on television, where in the commercials everybody is lolling around at beach parties drinking beer, or if they're not doing that, they're flying off to Hawaii or comparing the riding qualities of a Lincoln Continental with those of a Cadillac?"

"I think that does it," Gary said. "People get an outside look they never had before."

I asked about the rest of the family, and Tescher said that Cindy, the second oldest, is married and living in Beach. Barry, whom I remember as a four-year-old walking around the motel in Phoenix in boots, jeans, and a western shirt and under a Stetson that, Skipper Lofting said, made him look like an ant moving a soda cracker, was living with his sister and her husband and going to high school in Beach.

"Troy's thirteen and Bonnie's eight." Tescher said. "They'll be out of school in a few minutes, and they'll be in for dinner."

"Where is the school?"

"It's in a house trailer out back in the yard here."

"It's right here?" I said. "How does that come about?"

"Well," Tescher said, "there were the two of ours that go and Rodney Burnam, who's an eighth-grader with Troy. He lives across the river and comes over in the cable car, so because we have the two they moved it here."

"In other words, the school moves to the home place of the family with the most pupils?"

"That's right."

"And there's a teacher for just Troy and Bonnie and the other boy? Where does she live?"

"In the teacherage, in the back of the trailer," Tescher said. "We can go out and look at it later, if you care to."

When Troy and Bonnie came in and we were introduced, we sat down to dinner. Tescher said grace, and we had buffalo steaks and prairie hen, home-grown vegetables, home-baked bread, and homemade ice cream. After we had eaten, Gary started to carry some things to his car and I followed him out.

"Do you like this car?" I said. It was a Chevrolet Nova, not quite a year old.

"I like it fine," he said. "The only thing I have against it, it's not paid for."

It reminded me of his father. In Phoenix in 1964 I had watched him take out of the trunk of his car the bronc saddle he had paid $185 for in 1949 and had been using ever since. The leather was scarred and dry, and I had asked him what he treated it with.

"Just abuse," he had said.

"How far have you driven to rodeo this year?" I said to Gary now.

"I'd say about 100,000 miles."

"Do you share the driving with others, or do you do most of it alone?"

"Alone," he said. "North Dakota is kind of the armpit of the world as far as rodeo goes now, and there's not too many guys from around here."

"So to get to Abilene by tomorrow evening," I said, "you'll be driving most of the next twenty-eight hours. How do you stay awake?"

"I drink a lot of Coke," he said. "Coffee gives me heartburn. There's a lot of tricks, too. Eat sunflower seeds. Take your boots off. If you've made a good ride, though, you can drive around the world."

When he went back into the house to say good-by, I waited by the car, and when he came out his father was with him. They talked awhile, standing on the walk, and then he came over and I shook hands with him and wished him luck.

"Thanks," he said. "I sure hate to leave."

"I was the same way," his father said. "I always stayed too long."

We watched him drive out the gate for Abilene and then Albuquerque. When the car had disappeared down the slope, we started to walk slowly around the outside of the house.

"He's a fine young man," I said, "and I hope he makes it in rodeo."

"I've talked to two or three bronc riders who said he's goin' good," Tescher said, "but he just hasn't been drawin' good."

"Realizing how much he wants to win the world championship," I said, "and knowing how difficult that is, I've been wondering if I'm partially responsible. I mean, in that piece I wrote about you, I wrote how he wanted you to win it and how, when you just missed out that last night, he cried. I'm wondering if, focusing that attention on it, I may have helped to start him reaching for something he may very well never attain."

It is a responsibility that has concerned me for many years. A writer pries into many lives, and since what he writes and is printed and is read can alter those lives to some degree, he can only hope that, while it is accurate and the truth, it is also for the better.

"I don't think so," Tescher said. "I think he'd have tried anyway. I told him, 'If you're doin' it for me, don't do it.'"

"Do you give him any coaching, or any advice?"

"If I know the horse he's drawn. This one he's on in Albuquerque, I tried him out when Mike Cervi bought him. He's the biggest rodeo producer in the world, and Gary and I and two nephews went down to Spearfish to try out about fifteen horses for him when there was still snow on the ground in the arena. I just told Gary now that he's got to really hustle and keep throwing his feet ahead, because the horse really snapped, and you really have to hurry on him."

In Phoenix he had known them all, all he had ever ridden or just seen. He had studied them all, the way in big-league baseball the pitchers study the hitters and the hitters the pitchers, and in pro football the defensive backs keep mental book on every change of pace and fake and move of every receiver they have to face.

"You know what these are?" he said now.

We had walked around to the far end of the house. There were a half dozen large animal skulls, bleached an off-white, propped against the foundation.

"Buffalo," he said. "They're a hundred years or more old. We found them buried ten to twenty feet underground. Where the draws wash out you see a horn, and you dig it out. They died in the creek or were washed in, and where Roosevelt lived they found a hairy elk. There are people who pay money for these now."

"Those buffalo steaks we had," I said. "Where do you get those?"

"I bought ten buffalo calves three years ago," he said, "from the fella who restored Medora, and I've still got two left. Two years old is prime, though."

"What about the buffalo in the National Park here?"

"About a dozen years ago," he said, "they began to rebuild the herd. It got to 220 head in the south unit, and last year they shipped out over 100 head to Indian reservations and other parks. There's about 150 or 160 in the north unit, and when they're movin' them, we help round 'em up."

"You actually round up buffalo?"

"About eight or ten ranchers and a few rangers that can ride. Some are help, and some are hurt. You've got to be mounted real good, because they're hard to handle. You have to crowd buffalo a lot to get 'em started or to bend 'em, and if you're not mounted good, you don't dare get in there.

"They'll charge you real bad, the cows with the bulls and when the bulls get tired. You just have to outrun 'em, and I think the biggest thrill I ever had in my life was last year. Some other fellas were bringin' some in, and I had to run my horse real hard to help bend 'em, and it stepped in a prairie dog hole. It turned a somersault and skinned up its nose and head, and that takes a lot of drive out of a horse. It hurt my leg, but I remounted and rode in to help. One fella said, 'Look out, or that one cow will really take you.' She was the worst I ever seen. She charged me and she took me two hundred to three hundred yards through sage brush, and it was thick. I couldn't see downed trees or holes or whatever. She was on my tail, and my hat fell off and she turned with that. We had trouble with her for two days straight.

"They're more vicious than the bulls," he said, "and they're so strong. There was a brand new semi backed up there, and one took a run at another. Their horns come out straight and up, and they're terrible sharp. The one got its head under the other and threw her and the second one's horns went through the roof of this new semi. I remember the driver was kind of complainin', cryin' about his new semi. The biggest will go to 2,400 pounds and one bull hit the gate eleven times and broke it. They have no reasoning power, and the last half mile from the pens you have to go as fast as you can, hootin' and hollerin' so they can't turn back."

"And how long does one of these roundups take?"

"About three days."

My wife had come out of the house, and we walked down to the bunkhouse. There was a large main room, with a poured concrete floor and a fieldstone fireplace, and, at one end, two bunkrooms and a bath.

"Who built this?" I said.

"We put in the foundation," he said, "and hunters who come up here regular stayed for five days and put up the shell, and then we finished it. We've had two wedding dances in here, and they have the Christmas pageant in here, too."

"A Christmas pageant?"

"One year we had it back at the house in the living room," he said. "There's another school ten miles from here, and they combined. There were eight to ten kids, and the teacher took a part. All the neighbors will come from up and down the river, maybe thirty or so. Would you like to look in at the school?"

"I don't think we should go in while it's in session," my wife said. "I told Loretta we'll be going back to Medora for tonight, but we'll come out again tomorrow and stay over, if we may, and we'll see the school then."

"Fine," Tescher said. "Whatever you say. We're just pleased to have you."

Driving back out that afternoon, we were almost as hesitant as we had been coming in, afraid of taking a wrong turn, even of being stranded by a mechanical breakdown in this country where we did not see another vehicle or another person for the more than thirty miles. The next morning, after we had eaten breakfast again at Bud's Coffee and Gift Shop and I had checked out of the motel, we drove the Interstate and turned north once more. Now, knowing where we were going, we were relaxed enough to notice even the smaller bird life, the meadowlarks and magpies, and to appreciate the patterns of sunlight and cloud shadow playing across the grasslands and illuminating the buttes and down into the draws.

We were to sleep that night in the basement room I had shared, that night twelve years before, with Gary, and after I took the bags out of the car, Loretta led us down. There were the two bed-rooms, with the bath between, and what had been the kitchen and laundry, and off that, what had been the living room, all of it where they had lived for eight years under the flat roof of six layers of tar and tar paper.

After we had eaten that evening in 1964, Tescher and I had sat in the living room having a couple of drinks, and I had got him to talking about how, when he and his brother Alvin were living alone in the bunkhouse after the family ranch house had burned, someone would leave a horse with them to be broken. It would take them three or four weeks to get it roughed out and ready to handle, and then they'd take it back to the owner. That was how he got the thirteen dollars for his first pair of boots and ended his shoe wearing right then.

"We used to run wild horses, too," he said. "In those days these Badlands were full of 'em, and when I was seventeen I had forty-three head."

"In other words," I said, "when you wear those jeans and boots and that hat, it's not just a costume and you're not just acting."

Levi Strauss, a Bavarian sailmaker, brought blue denim and dungarees to the California gold miners in 1850, and the Ameri-can cowboy adopted them. In the 1950s the jeans, which when new will almost stand alone, became a prop for the newly pubes-cent and an excuse to go unwashed for the arrested adolescent. They have since been bleached and bespangled, hijacked, coun-terfeited, and even corrupted by couturiers into costumes for the chic.

"Just acting?" he said. "I guess that's right."

"I understand that some people don't know that," I said. "They told me in Phoenix that when you and Tom were rodeoing together, and somebody in a bar would start the abuse with that 'Where'd you park your horse, Tex?' it was a delight to see. They say that you two, wreathed in smiles, would just clean out the place."

"They told you that, did they?" he said.

"That's right," I said, and he was then on the Board of Directors of the Rodeo Cowboys Association. "I understand that last summer at Cheyenne this cowboy came up and shook his finger in your face and said, 'You RCA directors are a lot of fatheaded sonsabitches!' They say you knocked him on his tail, and he was still out five minutes later."

"I guess that's about right," he said.

"What about the night in Dickinson?"

"Well," he said, "Loretta and I were going to Fort Madison, and we stopped in this cafe to wait for Pete Fredericks, from Halliday, who was goin' with us. While we were eatin', there were three or four fellas in the next booth who got to arguing and cussing and finally the big guy challenged this little fella to go out in the street. I went out and the big guy just bloodied up the little fella somethin' awful, and finally he knocked him out.

"The big guy was feelin' pretty good now," he said, "and back in the booth he got to using some pretty rank language. Finally I said to him that there was a lady present, and I told him he should shut up. He jumped up and said, 'I'd like to have you shut me up!' I had my right hand on the top of the back of the booth, and I kinda pivoted on that, and I hit him a left.

"He went back over the table, but he came out of the booth and I hit him another shot and I flattened him. Then I picked him up and I threw him out. By then the manager had called the law, and when they got there, this manager said, 'It's all right now, officers. This gentleman has already handled it.' One of the cops said, 'Was that you threw him out in the street?' I said, 'That's right.' And the cop said, 'You know, as we come along in the dark, we thought you were throwin' out a saddle.'"

"I like that," I said.

"Then the manager wouldn't let us pay for the two dinners," Tescher said.

"What about that time in Dallas?"

"They told you about that, too?" he said. "Well, after the rodeo, we got paid off kind of late, and it was about two A.M. when I went to eat in this cafe right across from the hotel. There were about a dozen cowboys and a lot of others there, but there was only one waitress, and we had to wait. There was one fella there and he started that 'Tex' stuff. The longer nobody said anything the worse he got, and finally I'd finished eatin' and George Williams just kinda nudged me.

"So I said to this fella, 'Why don't you just get out?' He said, 'Maybe you'd like to try to put me out.' Then we went to it, and as soon as we did I knew he could fight. I guess we must have gone for three or four minutes until finally I hit him a good right, and he went down and he just lay there by some chairs. The other fellas got me out then, because they figured the law was comin'. Later, when I went back to pay my bill the manager said somebody had already paid it, but he said, 'Do you know who that fella is, you knocked out? He's the light-heavyweight champion of Texas.' I could tell he could fight."

"I used to think," I said, "that if I got cornered in a dark alley I'd holler for Rocky Graziano. Now I think I'd holler for you."

"I never look for it," he said, "but there's some people don't understand anything else."

In the pantry in that basement now, Loretta was showing my wife where she stacks on the shelves each year the 300 quarts she puts up of tomatoes, peas, beans, carrots, corn, and peaches, along with the thirty or more jars of jellies and honey. At noon we ate buffalo meat balls, and then, with Loretta and my wife in the car, I drove Tescher the seven miles to their nearest neighbors, the Harris Goldsberrys, where Tescher was to pick up the Caterpillar to bulldoze some cattle trails in his winter pastures.

When we got there, Harris Goldsberry, a slim, taciturn man, was working on the Caterpillar, replacing the hydraulic pump. While Betty and Loretta went into the ranch house, where they said later, they talked gardening with Margaret Goldsberry and had iced tea she had steeped in the sun, I watched the work on the

Caterpillar for an hour, and then we left Tescher to drive the machine back while we drove back in the car. By then the school was out for the day. Rodney Burman had taken the wooden-platformed cable car back across the river, and Troy and Bonnie were about their chores when Loretta knocked on the trailer door.

"May we come in?" she said.

The white trailer was set up between the white-painted chicken house and the white-painted privy. There was a basketball backboard and basket off to the right, and there were a couple of dozen white hens and a couple of roosters wandering around. Inside the trailer, after Loretta left us to go back to the house, Sandy Schulz, five years out of North Dakota State Teachers College in Dickenson, and in her fourth year of teaching here, showed us around. Her living quarters were in the back half of the trailer—the sofa-bed, a chair, a small television, the gas range and refrigerator, and the sink to which she would bring the water from a spigot outside. In the schoolroom half were her desk and the three others, bookshelves, a blackboard, and a wall rack of rolled maps.

"I suppose Bonnie gets reading and writing and arithmetic," I said. "What subjects do Troy and the Burman boy get?"

"The eighth graders?" she said. "We have reading, math, spelling, United States history, North Dakota history, and earth science."

"And your books?" my wife asked. "You're able to get whatever books you need?"

"Oh, yes," she said. "The county librarian sends out the boxes of the books you write for, and it's always exciting when we get new books."

It was getting toward six o'clock when we heard the Caterpillar coming up the road and into the yard. Tescher came in and washed up and changed for dinner and we had pheasant. After dinner we sat in the living room with the glass-topped wagon-wheel table, with the award buckles—several dozen of them—set between the spokes under the glass. The two National Finals award saddles were on their stands, and the rodeo trophies were on the mantel of the fieldstone fireplace.

"I gave away about sixty-five buckles," Tescher said "Some to relatives, some to rodeo fans, some to neighbor kids."

In the ten years he had rodeoed, he had won $160,000, but half of that had gone into expenses. Out of the rest he had built up the ranch, 6,000 acres now in three units with 350 head of Hereford and the two dozen registered quarter horses from which he sells three or four colts a year.

"We bought the place in the fall of '52," he said. "I sold a new Packard car to pay the $5,000 down payment. There was this old log house, sort of stuccoed on the outside. It was out where the school is now, and I remember sitting in the kitchen and tryin' to read the newspaper and having to hold it down so the wind wouldn't blow it away. It was cold. That first winter I trapped bobcats and beaver to buy our groceries, and we lived off that."

"Do you still trap and hunt?"

"That's right. We reload our own shells, and we get coyote and some bobcat and trap beaver and coon. The coon bring two to five dollars and coyotes forty. Their furs sell good over in Europe, and a fella told me a coat sells as high as $2,000 over there. Bobcat hide are up to $200 apiece, and the beaver run $25 or $35."

"And you've got your own bees and chickens," I said.

"We've got fifty hens," Loretta said. "We try to give the eggs away, but the neighbors give the children money."

"And the children, I suppose, have their chores?" Betty said.

"Troy gets up at six to milk," Loretta said. "Bonnie takes care of the chickens."

"And they break horses," Tescher said, "and they fill the creep feed."

"What is that?" I said.

"It's a bin in the calf bottom, where only the calves get in. It's oats and hay and they take care of that, every morning and night, from November first until about April twentieth. Then they have their own. Troy has three cows and a couple of yearling steers. When they get out of school, they have something to sell to go on to college if they want to.

"They're beef cows," he said, "and they all have their own brands, simple to put on, just straight irons and not writing all over the critter so they blotch. Barry helped brand this year, heelin' the calves and draggin' them out. There'll be three or four calf-rasslers—neighbors—and one dehorning and some vaccinating. One will do the castrating, and the women and children do the vaccinating."

"And how long does this take?"

"We'll do 300 a day, usually June 20 to July 4. You have to spend two weeks ridin' to bring them in before branding."

"And then you have to bring them all in close to here before winter?"

"In the fall you spend a week gathering your stock for sale. Then the last two weeks of December we're ridin' to get them out of the common pastures and into the private pastures."

"When there was that buyers' strike against beef prices about four years ago," I said, "did that hurt?"

"I actually think the cattle were too high," Tescher said. "Prices went up over the counter, and ours started droppin'. People thought we were reapin' in money, but we'd been losin' money for three years, and I think TV has a lot to do with it. I think it hurts the farmer and rancher, because just as soon as they hear one morning that round steaks went down in New York City, it's plumb across the country and cattle drop that much.

"You take cattle to market now, and you don't know what they'll bring. The next day it may be up, but otherwise supply and demand took care of it. This way it's just talk, and now our fat cattle are bringin' the lowest since 1953, and a lot of people are goin' broke. The land is so high that there's no way of payin' for it, and the wrong people are gonna end up with it, for a sideline and a tax deduction.

"It's sad," he said, "when a young fella who's willing to work can't go out and buy a ranch and make it pay for itself in twenty years. There are people who owned land for thirty years who are goin' broke. I'm sure that the supermarket gets a lot of it. I think, though, that three quarters of the people in the United States are livin' too high off the hog, includin' ourselves, and we've pure had to back off.

"I'll tell you," he continued, "I think it's a lot tougher world to live in now. Things are too easy, and that's why it's tougher to amount to something. Work don't pay all that well now, and there's millions of people who get paid for not working. There's no pride left in work. I think there's more pride left in ranching than in most anything else."

"Well you should be proud of what you and Loretta have done here," I said. "I remember twelve years ago when your back used to hurt you when you'd take some time to sit down."

"It's pretty good now," he said, "if I don't work too hard. Haulin' bales by hand, it hurts all the time."

"And if it goes out, you haven't got Benny Reynolds to snap it in."

"Once in a while the chiropracters could get it back in place, but most couldn't," he said. "Probably they weren't strong enough, but Benny could, and it sounded like snappin' a log chain."

"Speaking of hauling bales by hand," I said, "I remember you telling me that the children, when they were just little tots, would drive the pickup in low gear while you stood in the back throwing off the bales."

"That's right," he said. "They'd go with me feedin', and they'd drive when they were about three. When they wanted to stop, if we came to a tree or whatever, they'd just shut the key off. By the time they were third-graders they knew how to drive."

"That's amazing," my wife said.

"A lot of this amazes me," I said. "When I was out here before, you didn't have a phone. The nearest one was your dad's in Sentinel Butte."

"That's right," he said. "The phone came in in 1971, and it made the New York *Times* and *The Wall Street Journal*. There are a hundred people on the exchange—it's Squaw Gap Exchange and there's an exchange building up here in the middle of nowhere—and everybody else is long distance."

"And what about the mail?" my wife said.

"The mail comes Mondays and Thursdays," Loretta said. "The postman comes to the mail box across the river, weather permitting. Sometimes we'll go for several weeks without mail, but if somebody goes to town they pick up everybody's mail."

"Do you still mine your own coal?" I said.

"We dynamite in and use coal augers," Tescher said. "It's during Christmas vacation and the kids help. Five families get coal off my vein along the river bank, and we take out twenty to thirty ton a winter."

"How cold does it get here in winter?" my wife said.

"I've seen it 52 below," Tescher said. "In January, three weeks at a time it'll never get up to zero during the day, and it'll be 20 to 30 below most nights."

"How hot does it get at the height of the summer?" I said.

"I've seen it 110," he said. "It was 105 one day in early September, and three nights later it froze."

"How much snow do you get?"

"On March 23 last year," he said, "everybody was startin' to calve, and on March 25 it was 20 below, and it snowed."

Loretta had left the room. When she came back she had a leather-bound diary in her hand.

"I have it in here," she said, and she read from it. "Sixth of April, still snowing and raining . . . Eighth, still stormy . . . April ten was the last time it snowed. There were thirty-four inches."

"A lot of calves smothered in the snow," Tescher said "Some froze to death and some got pneumonia. Some were three weeks old, and never saw the sun. In weather like that you've got to be right with them. The mother can save the calf at 20 below, but in the wet and chill they can't get dry. You didn't pay any attention to when the day started or ended because you had to be up all night. Everybody lost. Throughout this area we lost 20 per cent of the calves, but in a way it done us some good, because everybody was overstocked.

"There was an old-timer lived down here," he said. "He came in 1904, and even guys like that say they'd never seen anything like it. Easter came and we couldn't get in or out, and we called a pilot who flies some around here to round up the horses. He went and got 'em up on top of a plateau about a mile from here, and the Goldsberrys have that Caterpillar and it had a plow on it. For six days that Cat wasn't shut off. We had to plow trails for the cows. It was the only way they could get to the feed."

"Do you ever get angry at the elements at times like that?" I said.

"No," he said. "I'm sure some people do, but I take it in stride, and make the best of it. I get down when the machinery breaks down and repairs are so high-priced."

"I guess the neighbors out here are all pretty special people," my wife said.

"If you don't neighbor," Tescher said, "you're not gonna make it. We had a bad winter in '64–'65 when we were isolated for seven or eight weeks. One winter it was longer than that. That road you came in on, it was closed from Thanksgiving to March. When we had the old roads, the only road we had would be to come up the ice in the winter."

"What about illnesses?" my wife said. "Are you able to get to a doctor?"

"The nearest doctor is in Beach," Tescher said. "That's 44 miles, but we usually doctor in Dickinson and Williston. The one is 95 miles, and the other 120."

"Beach has changed, though," Loretta said. "They have two new doctors."

"Cindy broke her arm while she was in the eighth grade," Tescher said. "She had this horse she was breakin', and it drug her around the corral and hit the feed bunks and hooked on a post. She was kind of out of her head in the barn, and I didn't know if she was hurt internally. It was about 4:30 and in February, and we'd never been plowed out. We had to go down the river and it was three to four feet deep and the water would go over the lights. We had her laid out in the back seat, and I'd given her a pain killer. We had to go six miles down the river, north and east, and across Beaver Creek to where the road was partially open, and we got to Beach at about eight o'clock."

"Then once, when we were snowed in," Loretta said, "Bonnie fell and hit her head on the fireplace. If we could have taken her in and she'd had stitches in it, it wouldn't have a scar now, but Jim taped it."

"What if you get, say, the flu, and you can't get out?" my wife said.

"I've given all the children and Loretta and myself penicillin shots for the flu and sore throat," Tescher said.

"How did you learn this doctoring?" I said.

"We have a Red Cross first aid book," Loretta said.

"It's livestock penicillin," Tescher said. "I asked a doc about it and he said, 'That's all right, but what do you do if you have a reaction?' I said, 'Give 'em some of that stuff we have for the cattle. Epinephrine.' He said, 'Yeah. You're on the right track.'"

The next morning at breakfast we had orange juice, fried eggs, and Canadian bacon, pancakes with whipped cream and buffalo berries, red and tart, on them, and coffee. After breakfast, Tescher and I sat for a few final minutes in the living room, talking.

"As you look back over what you've lived up to now," I said, "are these the best years of your life?"

"The best years of my life," he said, "were the '30s, my childhood. We were very hard up, with a house full of kids, but I was happiest then, ridin' and breakin' horses, ridin' to other ranches and helping them brand. Then the idea of responsibility started to invade, but when I was Troy's age it was the best years of my life."

"And when you first found out you could win money in rodeo," I said, "those were good years, too."

"That's right," he said.

He was eighteen, and his hero was Bill Linderman, who twice won the saddle bronc title, and he had told me about it that night, sitting in the basement. In those days he and his brother Tom, who is four years older, used to travel in Tom's twelve-year-old Ford with wood and cardboard in place of the broken glass in the windows and no starter and almost no brakes, but with a good motor and good tires. The first major rodeo they went to was in Sheridan, Wyoming.

"When we got there," he told me, "we saw that Bill Linderman and some other name cowboys would contest, and it just sickened us. We thought of comin' back home, and then we waited until a few minutes before the entries closed, hopin' they wouldn't let us in, but they did. Tom won a third in the bareback and I won the saddle bronc, and it paid $192 and I thought I'd never see another poor day."

"When I won in New York in 1955," he was saying now, "it was the highest my feet were ever off the ground. A lot of times I felt I was overpaid. I didn't know how it could be happening to me. Will Rogers said that he'd rather be lucky than good, but if you're good you're lucky. A lot of people work real hard and can't make it, but just having the determination to work hard is a stroke of luck, too, because I think a person gets a lot of satisfaction out of working."

"What do you think is going to happen to this country in the years just ahead?" I said.

"I don't know," he said. "I sure don't know, but I think that people have to learn again to have respect for their work."

We had said good-by to the children in the kitchen before they had started across the yard to the trailer school. We said good-by to Loretta and Jim Tescher standing by the car. We said that yes, we would hope that someday we would be able to get out that way again, and they said that, if they could get away from the ranch sometime, they might visit a sister of Jim's in the East, and then we would see them again. As we drove out of the yard and looked back they were waving to us.

"What a reassuring experience," Betty said, "just to know that there are still people like that in this country."

"They're what's left of an America that once was," I said, "and soon won't ever be again."

We drove mostly in silence, until we saw, about a quarter mile off to the right and coming off a rise, about a dozen antelope. When they saw us they turned, their white rump patches showing, and crested the rise. Then, just over the rise, they turned again and peered at us, like small children in a playground who see something of interest passing outside. The last we saw of them they crossed the road about a half mile ahead and disappeared down into a draw.

4

So Long, Jack

There are two honest managers in boxing. The one is
Jack Hurley, and I can't remember the name of the
other.

Damon Runyon

It was while we were still driving West, heading for Medora and
then Jim Tescher's. We were crossing the Red River on the wide,
many-laned bridge between Moorhead, Minnesota, and Fargo,
North Dakota, and it was midmorning.

"Are we going to stop in Fargo?" my wife said.

"Maybe on the way back," I said. "I'm not sure."

I have a friend named Walter Wellesley Smith, whose mother
called him Wells, and who is known as Red. He was born and
grew up in Green Bay, Wisconsin, and while he was running an
elevator in the Northland Hotel summers and going to Notre
Dame the rest of the year, he used to dream about sometime seeing a World Series, a heavyweight championship fight, and a Kentucky Derby. He writes a sports column for the New York *Times,*
and in close to a half century he has attended forty-four World
Series, fifty-four heavyweight championship fights, and thirty-
three Kentucky Derbies.

"When we drive out to Jim Tescher's," I was telling him several
months before, "we'll be going through Fargo. I'm thinking of
stopping there and seeing if anybody remembers Jack."

"Oh, sure," he said. "You've got to do that."

"I'll go to the sports department of the paper," I said, "and ask
somebody, 'Can you tell me where Jack Hurley is buried?'"

"Of course," he said, "and you'll get some young noodnik who'll say, 'Jack who?' ' "

"I'm not much for visiting graves," I said.

"Oh, but you've got to do that," he said. "You've got to get Jack in the book."

About ninety miles west of Fargo I turned off the Interstate where we saw several of those gas station signs on their high-legged towers, and got gas and drove into the adjacent restaurant for lunch. The waitress led us between two rows of booths, and in one of them a young man in his late teens, blond, blue-eyed and sturdy, was sitting, looking at the menu. He had on a freshly laundered, blue football jersey with the white numerals 54 and, in orange block letters, the name WASHBURN across the chest, and he was leaning back at ease the way in high school my football heroes used to loll in class.

"Oh, you're from Washburn?" I heard a woman say in a reedy, treble voice. She was one of three, all of them white-haired, that the waitress had started to lead between the booths and, while the others had gone on, she had stopped at the young man's.

"Yes, ma'am," the young man said.

"I used to live in Washburn," she said. "What's your name?"

"Tracy," he said.

"Tracy?" the white-haired woman said. "Tracy? Well, you're a younger generation. I don't remember a Tracy."

"But I'm from Washburn High in Minneapolis," he said, indicating the name on the jersey.

"Tracy?" she said. "It's been such a long time since I lived in Washburn. Tracy?"

The young man started to say something but then, embarrassed, he shrugged and looked away. The woman, still repeating the name, walked on and joined the others in the booth. I looked at my wife and shook my head, and when I glanced over at the other booth again the young man had left.

"She scared him right out of the booth," I said. "Jack Hurley should be here, and it would get him started on the creatures again."

It was Jack Hurley's contention that more fighters are ruined by women, whom he called creatures, than by opponents' punches, alcohol, or whatever. The affliction, as Hurley saw it, was epidemic, affecting not only fighters but all married men, whom he called mules, in all callings, and nothing reaffirmed this for him more convincingly than the sight of women of advanced years enjoying a meal in a public place after, he was certain, they had driven their husbands into early graves.

"On the way back," Betty said, "we'd better stop in Fargo. After all, Jack Hurley meant so much to your life."

Of all those I came to know in sports nobody else ever fascinated me as did Jack Hurley. He seemed to me to be a literary character, as if he had stepped out of the pages of a novel, and I put him in one about a prize fighter and his manager. A novel, of course, should be larger than life but there was no way I could make my Doc Carroll bigger than Jack.

There were the last days I spent with him in Seattle and Boise in September of 1966, and all week I kept telling myself that I had written the book ten years too soon. He was moving his last fighter then, a heavyweight name Boone Kirkman, and when I got off the plane he was at the airport. I hadn't seen him in eight years, but there he was at the edge of the crowd, tall and bony, craning his neck and then waving. He looked a lot older and thinner and paler, and there was dark green glass over the right lens of his bifocals.

"How are you?" I said, as we shook hands.

With Jack I always knew what the answer to that one would be. The moment I would ask the question, I would get the feeling that I was the straight man in an act.

"No good," he said.

That had to be the truth. He was sixty-nine then, and wracked with the rheumatism he said he picked up in France in World War I. In addition to that, the surgical profession had been whittling away at him for years. They had taken his tonsils and his appendix for starters, and then, after he retired Billy Petrolle—his one great fighter—in 1934, they took two thirds of his stomach because of ulcers. While they were still trying to cure sinusitis with surgery, he had twenty-three operations, and recently I had read in *The Ring* that he had had a cataract removed from his right eye.

"Who hit you in the eye?" I said.

"Ah," he said. "Cataracts, so I decided to go for the operation."

"Good," I said. "That's one they've become very proficient at."

"Don't I know that?" he said. "So what happens? When it's over, I say to the doctor, 'Now, Doc, I understand that after ninety per cent of these operations, the patient's sight can be corrected with glasses to 20–20. Is that right?' So he says, 'Well, that's about right.' So I say, 'But, Doc, I'm not gonna have 20–20, am I?' He says, 'Well, no.' So I say, 'All right. How good is my sight gonna be?' He says, 'Well, pretty good.'

"Now wouldn't you know that?" Jack said, that pinched look of disgust coming over his face. "Ninety per cent are successful, but I have to be in the other ten per cent. Why?"

"I don't know," I said.

"Now tell me something else," he said. "What does he mean by 'pretty good'? Just how good is 'pretty good'?"

"I don't know that, either," I said.

"I can't see a damn thing," he said. "Oh, hell. I can see some, but at the hotel I've already fallen down the stairs twice, and now I've gotta have the other eye done. How about that 'pretty good' though?"

Jack had been living in room 679 of the Olympic Hotel since he had left Chicago seventeen years before to manage a light-heavyweight named Harry "Kid" Matthews. He had also left his wife.

"So I'm hustling to make a living in Seattle," he told me once, "when one day these two detectives from Chicago show up. They've got a paper charging me with desertion, and they drag me back. Now I'm in Chicago again, and late one afternoon I come into the lobby of the hotel where we're living. All the creatures are sittin' around there—they've got nothing else to do—and as soon as I walk in I see them start lookin' at one another and their heads start going. One of them says to me, 'Oh, Mr. Hurley. When you get upstairs you won't find your wife there.' I say, 'Is that so?' She says, 'Yes, she's left you.'

"You see?" Jack said. "She can't wait to let me find it out for myself. So I say, 'Is that so?' She says, 'Yes, she's gone to Miami.' I say, 'Thank you.' I turn right around and I go over to the station house. I walk up to the desk sergeant, and I say, 'I want to report that my wife has just left me.' So the desk sergeant says, 'So what?' I say, 'So what? I'll tell you what. You know those two donkeys you sent out to Seattle to bring me back? Now I want you to send them down to Miami to bring my wife back.' You know what he said?"

"No," I said.

"He said, 'Listen, Hurley. You get out of here before I lock you up.' Now, isn't that terrible? What kind of justice is that?"

It was Hurley the teacher and ring strategist, however, who captured me. In boxing I knew three great teachers. Ray Arcel worked with seventeen world champions and, as one of the most gentle, kind, and refined of men, was concerned about the fighter as a person more than anyone else I ever knew. To him I would have entrusted a son. Charley Goldman worked on a fighter like a sculptor working on a block of marble, always trying to bring out all the truth within, and always afraid that if he did not go deep enough, he would leave some of it hidden, but also afraid that if he cut too deep, he would destroy some of it forever. Over a period of several years I watched him as, without destroying the fighters' gifts, he made a great heavyweight champion out of the awkward Rocky Marciano. Jack Hurley, the great ring strategist and perfectionist, as he crouched at ringside, squinting through those thin-rimmed glasses, saw a fight as a contest of the mind in which he was always moving his fighter a move or two ahead.

"I don't know why it is," Jack was telling me once, "but I can look at a fighter and know that he must do this or he must do that to lick the other guy. There are a lot of things I can't do. You can sit me down at a piano and I couldn't play 'Home Sweet Home' if you gave me the rest of my life, but I can just look at fighters and know what's right.

"Some people are just like that. Some years ago out in the Dakotas there was a kid playing third base for the Jamestown club in the Dakota League. Behind first base there was this high fence, and this kid playing third used to field the ball—and he had a terrific arm, and he'd not only throw the ball over the first-baseman's reach, but he'd throw it over the fence.

"So one day," Jack said, "the word got around that a scout for the Yankees was in town to look at the kid. Everybody laughed.

They said, 'What is this? He's wasting his time with a kid who can't throw any better that that.'

"The scout knew something, though. He had the ability to see something that no one else could. He took that kid and put him in at shortstop. He put him at deep shortstop, where the kid could cover a lot of ground and where he could make the throw. He played shortstop for the Yankees for a number of years. His name was Mark Koenig. I still don't know why it is that somebody can see something when everybody else can't."

Over the years, though, I came to know why Jack could see things in fighters and fights that others couldn't. I never saw his one great fighter, Billy Petrolle, in the ring, but fifteen years after Petrolle retired, Wilbur Wood was still telling me about his fights. Joe Williams, the Scripps-Howard sports editor and columnist, once wrote that, in twenty-five years of watching fights in Madison Square Garden, the greatest he ever saw there was the first Petrolle-Jimmy McLarnin fight. As I watched Jack work with other fighters, and listened to him for hours while he talked about Petrolle's fights, it was obvious that he could see what no one else could because he had analyzed and broken down the science that precedes the art.

Jack was born and grew up in Fargo, and he was thirteen when his father, who was a switchman on the Canadian-Northern, was killed pulling a coupling between boxcars. As the oldest of five children Jack had to go to work, and he started selling newspapers on Broadway and Northern Pacific Avenue where, to protect his corner, he had to fight. There was a gym in the basement of Saumweber's Barbershop across the river in Moorhead, and he started to hang around there, learning what he could by watching the other fighters. When he was fifteen he weighed 120 pounds, and he began boxing at smokers at night.

"I liked the boxing business," he told me once, "but I figured there must be an easier way. Then I got the idea of using the talents of others. I figured that if I could get a half-dozen kids and get them each a fight a month I could make more money than if I was fighting myself."

He was eighteen when he started managing fighters. He would go down to St. Paul and corner Mike and Tom Gibbons. They called Mike "The St. Paul Phantom," and Tom went fifteen rounds with Dempsey, and Jack would ask them questions, and as he watched fights, he would lift a move here and a move there, starting to build up his own library of moves and punches.

When World War I started, Jack got into it. He was in D Company of the 18th Infantry of the First Division that, a generation later, I would come to know in Normandy and the Huertgen and in Germany on both sides of the Rhine. For a while they were in Heudicourt in the St. Mihiel sector, and the British sent in a Sergeant Major named Cassidy, to teach the Yanks the bayonet manual.

"He was a miserable s.o.b.," Jack used to say, "but he knew his business. He would stand there unarmed with his hands down at his sides, and he'd say, 'Stick me!' You'd have your rifle with the bayonet fixed, and you'd make a lunge at him and you'd miss. Maybe the next time your rifle would go up in the air, or you'd get the butt of it under your chin. He did it all with feinting and footwork. He'd draw you into a lead, and that would be the last you'd have to do with it. You'd have the bayonet, but this Cassidy, without even touching the bayonet, would be controlling it.

"I used to go and see this guy at night," Jack said. "His stuff fascinated me, so one night I said to him, 'This puts me in mind of boxing.' He said, 'The bayonet manual was taken from boxing. If you're standing in the on-guard position, and I take the rifle out of your hands, you're standing like a boxer. Now I put the rifle back in your hands, and at the command of 'long point' you make a left jab. Now you move the opponent out of position, and you come up to hit him with the butt. Isn't that the right uppercut?'"

It was the footwork that impressed Jack, though. As Jack told it, this Cassidy would stand right there with his feet spread, and he wouldn't move them more than a couple of inches and still they couldn't reach him with the bayonet.

"If a boxer would master this style," Cassidy told Jack, "he'd save thousands of steps. He'd be just as safe as I am, and he'd save all those fancy steps."

"And can't you see it now?" Jack would say. "As you look back on Billy Petrolle, can't you see where I got that famous shuffle step?"

Jack would forget, of course, that I had never seen Petrolle fight, that I was a high school kid at the time, but I had built up such a book on him, listening to Jack and others talk about him, that it was as if I had been at all those fights. Even now, after watching thousands of fights, I can "see" those Petrolle fights, punch by punch, as I have seen few fights.

There was the first McLarnin fight, that Joe Williams cited as the greatest he ever saw in the Garden. One of the moves that Jack had taught Petrolle was the knack of turning away from a right hand and throwing a right hand back, and just before the fight he sat down with Petrolle to map it out.

"Now remember," he said, "you can't turn away from McLarnin's right because he punches too long and too sharp. You'd be too far away from him to hit him. With this guy you have to resort to an amateur move. He won't expect it from you because he knows you're a good fighter, and he thinks you know too much. What you've got to do is drop the left hand. He'll throw the right, and you lean down under it and counter with the left instead of the right. He won't be looking for it, and you can't miss him with it."

Petrolle started drawing the right and countering with the left, and McLarnin didn't know where those punches were coming from. He knew they weren't coming from Petrolle, because Petrolle wouldn't do a thing like that and, as Joe Williams wrote later, at one point he looked at Patsy Haley, the referee, as if to ask, "Are you hitting me?"

"But McLarnin was some fighter," Jack said and, of course, McLarnin went on to win the welterweight title, "and after a while he figured it out. Then I had Petrolle switch. He walked out there and started jabbing and missing, jabbing and missing. McLarnin thought he had him all figured out again, and he tried to anticipate Petrolle and moved in. He came in, right into a right that Petrolle had been building up all the time, and down he went."

Petrolle won that decision, but Jack always said his greatest fight was with Justo Suarez in the Garden seven months after McLarnin. Suarez was out of the Argentine, a bull of a lightweight, and they called him "The Little Firpo." After he came to this country and licked three of the best lightweights around, no one wanted to fight him, but Jack took him for Petrolle.

"After the match was made," Jack used to say, telling about it, "I went up to the gym to get a line on Suarez. He used to box sixteen or eighteen rounds a day without more than breaking a light sweat. The day I was watching him, he fell out of the ring and landed on his head and got up and went right back in. I said, 'Oh-oh, this is going to be it!'

"Well, Petrolle was some hooker, you know, and in the first round he had Suarez down three times. At the end of the round Suarez had Petrolle back on his heels, and when Billy came back to the corner, I said, 'Now don't hit him on the chin again. When you leave this corner you bend over and you punch with both hands to the body.' Petrolle used to follow orders to the letter, and for six rounds it was the most scientific exhibition of body punching anybody ever saw. At the end of the seventh round Petrolle said to me, 'Jack, I think he's ready.' I said, 'Not yet. Stay right down there and punch up.'

"At the end of the eighth round I said, 'All right, now is the time. Start this round the same way, and after three or four punches to the body, raise up and hit him a right hand on the chin. If he don't go, get down again and then raise up and hit him a left hand on the chin. If he don't go, you stay down.'

"Petrolle went out, belted that Suarez three shots in the body and then came up. He landed the right hand flush on the chin and he shook Suarez. Now, another fighter would have been tempted to throw another right, but Petrolle went back to the body, and the second time he rose it was with the hook, and Suarez went over on his head. Hell, it was easy, if they'll only do what you tell them. The other fella doesn't know what he's doing. He's just guessing, but you know, because you've got it figured."

What Jack meant was that Jack had it figured. Crouched there below the corner he wouldn't be watching his own fighter, because he knew what his own fighter could do. He would be watching the other fighter, and not slipping or ducking any punches, he would be studying the other fighter's moves and analyzing his errors.

"So tell him about the Eddie Ran fight," Wilbur Wood said to him one day. We were in one of the dressing rooms at Stillman's

Gym when Jack had Vince Foster, who looked like another Petrolle until Jack lost his grip on him to whiskey and women, and at the age of twenty-one, he died one night in a highway crash near Pipestone, Minnesota.

"Yeah," Jack said, "but the thing about Petrolle was that people never knew how good he was. They thought he was a lucky fighter, but what he did he did because it was planned that way. It wasn't any accident when he won a fight.

"Petrolle, you know, wasn't easy to hit. He gave the impression that he was easy to hit. Sure he did. He invited you to hit him. Do you know why? Because then he could hit you back. Petrolle would go in there and put it up there where you could hit it. He'd take two or three jabs, and then slip under and let go with the heavy artillery. That's a good trade any time you can take three light punches to let go with the heavy stuff. What gave people the impression that Petrolle was easy to hit was that he was always on the edge of danger. That's the place to be. Be in there close where you can work, where you take advantage of it when the other guy makes a mistake, and . . ."

"And don't pull back," Wilbur said. "That's where they get hurt."

"Certainly," Jack said. "For fifteen years I've been schooling myself. If I ever get into a theater fire I'm not gonna get up and rush for the exit. What chance have I got? Like the others, I'm gonna be trampled to death. Do you know what I'm going to do? I'm gonna sit right in my seat for thirty seconds and figure it out. Then I'm going to get up and walk over the others and pick my exit."

"But tell him about the Ran fight," Wilbur said.

"Sure," Jack said, "but, you see, it's like that when you fight. You're safest when you're closest to danger. You're inside where you may get your block knocked off if you don't know what you're doing, but if you know what you're doing it's a cinch. You look so easy that the other guy has to try to hit you. Don't you see? He can't help himself, and then when you've got him coming, you work your stuff, you let the heavy stuff drop. Why, Petrolle used to just sit there in that rocking chair and belt them when they came in."

"The Ran fight," Wilbur said.

"Yeah," Jack said. "In the first round he had Ran down a couple of times with hooks. When he came back to the corner I said, 'You're not going to drop him with a hook again. You've got to get him to throw the right. You've got to slip it like this . . .'"

He had his hands out in front of himself, and he moved his head as if he were slipping a punch.

"Do you know," he said, "that we had to wait until the sixth round for that chance for Petrolle to get that opening for his own right? He went out there, jabbing and jabbing and hooking light and sticking it right out there, and Ran wouldn't do anything. All of a sudden, though, Ran fired that right, and Petrolle slipped it and let his own go. It was really a hook with the right, and Ran went down—like this—like he'd been cut down at the knees with a scythe.

"After the fight, though," Jack said, that pinched look of disgust coming into his face again, "do you know what they said? They said Petrolle was lucky. They said, 'My, what a lucky punch. What a lucky fighter.' It wasn't luck. It was the work of an artist, and after Petrolle got dressed he went into Ran's dressing room. Ran said to him, 'Billy, I'm embarrassed.' Petrolle said, 'Why?' Ran said, 'I'm embarrassed of Eddie Ran. I knew you were gonna do that to me, but I couldn't help myself. You made it look so easy I just had to throw that right.'

"Then when he came out," Jack said, "Petrolle says to me, 'Jack, we'd better not fight them again. They're hep.'"

I wrote that for the next day's paper, the conversation in the dressing room with Jack talking and making the moves and Wilbur Wood cueing him. A couple of days later the old, white-haired receptionist at the paper who, it seemed to me, must have been there when they ran the headline that Lincoln had been shot, came shuffling into the sports department, and he had the name on the slip of paper and he said, "There's a Mr. Eddie Ran here to see you."

"Oh?" I said. "Send him in."

Seventeen years had gone by since the fight. How many times Eddie Ran had refought that one I had no idea, and how does a man react when, suddenly in a newspaper, he reads a description that brings back a night when he was knocked out?

"Mr. Heinz?" he said, walking up to me and putting out his hand. "I'm Eddie Ran."

He had on heavy work clothes, brown pants and a brown windbreaker and heavy work shoes. He was slim, and his face was tanned.

"I'm glad to meet you," I said, shaking his hand and waiting.

"I'm glad to meet *you*," he said, and then he smiled. "Gee, that was some column you had in the paper yesterday. I'm working on the docks over at the river, so I just had to come in and tell you."

"All I did was write what Jack Hurley said."

"Hurley told you the truth," he said. "That was some fight, and like Hurley said, I knew Petrolle wanted me to throw that right, but I just couldn't help myself."

Jack named Petrolle "The Fargo Express," and gave him one of the great trade names of boxing. Petrolle was of Italian descent, but he had high cheekbones to go with his black hair and dark eyes, so Jack gave him one of the great trademarks—an Indian blanket—to wear into the ring. When Petrolle retired after 255 fights and built a home in Duluth, he wanted to hang that blanket on the wall of his den.

"But it has blood on it," his wife said.

"Only some of it is mine," Petrolle said.

All Petrolle and Jack ever had for a contract was a handshake, but after thirteen years Petrolle retired during the Depression with $200,000 and an iron foundry in Duluth. When I met him years later, he owned a religious goods and gift shop in Duluth, and he was the chairman of the board of directors of the Pioneer National Bank.

After Petrolle retired, after his hook was gone and after his legs had left him, Jack announced in Duluth that he was looking for somebody to take the place of "The Fargo Express." The story went out over the Associated Press wire, and within the next week six hundred candidates showed up in Duluth.

"I forgot what it cost me to get them out of town," Jack used to say. "The Police Department came to me and said, 'Look, you got Michigan Street loaded with guys stranded here.' I had to pay the fare home for half of them, and there wasn't a fighter in the lot. Most of them should have been arrested for even entertaining the thought that they could be taught to fight."

There were very few people in the fight business then who wouldn't have found a way to make some money out of those six hundred, but not Jack. To Jack a fighter was a tool, and he was always looking for the tool that, when he finished shaping it and honing it over the years, would be the perfect tool to do the perfect work. He put all of himself into it, and when a Hurley fighter went into the ring Jack took every step with him. That fighter was what Jack would have been if he had had the body for it, and that is why it took so much out of Jack when, under pressure, the tool broke.

The best Jack had after Petrolle was Harry "Kid" Matthews, who had had seventy fights in twelve years but was getting nowhere when Jack took him on. Before he was done with him, Jack actually started a Congressional investigation into why the International Boxing Club wouldn't give Matthews a fight in the Garden. When they did, they put him with Irish Bob Murphy, who was belting everybody out, and they gave Murphy to Jack because nobody else would take him.

"Well, you're in," somebody said to Jack. "All you have to do is lick this guy and you're in."

A half a dozen of us were sitting around in the boxing office on the second floor of the Garden. We had just been making small talk when Jack had come in. He was fifty-three then, and Royal Brougham had written in the Seattle *Post Intelligencer* that he looked like a stern-faced deacon passing the collection plate at the First Methodist Church.

"Sure, we're in," Jack said, those ice-blue eyes narrowing behind those glasses, and a hurt look coming over his face. "We're in with a murderer. This guy never lets up. He rips you and slashes you and tears you apart inside. He's rough and strong, and you can't hurt him."

Jack turned and started to leave. He got as far as the door, and then he turned back and his eyes were big now behind the glasses and he had fear all over his face.

"That's the kind of guy you have to fight to get in here," he said. "Why, we're liable to get killed."

He left then. Pete Reilly was sitting there, and he had been around for so many years and worked so many a deal that they called him "The Fox."

"Listen to Hurley," Pete said, smiling and shaking his head. "When Jack talks like that you know he's got it figured. You know he's ready to slip one over. You can bet your bundle on that."

The smart money bet the bundle on Murphy, and it was some licking that he and they took. Matthews would draw a lead, and then he would slide with that shuffle step into one of those Hurley moves and he would belt Murphy so that the cops with the duty out on Eighth Avenue must have felt it. It was the greatest exhibition of body punching I have ever seen, and all the time that it was happening to Murphy there wasn't any way that Murphy could avoid it without turning his back and walking out.

The next day, up in the Garden, everybody was crowding Jack. They were slapping him on the back and telling him it had been years since they had seen anyone who could punch like that, and that it had been some fight.

"When I got home last night and went to bed," Irving Rudd was telling Jack, "it was like I had just finished a great book. I kept seeing it over and over, and I couldn't get to sleep."

"Why, in the ninth round," Jesse Abramson said to Jack, and Jesse was writing for the *New York Herald-Tribune* then, "your guy hit Murphy seven solid hooks without a return. I counted seven terrific hooks to the body, and Murphy couldn't help himself. It was wonderful."

"Yes, wasn't that wonderful?" Jack said, and now that pained look came into his face again. "Why, that was stupid. After he'd hit that Murphy with three of those solid hooks and turned him around, if he'd just thrown one right-hand uppercut he'd have knocked that stiff out."

"But it was a still a great fight," somebody said.

"And he'll do the same with that Marciano," Jack said, "if I can get him the fight."

That was one I never wanted for Jack, and I tried to talk him out of it. Putting Matthews against Marciano was like sending an armored jeep against a tank, but by the time Jack had sold the press and the public on Matthews he had also sold himself.

"I've been watching Charley Goldman working with Marciano," I told Jack. Jack had come into New York and we were having lunch in one of the booths in Muller's across Fiftieth Street from the Garden.

"Oh?" he said.

"Charley's really making a fighter out of him," I said.

"He is, is he?" Jack said.

"That's right," I said. "He's got him moving inside now and punching to the body, and you know he can sock."

"Ah," Jack said. "You know what you do with those body-punchers? You belt them right back in the body, and that puts an end to that."

"But this guy is too strong for your guy," I said. "You can't hurt him."

"Ah," Jack said, and there came that look, as if he had just bitten into another lemon. "Matthews will do to that Marciano just what he did to that Murphy. It'll be the same kind of fight."

Jack really believed it, and he had $10,000 bet on Matthews when they climbed into the ring in Yankee Stadium that night. I had to give Matthews the first round, because there he was, drawing Marciano's leads, moving off them and countering in that Hurley style, but all the time that it was going on, Marciano was backing him up. Matthews was winning the round, but losing the fight, and then, just as the bell sounded, Marciano hit him a right hand under the heart and Matthews bent under it, straightened up and started for Marciano's corner. Jack hollered at him, and he turned and walked to his own corner and I knew it was over. Early in the next round, and with a left hook, Marciano knocked him out.

"So are we going to stop in Fargo?" my wife was saying now. "We'll be there well before noon."

Driving back now from Jim Tescher's, we had got as far as Bismark, and had spent the night in a motel on the outskirts. We were having breakfast, and I was looking at the front page of *The Forum,* the Fargo-Moorhead paper. There was a two-column picture of a farmer standing thigh-deep in a fissure in his alfalfa field near Durbin, North Dakota. The farmer's name was Richard Hillborn, and it said in the caption under the picture, that he couldn't recall conditions ever being so dry, even in the drought of the 1930s.

"I guess so," I said, "but as it's a Saturday, there may not be anybody in the sports department of the paper. They may all be out covering football games for the Sunday paper."

"But I'm sure there'll be someone there in some department," she said. "You'll probably find someone to ask."

"I'd like to find somebody in sports, though," I said. "I doubt that anybody on the city side will remember Jack, but I'll find out."

When we passed the turnoff to Jamestown, and I saw the high-towered gas station signs on the left now, it reminded me of the white-haired woman who had flushed the high school football player out of his booth. The last we had seen of him he had been having a sandwich across from the cashier's counter when I had stopped to pay the check. The last we had heard of her she was still rasping, as she had been throughout our lunch, about ailments, not only her own but those of what must have been a whole battalion of invalided friends or acquaintances, none of whom, as walking wounded, could compare with Jack.

"Now isn't this something?" Jack was saying outside the Olympic when we got out of the cab that time he met me at the Seattle airport. "I checked in here for a week to manage that Matthews, and I've been here seventeen years. You have to remember, too, that I've got the two worst things in the world for this climate—rheumatism and sinus."

He waited while I checked in, and then we followed the bellhop up to the room. The bellhop went through all the business with the window shades and the closet doors and the bathroom light, and Jack beat me to the tip.

"All right," he said, when the bellhop had left. "Let's go down and get something to eat."

"Eat?" I said. "It's the middle of the afternoon."

"You know me," Jack said. "You know I have to eat every three hours."

Jack hated to eat alone, and that was how Ray Arcel came to call him "The Life-Taker." Jack was still around Chicago at the time, and it was just after they had taken two thirds of his stomach and he had to eat six times a day.

"It was during the Depression," Ray told me once, "and Jack had just retired Petrolle and had money, so he'd take these poor guys who were half-starving to eat with him. Jack would have a bowl of soup, or milk and crackers, but they'd order big steaks. One guy ate so much that Jack had to buy him a new suit of clothes, and another one actually ate himself to death."

They used to say around Seattle that while Jack had Matthews he would spend $1,000 a month feeding sportswriters and cops and press agents and hangers-on. Whenever he had it, he spread it around.

"When Petrolle was fighting," he told me once, "I loaned out $60,000. I had it all in a little book. Then, when I had the ulcers and I went into the Mayo Clinic, I sent out eight letters and six telegrams to guys who owed me $500 and up. I never got one reply, and I've got $75,000 more standing out since."

That first afternoon I walked Jack down Fourth Avenue to his favorite cafeteria, and watched him have a bowl of soup and a sandwich and a cup of tea. Then we walked over to the Eagles Temple at Seventh and Union, where the fighter trained, and all along the way people recognized Jack.

"How are you, Jack?" they'd say.

"No good," he'd say.

"Why, Jack!" they'd say. "How are you feeling?"

"No good," he'd say.

One noon we sat down in the restaurant in the Olympic Hotel. He had been living in that hotel for so long by then that just about everyone on the staff knew him, and when the waitress came over she was smiling.

"Why, Mr. Hurley!" she said.

"Hello, Hilda," Jack said.

"Mr. Hurley," she said, "you won't like what I'm going to say."

"What's that?" Jack said, squinting up at her.

"You're looking much better than the last time I saw you."

"Isn't that terrible?" Jack said to me. "You know I set the

world's record for those sinus operations. They found out with me that there's no sense in operating. I was a guinea pig for medical science, just a living sacrifice to make the world safe for guys with bad noses."

That first afternoon at the Eagles Temple, I could see why Jack was high on the fighter. He was a dark-haired, dark-eyed kid who looked right at you, and you could tell that he was not going to be cowed by anybody or anything. He had a good pair of legs, but the best of him was up in the arms, chest, and shoulders, and he was just the right height to carry 195 pounds and still get under tall jabbers who stick out a left hand and think that they're boxing.

"So he was the 1965 National A.A.U. heavyweight champion," Jack was saying while the fighter was getting into the ring, "but he was like all amateurs—awkward and over-anxious, and just a wild right-hand swinger. For six months, every day, we worked on the footwork. His stance was too wide, so I had to tie his feet together with shoe laces and a piece of inner tube that would give about six inches. He'd walk with it, shadow-box with it, and this is a long tedious thing. You get sick and tired of it, but it's balance and leverage that make punching power.

"All right," he said to the fighter. "Move around. Let's see how fast you can move. Now slow it down. Good.

"You see?" he said to me. "He slows the action down to where he wants it—to one punch. I've taught him that speed is detrimental, because if you're moving fast you're also moving your opponent fast. If you're out hunting, would you rather shoot at a slow-moving or a fast-moving target? It's the same thing. He's been taught how to put two thirds of the ring behind him. He doesn't want it, but those jabbers and runners do, and he deprives them of it."

Jack had the fighter box three rounds then, but there was the same shortage of fighters in Seattle as everywhere else, and the light-heavyweight he was in with had been around Jack and the fighter too long. As soon as the fighter would start to build up a move the light-heavyweight would know what was doing, but you could see one thing. You could see that this was another Hurley fighter, and if you knew anything about boxing you could tell a

Hurley fighter from the others as easily as an art expert can tell a Rembrandt from a Harry Grunt. There was that shuffle step, that came out of Heudicourt and the bayonet drill that Jack perfected with Petrolle, and there were those moves, with the hands low and in punching position, inviting you to lead and have your block knocked off with the counter.

"But don't you see?" Jack was saying to the fighter when it was over. "You were jumping in instead of sneaking that right foot up. You gotta sneak it up so they don't know it's coming. They think you're just jabbin', but that's only the camouflage so you can move the artillery up behind the jab. I don't even care if the jab misses."

With Jack eating every three hours and not going to bed until two or three in the morning because he had trouble sleeping, we spent a lot of time sitting around restaurants and cafeterias and the lobby of the Olympic with Jack's cronies, talking about the way things used to be and what the world was coming to. That was Jack's hobby.

"Isn't it terrible, the condition the fight game is in today?" Jack would say. "You wouldn't believe it, would you? A lot of Johnny-come-lately booking agents who call themselves managers and don't know the first thing about it. Amateurs! Why, amateurs just clutter up the world. They louse up everything they put their hands to.

"Look at what that television did, too," he'd say, "and it'll do it to pro football next. Why, you can't give your product away free and have people still respect it. That TV cheapens everything it touches. It would even cheapen the Second Coming."

Late every afternoon, of course, we would be over at the Eagles Temple, with Jack hounding the fighter. No matter what the fighter would be doing—boxing, shadow-boxing, punching the bag, or skipping rope—Jack would be after him.

"No, no," Jack would say, the fighter shadow-boxing around the ring. "Don't set your feet. Just walk. Now the left hook to the head. You're too tense. Just turn with it. All right. Now you jab, and the guy is a runner, so you're too far away. Now you gotta step again. Now the guy is pulling away, so you gotta throw three punches, but only one is gonna land. Now you're with a guy throws an uppercut. Now turn away so it misses, and throw the right hand up into the body. Good.

"You see?" Jack said to me. "He's like a pool player, practicing those draw shots. He's gotta get that ball back there, so he practices hour after hour until it becomes instinct. Like a pool player, he's also playing position at all times, and you know how long this practice lasts? His entire career. He'll still be practicing it when he quits, and you know something? If he's having trouble hitting a left hook to the body, it's nothing for me to sentence him to two weeks of doing nothing else. He wants to learn it to get rid of me.

"All right now," he'd say to the fighter. "You're in there with one of those runners, so you don't want to scare him or he'll start running again. Easy now. Left hook to the body. No, no! Let him see it. Start it back farther so he'll be sure to see it, because you want him to drop his hands. Good. Do that again.

"You see?" Jack said to me. "Other guys breed fear, but it's like cornering a frightened pig. This guy has been taught to encourage them, to make them feel safe. He'll sometimes miss a jab to give 'em courage, and Petrolle even had the facial expressions to go with it. The first thing you knew, he'd catch those suckers moving in."

The last afternoon, though, Jack was discouraged. We had to be in Boise the next day so Jack could go on TV and radio and talk up the fight. The fighter was going to come in two days later, just in time for the weigh-in, with Marino Guaing, the little Filipino who was training amateur fighters around Seattle and helped Jack.

"No, no," Jack was saying to the fighter, watching him hit the big bag. "The left hook is too tight. It's got to be looser. Just throw it up there. No good. Your feet were off the floor. No. Bend those knees a little. It's like you're on stilts.

"Isn't that terrible?" Jack said to me, turning away from the fighter and shaking his head. "He never did that before. You gotta watch 'em every damn minute of the day.

"Now start soft," he said to the fighter. "Easy. Now increase the power a little. Now your stiff-legged again. Start over."

The sweat was dripping off the fighter's chin. The floor under the bag was speckled with it, but Jack was still unhappy walking back to the hotel.

"Now where would he have picked that up?" he said. "You see what I mean? He picks up a bad habit, or he goes on the road and he steps on a pebble and he turns his ankle. He's liable to sleep with the window wide open and catch a cold. He comes to the gym and he may get his eye cut or hurt his hand. That's why, when you manage a fighter, you end up with cancer, heart trouble, or ulcers. I took the least."

"But look at the rewards," I said, hoping to kid Jack out of it. "How about all that fame and fortune?"

"Yeah," Jack said, "You raise him like a baby. That ring is a terrible place to be in if you don't know what you're doing in there, but you teach him how to survive. You teach him how to make his first steps, and you bring him along until he becomes a good fighter and starts to make money.

"Now, when you come into the ring with him you don't do nothin'. He's a professional fighter. He doesn't need people pawing at him and dousing him with water and tiring him out. He needs a little quiet advice, but no one sees that. So they see me up there, and they say to the fighter, 'What's *he* do for you?' Twenty guys say it, and it means nothin'. By the time eighty guys say it, though, the fighter forgets. This one will too.

"I'll tell you," Jack said. "Regardless of the outcome, this is my last fighter."

At 7:30 the next morning I met Jack in the lobby, and a bellhop named Harry carried our bags out and wished Jack luck. In the cab on the way to the airport Jack was looking at the heavy traffic heading into town.

"Look at the mules," he said. "Isn't that terrible? At 4:30 they'll all be heading the other way to take those paychecks back to the creatures. When I started out, my mother wanted me to get a steady job. I said, 'Mom, a steady job is a jail. I see these fellas I grew up with here, and they're in prison ten hours a day. I want to see something, go somewhere, and I can make a living doing it.' You care where you sit on the plane?"

"No," I said.

"I like to sit over the wing," Jack said. "It kinda gives you the feeling you've got something under you. Besides, I couldn't sleep last night. I think I slept an hour, so I want to grab a little nap."

We were the first in line and the first on the plane, and I had Jack take the window seat where he wouldn't be bothered by the traffic in the aisle. I reached up and got him a pillow, and he had just settled his head back and closed his eyes when I heard the small voice right behind us.

"Eeee choo-choo, Mommy?" the voice was saying, "Eeee choo-choo?"

"No," the woman's voice said. "Not choo-choo, dear. Airplane."

"Eeee choo-choo?"

Jack opened his eyes. He had that pinched look on his face again, and he sat up.

"Isn't that something?" he said, shaking his head. "With the whole plane to pick from I gotta draw a creature and her kid. Wouldn't you know it? Ninety per cent of those eye operations are successful, too, but I gotta be in the other ten per cent."

It didn't make any difference, because Jack wasn't going to sleep anyway. We weren't off the ground more than twenty minutes when Jack's rheumatism started to act up, and he had to stand in the aisle, holding onto the arm of my seat, almost all the way to Boise.

"Isn't that terrible?" Jack said, as we were getting off. "A whole plane, and that creature and the kid have to sit behind us."

"But he was a cute kid," I said.

"Yeah, you're right," Jack said. "I took a look at him, and he was."

Then Jack really went to work. After we checked into the hotel we walked down Main Street, with Jack saying he couldn't see a thing in the bright, shimmering sunlight and with me helping him up and down the curbs, to Al Berro's. Al Berro was promoting the fight, but for a living he was running the Bouquet Sportsmen's Center. The Bouquet had one of those long Western bars down the right side, with the meal for the day chalked on a blackboard at the far end, and along the opposite wall a half dozen tables with faded green baize covers and the nine-card joker rummy games going.

"Am I glad you're here!" Berro said, shaking Jack's hand.

"How's it look?" Jack said.

"Pretty good," Berro said.

"There goes that 'pretty good' again," Jack said to me.

"I think we'll do all right," Berro said, "but I've got you lined up for the radio and TV. You ready to start?"

In the next eight hours, with Berro driving us around town, Jack was on two television and four radio stations, and at 9 o'clock that night he was over at the *Idaho Daily Statesman*.

"Now what brings you to Boise?" one of them, interviewing Jack on the TV or the radio, would say, as if he didn't know.

"Well, I've got Boone Kirkman boxing Archie Ray, from Phoenix, at the Fairgrounds arena on Thursday night," Jack would say. "My best friends in the boxing game tell me I may be making a mistake, though, because my fighter has had only four fights and Archie Ray has had twenty-three, with eighteen wins, ten by knockout."

"What's going to happen at the Fairgrounds arena on Thursday night?" another would say.

"Well, it's hard to tell," Jack would say. "All the people in the fight game tell me Archie Ray is gonna lick my fighter for sure, but of course I don't think so."

"Jack, is Boone going to shoot for a first-round KO," another would say, "or is he going to play with this fella?"

"He doesn't play with anybody," Jack would say. "You see, all my boxing friends tell me Archie Ray is gonna be too much for my guy, but we'll find out Thursday night at the Fairgrounds arena."

Jack did some job. Knowing how he felt, and that he hadn't slept much the night before, I was amazed that he got through the day.

"Ah, I don't have the enthusiasm for it anymore," he said when we got back to the hotel.

"You've got me beat," I said.

"I'm old and I'm sick and I'm tired," he said, "but you can't let the bastards know it. They'd kill you."

On the day of the fight, the fighter and Marino, the trainer, got in about twenty minutes before the one o'clock weigh-in at the State Capitol. The elevator operator who took us up was a middle-aged woman wearing a white uniform blouse and dark skirt.

She was sitting on a stool in front of the panel of buttons and, open on her lap, was an instructional volume of the Famous Writers School.

"Do you subscribe to that course?" I asked her on the way down.

"Yes," she said, looking up at me and her face brightening. "Do you?"

"No," I said, "but I've heard about it."

"I think it's just wonderful," she said. "I'm really enjoying it."

"Good," I said.

"What was all that about?" Jack said to me when we got off.

"She's taking a correspondence course in how to be a writer," I said. "It costs over four hundred bucks, and I think that, for the ones like her, it's a lonely hearts club."

"That figures, don't it?" Jack said.

When we got back to the hotel, Jack had the fighter rest until 3:30. Then we took him to the restaurant across the street.

"You'd better bring him two of your top sirloins," Jack said to the waitress, "and a baked potato and hot tea."

"The baked potato doesn't come on the menu until five," the waitress said.

"In Idaho?" the fighter said.

"Isn't that terrible?" Jack said, looking at me. "They want you to eat what they want you to eat when they want you to eat it."

After the fighter finished eating he took a walk with Marino, and Jack and I went down to a cafe he liked on Main Street, and he had a ham sandwich on whole-wheat bread, sliced bananas, and a cup of tea. At 7:30 Jack was sitting in the hotel lobby when the fighter and Marino came down from their rooms with Marino carrying the fighter's black zipper bag.

"Listen," Jack said to the fighter, "when you finished eating across the street there, did you remember to tip the waitress?"

"Gee, no," the fighter said. "I forgot."

"Here," Jack said, handing him a bill. "Go over and do it now."

When the fighter came back we all got in a cab and went out to the Fairgrounds. In the dark the cabbie missed the main entrance, so we rode around between a lot of barns before we got to the arena with the sign SALES PAVILION over the door.

"You see?" Jack said when we got inside, the customers milling around us. "It's like the old Cambria in Philadelphia."

From where the ring was set up in the middle of the floor the solid planking of the wooden stands went back and up like steps on all four sides to where the walls and the ceiling rafters met. The stands were about half full, with more customers climbing up and sliding along the rows and sitting down.

"You gonna fill up?" Jack said to Al Berro.

"I don't know," Berro said. "I've got eleven hundred and fifty bucks in, and I've only collected at the Stagecoach, Hannifin's and a couple of others. I've got Homedale and Mountain Home coming in yet, so we'll do pretty good."

"There goes that 'pretty good' again," Jack said.

They had the fighter dressing under the stands in a small room with a wash basin and a toilet in it and a shower without a curtain. There was no rubbing table, only a green painted bench, and when the fighter stood up, he had to be careful not to hit his head on the naked light bulb sticking down from the low ceiling.

It was hot in the room, so the fighter had stripped down and was in his black trunks with white stripes. He had put on his white socks and was lacing his ring shoes. Through the wall you could hear the ring announcer bringing on the first preliminary.

"Marino," Jack said, "tell them I'm gonna start bandaging and to send somebody over here if they want to watch."

"But I just there," Marino said. "They don't come in yet."

"Then the hell with them," Jack said. "I'm gonna start anyway."

"Oh, excuse me," one of the customers said, looking in. "I thought this was the men's room."

"Next door," the fighter said.

"This will go on all night," Jack said. "They sell a lot of beer here."

With his bad eyes Jack had to squint to see what he was doing, but after bandaging fighters' hands for a half century, he could have done it with his eyes closed. While he was putting it on—the gauze around the wrist, and then across the palm and between the thumb and index finger, and then back around the wrist and around the hand and across the knuckles, and then the tape—we could hear the crowd hollering and then, over our heads, the stamping of feet.

"All right," Jack said to Marino when it was over. "Grease him up."

Marino rubbed the cocoa butter on the fighter's arms and shoulders and chest and neck and face. When he had finished, Jack sent him to watch the other people bandage and put the gloves on. The fighter was sitting on the bench, his bandaged hands in his lap, serious now.

"The hell with them," Jack said after a while. "We might as well get into the gloves. Then you'll have plenty of time to loosen up, because they take that intermission to sell more beer."

"Good," the fighter said.

Jack helped the fighter into the right glove first, the laces down the palm and then around the wrist, then tied the ends and put a strip of tape over it. When he had finished with the left glove, Marino was back.

"They all done now," he said.

"All right," Jack said to the fighter. "Loosen up, but be careful of that light. Now jab . . . hook . . . jab . . . move up behind it. All right, but don't stand there. You gotta move right up behind it. And another thing, if you start to miss punches just settle down and start over again."

"I know," the fighter said.

"We're ready to go Jack," Al Berro said, sticking his head through the doorway after the fighter had had about five minutes of it. "You ready?"

"Yeah," Jack said, and then to Marino, "You got the mouth-piece?"

They went out and down the aisle, Marino first, carrying the pail, and then the fighter and then Jack. The aisle was crowded, some of the customers still trying to get back to their seats with their containers of beer, and then the calls started from the stands.

"Hey, Jack! How many rounds?" . . . "Good luck, Jack!" . . . "Hey, Kirkman, how about our money's worth tonight?"

When the bell rang, Jack's fighter walked out in that Hurley style, hands low and in punching position, and he walked right to Archie Ray. Archie Ray was a straight-up fighter, with a pretty good jab and a straight right hand, and he started out to make a fight of it. He punched right with Jack's fighter, and I gave him that first round. Jack hadn't said a thing, but now he was up in the corner, bending over the fighter and lecturing him, and when he came down the steps at the start of the second round I could see he was still mad.

"Hey, Kirkman!" some loudmouth was hollering. "You're gonna get yours tonight!"

"His stance was too wide, and his feet are too flat," Jack said. "What's the matter with him?"

"He's tense," I said. "He'll fight out of it."

"Tense, hell," Jack said. "He's never been like this before."

He didn't fight out of it. In the second round you could see he was trying to settle down and put his moves together, but he was still too anxious. The young ones, if they're really fighters, are usually that way. They know what they're supposed to do, but then they are hit with a good punch, and they widen that stance and start swinging because they want to end it with one. Jack's fighter was still throwing punches from too far out, but he was hurting Ray with right hands. You had to give him that second round and the third, too, although he came out of a mix-up he should never have been in with his nose bleeding.

"Hey, Kirkman!" the loudmouth was hollering when he saw the blood. "How do you like it now?"

"Isn't this terrible?" Jack was saying. "All he's got to do is jab and move up before he lets those right hands go. What's the matter with him?"

"He's still trying too hard," I said.

"Hell," Jack said.

In the fourth round he had Ray against the ropes and then through them, but he couldn't finish him, and in the fifth round he dropped him with a nice inside right hand to the body and still couldn't put him away. Ray looked like he was in there just to stay now, and by the sixth round you could see Jack's fighter tiring, the way they all do until they learn pace. He would be all right for the first half of a round, but then he would flatten out and start to flounder. In the eighth round, though, he made one good Hurley move. He drew that right hand of Ray's and, when it came, he turned from it and turned back with his own. It was a little high—on the cheekbone—but it caught Ray following through and moving into it, and Ray's knees started to go as he backed off.

"He's got him now," I said to Jack.

"And everybody in the house knows it but him," Jack said over the roar, and by the time he said it, the chance was past. "Isn't that terrible?"

That was the last round, and it had been enough of a war so that the crowd liked it. Jack's fighter got the unanimous decision, but when we got to the dressing room he was still disgusted, and Jack was, too.

"I swear I can fight better than that," the fighter was saying to two of the local sportswriters. "That's the worst fight I've ever had."

"He was in a trance," Jack said. "He couldn't even follow orders, and he always follows orders to the letter."

"I didn't even feel like I was in a fight," the fighter said. "I can't understand that."

"The hell with it," Jack said finally. "Let's get out of here."

And hour later we were still sitting in the restaurant across the street from the hotel. The fighter had a milk shake, and Jack was nibbling on a ham and cheese sandwich on whole wheat and still going over the fight.

"He comes back at the end of the first round," he said to me, "and he says, 'I'm not sick, but something's the matter with me.'"

"That's right," the fighter said.

"So I said, 'It's too bad, but you're here. You're having a bad night, but you'll fight out of it. You're punchin' from too far back. Jab and move up and then wing those right hands.'"

"So you've got him against the ropes," Jack said to the fighter now, "and he's lookin' for the punch, ready to duck it, and you give it to him, instead of the jab. Let him duck the jab and into the right."

"I know," the fighter said, shaking his head.

"Now you know what it takes to be a fighter," Jack said. "You've got to settle down and live it and sleep it and eat it."

"But I do," the fighter said.

"But you've got to do it more," Jack said. "You can't afford bad nights like this."

"I know," the fighter said.

The fighter left then to pick up a couple of the display cards with his picture on them that Al Berro had for him. That is how new he was, and Jack took another bite of the sandwich and then left the rest of it and we walked out onto the street.

"That's the worst I've seen him," Jack said. "He knows how to do those things. Why couldn't he do them? How could he possibly be that bad?"

"Don't get sore," I said. "When you figure it out, he's had six rounds of professional boxing before tonight. You know it takes time."

"But I haven't got too much time," Jack said. "Hell, I think I'll walk down to Berro's and find out how much they took in tonight. Maybe I'll finally find out how good that 'pretty good' is."

"I'll go along with you," I said.

"No," Jack said. "You've got that early plane to grab. You've got to get some sleep."

"I'd rather go with you."

"I can make it alone," Jack said. "Hell, the way the eyes are now, I can see better at night than I can in that damn sunlight."

"If you say so," I said, and we shook hands, "but take care of yourself."

"Yeah," Jack said, "but wasn't that terrible tonight?"

The last time I ever saw him I watched him then, old and half-blind and aching all over, start slowly down the empty Main Street of Boise, Idaho, at one o'clock in the morning, heading for the Bouquet Sportsmen's Center to find out how much money there had been in the house. Once, after that, I did see him in a way. Four-and-a-half years later, I sat in a theater and watched as George Foreman, too big and too strong for Boone Kirkman, took him apart in two rounds. It was the armored jeep against the tank again, and the old Hurley moves never got started. The old dreamer that was in the old pragmatist had dreamed too much too late, and Jack's forty-year search for another perfect tool like Billy Petrolle was over.

When we turned off the Interstate now, my wife had the *Rand*

McNally Road Atlas in her lap. There was a two-page spread of the Dakotas, and a street map of Fargo, and the Saturday traffic was light. We found *The Forum,* and I parked in a black-paved lot across the street.

"I don't know how long I'll be," I said. "If there's no one in there who ever heard of Jack, that'll be the end of it, and I'll be right out."

"Take your time," she said. "I'll just wander around."

Off the lobby on the left there was a door identifying the classified advertising department, and I opened that. It was a large room, with a counter along the right and a lot of desks. Behind two of them, and facing the counter, two young women were sitting, and when I walked in they looked up.

"Excuse me," I said, "but can you tell me where your sports department is?"

"The sports department?" one of them said. "That's on the second floor?"

"And I go up these stairs out here?" I said. "And then it'll be on the left or right?"

"The left or the right?" the same young woman said, and then she stood up. While I watched, she turned her back to me and she pointed with one hand one way, and with the other hand she pointed the other, and then she turned around again. "It'll be on the left."

"Thank you," I said. "Thank you very much."

"You're welcome," she said.

Jack should have watched that, I was thinking, walking up the stairs. Out in Seattle that last time, before we flew down to Boise, we were sitting around the lobby of the Olympic with some of Jack's cronies one night, and Jack was expounding again on all the hazards and all the heartbreak in trying to make and move a fighter.

"And how about women?" I said to him, playing the straight man again. "Have you explained women to this fighter?"

"The creatures?" Jack said. "I've explained it all to him. I've told him, 'Look, marriage is for women and kids, and it's expensive. You've got to be able to afford it. Your best chance to make a lot of money is to become a good fighter, and then you'll be able to afford marriage.' He understands that point.

"Did I ever tell you," he said, "about the fighter I had who started looking at the creatures, and one day he went to the movies? When he came back, I said, 'How was the picture?' He said, 'It was good. It was a Western.' I said, 'Any dames in it?' He said, 'Yeah, one.' I said, 'How many guys were after the dame?' He said, 'Three.' I said, 'Anybody get killed?' He said, 'Yeah, two.' I said, 'The dame one of them?' He said, 'No. Just two of the guys.' I said, 'There! Doesn't it figure? Don't you see how the odds are stacked for those creatures?' It didn't do any good.

"Then I had another one." Jack said, "who was starting to think he was in love. You can tell when they don't have their minds on their work, so one day we're walking along the street and the light changes and I said, 'Wait a minute.' Next to us is this creature with a little creature, about three or four years old, and the little creature is all dolled up and has a little pocketbook. I nudge the fighter, and I said to the little one, 'Hello, little girl. That's a very nice pocketbook you have there. Do you have any money in it?' So she says, 'Yes, three pennies.'

"So the light changes again and they go on their way, but I say to the fighter, 'Don't move.' Here comes another creature now with a little boy, and the light changes again, and they stop. I nudge the fighter again, and I say to the little boy, 'Say, son, that's a nice new suit you're wearing. Do you have any money in your pocket?' The little kid looks up at me, and he shakes his head, and he says, 'Nope.'

"So I say to the fighter, 'You see that? That little creature with the pocketbook is being educated in how to handle money. This poor little mule here is being taught nothing. All he'll be taught when he grows up is to bring the paycheck home each week to the creature. Don't you see that?' You know what the fighter said to me?"

"No," I said.

"He said, 'But, Jack, my girl is different.' Now the light changes again, and this time I go *my* way. Isn't that terrible?"

At the top of the stairs now I turned left and walked into the city room, almost somnolent now on a Saturday morning. Across the room, at the far right, a young man, bearded and in a short-sleeved sports shirt, was typing. On the left two others, older, were sitting at their desks and talking, and from the right another was walking toward them.

"Excuse me," I said to him, "but I'm looking for your sports department."

"Over there," he said, pointing, "where you see that young fella."

"Thank you," I said, and I walked over between the desks. I waited until he stopped typing and looked up at me.

"I'm sorry to bother you," I said, "but can you tell me where Jack Hurley is buried?"

"Jack Hurley?" he said. "I don't know, but that man over there can probably tell you."

"The one in the white shirt?" I said, thinking that well, at least he had heard of Jack.

"Right."

"Thank you," I said.

"Okay," he said, and as I turned he went back to his typing.

The one in the white shirt was still talking with the other at the next desk when I walked up. He stopped and turned toward me.

"Excuse me," I said, "but can you tell me where Jack Hurley is buried?"

"Jack?" he said. "Gosh, I don't know. It's in one of the cemeteries around here, but I forget which one."

"There are several?"

"Three," he said, and he reached into a drawer of his desk and brought out a telephone directory. He started to turn through the yellow pages, and then he said, "Wait a minute. His brother Hank is still around town."

"He is?" I said.

I had known that Jack was the oldest of five children, but he had talked little about the others. It had been as if it would have detracted from his pose as an opponent of all domesticity.

"Sure," the one in the white shirt said now. "He's got a religious goods store. Here it is. It's at 622 Second Avenue, only a few blocks from here."

He gave me the directions and I thanked him and I went out

and walked over. At the address he had given me, the store was vacant.

"Excuse me," I said, "but I'm looking for Hurley's religious goods store."

He was standing in a doorway. He needed a shave, and he looked as if he were coming off a bad night, or several of them.

"It ain't here any more," he said. "They moved around the corner there to Broadway, just up there."

"Thank you," I said.

"Yeah," he said.

The sign outside made clear that it was a gift shop and religious goods store, and the shelves and the counters displayed dishes and glassware and household ornaments. When I walked in, a woman, smiling, came forward to meet me.

"May I help you?" she said.

"Is Mr. Hank Hurley in?" I said.

"Hank Hurley?" she said. "No, he's not. He doesn't own this store any more. Mr. Donald McAllister owns it now."

"Oh?" I said. "Do you know where I might find Hank Hurley?"

"I don't," she said, "but maybe Mr. McAllister can help you. He's back there in the office."

He was coming out of the office as I walked toward it. I introduced myself, and told him I was trying to find Hank Hurley.

"Hank?" he said. "He lives in the hotel right around the corner here. The college has taken it over, but they're letting him keep his room for a while. Maybe I can get him on the phone."

He picked up the phone and he dialed and he asked for Hank Hurley. He waited, and then he put the phone down.

"He's not in his room," he said. "He's probably at the Elks Club, having his lunch. He always eats early, and we could try him there."

"That's all right," I said. "I can try him at the hotel later, but I'd like to know where his brother Jack is buried."

"Jack?" he said. "I think it's the Holy Cross Cemetery. It'll be right here in the book from the funeral."

From a drawer of the desk he took out the book with its light gray watered-silk cover. He opened it on the desk.

"This is Hank's desk," he said. "A year and a half ago he sold the business to me, but I've still got the desk and Jack's trunk down in the basement. It's full of scrap books and I don't know what."

"I can imagine," I said.

I remembered the trunk from room 679 at the Olympic Hotel. The room was just big enough to contain the bed, the steamer trunk, the footlocker for Jack's files and the desk where, on the thirty-year-old Corona portable, Jack pounded out the publicity. While he was making Harry "Kid" Matthews into a leading contender and starting that Congressional investigation, he was spending $10,000 a year for stationery, stamps, and the newspapers that carried stories about him and the fighter that he used to clip and send to sportswriters throughout this country.

"Don't write about me on Sundays," he used to tell his friends on the sports pages. "Sunday papers cost more, and you're running up my overhead."

"Here it is," McAllister said now, reading from the book, " 'Holy Cross Cemetery, West one-half, lot 35, block 7, old section. Laid to rest, November 21, 1972, 12:15 P.M.' Say, you almost made it!"

"Made it?" I said. "Made what?"

"You almost made 12:15 P.M. It's 12:45 now."

"How about that?" I said.

" 'Born December 9, 1897,' " he said, reading from the book again.

" 'Died November 15, 1972.' Then here's all the relatives and friends who came and signed their names."

"May I look through those?" I said.

"Sure," he said. "I've looked at this before. These two sisters have died since, but here's Billy Petrolle's signature. He was here."

"Good," I said, "and I'm glad to see that so many came."

"Well," he said, "let's count the pages here. There are, let's see, nine pages of signatures. Now let's count how many signatures there are on a page. Eighteen. Just a second."

He reached over to the adding machine. He punched some numbers on it, and looked at the tape. He went back to punching numbers again.

"I'm not doing something right," he said, "but there must have been about 160–75 attended."

"I make it 162," I said.

"Right," he said. "You know, Hank goes out to the grave twice a week to water and put flowers on it. It's been so dry that he's been doing it every night. In case you don't find Hank, I'll draw you a map of how to get there."

On a page from a desk memo pad, he drew the map showing how we should go north to the airport and then turn left. The page bore the imprint of the Muench-Kreuzer Candle Co., Inc., of 4577 Buckely Road, Liverpool, N.Y., 13088.

"You've really been most kind," I said, as we shook hands, "and I thank you."

"Glad to do it," he said, smiling. "I guess Jack was quite a guy."

"Yes," I said. "He was."

I walked around the corner to the hotel and, when I had the college student at the desk ring the room, Hank Hurley answered. He said he was amazed, and he sounded it, that I should be right there in the lobby. He had been about to take a nap, he said, but he would be down as soon as he dressed. I told him I would walk back to *The Forum,* where my wife would be waiting in the car, and he said he would meet us in the parking space across from the hotel. When we got out of the car he walked up, shorter and with more weight on him than Jack, but with the same look in the eyes and the same mouth. He took us to lunch at the Elks Club, and while we ate, he talked about Jack.

"You know," he said, "Jack used to say to me, 'When the good Lord takes me, I hope he does a clean job.' I told my sister, 'He couldn't have done a cleaner job.' If he'd had all his marbles and been in one of those nursing homes, he would have been oh, so unhappy.'

"How did he go?" I said.

"At the Olympic," he said, "Jack was always there at the front desk when the four o'clock mail came in. When he wasn't there, and it got to be 4:45, somebody got the assistant manager and they found him dead at the foot of his bed in that room 679."

It was out of that room that, in 1957, Jack also promoted the

Floyd Patterson-Pete Rademacher fight for the heavyweight championship of the world. Cus D'Amato was protecting Patterson then, and he accepted Rademacher, who was the Olympic heavyweight champion but had never had a professional fight, as a likely victim and Jack as the logical promoter. Jack forgot for a while that he had no use for amateurs and, out of his pockets and a box under the bed, he sold $74,000 worth of tickets out of the $243,000 they took in, and Rademacher, green as he was, had Patterson down in the second round before Patterson put him down six times and then, in the sixth round, knocked him out.

"Just think," Jack said, after it was over. "An amateur did this for me. I guess it just goes to show there's some good in everybody. Somebody told me that he went to a college, too, and took a course in how to be an animal husband. Now what kind of a college course is that?"

"At the Olympic," Hank Hurley was saying now, "they put a floral display on the door of the room. In the dining room, at the table where Jack always sat, they had a black ribbon and a single rose and a card that said, 'Reserved for Jack Hurley.' At a chair at the counter they had another single rose and another card, and they kept them there for a week."

"They thought a lot of him there," I said, "and I remember he used to tell me, 'You know I've got my plantin' suit. I've had it for years, and every now and then I try it on to see that it still fits.' "

"He had several plantin' suits," Hank Hurley said. "Every now and then he'd buy a new one."

"He said he had sent you an insurance policy and told you, 'When I check out, this is for the burial, but nothing fancy. Just have them sharpen my feet and drive me into the ground, and I hope it's not during the winter.' "

"That's right," Hank said, "he used to tell me, 'Don't make a production of it, and don't open the casket except for you and our sisters and a couple of friends. Nobody else knows me there.' We did open it for our sisters and Billy Petrolle."

After lunch he drove us out past the airport and then turned left onto a gravel road past two cemeteries on the left and then into the third. He stopped the car about 150 feet inside the gate, and we walked over the sun-baked sod, the dried yellow grass making a sound under our shoes. Backed by two spruce, there was the gray granite headstone with Jack's father's name on it and a cross on top and a red geranium at the base. To the left there two granite markers, one with Jack's mother's name on it and the other with his sister's. On the right was the marker that said "John C. Hurley." So severe was the drought that there were cracks about an inch wide in the black topsoil and they outlined in a rectangle the shape of the coffin.

"Jack hated that name John," Hank Hurley was saying. "Oh, how many fights he got into in school when somebody called him 'Johnny.' I guess I made the mistake. On the memorial card it said 'Jack C. Hurley,' and I sent it out to the stone-cutter. When I saw this I called him and he said, 'But you ran a line through it and wrote "John."' I guess it's my fault."

"Forget it," I said. "It was the name with which he was christened. That makes it right."

"I don't know," he said. "I don't remember doing that, but I guess it was my fault."

After he drove us back to our car and we thanked him and said good-by, I drove back through the city and out to the Interstate once more. I was seeing again that rectangle in the ground.

"I can just hear Jack," I said to my wife. "I can hear him saying, 'Wouldn't you know it, Ninety per cent of the people get planted and everything goes all right. They plant me, and they have this drought. Why, there's a farmer in Durbin, North Dakota, who says it's worse than it was in the '30s. Isn't that terrible? How can you explain that?' "

5

The Onion Farmer

> Who made them serfs of the soil? Why should they
> eat their sixty acres, when man is condemned to
> eat only his peck of dirt? Why should they begin
> digging their graves as soon as they are born? They
> have got to live a man's life, pushing all these
> things before them, and get on as well as they can.
>
> Henry David Thoreau, *Walden*

There is a stretch of narrow blacktop road that runs northwest out
of Canastota, New York, and it had remained in my memory for
twenty-one years. Whenever I would see his name in print or hear
it or he would otherwise come to mind, I would remember the
road, straight and raised above the flat black fields that reach toward the horizon on either side. The fields, known as the
Muckland, had been reclaimed from swampland many years before, and had been planted ever since in corn and potatoes, but
mostly in onions. Each year, during the growing season, the
families of workers would move out of town to live in the two-
story square, weathered-gray shacks spotted every hundred yards
or so along the road.

"Everybody worked—my father, my mother, all of us kids, everybody," he had told me, when he had driven me slowly along
that road for the first time more than two decades before. "In the
spring we'd plant by hand. It would be wet and cold, and my ma
would take old inner tubes and sew patches on the knees of our
overalls so they wouldn't get soaked. In the hot summer we'd
weed on our hands and knees. We'd get up at five in the morning

and work till nine. Then we'd start again at 3:30 and work until nine at night.

"In the fields we used to talk what we called 'wish-talk.' We'd see a kid go by on a bike, and one of us would say, 'I wish I had a bike.' Then we'd imagine where we'd go if we had bikes. Sometimes tourists would stop their cars on the road and look at us. It was something they'd never seen before—a whole family of people, little kids and all, on their hands and knees in the hot sun. One of us would say, 'I wish I had a car.'

"One day," he had said, and this I shall never forget, "I'd had enough. I stood up, and I had a handful of onions and I threw them on the ground. 'Hey!' my pa shouted. 'What do you think you're doin'? I said, 'I'm tellin' you, Pa, I'm all done workin' on onions.' So he said, 'So then what you gonna do?' I said, 'I'm gonna fight professional.' He said, 'And you gonna get plenty lickin's.' And I said, 'Sure, and I'll give plenty too.'"

And he did. Of the fighters who won titles in my time, none took more punishment while delivering more than Carmen Basilio, who twice won the welterweight championship and beat Ray Robinson for the middleweight crown in the first of their two brutal fights. He walked into the guns to bring his own into range, fearless and ferocious, and over his career of seventy-eight fights they sewed more than two hundred stitches into his face. His fights were described as blood-lettings and all-out wars, and I still see them not as action flowing, but as a succession of still photos snapped in a thousandth of a second by the mind, of head punches landing, faces distorted, necks strained, the spray of sweat and sponge water flying off the heads and shining under the overhead lights, and his own eyes slits between swellings above and below. Most of our fighters came out of the poverty of our ghettos, but this one fought to escape the imprisonment of the Muckland of mid-New York State.

LeMoyne College is on the eastern outskirts of Syracuse, and it was started by the Jesuits in 1946. It is coeducational, with an enrollment of about 2,000, and it stands on a hill, its red brick, flat-roofed buildings still devoid of the patina and ivy of age, overlooking the Athletic Center and the playing fields below. He has been an instructor on the athletic staff there since September

1961, four months after he lost a fifteen-round decision to Paul Pender in a third attempt to regain the middleweight crown.

"Wait till I get my schedule," he had said on the phone, and then, "Let's see. I'm off at noon, but if there's a game—like today I watched the soccer—I'll be there. I think they've got a baseball game scheduled that afternoon, but whatever it is, I watch them all. I love it, and you'll find me somewhere around."

It was early October, but across the black asphalt parking lot from the Athletic Center there was a baseball game under way between LeMoyne and Cortland State. There were about a hundred students and others in the low wooden bleachers along the third base line, and I recognized him—the Roman nose, the heavy brows, but the narrowed eyes now behind metallic-rimmed glasses, and the face a little fuller. He was sitting on the top row, wearing a dark green wind-jacket, watching the game but turning to talk with a dark-haired young man standing behind the low seats.

"Hey, how are you?" he said. I had walked around behind him, and he introduced me to the young man. "This is my heavyweight, Greg Sorrentino. Come on around and watch this game. It's all tied up, 3–3."

I climbed up the half dozen rows and sat down. When I did Sorrentino excused himself and left.

"He's a good kid," Basilio said. "He's twenty years old and he was a hell of a football player for the University of Vermont. He was only a freshman, but he was playing fullback when they gave up football. He came to me and I said, 'I know a lot of people at Syracuse, and maybe I can get you in there.' He said, 'I don't want to play football. I want to fight.' I said, 'I'll work with you for a month if you'll do everything I tell you, including at the end of the month if I tell you to pack it in.' At the end of the month he surprised me, so I took him for two months in the gym. He's just learning how to bob and weave now, but he's got four pro wins and one draw, and he really won that draw."

"How big is he?" I said.

"He's 196."

"Six feet?"

"Just about. I wish he was six-three, six-four. I wish he'd quit fightin'. Managing isn't my bag, but he's such a good kid, I don't want to see him hurt."

"Excuse me, Carmen," someone said. It was a middle-aged man standing behind the bleachers, and Basilio turned and shook hands and they talked for a minute or so and then the other left.

"He's from Chittenango," Basilio said. "It's for St. Patrick's Church, and he wants me to show films. I'll show one that I won."

"Because those are the only ones you have," I said.

"No," he said. "I bought a couple of losses, too."

"Tell me," I said, "how you became associated with the college here."

"In a second," he said, and LeMoyne was at bat in the fifth inning with a runner on first. "Watch this kid steal now. He's a great base-runner."

The runner was leading off first, feinting and hazing the pitcher. When he took off on the next pitch the catcher's throw was on a line, and he was out sliding.

"He got a bad start, but he can really run," Basilio said. "About the college, I always knew a lot of priests. I made a lot of appearances for charity and at breakfasts and things, so after I fought Pender and retired they talked to me about coming here. It's a great college, and when a kid walks out with a degree from LeMoyne he doesn't have trouble getting a job."

He himself had quit high school before his eighteenth birthday to enlist in the Marines in March of 1945, but when I had first heard of his association with the college it had not surprised me. As ruthless as he was in the ring, as rough on his sparring partners and opponents, he was as compassionate outside it. I knew that while he was fighting he had appeared often for charity, had spoken at the graduation breakfast of the Canastota High School, was an assistant scoutmaster and the sponsor of a Little League team, and that on a visit to the Syracuse Cerebral Palsy Clinic he had been unable to fight back the tears. To me he had always represented the ambivalance I had found in some of the roughest fighters I had known.

"What are your duties here?" I asked him now.

"I've got ten physical fitness classes," he said, "and it's compulsory for freshmen. They can't graduate unless they complete it.

We use the Marine Corps physical fitness test as a barometer, and if they score over 325, they're over the average. The most you can get is five hundred points, and we have a few kids around four hundred. The only kids I have are 325 and down, in other words average or below average. They get four cuts a year, and I tell them, 'Don't use your cuts in this good weather. Save 'em until the weather is cold and snowing, and you don't want to walk down that hill.' "

"You'd know about that," I said, "from when you used to do your roadwork in the winter."

"Right," he said. "I used to wake up mornings and I'd look out the window and it'd be snowin'. It's zero or five above, and I'd think maybe I shouldn't run this morning. Then I'd think of that other guy down there where the weather is better, so I'd better run. I'd talk myself into it.

"Then I'm in charge of the intramural program," he said. "We've got football for seven weeks, soccer for four weeks, and basketball lasts from December to the end of March. I'm also Athletic Physical Fitness Co-ordinator, and I pre-condition all the athletic teams before their season starts. I give them push-ups, run, stop, backwards, sideways. I teach a lot of them, basketball players particularly, to skip rope. It strengthens the ankles and builds up the cardio system. Ten minutes of good rope skipping is equal to thirty minutes of jogging at a good pace. It's in a medical report, and you can look it up."

We left the ball game at the end of the seventh with the score 4–4. As we walked toward the parking lot, he noticed two small boys wrestling on the grass about twenty yards behind the backstop.

"The kids here worry me," he said. "I'm always afraid one of them is gonna get hit on the head with a foul tip."

While he went into the Athletic Center to call his wife, Kay, I waited in the parking lot, watching the frantic flow of an intramural touch football game on a field just beyond, the players lining up, then dispersing in crisscross patterns, arms waving, and the ball arcing through the air and bouncing off hands. He had told me that his wife worked afternoons and into some evenings in the office of an automobile agency, and I had asked him to see if she could join us at dinner.

"She can't make it," he said. "She hasn't been too well and I was supposed to clean the house, and now she's mad at me because I didn't do it. She's a hell of a person, I'll tell you that. She got an ulcer while I was fighting, and when I quit she got rid of it. Anything that had to be done to better me, she was for it."

I remembered it well. They had met while she was a waitress in the Kirk Hotel in Syracuse, and been married early in 1950. They had moved into a three-room apartment in a two-family house on the south side of Syracuse, and there they had battled a series of misfortunes together.

"One weekend early in 1951," he had told me years before, "we had exactly thirty-nine cents between us. She wanted to sell her engagement ring, but I wouldn't let her because I'd sold my ten-year-old car to buy it for her. I'd broken the first metacarpal bone in my left hand when I fought Vic Cardell, and I had a cast on my wrist. There was a big snow storm in Syracuse, and they put out a call for snow shovelers. It paid a dollar an hour, and I shoveled for three nights from eleven o'clock until seven the next morning, with the temperature around zero."

Not he, but someone else, had told me that on one of those nights a friend, who was later to become his accountant, had happened along and had seen him. He had offered to lend him eight hundred dollars, but Basilio had refused it.

"When I got the twenty-four bucks for shoveling," Basilio had told me, "I thought I had a million dollars. I paid ten dollars on our rent and five dollars on a bill we owed."

I remembered, too, how weeks before his fights, his wife would get up with him at five o'clock each morning to follow him in the car while he ran on the hilly Chittenango Falls road. Afterward, when he came home with his face swollen or cut and with bursitis paining his left shoulder, she would apply the ice bag and hot packs until the early hours of the morning.

"She's mad at me, too, for managing this kid," he said now, "but he's such a nice kid, and he could be a hell of a fighter sometime."

"I'm sorry she hasn't been well," I said as we got into his car, a two-year old orange compact Oldsmobile Omega. "I seem to recall that she had a hearing problem."

"That's right," he said. "Otosclerosis. In the inner ear the windows were completely plugged with calcium. They opened them up and put in a metal plate and then covered it with flesh from the ear lobe. I think they call it fenestration. Something like that."

"It means to make a window, or opening."

"Fenestration of the stapes," he said, driving out of the parking lot. "Now she hears through walls. She hears me think, but that was twenty years ago. In 1972 she had two heart attacks. The second one she was in the hospital on the monitor, and when that went flat, in twenty seconds there were two nurses and a doctor right there. They put her on that electric thing, and they were pounding on her chest and rubbing her ankles, and the doctor said she was out two minutes, and in one more minute she'd of been gone. That's when they called it a real cardiac arrest, and that was a fabulous guy who brought her back and we've got a great internist, too, and I'm forever grateful to them."

"Which is why I make doctors more important than writers or fighters."

"You can say that again," he said. "Now she's all right, but she's got all these pills she takes and she pops those nitroglycerins like they're candy, God bless her, and then she takes all that bull I put out while I'm runnin' around trying to make ends meet."

"What do you do while college is out during the summers?"

"Public relations for the Genesee Brewing Company. I travel with the salesmen full time, so I'm away a lot."

It is a small Italian restaurant with the bar on the left. As a waitress led us back to a table near the kitchen, several at the other tables waved or nodded to him. When he was fighting he was, of course, lionized locally. Two years before he won his first title the members of the Knistestota Club, a men's social organization in Canastota, staged a testimonial dinner for him, hoping to raise enough money to present him with a traveling bag. In two hours they collected enough for him to buy a new car. After he won the welterweight title, his followers gave him a $3,900 convertible, but it seemed to me that the ultimate unique proof of his popularity was demonstrated when, in several hours at the Schisa meat markets in Syracuse, he autographed 2,000 photographs of himself, and attracted 7,000 entries in a drawing for boxing gloves and other prizes while the markets sold 49,510 pounds of meat, 26 per cent more than they had ever sold on any day in their ten-year history.

"They still remember you here," I said now, as we sat down. "What about the kids at the college?"

"They were too young," he said, "but their fathers remember. Just today one kid said, 'My father remembers you. He used to watch you fight all the time.'"

"Drinks, Carmen?" the waitress said. "Would you gentlemen like a cocktail?"

"An orange juice for me," he said, and after she had taken my order and left, "Would you believe I got an ulcer? I found out two weeks ago."

"The stress of modern living," I said. "Now you have to follow the diet and learn to relax."

"Yeah, but I have to scramble, too," he said. "I bought a motel in the Thousand Islands, and I lost $70,000 up there and that wiped me out. I didn't touch that property we live on, or I'd really be wiped out. I almost took a mortgage on it, but I changed my mind. I've got ten-and-a-half acres, all building land, in Chittenango and six acres at the other end of town that I own, but the taxes are close to $4,500 a year. The biggest rap is school taxes, and they keep building on them like they're country clubs. I went to a little nothing school, and I learned just as much as they do."

"Yes," I said, "you learned how to fight by beating up on all the other kids."

"No," he said, shaking his head. "Not me."

He was being the college instructor now, but I was remembering the fighter with whom toughness had been an obsession from childhood on. He had told me once how he had had a fight every day he had gone to school.

"I used to go home for lunch period," he had said, "and I used to think, 'Now, who am I gonna have a fight with?' Then I'd go back and bother somebody. I'd push him or shove him. Then the other guy would swing, and we'd fight. Sometimes I'm ashamed when I think of it now. I had no pity because I had to prove my toughness."

"Come on, Carmen," I said now. "You were a terror in school when you were a little kid."

"Yeah," he said. "There was one kid I gave a lickin' to once a week from kindergarten through the eighth grade, but it wasn't my doin'. He'd say, 'Come on, you Wop. I'm gonna kick your tail for you.' He lives in Oneida, New York now, and I run into him and he's got a good job. He'd come into my house and he loved spaghetti and meat balls, and whenever you came into my house my ma always had to feed you. She's still the same way, and this kid would sit down and we'd eat, and then he'd go home and we'd have that one fight a week."

"When did you first think that some day you'd be champion of the world?"

"When I was little," he said. "You know who my idol was? Jim Braddock."

"A wonderful guy," I said. "During the Depression when he got laid off on the docks he had to go on relief. After he won the heavyweight title he paid that money back. I don't know anyone who didn't admire and like him."

"I had just started reading the sports pages," he said, "when he won the championship from . . . uh . . ."

"Max Baer."

"Right, and my pa had this rule that you had to be in bed by 8:30. Braddock was fightin' Louis, and they had the fights then on the Adam Hats radio program. I said, 'Pa, let us stay up.' My two brothers and me, we sat on the floor, and when Braddock got knocked out in the eighth round I walked up the stairs cryin' and sayin', 'Someday I'm gonna be a fighter, and get big and lick Joe Louis.'

"Now I'm fightin' in Syracuse and I'm working for the Autolite Company, assembling parts for radios and things. The guy next to me says, 'You fight a lot?' I said, 'Yeah.' He said, 'What do you think you're gonna do fightin'?' I said, 'I'm gonna be champion of the world some day.' He looked at me, dropped the tools and walked away. We got laid off then, and after a couple of weeks I came back, but he wasn't there. I often wondered what he thought when I became champion of the world. He walked away as if to say, 'This sonofabitch is crazy.'"

"Man has to dream," I said. "It's like your 'wish-talk,' and sometimes his dreams come true."

"When you stop dreaming you're done," he said. "Who else are you going to talk to for this book?"

"Fighters?" I said. "Among those you fought, well, Lew Jenkins, and . . ."

"Lew Jenkins?" he said. "Every time I pick up something he's knocking the stuff out of me. He says I couldn't fight enough to keep warm. He calls me a bum. What's wrong with him?"

The two fought in Syracuse on March 6, 1950. Basilio was twenty-three, and a future champion on the way up. Jenkins was thirty-four, and a former champion on the way out. After he lost that ten-round decision to Basilio, Jenkins was knocked out by Beau Jack in Washington, and then he enlisted in the Army for his second war. He went to Korea where, his general told me later, he was a great combat sergeant, and where he won the Silver Star.

"I don't know what he's got against you," I said, "but he came out of the cotton fields of Texas just like you came out of the onion fields around here, and you two should really like each other."

"Who else are you going to see?"

"Ray Robinson," I said, "and there's someone *you* don't like."

After he beat Robinson in that bloody combat in Yankee Stadium in 1957, when he was thirty and Robinson thirty-seven, Robinson regained the middleweight title with a split decision over him the next year in Chicago in another savage battle. Then the two went head-to-head over the terms for a third fight, which never came about.

"I don't dislike him," he said now. "What I really believe is he was afraid of me. In that second fight I fought seven rounds with one eye. The referee gave me the decision and the two judges voted for him, but I walked to the dressing room and they had to carry him. He had a $600,000 guarantee for the next fight, and I'd got $300,000. At that time it was the hottest match in the world, so he lost his title to Paul Pender for $65,000."

"At his peak he was a great one," I said, wanting to go beyond that, for Robinson was the greatest I ever saw.

"The greatest I ever saw," Basilio said as if he had read my mind, "was Willie Pep."

"He was certainly the greatest creative artist I ever saw in a ring," I said, "and I'm going to look him up, too."

"He won't agree with you," Basilio said. "Whenever I see him and we start to talk and I say something, he says, 'No.' It doesn't matter what it is, he always says, 'No.' Why would he do that?"

"I have no idea."

"The smartest guy I ever fought was Billy Graham."

It was his two fights with Graham in 1953 in Syracuse that started Basilio on his way to his titles. Norm Rothschild was trying to build boxing in the area, and Ray Arcel was trying to build an audience for his Saturday night fights on TV, and they talked the New York State Athletic Commission into recognizing the fights as deciding the New York State welterweight title. Basilio won the first, and the second was declared a draw.

"I'll see Billy, too," I said. "I once spent three weeks with him in camp."

"He couldn't break an egg, but I learned more in three fights with him than from anybody I ever fought. I hit him with punches that would knock other guys dead. I fought him in Chicago, and he said, 'You hit me a punch, and I went back to the corner and my feet were tinglin'. In Chicago I was coming off mononucleosis, but I got him back in Syracuse."

"Whenever you think back on your career," I said, "do you ever fasten on one moment as the greatest?"

"There's nothing like winning a world championship," he said. "That has to be the greatest moment, but there was one key bout. In 1956, March 14 in Chicago, when I had the title and I fought Johnny Saxton. I had him hurt, and in his corner they took a razor blade and cut his glove and held up the fight. They gave him the decision, and they made the fight back in Syracuse. Now, if I don't win the welterweight title back, I never fight for the middleweight championship, and after I beat him I was cryin', it meant so much to me.

"In the ninth round," he said, "I come out and I hit him a right hand and he staggered into the ropes. Instead of going for his head, I hit him a left hook to the solar plexus, and his knee came up and I knew I had him hurt bad. He went into the ropes again, and I was gonna hit him a right hand and Al Berl grabbed my hand. I hollered, 'Let me go! I wanna flatten the sonofabitch!' Then in my corner I was crying and I said, 'I finally got him. I finally got him.'

"Now, after the Ali-Norton fight in the Yankee Stadium I was in Ali's dressing room, and Saxton was there. He was big as a horse. He said, 'Hey, Carmen, how you doin'?' I said, 'All right. You still with that youth program in Harlem?' 'No,' he said. 'I'm not workin'.' I felt sorry for the guy, and I'd like to send him a thousand, but I haven't got that kind of money."

I, too, had often felt sorry for Saxton, for he suffered from Robinson's syndrome. As every great artist in any field acquires a host of imitators, so did Sugar Ray and, just before him, Henry Armstrong. When Armstrong held three titles at the same time— the only man ever to do so—you could walk into the Uptown Gym on 116th Street in Harlem and see a dozen Armstrongs. Then came Robinson, and the gym was filled with young Robinsons.

One afternoon I got to the gym early, and over in a corner, in the half light, I saw Robinson working on the big bag. I stood there and marveled at his natural grace, the speed and fluidity with which he turned on his variety of combinations. It seemed to me that at the age of thirty he looked better than ever, and then he stopped and turned around. It was Johnny Saxton, and a week or so later, I watched him box Joe Miceli at the St. Nicholas Arena. For the first five rounds he did his best to look like Robinson, and he took a beating. After the fifth round they sent him out to fight his own fight, and he knocked Miceli down and managed to pull out the decision, but I knew his problem after that night.

Saxton went on to win the welterweight title, not once but twice, but it was my opinion that he never became the fighter he should have been because of Robinson. I once expressed this to Sugar Ray.

"That's right, and it's too bad," he said. "I used to work with the boy when he was first starting. I showed him a lot, but there's things you do that you can't show another man. You do them in a fight, and you don't know why you do them. You do them without thinking. You do them because you just have to, and you can't explain that."

While we were eating I asked about the two boys Basilio and his wife adopted. They are the sons of his wife's sister, and one was five and the other five months old when the Basilios became their foster parents.

"They're fine," he said. "The one is twenty-four and manages a marina up in Cape Vincent, and he's married and has a boy and a girl. The other is twenty-nine and works for an electronics firm in Marysville, California, and is married and has two daughters. I love them like my own, and I told them, 'I made a lot of mistakes and I lost a lot of money, but if you need anything just call on me.' "

"You mentioned your mother . . ."

"She's eighty-three now, and my pa died two years ago. He was eighty-eight, and the nicest man in the world. He'd give you the shirt off his back. We were ten kids, and he'd do without to be sure we had shoes on our feet, clothes on our backs."

I recalled how, when Basilio was six years old, his father had driven a truckload of onions into Albany, and returned with a set of four boxing gloves. Basilio had told me, "When he opened that box, it was like seeing gold. We kids boxed for three hours that night. Then my old man used to have friends in, and we'd box for them in the living room. My older brother, Armando, would make me cry, and I'd make Paulie cry. The old man would say, 'O.K., rest period.' Then they'd give us a hand. That was their TV."

"What a sweetheart he was," he said now. "I didn't know a person who didn't like him. When he died in that little town, the undertaker said it was the biggest funeral he ever had, the most people that ever came to a wake."

"It's good to have that to remember."

"It's a hell of a thing to brag about," he said.

"Excuse me," someone said, and when we looked up he was standing at the table, slim, his dark hair starting to gray. "I don't like to interrupt."

"That's all right," I said.

"Carmen Basilio," he said, offering his hand, "You're my hero."

"Thank you," Basilio said, taking the hand, "but . . ."

"You don't understand," he said, stepping back, and then to both of us, "Jimmy Lombardo. For twenty years I want to meet Carmen Basilio. To me he's just a great man. I have this friend Frank, and he eats here. Last week he tells me that sometimes Carmen Basilio comes in to eat here, too. I said, 'Do you think I could meet him, Carmen Basilio?' He said, 'Sure.'

"Now listen to this," he said. "He told me, 'Now next Wednesday I'll meet you at this restaurant, and we'll have veal scallopini and maybe we'll see Carmen Basilio.' So Wednesday is tomorrow, and we're supposed to meet here, and what happened? He just called me up and he said, 'I'm here and I'm having veal scallopini, and Carmen Basilio is here. Come quick.' It was supposed to be tomorrow."

"And he called you," Basilio said, "and you came over?"

"Of course. And I never thought that today, after all these years, I would meet you, a great man, and here I am and I shake your hand."

I was watching Basilio. He had taken his glasses off and placed them on the table, and with his forefingers he was rubbing his eyes.

"What's the matter?" the other said, looking at him. "What happened?"

"Carmen Basilio is crying," I said.

"You made me cry," Basilio said, blinking his eyes, and trying to smile.

"I'm sorry," the other said. "I didn't mean to make you cry."

When I drove into the campus the next morning and parked by the Athletic Center and got out, a pale sun was shining between white, fleecy clouds. A light breeze was blowing out of the south and the air was fresh and warm, and a workman on a garden tractor with a rotary cutter beneath it was mowing the playing field where the touch football game had been under way the afternoon before.

In the lobby of the Athletic Center I stopped by the trophy

case. In the middle of it, behind the glass, there is an oil portrait of Basilio, gloved and wearing boxing trunks and in a fighting pose. On either side are trophies for the Queens-Iona Relays . . . the Canisius College Run . . . the Harpur Invitational Golf Tournament . . . the basketball from LeMoyne's 300th win on February 24, 1971, when they beat Cortland 72–70 . . . another with LeMoyne's individual college scoring records painted on it in white . . .

The coaches' office is down a hallway to the left of the main gym, and Basilio was sitting at one of the four desks. He introduced me to Dick Rockwell, the baseball coach, Tom Mooney, who coaches basketball, and Whitey Anderson, the sports information director, and when he came out of his private office, to Tom Niland, the Athletic Director.

"That ball game yesterday," Basilio said. "We won it 5–4 in the ninth when that kid I told you about, who was thrown out at second, stole home on a double steal. I told you he can run."

"Very good," I said.

"Hey!" he said, looking at his wristwatch. "I've got my class."

He was wearing his instructor's uniform, gray trousers with a dark green stripe down the legs and a gray top. He picked up his attendance book at his desk and walked out to where, just inside the doorway of the main gym, five of them in dark green shorts, white tops, sneakers and socks were waiting for him.

"How many here?" he said. "Five? Wow, there's supposed to be eight. You guys do your five laps? Good, so let's go."

He followed them across the hall to a square, almost barren room next to the weight room. With his attendance book in hand, he called off the names.

"O'Reilly here? Tiberio not here? Okay, who's gonna tell me why we do these silly little exercises? To stretch out? What? To loosen up the muscles? Right, so we don't get muscle spasms. Okay, so let's start off with some jumping jacks . . . one, two, three, four . . . one, two, three, four . . ."

He put them through toe-touches, waist twists, running in place, and squats. On the push-ups, after the first half dozen or so, most of them started faking it, skipping a count and then two counts and not going all the way down.

"Okay," he said. "You know you're going to have to do thirty. If you don't do them here, you'll never do them on the test, so when you're here playin' basketball or whatever, come in here and work because this half hour isn't enough. Okay, now the sit-ups, and four guys hook their feet under that bar over there and I'll hold this one on the mat here . . . C'mon . . . one, two, three, four, five, six . . . Bounce off that mat . . . eight, nine, twenty-four, twenty-five . . . only nine more to go . . . thirty-four, thirty five. . . . Okay, now go out in the gym and do ten laps and sprint the last one, and a couple of months from now you guys will be tigers."

He followed them out and into the gym where two middle-aged men in gym shorts and T-shirts were going one-on-one at one of the baskets. We sat down on a bench along a wall and watched the small pack of five start out together, the slap-sound of their sneakers fading, and then in the hollow silence of the gym the thump of the basketball coming through.

"Those two guys are professors here," Basilio said. "They don't have classes in the morning, and they've been doing this for two years."

"That's a pretty stiff set of exercises you put these kids through," I said. "Ages ago in college we didn't have anything like this."

"It started with the Kennedy fitness program," he said. "It's amazing how these kids will improve in three or four months, and in the fifteen years I've been here, there haven't been two or three kids I didn't like. You know what's gratifying in this job? Next May a lot of these kids will come and say, 'Thanks a lot, Carm. I never thought I could be above average.' Some guys who graduated ten years ago say, 'You were a tough bastard, but you helped me.' "

"You had better help this kid," I said.

One of them had come off the floor to our right, gasping for air, his face contorted, and he was bent over now, an arm and his head against the wall.

"You'll be all right," Basilio said, getting up and walking over and putting an arm around the young man's shoulders. "Here. Sit down. No, put your head down between your knees. Take short, fast breaths. That's right. Good."

The others were finishing their ten laps now, strung out, the last two unable to sprint. Basilio got up and saw that the one on the bench was sitting up now, still breathing heavily but his face starting to relax.

"Okay," he said to the others. "If you need clean towels, remember I can't give you a clean one if you don't turn in a dirty one."

From behind the counter in the equipment room he handed out the clean towels, and we walked back to the coaches' office. Whitey Anderson was sitting at his desk and he looked up.

"Here comes the matchmaker," he said.

"The what?" Basilio said.

"The matchmaker," Anderson said. "Didn't you tell him about Chuck Davey?"

During the early 1950s, Chuck Davey was the darling of the college-cultured who, through him, discovered boxing on television for the first time. A lithe, blond graduate of Michigan State, with his masters in physical education and his boyish looks, he attracted to the sport a whole new audience, women as well as men. With his flitting, in-and-out, spring-kneed southpaw style he confused and defeated a succession of opponents until he flunked his doctorate trying for the welterweight title against Kid Gavilan. Basilio fought Davey twice, first in May of 1951 in Syracuse, where the fight was called a draw, and two months later in Chicago, where although he opened deep cuts on Davey's left cheek and over his right eye, Davey was declared the winner.

"Chuck Davey?" Basilio said now. "He's doing all right. He's on the boxing commission out there, and he's making a mint in the insurance business, and he's married and got kids. In Chicago I put him in the hospital, and while he was there he met this nurse and he married her. Two years ago I went down to Philadelphia where all the champions boxed each other—we did it for expenses and made $35,000 for cerebral palsy—and Chuck was there with two of his boys. I said to them, 'If it wasn't for me you wouldn't be here.' Chuck said, 'Hey, he's right.'"

After his 11:30 class he and Dick Rockwell, the baseball coach, teamed up for three games of paddle-ball against Mike Yost, the dean of students, and Jim Welter, a biology professor, on a court separated from the main gym by a sliding wall. He is a natural southpaw who seldom reverted in the ring, but he kept switching the paddle from one hand to the other as he tried to overpower the ball against the wall even as he had tried to overpower every opponent he had ever fought.

"I love this game," he said, after he had showered and changed. "It's like golf. It's a disease. I wait to play it, like yesterday I played six games. I won four of the six, and they were cut-throat games—not two-on-two, but two-on-one. It's great exercise."

He had no classes that afternoon, and I had asked him if he would drive me out again to that road raised above the Muckland from which he had fought to escape so many years before. We stopped for roast-beef sandwiches in one of those gaudy, plastic, however immaculate fast-food eateries that one finds among the gas stations, laundromats, drive-in banks, and furniture outlets on the outskirts of our cities. As we ate in the small booth, I could look over his shoulder and see, across the parking space, an automobile muffler shop with three lifts and a mechanic in uniform working under a car raised on one of them.

"Have you had to get a new muffler lately," I said as we walked toward his car, "and discovered what they rap you for one now?"

"You're telling me?" he said. "I need one and I saw this ad for mufflers for $16.85. I went and got one, and then the guy who was gonna install it said it wasn't just the muffler but the piece of pipe, and you couldn't just buy that piece but you had to buy the whole assembly. Then he ripped me off on the labor—$28 for forty minutes—and the whole thing came to $98.75 when it was finished."

As we approached the car I noticed for the first time his New York license plate: KO 1.

"I knew the fellow who had Massachusetts KO 1," I said. "Rocky Marciano."

"I've had that since 1955," he said, "but it wasn't my idea. After I won the welterweight title they gave me that car, and Norm Rothschild and an assemblyman who's dead now got me this plate."

"They used to give you cars," I said, "and now when you want to buy a muffler they give you a going-over."

."I don't want anything for nothing," he said, "but I don't like to get rolled."

The blacktop road from Syracuse to Chittenango is bordered on the left in places by the Erie Canal which, a century and a half ago, linked the Hudson River to the Great Lakes and tied the industrial Northeast to the agricultural Midwest. It was one of America's life lines, and now, along here, the tow path on the far side has been converted into a bicycle path, and we could see an occasional rider and sometimes two or three, with the pale sunlight glinting off the brightwork of their bikes.

"I'll just whip in here for a second," he said, turning right up a driveway on the outskirts of Chittenango, "and you can see where we live."

It is a two-storied house, with weathered shingles and white trim, standing on a slope that rises behind it. It is hidden from the road and the house next to it by trees and bushes, and there was a car in the driveway.

"My wife's still here," he said, backing around, "so I guess she's not feeling too good. She has a hard time mornings and afternoons, or I'd take you in. Also four years ago I moved the furniture from the fourteen-room house in Alexandria Bay into these nine rooms, and I've got stuff piled up all over the place. I gotta have a garage sale, and she said, 'Don't bring anybody in this house. It's a mess.' She's a sweetheart, though. When I had a fight coming up and I'd start to get edgy, I'd take it out on her. I'd start snappin' at her and she'd say, 'I know you're ready.' Twenty-six-and-a-half years we're married, and we've had our ins and outs and our little spats now and then, but I still love that gal.

"What we've got here, too," he said, "is apple trees. We had bushels of apples this year, and I asked a lot of people if they wanted any. They all said, 'Sure.' Then nobody came and got any, and they just rotted."

"They wanted you to pick them for them, and then deliver them."

"That's it," he said. "You're right."

We drove through Chittenango and from there to Canastota,

towns that, like their counterparts all over America with populations of about 5,000 or less that are still apart from the mainstream of commerce, do not change much over the years. On the main streets the places of business are low and flat-roofed, only their modernized facades and their signs differing from the fronts in the old photographs of three quarters of a century and more ago.

The road itself had not changed much either since the last time I had been there, the straight blacktop running northwest toward Oneida Lake and raised several feet above the flat fields of black soil on both sides. Where the onions had been harvested more than a month before and the ground retilled, it looked the same, but I had not remembered that there had been so much corn, the stalks standing golden brown in the October afternoon sun.

"You're right," he said. "There's a lot more corn now where there used to be onions. The onion business is dying because the families don't work like they used to, and the growers can't meet the labor costs. There's still some, but they're growing them now in Florida and Texas and California."

"Do you still have the scars on your hand?" I said, remembering that he had told me how, before the harvest, his father would sharpen the knives until he could shave the hair off his arms with them. During the haste of the harvest their hands bled each day, and he had shown me the fingers of his right hand crisscrossed with small white scars.

"Oh, yeah," he said, and he had turned off on a gravel road, "but I'm not the only one. Pop, everyone of the kids had them, so I'm not feeling sorry for myself. You see along here? This was my pa's land, ten acres, and while I was still fighting I bought it from him. It was all onions, and now look at it."

It was covered with scrub growth, mostly box elders. A few of them were fifteen or twenty feet tall and a foot or more in diameter, and others had fallen in wind and ice storms.

"Some of that could be cut for fireplace wood," I said.

"I know," he said. "I told some people who have fireplaces, 'You want some wood? Help yourself.' They said, 'Sure.' Then they don't do it. It's like the apples. They want you to cut the wood for them, too. You see where that one big tree is standing now? We used to have our house right there. It was only four miles from town, but in those days it was like a hundred miles, and the idea was you could get up in the morning and walk right out the door and start working. You see this stream here? Sullivan Creek."

He had stopped on a narrow, steel-framed bridge. The stream, about fifteen feet wide, it's banks overgrown, was almost still, its waters an olive green.

"Right there," he said, pointing, "is where we used to go in at the end of the day. My pa would give us soap, and we'd soap ourselves and jump in. One day I was just a little kid, and I'm standing up to my waist in the water right there and all of a sudden I let out a yelp. I hollered, 'Hey, Pa! A fish just bit my pecker!' Everybody just howled. I was such a little kid but I still remember it, and this was the only place we could get clean."

"When I was writing about ballplayers and fighters," I said, "I used to wonder if the people who went to the events ever conceived of the athletes as being other than as they then saw them. I mean, the ballplayers weren't born with a glove and a bat and a ball in their hands and wearing Yankee pinstripes, and the fighters didn't come into the world wearing white trunks and 8-ounce gloves. I'm thinking of that now, as you describe yourself as a kid bathing in this creek here."

"That's right," he said. "Who the hell ever heard of an onion farmer comin' out and fighting in Yankee Stadium?"

About a quarter of a mile down the road he stopped again. In the field on the left the corn had been harvested for silage, and only the stubble, clean cut about eight inches above the ground, remained. He rolled down the window on his side and pointed to about two dozen Canada geese resting among the cropped rows, some fifty yards from the road. He let out a couple of harsh calls, but as we watched the black heads with the white chin patches just visible and the black necks, there was no movement.

"I haven't got my voice in shape yet," he said.

"Do you still do some hunting?"

"Pheasant and deer," he said. "I fish for trout, too. I go up around Osceola, New York. I had a hundred acres I paid $3,200 for in 1956, and after I put $500 into the house and built a trout pond, I sold it in 1971 for $4,000. I stopped by there, and a guy said, 'Carmen, you should have held it. They're gettin' $1,000 an acre now.' They were breaking into the house, though, and shooting down the TV aerial, so that's what you call the breaks of life."

He drove back to the blacktop and back into town. The houses on North Main Street are modest, standing on small pieces of ground with well-kept lawns between them and the sidewalk. He stopped in front of one on the right, narrow and two-storied with new dark green asphalt shingles and with white trim that looked like it had just been repainted. On the small patch of grass between it and the sidewalk, a young man was sawing a piece of 8×4 plywood that was resting on two saw horses.

"Two eleven North Main Street, Canastota," Basilio said. "I was born in that house. Six of us out of the ten were born in that house. You see where that bay window is downstairs? When my mother was ready, my father would move the bedroom in there. It was a bigger room for the doctor to operate on her."

Near the center of town he turned right and drove down the street and pulled into the parking lot in front of a flat-roofed blue-and-white-sided building. A woman in a ground floor window in the house next door was peering between the white curtains.

"Carmen Basilio's Hot and Sweet Sausage," he said, and he got out and tried the door and came back. "They're delivering now, Paul and Armando. They also make frozen meat balls, and we're going to start canning sausage with sauce and meat balls with sauce, and ship it around the country. We'll see if my ma is home."

Down the street he pulled into the driveway next to another narrow two-storied house, this one white-shingled with white trim. I remembered his mother well, a short woman, only 4 feet 10, who also had told me what it was like in the onion fields. For three years, beginning in 1934, Basilio's father had been invalided by sciatica, and the rest of the family had had to work the farm without him. Some years a blight, caused by early morning fogs and burning sun, had ruined the crop. Other years the price of onions had dropped to a point where the growers had decided to hold out and, finally, to dump their crops rather than sell.

"You take the gamble and you lose," she had said. "You can

smell those onions decay, and you think, 'A whole summer's work for the whole family, and the seed and the fertilizer, too.'"

"Raising a family through all those hard years in the onion fields," I had asked her, "what dreams did you have for your children?"

"We had no dreams," she had said. "None. We just tried to bring up our children to be good."

There is an enclosed porch at the right of the house, and when Basilio opened the door and we walked in, she came out of the kitchen to the left. She seemed even smaller than I had remembered, bespectacled and wearing a black dress. We shook hands, and she led us, moving slowly, into the kitchen. In the front room, off the kitchen, a television was on.

"How are you feeling?" Basilio said.

"All right," she said, sitting down at the kitchen table with us. "With the arthritis I can't do so much, but I'm all right. I don't see you, though, for a long time."

"I know, Ma," he said, "but I'm busy. I gotta keep hustlin'."

"I know," she said.

"She's eighty-three now," Basilio said to me. "She came here when she was four. In 1914 she and my pa went back to Italy to see his family, and they drafted him and he fought in the Italian Army. They didn't get back here until 1921, and my sister Matilda and my sister Anna were born in Italy, in Veroli, north of Rome, where my pa came from."

"We didn't go where I came from," she said.

She had got up from the table. While they talked about the family I watched her. She had taken a jar of tomato sauce and two pork chops out of the refrigerator, and she had filled a pot with water and carried it to the range.

"She's starting to cook," I said to Basilio.

"What did I tell you?" Basilio said, nodding. "I said you can't come into the house without her feeding you."

"We can't eat now," I said. "We just had lunch."

"Ma, we just ate," Basilio said.

"So eat again," she said. "You should have something to eat."

"We can't, Ma," he said. "We just ate lunch. Really."

"No?" she said and, moving slowly, she put the chops and the jar of sauce back in the refrigerator, and sat down at the table with us again.

"Mrs. Basilio," I said, "I remember you the night that Carmen won the welterweight title in Syracuse from Tony DeMarco."

This was a television first, long before presidential candidates paraded their families through campaigns and capped their acceptance speeches and concession statements with connubial kisses. After Harry Kessler, the referee, had stopped that fight with DeMarco helpless in the twelfth round, more than 32 million viewers had seen Basilio drop to his knees, cross himself and pray. When he arose, they saw his wife standing on the ring apron and they watched him embrace her. Then this small semi-stout elderly woman in a black dress and an aging, bald man—Basilio's parents —had been helped into the ring from the other side. For weeks after that Basilio received mail from strangers throughout the country who had been moved by the scene. When he went to New York, others stopped him on the street to talk about it, and when he appeared on Ed Sullivan's TV show, Sullivan commented on it. What the television audience had sensed without completely understanding was all the family hardship that had gone into the making of that moment.

"I remember you in the ring," I said now, "and how many people throughout the country were impressed by that."

"Yes," she said. "Many people saw it, but it is getting to be a long time ago."

As we drove back toward Syracuse, we talked about some of his fights, the two late in his career with Gene Fullmer that had been halted by the referee in the late rounds and how he had protested, he was saying now, because he had never been stopped and it was a matter of pride. In his last fight, the one with Paul Pender, his final attempt to regain the middleweight title, he had fought with a torn cartilege in his left shoulder, suffered in training. It had deprived him of his best punch, the left hook, and he had lost the fifteen-round decision.

"I should have had a couple of cortizone shots," he said, "but I didn't know then. I only learned now, sitting around the field house and hearing these guys with degrees talk."

"How much do you miss it?" I said. "I mean, an athlete always knows it's going to end some day and yet, when that day comes, he will never again be able to do that which expresses him best and fulfills him the most. How often do you think back?"

"I really don't have the time," he said. "Sometimes I go back and eat my heart out about fights I lost that I shouldn't have lost, like the Pender fight, but you can't live that way. I see fights now, and it makes my heart sick. The good trainers are gone. They don't know how to set up, how to hook off the jab. I wasn't what you call a clever fighter, but I could put combinations together, but all that's gone."

We were in the outskirts of Syracuse again now. The late afternoon truck traffic was heavy, with an ambulance, its red roof light turning and its siren going, trying to get through, and in the stretches between the traffic lights, the drivers of the passenger cars cutting back and forth between lanes.

"So much is gone," I said. "You buy a muffler and the ad misleads you. Then they phony the labor cost and rip you off. The kids today, they don't want to work like you did. I don't mean in the onion fields, because that should never be again, but how many of them would work and sacrifice like you did to succeed?"

"Some of it we don't like," he said, "but some of it I do. The kids go around with long hair and all that, but they just want to be one with the crowd. They're really good kids, and I believe in them. Speaking of hair, though, my wife said this morning, 'And don't come home without getting a haircut today.'"

6

The Unsinkable Mister Brown

"The next best thing to a lie," Joe Palmer wrote, "is a true story nobody will believe," and anybody who would believe the story of Freckles Brown ought to report himself.

Red Smith

One of the secrets of selling whiskey is to make a secret of time, and so in the cocktail lounges of this country an eternal twilight prevails. It was midafternoon when we walked into the lounge of the Holiday Inn West in Oklahoma City, and before our eyes could adjust to that light-damped eventide, we could hear them.

"Hey, there's Brownie!" . . . "Hey, Freck, come over here!" . . . "Hey, Brown, you old dog, have a drink!" . . . "Come sit down, Freck! Somebody find a chair for Brown."

It was the first week in December, and the National Finals Rodeo was in town. The lobby had been crowded with them in their quilted vests and jackets and under their big hats, and in the lounge they were sprawled in the chairs they had pulled up to the tables they had rearranged, leaving the waitresses, holding the drink trays over their heads and perspiring and suffering like bearers on safari, to pick their way through an underbrush that was constantly closing ahead and behind them.

"You want me to tell you something?" one of them said to me. "You want to listen to me?"

"Why, certainly," I said.

There were five of them at two tables they had pulled together just inside the door, and Freckles had introduced me and we had sat down. We were waiting for one of the waitresses to make her way to us and take our order.

"This man," he said, sweeping an arm toward Freckles, "is an immortal. Did you know that?"

"Yes," I said, "I did."

"You did?" he said. "How well do you know this man?"

"Aw, old Bill knows me," Freckles said, embarrassed. "He's been out here before."

"That's right," I said. "During the Finals in '68 I followed Freckles around for nine days and . . ."

"And I was fallin' off everything," Freckles said. "I sure was ridin' sorry."

"That don't matter," the other said to Freckles, and then to me, "And I want to tell you somethin' else, too. This man has a million friends, and not an enemy in the world. Did you know that?"

"Aw, not that many," Freckles said, "and I'm sure there's some don't like me."

"Listen," the other said to Freckles now. "What I said is right. You haven't got an enemy in the world."

Stay with it, Freck, I was thinking, and you'll win this by making an enemy right now.

"Well, I just try to live with people," Freckles said, still embarrassed.

"You want to know something else?" one of the others said to me now. "You are in the presence of a legend. Did you know that?"

"Yes," I said. "That's why I'm here."

He was, as Red Smith wrote, the most improbable athlete in creation, a smiling little chipmunk of a man who was two months from being forty-eight when I trailed him for those nine days and watched him as he spent more time in the air and on the ground than he did on the back of the bulls he drew until he finally rode one. Each time he came out of the chute, a sudden silence would descend over the packed seats of the Fairgrounds Coliseum, for they had been watching him, or had been reading about him, for years, and when I added up the injuries he had sustained over a quarter of a century they surpassed the seasonal totals for a couple of National Football League squads.

He had had his right leg broken four times, and his left leg twice, his left ankle once, and his right ankle twice. He had had his left foot smashed a couple of times, and his neck broken twice. There was a piece of tendon from his upper left leg tied to the tendon in his left ankle, and the severed tendon in his right arm had been retied. There was a metal screw in his left ankle, and his neck was held in place by a plug made out of a piece of his hip bone. He had had ruptured blood vessels in his right thigh, and pulled muscles and ruptured vessels in his groin. He had suffered three concussions, and there is a scar over his upper right lip where it was hooked by a horn.

"You know what I do when I get into one of them strange hospitals?" he said to me one night. "I get ahold of one of them old head nurses and I ask her, 'Who's the good doctor around here?' Those interns sittin' around there, they don't know, and if you get one of them, it's like havin' a court-appointed lawyer."

I took that to be the considered opinion of the world's leading expert on the subject. He had been in more strange hospitals than most people have motels. He had known three cowboys who had been killed by the bulls, and in Sidney, Iowa, in 1963, he had almost lost his friend Tex Martin. They had been going down the road together, as they say in rodeo, for two years when a big brindle threw Martin and then came down with one of its hind feet on his chest.

"He stepped plumb through Tex to the back of his rib cage," Freckles was telling once, "and when he brought that leg up, Tex was on it. It was like pullin' a cork, but there was a doctor right there, and he had the guys hold Tex out straight in the air and he just kept wrappin' the bandage around him.

"I got into the ambulance with Tex, and he was hurtin'. On the way over to the hospital in Hamburg he got to gaspin' and sayin', 'I can't breathe.' I told him. 'You sorry little sonofabitch, take a deep breath.' He said, 'It hurts.' I said, 'The hell it does. You sorry little bastard, keep breathin'.' Later, after he was gettin' better, that ambulance driver told him, 'You know, I never heard anybody talk to a dyin' man like that friend of yours was talkin' to you.'"

That next afternoon at Sidney, Freckles drew the same bull and rode him to get second money of $260 on him. The year before, in Portland, Oregon, he himself came close to being killed when a big spinning bull named Black Smoke threw him after the whistle and then butted him.

"I lit with my face in the dirt and my butt up," he said, "and he just kinda mashed my hips and head together. In the hospital, after they X-rayed me, they shaved my head and drilled holes in my skull and they put these tongs—like ice tongs only littler—in there. Then they had a rope comin' off those tongs to a pulley with some sand bags hangin' on it, and it felt like somebody had their fingers in my head and pressin' all the time. One of my friends come to see me there, and he took one look and got so sick he had to run to the men's room and vomit.

"They found my neck was broken, that the bones was just pulverized, and there were two bone specialists there that said I'd never be able to ride again. There was this neurosurgeon, though, who'd been learnin' this front neck fusion—what they call it—and the two bone specialists were against it, but I told him to do it. He took all that broken bone out of there, just cleared it out, and took that piece of my hip bone and put it in there instead. I was in that rig for thirty-four days, and they had me on sheepskin. Every five hours they'd tip me one way, and then in five hours they'd tip me the other way.

"Before I left," he said, "they stood me up and they put a cast on me from the top of my head down to my hips, with just my face and my ears and the top of my head stickin' out. For about two days, until a cast cures out, it's real tight, and when they were puttin' it on, I kept tryin' to keep a little air in my lungs and this nurse kept givin' me smelling salts. The doctor was standin' on his toes, and he said, 'I'm glad you're not any taller than you are.'"

He was in that cast for three months. He was in it at the National Finals at Los Angeles when they named him World Champion Bull Rider for 1962. By the time that bull had butted him at Sidney, he had been so far ahead in prize money earned that year that the competition had never caught up.

"But that neck kept me out for six months," he said.

He was telling me this in '68, sitting around the Wiley Post Suite that Skipper Lofting and I were sharing in the Sheraton Oklahoman. After the evening go-rounds at the Coliseum, he would come up to have a drink and answer my questions and just talk.

"And he came back," Skipper said, "in a little rodeo in Claymore, Oklahoma, just before Cheyenne."

"That right?" Freckles said.

"When he got on that bull in the chute," Skipper said, "and they announced his name, it was so quiet that you could hear cars a mile away on the highway."

"That's right?" Freckles said.

"He rode that bull," Skipper said, "but he bucked off a saddle bronc and landed on his shoulders."

"Yeah, I did," Freckles said.

"Those other guys just held their breath," Skipper said.

"But when I got up," Freckles said, "I was all in one piece."

Three times over the years he had been knocked unconscious. In Lawton, Oklahoma, he was out for an hour. At Odessa, Texas, he woke up in the hospital at 4 A.M. with no memory of his ride.

"When the nurses came in in the morning," he said, "I said, 'What the hell am I doin' in this hospital?' They said, 'Don't move.' Then in Chickasha, Oklahoma, a bull knocked me out. I was in the wild horse race after the bull ridin', so they poured water on me. I rode in that and we came in second, and that night we were sittin' in a cafe in Lawton, fifty miles away, when I come to. I didn't remember that race."

In 1965 he got into Springdale, Arkansas, at three o'clock one morning, and at the motel he left a call for five. There were so many entries in the bull riding that, as they say in rodeo, they were riding the slack off at six. He got up and showered, and drove out to the arena.

"I hadn't warmed up and got the circulation goin' and I was cold," he was telling. "When I ride I take my hold with my left hand, and I was on a real arm-jerker. He was really stout on that rope, and after the ride, I was puttin' up my rope when I noticed something lyin' like a big lump near my elbow. There was just skin and bones above, and that was my bicep lyin' there. This tendon had pulled in two, and this doctor went in and grooved the bone and tied the tendon back together at the shoulder. I carried my arm in a sling for ten days, and I was squeezin' a rubber ball. I thought I could win somethin' ridin' with my right hand, but that was a mistake. I couldn't ride so good."

"But don't you ever have any fear?" I asked him one night. "You've known cowboys who were killed. You almost lost Tex Martin, and in Portland you were close to being killed yourself, and could have been paralyzed for life."

"Bein' afraid?" he said. "Nope. I've never been afraid ridin' a buckin' horse or a bull. If you're gonna ride, you have to ignore it. You couldn't be thinkin' about it. Some of them guys, they like to find out what they drew so they can worry all night, I guess, but there ain't nothin' you're gonna do about it. And it ain't courage, either, because I think you got to be scared to have courage."

"When you were just a kid," I said, "what were you afraid of? Children have fears."

"Nothin' but the dark," he said, "but I could go anywhere if I had an animal with me, a cat even. I could get on a horse and ride all night, but I didn't tell anybody."

So he has that ability, of which Hemingway wrote, to suspend the imagination and thus supress the fear. He has, a doctor once told him, a high pain threshold, and so he is able to live with the aftermath of his injuries without being a semicripple or even a complainer. He is one, however, whom I wanted to see again, as I had wanted to see Jim Tescher, to reaffirm, while I watch society go soft all around me, that a man, not with just that indefinable courage but with determination, can survive poverty and deprivation and still ride adversity out to the whistle.

He was born Warren Granger Brown in Wheatland, Wyoming, between Lingle and Fort Laramie on the North Platte, on January 18, 1921. The family homesteaded on 160 acres, raising sugar beets, corn, beans, potatoes, alfalfa, and hay.

"We lived in this house of cottonwood logs that Poppa had built because there wasn't any real lumber around," he said, "and we had this tarpaper shack, what they call it, about thirty yards from the log house. My two oldest brothers had died before I was born, but my other two brothers and me slept out there. We had a pot-bellied stove and a coal oil lantern, but in the winter it would get thirty below, and it was cold. When I was nine, we built a new house with two bedrooms in the basement where my brothers and me slept. There was a bathroom and a windmill and a pump, and if the wind was blowin' you had water in the house. Otherwise somebody had to go out and pump.

"We always had plenty to eat," he said, "but otherwise we were poor. We had none of the things kids get today."

"What about Christmas?" I said. "What would you get on Christmas?"

"One year I got a mouth harp," he said. "One year I got a horn. One year I got a little wagon, and then one year I got pants and a shirt."

"You were outgrowing toys," I said. "How far did you go in school?"

"I went a month in the ninth grade," he said. "I run off to Nebraska and got a job pickin' spuds. My folks and I got along fine, but there was this superintendent's boy, and we were playin' football and I tackled him and he skinned his face. He told his dad, and his dad jerked me up by the ears. My feelings were just real hurt, and the next morning I let the school bus go by and I jumped on the hay rake. My dad said, 'You go to school. You got to go to school tomorrow.'

"The next morning my dad waited to be sure I got on the school bus, so I put on two pairs of pants and two shirts and I rode the school bus six miles into Lingle. Then I got off and I walked over to the highway and I hitch-hiked to Mitchell, Nebraska. I had a job pickin' spuds that evening."

"Tell me what that was like," I said.

"Well, you pick in a basket and dump 'em in a sorter. There are ten guys pickin' and each man is on a row, and you got to keep your row up because at the end of the day they count the sacks and divide by ten. It was mostly Mexicans, because them beet workers don't want to pick spuds, and we were in the field before eight until dark. You could make around two dollars a day.

"I'd never been away from home before, except for one or two meals in a restaurant, and after two weeks I wrote my folks that I wasn't goin' to school no more. They wrote there was plenty of work at home, so I come back, and when I walked in they were at the table eatin' and all Poppa said was, 'You're late for supper.'

"Then we moved to Arizona," he said. "My mother had arthritis real bad so we went to Tucson, and there were just hardly no jobs. I got a job for ten dollars a month with board and room milkin' cows at a dairy. Three of us milked sixty cows twice a day and cleaned the barn and washed the equipment, and your hands would swell up sometimes so you'd have to soak them in cold water.

"Mr. St. Denis, he had the dairy and he pastured some cattle up in the mountains twenty miles from Tucson. He put me up there in a line camp for two and-a-half months. You want to hear about that, or am I talkin' too much?"

"You're doing fine," I said. "I want to hear about all of it."

"Them line camps," he said, "is where them big ranches will put a guy, or sometimes two, and they'll bring him out his groceries and he batches and cooks there for two or three months. I was fifteen, and they put me out there, livin' in this tin-roofed shack with this kid who was nine years old and what you'd call like retarded now. He'd just piddle around and follow me because he was scared of the dog. We had beans, and I'd shoot cottontail rabbits and make fry bread in a skillet. I was really put there to see that the cattle had water, and to clean out the spring after they tramped sand into it.

"So this one day we were on our way in the wagon with the two mules to the spring to haul two barrels of water. We were goin' along where there was a kind of a ravine on the side and I got to noddin'. When I sort of woke up and looked around this kid was walkin' behind the wagon. I said, 'What are you doin' back there?' He said, 'I thought you was asleep and that the mules might drive you over the edge, and I'd get your boots.' Hell, you couldn't have driven them mules over that edge, but he liked my boots."

"That kid must have been great company," I said.

"Well, they talk about them line camps and being lonely," he said, "but I'll tell you somethin'. I've never been so lonely in my life as I was in New York."

"So where did you go after Tucson?" I said.

"Well, in Tucson," he said, "I worked some on and off for Mr. Hulen McMinn, helpin' him break horses. He really taught me—how to put a hackamore on, and how to pull one's head around and when to leave 'em alone and when to keep on makin' them do something right, and how to teach 'em to turn and to come to the run. He had no money, and I just got board and room, so I rode the freight to Colorado to find work."

"How old were you then?" I said.

"I was still fifteen," he said. "My brother Bryson was eight years older, and he'd taught me how to do it. You run as fast as you can and catch the ladder at the front end of the boxcar. I caught one in Tucson and then one out of El Paso, and I'll bet there were two hundred guys on it. There might have been thirty professional bums, but most were guys tryin' to find work. I got to Tucumcari and rode one from there to Denver, and in Englewood I got a job on a dairy and wheat farm for thirty dollars a month and board and room. I worked there for two months that summer, and then McMinn wrote me he had a bunch of horses and he'd give me a job for the winter.

"I went back to Tucson for the winter and worked for McMinn, but there just wasn't any money. Nobody had any, and my brother Bryson had sewed sacks on the wheat harvest in Walla Walla, Washington, and he thought we should go out there, so we did."

"What was that trip like?"

"It was in July, and we had all our clothes in one suitcase, and we hopped a freight. We had no money. I mean I had fifteen dollars, but we ate that up this side of Denver. We'd go knock on doors and ask them if we could chop wood or mow the lawn for somethin' to eat. We'd find a boxcar with a lot of paper in it, packing paper from crates, and we'd wrap up in that. We had a bar of soap, and we'd wash in the water troughs for cattle. We hitchhiked, too.

"In La Grande, Oregon, this railroad bull ran us out of the yard. He told us he'd give us thirty days for vagrancy, so we tried all morning to hitchhike, but nobody would stop. Finally my brother Bryson said, 'We'll split. You're a lot younger lookin' than I am, and somebody will probably pick you up.' So he took the suitcase, and went down around the curve in the road, and sure enough, pretty soon this car came along. There were these two old ladies in it, and it was a real long expensive car, and they picked me up. They were goin' real slow, and when we came around the curve, there was my brother Bryson standin' with his thumb in the air, and he looked real dejected. I said, 'That's my brother Bryson there, and we're travelin' together.' But they didn't stop, and it was two-and-a-half years before I saw my brother Bryson again.' "

"What happened to him?"

"Well, we were gonna meet in the park in Pendleton, and I waited three days, walkin' from one part to another. I piled grass between two cross ties in the railroad yard and slept between them, but Bryson got a job stackin' hay for a farmer who gave two dollars a day for two weeks, and I got a job breakin' horses at a dude ranch fifty miles from Cody, and I was there until I got into the Army."

"What was that job like?"

"It was the first good job I ever had," he said. "When I got there my shirt was torn down the front and I had on these old brogan shoes, but they needed horse-breakers and I told them I could break. They said, 'We'll try you in the mornin', kid.'

"There was this long bunkhouse and they gave me a real good meal. For breakfast there was hot cakes, eggs, anything you could eat, and after we ate we went out and they cut me this bay mare out. I went up to her and put a hackamore on her and got on her and turned her, and they didn't say nothin'. They got to cuttin' me horses, and they cut me twenty-one head—not all the same day— and I rode them all. They give me sixty dollars a month and board and room, and I thought that was the highest a guy could ever get. I was the tickledest kid you ever seen, and I worked there from 1938 to February of 1942.

"My folks were real poor and my mother needed medicine, so I sent home money every month, and I bought a 1936 Chevy car and a saddle and an eiderdown sleepin' bag and a good hat and boots. Simon Snyder owned the ranch, and he was tough, but he didn't drink or smoke, and I was a kid who could have been influenced. I was ridin' those colts and they were buckin' me off, but I was gettin' back on. There were some bad horses, too, but I wasn't afraid of hittin' the ground, only that when they bucked me off that made them much worse.

"You gathered horses in the spring and fall, and some got away. There was this big sorrel horse, about twelve years old, that the riders used to let get away on purpose, but I rode him fifty miles to Cody to that rodeo, and it was the first bull ridin' trophy I won."

"And didn't you have your leg or your foot broken in that rodeo?" I said.

"No," he said. "What happened was, a bull kicked my right leg, and the muscle and tendon swelled up so I couldn't put my foot in the stirrup, and I rode back to the ranch with my leg stickin' out straight."

"The fifty miles?" I said. "How long did that take?"

"About nine hours," he said, "but I felt real good. I'd won a little over $200, which was a lot of money, and that trophy."

"And you left that job in February of '42?"

"We had just got into the war then," he said, "and Simon Snyder said to me, 'The government is allowin' me one man, and you'll be it if you want to stay out the war.' I felt awful bad leavin' him, but I'd of felt awful guilty if I hadn't been in. I sold my 1936 Chevy and got $200 for it, and went to Cheyenne and enlisted."

"What were you in?"

"I was in Fort Sill in the horse-drawn artillery, and then I transferred into mule pack as a horse-shoer. Hulen McMinn, he'd taught me, and then they sent me to the horse-shoein' school at Fort Riley. I seen right away there that a man could learn a bunch, and I wanted to learn.

"They made you sit at a desk and dissect feet for a week, and they had these feet in formaldehyde and they stunk like hell. You had to do that before you got to the blacksmith shop, and then you worked one of them forges for two weeks before you even picked up a foot. I had the highest grade ever graduated from that horse-shoein' school, and then they was wantin' people for the OSS, and they come around. They were gonna jump into Mongolia and go work with the Chinese and use little mustanglike horses. This major and this colonel that come to interview us, they asked me if I'd be afraid to jump out of an airplane and I said, 'I don't know. I never was up in one before.' "

"I like that," I said. "I hope the colonel and the major did."

"That was the truth," Freckles said. "How could I know? It's like when I was growin' up, my dad taught me things like that. He would point and say, 'What's that over there?' If I said, 'That's a cow,' he would say, 'You should say, 'I believe that's a cow.' Don't make it a fact unless you're sure.' Today when somebody says somebody throwed a steer in six seconds, I say, 'I think it was six flat.' "

"So did you jump?"

"Only in trainin'. They sent me to a school in Washington, D.C., to learn to talk Chinese in two months, and I was the only guy I knew that didn't have a college education. Then they flew us to Kunming, where we trained. We took our trainin' jumps, and I was in the Seventh Commando with 120 Chinese and seven or eight Americans, but the war ended before we had to jump behind the lines, except there were no lines really.

"In Kunming, when we were alerted to jump in, they had this rodeo. The Red Cross sponsored it and the boys in the mule pack put it on. Them mules really bucked, and I won the bareback mule ridin' and got second in the saddle-mule ridin', and I won the all-around. The G.I.s just swarmed that thing, and I think I won forty-six dollars. It cost you $2.50 an event, and they paid us in Chinese money, and we got a whole slew of that."

"Now, you'd been on the backs of animals since you were about two years old," I said, "but you'd never even been up in a plane until you volunteered. Weren't you nervous about that first jump?"

"No," he said. "There wasn't nothin' scary about the whole thing. I just figured that, if them other fellas could do it, I could do it. That opening shock shakes the hell out of you, but from then on you wish it was ten thousand feet because it's the most beautiful feeling."

During those nine days that I spent with him in '68, around the hotel and out at the Coliseum, it was like being with Vince Lombardi in Green Bay or Jack Dempsey on Broadway. At the Finals the year before, the first bull he had drawn had been Tornado, which had never been ridden in 185 times out of the chute. Freckles rode him, and they gave him three standing ovations. He rode five other rank bulls, and that last night, when they named him winner of the bull riding, the walls shook. Freckles came running out, tugging off his big hat, and the clowns, who are out there not just to amuse the crowd but to divert the bulls from the grounded riders, wrestled him down and rolled him in the dirt while the band played "Oklahoma."

Now, a year later, everywhere he went heads turned. People nudged one another and eyes followed him as he loped along, always seeming to be in a hurry, with that gimpy side-to-side gait that derives from all the broken and chipped bones in the legs, ankles, and feet.

"Down home," he said once, meaning in Soper, Oklahoma, where he ranches, "I run everywhere. You get your pickup stuck, and you gotta get the tractor, so I run and get it. You gotta get your bucket, so I run to it. If it's too far, I just run awhile and then walk a while. On the way to the house, after I've fed the calves before breakfast, I may drop down and do fifty push-ups, too. I can come in at night and be tired, and I'll just jump down there and do thirty push-ups, and it just seems like it makes me feel better.

"I learned that in the Army," he said. "If you messed up, if you took a wrong step in the dummy plane or didn't tumble right on the tower, the jump master would say, 'Give me fifty push-ups.' We did a lot of runnin' and jumpin' and tumblin', too, and when I got out I just felt it was kinda foolish not to stay in shape."

"How many push-ups can you do going on age forty-eight?" I said.

"I've done about seventy-five," he said, "but I never did try to see how many I can do. If somebody said that I'd have to do sixty after I'd done fifty, it would be a lot of effort."

During the Finals his wife, Edith, slim dark-haired and dark-eyed, had been with him. They had met and been married in 1942, while Freckles was at Fort Sill, and they have a married daughter.

"There was this buddy of mine," Freckles said once, "and he said, 'My wife works in a dime store and there's this black-haired girl there she could get you a date with.' We been married twenty-six years now."

Over a lot of those twenty-six years Edith had sat in a lot of those bleachers in a lot of those little towns where there would be more people in the trees than in the stands. She had sat up in the good seats in the good arenas, too, wherever it was just waiting for that chute gate to open again, and Freckles to come out once more on the back of another bull or another bucking horse.

"With everybody else in the place holding their breath while Freckles rides," I said to her one night, "I don't know how you can stand it. Have you ever talked to him about retiring?"

"No," she said. "That's up to Brown."

When she doesn't call him Brown, she calls him Brownie or Mister Brown and, of course, she knew what Casey Tibbs knew. Casey Tibbs won nine bronc riding championships between 1949 and 1959, and one day he was talking about Freckles.

"He's just like an old hound dog," he said. "You pen him up and take the others out huntin', and he'll howl himself to death."

In 1974, at the age of fifty-three, Freckles finally hung up his rope. The following year at the Finals they built an act around him. Red Steagall, the country singer, had written a ballad about Freckles' famous 1967 ride on Tornado, and with Steagall singing, Freckles came out under a spotlight and then they brought out a trained bull. The next year that act was over, too, and when I got out there they had a job for Freckles. During the performances he stood at the back of the announcer's stand with a headset on, co-ordinating with the stock contractors and the others back by the runways and the chutes, the stock and the riders for the various events.

Freckles and Edith had driven the two hundred miles up from Soper seven miles north of the Texas border, to Oklahoma City in a red-and-white pickup with a camper on it that belonged to their daughter, Donna, and her husband, Wiley Harrison. In a trailer behind, they had hauled two of their quarter horses for cowboys who did not have their own mounts with them to ride in the Grand Entry that opened each performance. For that they received two tickets for the week.

The Finals ended on a Saturday night, and I met them in the

motel lobby at nine o'clock the next morning. Freckles had already been out to the Fairgrounds to feed and load the two horses, and he had carried Edith's and his luggage out to the parking lot and stacked it behind the seat of the pickup. There was no room in the cab for my bag, and now he was trying to unlock the door at the back of the camper to stow it there.

"Somebody tried to jimmy this lock last night," he said. "Looka here."

Around the lock set in the metal door you could see someone had been trying to pry it open. The metal of the frame was bent and jagged.

"But there's nothing in there," I said, looking in a side window.

"Just a spare tire," he said. "They were tryin' to get that."

That was all he said. We watched him work with the key for three or four minutes until he finally opened the door.

"But doesn't he ever get mad?" I said to Edith, while Freckles was lifting my bag in. "I'm ready to turn the air blue."

"No," Edith said. "He always says, 'There's no cryin' over spilt milk. There's another rodeo tomorrow.'"

The temperature had dipped just below freezing during the night, and as Freckles drove, with Edith sitting between us, east out of Oklahoma City and then south, there were places where a heavy frost had covered the road. It had coated the grasses along the sides of the road and in the fields, and they glinted amber now in the pale morning sun.

"Is there a trick to hauling horses?" I said to Freckles, thinking of the two standing side by side and mute in the streamlined trailer behind us.

"Just to give 'em a little warning," he said. "When you want to slow, you kind of touch the brake easy at first, and when you're gonna turn you give the wheel a little touch first, so they can set theirselves."

"Tell me about your last bull," I said, "and why you finally decided to pack it in."

"My last bull was in Tulsa in '74," he said. "He bucked me off, and I lit on the back of my head. I went to this doctor, a real good bone specialist who took care of me after I come back from that time in Portland. He didn't say too much to me, but he told Edith that I had arthritis real bad, and one of them falls was liable to kill me. The neck wouldn't bend. It wasn't limber enough to stand one of them falls."

"So you told Freck?" I said to Edith.

"No," she said. "I said to the doctor, 'Did you tell him?' He said, 'You tell him.' I said, 'I'm not going to.' I told Donna, and she said, 'Tell him.' I said, 'I won't. He'll find out for himself.' And he did."

"I didn't want to rodeo that much anyway," Freckles said. "I needed to be home."

"I think he pleased a lot of people who wanted him to quit," Edith said.

"It got so," Freckles said, "that everybody was thinkin' of me like I was a soft-boiled egg."

"Do you miss it?" I said.

"No," he said. "I teach some in rodeo schools, and I judged Louisiana and also Oklahoma and the National High School Finals. I go some to banquets and talk to them kids."

"What do you tell them?"

"Well, I tell him how rodeo got started, and then I tell them you need to think you can win. I tell them not to think themselves off before they get on, and to try to stay away from them guys who've got a negative attitude. In the schools, though, when you try to teach those kids but they keep buckin' off, you want to show 'em. You want to ride 'em so bad—but I don't."

Soper has a population of 380, and it is one of those crossroads towns, two dozen or so of those low buildings of weathered white stucco or clapboard planted back from the four corners. There are a couple of grocery stores, a garage, a coin laundry, a liquor store, a dry goods store, the post office, and four churches. In 1964 Freckles and Edith bought the five hundred acres two-and-a-half miles outside of Soper on the Boggy River three miles south of where the Muddy Boggy and the Clear Boggy creeks come together. They put a native stone and knotty-pine house on it, with Freckles doing all the stonework in the foundation and fireplace and chimney.

"Before we moved to Soper," Freckles said once, "we had that place in Lawton. When we bought it, the house was just a shack, unpainted and with no windows and the floor fallin' in. It had no basement, and it was just sittin' on rocks. There were three rooms and we closed in the porch for a small room for Donna and I built a barn and a privy. This privy had no door yet, but I told Edith that if I rode my bull in Madison Square Garden in New York we'd drill a well and put in an electric pump and a bathroom, but if he bucked me off I'd just put a door on the privy. I rode him and it meant $1,300 to me, and we put in the well and I did the plumbing."

After we had driven into the yard now and carried the luggage into the house, Freckles unloaded the two horses and turned them out to pasture. Then he changed into old jeans and a jacket, and we went out and got into the 1961 pickup to feed the cattle. The two horses were grazing now near the barn.

"When your horses get old," I said, "and have to be destroyed, who does it?"

"I do," he said. "I give 'em a shot, and they just go to sleep."

"How do you dispose of them?"

"In a pit," he said. "I dig it with the scoop on my tractor, and I take the horse to where I dig it, and I just roll it in. I don't ever tell Edith, though, because they become like members of the family. I usually wait until she's goin' somewhere, and I tell her it just died."

While Freckles and Edith had been in Oklahoma City, their brother-in-law, Shorty Gordon, had been feeding the 270 head of cattle. Now Freckles drove the pickup over the rutted, red-clay road and into the first pasture. He backed it up to the open-sided hay barn and got out and loaded a couple of dozen of the seventy-five pound bales onto it.

"Doesn't lifting those bales ever bother you?" I said. "I mean, with all those broken bones you've had?"

"No, not a bit," he said. "I've got that arthritis in the back and neck though, and if I'm ridin' the tractor and lookin' back, it hurts that night."

"How about the push-ups?" I said. "Are you still doing them?"

"At night before I go to bed," he said, "and sometimes in the morning. I do about twenty-five, but I don't do near enough."

He had driven out into the pasture where, ahead, we could see the cattle, grazing in groups, over the dried, close-cropped grass. They are an off-white Charolais crossed with white-faced Herefords and Black Angus, and when he sounded the horn, they raised their heads and, seeing the truck, started toward us.

"I'll put it in low," he said. "You think you can drive it out there and around that oak and back again so I can unload?"

"I would think so," I said. "After all, Jim Tescher's kids started driving the pastures before they were three."

"That right?" he said. "How about that!"

He got out and climbed up in back with the cutting pliers to cut the wire bindings on the bales. As I drove slowly toward them, the cattle came toward us like children following a leader, and then, as I drove into them, they spread into two mooing, advancing lines to crowd against the sides of the truck. After I had made the turn beyond the oak, I could see the route we had come, the bales tossed to either side and the cattle, strung out and around the bales, forming a long aisle.

He had jumped down from the back of the truck now, and he came around to the driver's side and I moved over and he got in. He drove down to where a lone cow was standing, watching us, near some scrub growth. He got out and got a half-bale out of the back, but when he started toward her, the cow retreated into the brush. He walked in after her, and came out without the hay.

"She had a calf," he said. "A good big one, about an hour ago, and she ain't cleaned out yet. If she doesn't clean out, I'll take her into the chute and clean her and put a bolus up there as far as I can so she don't get an infection. I was just countin' the calves, though, and there were seven when we left and there's eleven now."

We went back to the hay barn, and he loaded again and we fed the cattle in two other pastures. In one of the pastures he emptied bags of commercial feed into a trough, the cattle crowding it, and when we got back to the house he started a fire in the fireplace while Edith opened the mail.

"Why, Brown," she said, "here's a letter from Mabel Dobbins, and Carlina's being married."

"That right?" he said. "Carlina?"

"Why," I said, "I remember Mabel Dobbins and Carlina."

It was a story he had told in '68. It had happened in April of 1952, while they were living in Lawton.

"I was getting ready to rodeo," he had said, "but I had this field I was gonna harrow. I was crossin' this ditch when this tractor turned over backwards on top of me. It pinned me under and broke my leg. The exhaust pipe was stuck into the ground, and that killed the engine, but the gasoline and the battery water were runnin' over me, and I lay there quite a while.

"About a hundred yards away there was this neighbor's house, and Edith was there, talkin' with Mabel Dobbins while Mabel was doin' her laundry in the washing machine in the garage. Mabel's daughter, Carlina, was four years old then, and while they were talkin' she kept runnin' in and sayin', 'Come see what Brown is doin'. Come look at Brown, and see what Brown is doin'.' Well, finally they come out, and when Edith saw that tractor upside down she run right out of her shoes. She run through some stubble and skinned her feet, and I told her, 'Go find somebody to come with a jack.' By the time they got there, though, I had got the seat out from under me and crawled out, but it was the most painful break I ever had.

"Then I was tryin' to hire somebody to drive that tractor, because I was gonna put in sweet feed, but everybody kept puttin' me off. Then one morning I got up and I heard this racket outside and there they were. There were twenty-eight big tractors with the operators, and the women brought in the food—meat loaves, lots of chicken, vegetables. Each woman brought what she had fixed for the family, only more, and they had the table out in front of the house. Those tractors started at 8 A.M., and some of them worked until dark."

That was typical. When Freckles got out of the Army he hired out to break horses, and he shod horses, rodeoed, and did janitor work in a taxi garage in Lawton. When he bought the land in Lawton, Andy Jordan, the taxi owner, loaned him $2,000—"with no note or nothin'," Freckles said—to buy twenty-five cows. Todd Whatley, a bull rider and steer wrestler, loaned him $32,000—"on just my word"—to buy the place in Soper, and he paid each loan back within a year.

"Last year," Freckles was saying now, "Wiley, my son-in-law, was helpin' me and we were gonna go and spray the cattle for lice and flies. We got a hose, and we were runnin' water into a barrel, and Wiley left the tractor in second gear. I reached down and clutched it with my hand and pulled the power take-off lever on it. It ran straight up my feet and right up my belly and right up my chest and right over my head, jaws, and ears. It mashed my chest in, and it was quite a while before I could get any wind.

"I got up to the house, and I could see kind of a blur and I lay down on the bed. Edith, she called the doctor. I went into the hospital and they X-rayed me, and it was nothin'. Shorty, my brother-in-law, thought we were playin' a joke on Edith, and he said to her, 'What will those bastards think of next?' "

"Those tractors," Edith said, "scare me more than those bulls."

The next morning, after breakfast, we went out and Freckles scraped the heavy frost off the windshield of the truck and I drove over the frozen ground while Freckles fed the cattle again. Then we came in and sat in front of the fire and talked while we waited for Skipper Lofting to drive down from Oklahoma City and pick me up.

"Tornado," I said, mentioning the bull on which Freckles made his greatest ride, "I think I read that he died."

"That's right," Freckles said. "They retired him in '69 and he died in '72, I think, and they buried him at the Cowboy Hall of Fame in Oklahoma City. I read it in the paper. There was just a little piece about him, but the cowboys liked him. Some bulls they don't like, but he looked good when he bucked, and he throwed everybody a long way off and he fought the clowns. He bucked some guys off and stomped on them, but he wasn't a dangerous bull, and when I read that he died I was a little sad."

"Well, he helped to make you famous in rodeo," I said. "When you were growing up, did you ever want to be famous?"

"No, no," he said. "Not at all. I just wanted to be a good hand."

"I wonder today," I said, "How many of the young want to grow up to just be good hands. What do you think is happening in this country?"

"This country?" he said. "I worry about it some. When I was growin' up, my mother and dad, they taught you everything you needed to know before you left. They taught the girls how to cook. They taught the boys how to build a fence, how to set post holes right, how to fix a corner fence, how to stack hay, how to harness and how to do up lines. I was probably seven or eight years old workin' teams.

"Kids don't know how to do things with their hands now. Then I see kids get thrown off, and they lie there and moan and beat the ground. When I was four years old, they were gonna let me go to school and visit one day. I was tryin' to get on this horse, by the potato cellar on the bank, and I threw a leg over and slipped off and the horse stepped on my leg. I started to cry, and my sister Ella said, 'Stop cryin'. Momma will hear you, and she won't let you go to school.'

"That's the way we were brought up then," he said. "We had a Great Depression, and we had no money. Nobody had no money, and the younger generation, if they had to go to work for almost no money, I don't know what would happen. Some could handle it, I guess, but a lot couldn't."

There were some, of course, who couldn't handle it then, either, but this one did. When Skipper Lofting drove up and came in, Edith made coffee, and after we had talked for a while, Freckles walked us out to the car.

"Now take care," I said, as we shook hands, "and stop fighting those tractors."

"Yeah, I will," he said, "and you come see us again. We'd really enjoy it."

"I would, too," I said.

We drove out the rutted, red-soil driveway that was softening into mud now under the midday sun. We were heading for Cut and Shoot, Texas.

"I'll probably never see him again," I said to Skipper, "but after I've been with him I feel a lot better for it."

"I do, too," Skipper said. "The old coot is something special."

7

The Backwoods Battler

They are a God-fearing people who cling to an old
order even though schools, power saws and bull-
dozers are moving them into oblivion. For decades
they rightly assumed that the land was theirs for the
hunting, whoever might have the title.

Supreme Court Justice William O. Douglas

We drove west out of Soper to Durant and then south across the
Red River and into Texas. It was midafternoon when we saw
Dallas rising in the sunlight out of the level plain like a cropped
Camelot, its rectangular and flat-topped corporate towers short of
the clouds where men's dreams lie, for there is a difference between aspiring and dreaming, and corporations aspire. We skirted
the city on the by-pass and put up in Corsicana, and the next
morning we drove the Interstate through the mist and rain into
Conroe in time to have lunch at the motel.

"Did you get him?" Skipper Lofting said when I came off the
phone.

"Yes," I said. "I went through two secretaries at Roy Harris
Real Estate, and it turns out that he not only runs that, but he's
also the clerk of Montgomery County. He'll see us at the County
Court House after lunch."

"Doesn't he kind of surprise you?" Skipper said.

"Everything about this story surprised me," I said. "After all,
how many times in his life does a reporter sit down with a subject
and say, 'Now, tell me about the time your Uncle Bob cut a man's
head off.'?"

"Well, not every day," Skipper said. "Sometimes not even once a week."

In 1957 Roy Harris was the fifth ranking heavyweight in the world and moving toward a fight with Floyd Patterson for the title. What interested *The Saturday Evening Post,* though, was not how well he could fight, but that he was out of a place called Cut and Shoot, Texas, on the western fringe of the Big Thicket where time, apparently, had come to a halt at the turn of the century.

In June of that year I flew out of New York to Houston on a dinner flight, and I checked into the Rice Hotel, and the next morning Lou Viscusi picked me up. Lou had managed Willie Pep to the featherweight title, and he had Joe Brown, who was then the lightweight champion, and he was also promoting fights in Houston. In his powder-blue, air-conditioned Cadillac we drove the forty miles north to Conroe, and then turned right onto Route 105. After a couple of miles we turned right again onto a farm-to-market and then off that and right once more onto a dirt road. We had gone about three tenths of a mile and were coming out of a grove of tall pines when he stopped the car.

"Well, there it is," he said. He is a stocky, broad-chested man, but his voice is rather high and laughter was in it now.

"You're kidding," I said. "That's the set from *Tobacco Road.* You had it hauled in here, and this is a gag."

"No, no," he said still laughing. "This is the way they live, and this is the way they are."

Strung out in the clearing about fifty yards ahead of us was a tin-roofed combination of log house and clapboard cabin with a porch running across the front, all of it raised about a foot and a half on piles. A wisteria vine was climbing one of the two-by-fours that supported the porch roof, and there was a traffic of hound dogs, chickens, and a couple of hogs in the yard. On the porch, and sitting in what turned out to be rope-bottomed chairs, were three men, one of them in bib overalls, another in a flowered sports shirt and chinos, and one bare-chested, and there were two women and a couple of children.

"They're eying us pretty good," Lou said. "I'd better drive in and introduce you before they come out after us."

"Hell, yes," I said, "and I wish we'd come with a horse and wagon instead of this Caddy."

It was mid-June and warm and humid, and we left our jackets in the car, and walked across the ground that was strewn with dried corn cobs, several worn automobile tires, a couple of rusting wheel covers, and sections of inner tubes, the hounds sniffing at us and the chickens scattering ahead of us. Big Henry, Roy's father and in the flowered sports shirt and chinos, came down off the porch and Lou introduced me. Then Big Henry introduced Uncle Cleve, in the overalls, Roy's older brother, Tobe, bare-chested, Roy's mother, and three of his four younger sisters.

"You from New York?" Big Henry said, as we sat down.

"Yes," I said, and then, trying to get out of the big city as soon as I could, "but I live in Connecticut."

"Ever been to Texas before?"

"No," I said, "but I have a couple of good friends who are Texans and whom I greatly admire."

"That right?"

"Oh, yes. One of them is General James Earl Rudder, who's the Texas Land Commissioner now, and who on D-Day led 250 Rangers up a ninety-foot cliff in Normandy. I think he's Roy's CO in the Army Reserve now."

"You know him?"

"Very well," I said. "Two years ago I took him and his thirteen-year-old son back to Normandy and the cliff for an article for the tenth anniversary of D-Day."

"You did that?"

"Yes, and the other Texan for whom I have great respect is Lew Jenkins, who was once the lightweight champion of the world."

"You know Lew Jenkins?"

Here we go, I thought. For the next fifteen or twenty minutes I told stories about Lew Jenkins. I told how I met him off Normandy when he was in the Coast Guard and had put the infantry ashore in Sicily and Salerno and the British ashore behind the Jap lines in Burma and then again in Normandy. I told how he was ashamed because he left them there to be killed and wounded and how he told me that if there were ever another war and we were in it, he would join the infantry. There was, in Korea, and he enlisted in the infantry and won the Silver Star, and I told that and some stories about Lew as a fighter, scrambling, as one of those the nesters in the Big Thicket used to refer to as "those town-raised bastards," for rapport.

"I got along fine with Big Henry," I was telling Skipper at lunch now, "but the cultural shock of re-entry from a champagne dinner flight and an air-conditioned Cadillac to that was something."

There were nine rooms in the log house and the clapboard cabin that the Harrises had jockeyed together fifteen years before. There was a naked light bulb centered in the ceiling of each room, and in the kitchen there were a refrigerator, a freezer, and a washing machine. Loose screening hung over the windows in the clapboard section, but the others were open to the flies, moths, and mosquitoes. Behind the house there was a hundred-gallon water tank on twelve-foot pipe legs, and it supplied the faucet in the kitchen and an outdoor spigot. The water was forced up into the tank under gas pressure from one of the oil wells that dotted the area and that Big Henry tended, and it tasted as if it were laced with gasoline.

"For an hour or so," I was saying, "Lou Viscusi and I sat on that porch and Big Henry answered my questions, and then they invited us in to lunch. The men sat down and the women served. They brought on these ham steaks, about three-quarters of an inch thick. The men, bearing down on their forks, cut right through the steaks, but I couldn't make it. I looked over at Lou and he was having the same trouble, so I said to Big Henry, 'I'm sorry, but may I have a knife?' He nodded to his wife and she went into the kitchen and came back and handed me a wooden-handled butcher's knife. Lou and I passed that knife back and forth. And then there were the flies. I kept shooing them off my food, but I noticed that the others paid no attention to them. They'd cut a piece of ham steak and then, as they brought it up, flip it or something, because the flies would leave before the food went into the mouths."

"Are you planning on us dining out there this trip?" Skipper said.

"I don't even know if anyone lives out there now," I said, "but I sure want to revisit the site."

About fifty feet from the house there was a weather-beaten boxing ring, and beyond it, on the shore of a mustard-colored fish-and-alligator pond, the upper half of an old, heavy punching bag hung from an elm festooned with Spanish moss. From another branch a climbing rope dangled, and a light punching bag on its support was affixed to a limb of a sweet-gum tree. Over the pond Big Henry had rigged a natural gas flare that burned night and day to attract insects that, singed by it, dropped into the pond as food for the perch, bass, catfish, and bream.

"The boxin' started here," Big Henry was telling me that first day back in '57, "when I had some old ducks. Tobe said, 'Can I have those ducks?' He took 'em down the road, and when he come back, he'd traded them for a set of boxing gloves."

"Then Roy and I started pokin' one another," Tobe said.

"We put that ring up seven-eight years ago," Big Henry said, "but they never did use it much. They fought all their lives barefoot on the ground. We made sort of a ring there. Two sides were barbed wire from the vegetable patch, and the other two sides were ropes, and others used to come in. What I did was run me up a gas flare over it, and they'd box under that, startin' every afternoon at five o'clock. We'd have six to a dozen here every night, with just me and Uncle Cleve settin' up here on the porch in these chairs and watchin'."

"And how long would these sessions last?" I said.

"Maybe to midnight," Big Henry said, "dependin' on how many arguments started. Then I used to go in and haul the bullies out of those honky-tonks. You know, those I-kin-whip-anybodies? I'd haul 'em out here and put 'em in with the boys, and the boys'd lick 'em."

Big Henry was six-feet-two-and-a-half inches, handsome, and at age forty-seven weighed 237 pounds. He said that when he was in his twenties he weighed 210, and had a thirty-three-inch waist, a seventeen-and-a-half-inch neck, and sixteen-inch biceps, and I used to imagine him—rather than his six-foot, 190-pound second son—fighting Floyd Patterson.

"Each community had their strong boy then," he said, "and their best roper and their best rider. I was their stout boy, and I never was beat."

The Harris clan had been led out of Oklahoma early in this century by John Wesley "Cussin'" Harris. He had made the land rush there in 1889, but when the Territory became too crowded for him he moved south into Palestine, Texas, then into Conroe and finally, in 1913, into the Big Thicket. During the next twenty-five years, three of his sixteen offspring—Jack, Bob, and Henry—established themselves as the best fist, knee, knife, club, and heel fighters in the area.

"Is it true," I asked Big Henry on the second day that Lou Viscusi had driven me out there, "that one afternoon Bob laid out fourteen men with an ax handle?"

"Don't know how many Bob got himself," Big Henry said. "I remember they took sixteen to the hospital. After it was over, there was a tuft of brown hair here, a tuft of black hair here, teeth over there. Lookin' at that piece of ground, you'd think men fought over it for ten hours."

"How long did the fight last?" I said.

"Ten minutes," Big Henry said, "but I'd rather not talk about that kinda thing. I don't want no damn family fracas startin' up again."

I had bought this, and all else that was to follow, because I had been prepped by Ed Watson, the editor of the *Conroe Daily Courier,* who had led me to J. T. Montgomery, then the principal of Conroe's William B. Travis Junior High School and a local historian. He, in turn, had referred me to Guy Hooper, a former sheriff. Twenty-five years before, Hooper had had a stockade erected to hold the Harrises and the other nesters of the Big Thicket they led on horseback into open warfare against the invaders who had discovered beneath the sandy loam and clay the nation's third largest and richest oil field. Now Hooper was retired on an oil fortune, and we talked on the phone.

"The Harrises are really great people," he said. "They fight like hell, but they're honest. They never lie."

I visited J. T. Montgomery at the junior high school, and found him affable, filled with his subject, and hoping to write a book about the Big Thicket. It is one of this continent's natural phenomena, for within its five thousand square miles there are more than one hundred kinds of trees, among them fifteen that are the tallest known specimens of their species, thirty species of ferns, four types of insect-eating plants, thirty species of orchids and nine hundred varieties of other flowering plants. There are an estimated one thousand species of algae and fungi and at least three hundred bird species, and for a hundred years it was a refuge for those who just wanted to get away—Indians, runaway slaves, Confederate Army deserters, outlaws, and moonshiners.

"Cut and Shoot got its name from a church squabble they had there in 1910," Montgomery told me. "There were two factions in the Baptist Church on the banks of Caney Creek, and I don't know how much cuttin' and shootin' there was, but Alfred Morris, a lawyer here in Conroe, named it, and the name stuck.

"I'll tell you one thing about those people in the Big Thicket, though. When they like you, they're for you all the way, and Henry Harris is the best friend I've ever had in my life. When they don't like you, though, you don't know it until you wake up in the hospital or with somebody throwin' cold water on your face. You never know what those people are thinkin'.

"You have to remember that they're independent people. That's why they went into the Thicket—to maintain their independence. They've always believed in the law, but their own law. They've got an extremely high code of honor, and they've always fought for it. You ask Roy about that. Ask him about the time his Uncle Bob cut a man's head off."

"Ask him what?" I said.

"Ask him about the time his Uncle Bob cut a man's head off," Montgomery said. "He'll tell you about that."

"You're not stringing me?" I said.

"No, no," Montgomery said. "You just ask Roy. He'll tell you the truth."

Roy was twenty-four years old, mild-mannered, polite, and it seemed to me, the least likely of the Harris adult males to be challenging for the heavyweight championship of the world. He had been an honor student in junior high and high school, and the year before he had been graduated from Sam Houston State Teachers College in Huntsville, thirty miles north of Conroe. When he was not boxing he was teaching spelling, reading, writing, arithmetic, and geography in the Stephen F. Austin Elementary School in Cut and Shoot. He also taught in the Seventh-Day Adventist Church and was a second lieutenant in the Army Reserve.

I had met him that second day—he had returned the night before from two weeks of maneuvers with the 90th infantry Division at Fort Polk, Louisiana—on the porch of the Harris homestead. While in his senior year at Sam Houston State Teachers, he had married Jean Groce, whom he first met in a homemaking class in high school, and they were living in a new white, blue-roofed, three-rooms-and-bath cottage just beyond the fish-and-alligator pond.

"This pond," I said to him, as we skirted it on the way to the cottage. "Are there any alligators in it now?"

"Only a couple," he said.

"How big are they?" I said, eying the pond.

"Well," he said, "about six years ago Tobe went over to a lake about ten miles from here, and he got out in a boat and he roped one. The 'gator turned the boat over and he dragged Tobe through the water for a while, but finally Tobe got ashore and he tied the rope around a button-willow tree, and he came home.

"All that night that button-willow tree played that 'gator like a fish pole, and the next day my dad and Tobe went down in the truck. They horsed that 'gator with the truck for a while to tire him out some more, and then they pulled him out and brought him over here. He was fourteen feet, two inches, and weighed about a thousand pounds. Then he ate a couple of our dogs, so Bob shot him."

"After all that trouble getting him in here?" I said. "Does that sort of thing go on all the time?"

"We had a couple in here that were eleven-and-a-half-feet and nine-and-a-half feet," he said. "We had this English Bull six weeks old, named Rowdy, and he'd go down to get a drink, and one morning we couldn't find him. A week or two later we had a hound pup, three or four months old, that disappeared. We had these fox hound puppies and one was sleepin' and a 'gator got him. The other puppies got scared and ran to the house, and they bayed that pond for two weeks. They got fifteen or twenty of our hogs, too, but my dad didn't care. We had lots of them, and they were mixed breeds."

The cottage was immaculate, and we talked at the kitchen table. I asked him about his schooling and about some of his fights, amateur and professional, hoping meanwhile that I would be able to maneuver the dialogue so that I might gracefully, if that could be possible, bring up the subject of his Uncle Bob and the other man's head.

"I've spent some time with J. T. Montgomery," I said. "He has great respect for you Harrises, and he was telling me about some of the fights your folks have had. What brought those fights on?"

"Mostly," Roy said, "they'd come about when somebody'd invite them not to come to a dance."

"They'd invite them *not* to come?"

"That's right," he said. "Once they invited Jack not to come to a dance, and he and Henry and Bob went. Jack, he went around and asked each lady to dance, and none of them would. Then he walked to the middle of the floor and he said, 'There isn't a lady here wants to dance. I asked them all, and before I let any of you make 'em dance, I'll die and go to hell.'

"One of them pulled a pistol on Jack, and Jack took his pistol and beat it to pieces on him. That pistol was pretty shackledy when he got done, and that fella was bleedin' from the mouth and ears, and if Bob hadn't turned him over he'd a drowned in his own blood. Then another one ran up behind Jack and hit him with a rail off a rail fence, and Jack grabbed it and hit him across the back and broke his back. You see, when people came out to Cut and Shoot to a dance and got back in one piece, they thought they'd really done something."

Well, I was thinking, this is it. If I don't ask it now I may never, and even if I do and get an answer and write it, they may not believe it in Philadelphia.

"J. T. Montgomery," I said, "told me to be sure to ask you about the time your Uncle Bob cut a man's head off."

"There was this gang of boys," he said, and it evolved as if I had asked him to tell me about trapping a fox or treeing a coon. "They had beat up several people in town. There were eleven of them, and one night they called Bob out on the road to give him a drink of whiskey. When he turned it up to drink, they hit him over the head with a car jack, and then one of them jumped Bob on the ground and started knifin' him.

"Bob, he opened his own knife with his teeth, and he cut that fella's neck through on one side and then the other. That fella got up and ran in a circle about fifteen feet, like a chicken with his head hangin' back, and then he fell dead. But he'd cut Bob to the holler in thirteen places."

"To the what?" I said.

"To the hollow parts of his body," he said. "They thought Bob was gonna die, but he didn't. They ruled it was self-defense, and Bob always said that other fella was the best one of the bunch, and he was sorry he'd had to kill him. He said the others had talked that fella into it. About four years ago one of them came up to his daddy's funeral, and Bob told him to leave, that the county wasn't big enough for both of them.

"Bob," he was saying now, "he got in fights with his knife a lot of times. My dad has a place in his head you can put your two fingers in, but Bob is shorter and active and fast. He used to run the hundred in less than ten seconds, and he could turn a flip backwards and forwards easily. I can turn a front flip, but I never could do the back flip too good. Bob is fifty now, and there was this mound of soft dirt, and he hadn't done a back flip in ten years. He went six feet in the air and landed on his head."

"From what I've heard," I said, "from your dad and J. T. Montgomery and Ed Watson, at the paper in Conroe, you're not of the same temperament. Have you ever had any fights outside the ring?"

"Only one, really," he said.

"Tell me about that one."

"Just a second," he said, and he stood up and was looking out of the window. "There's a squirrel come in and stole an ear of corn. Let me holler to Bob and let him go over there and kill him. Hey, Bob! Hey, Henry! There's a squirrel in the corn!

"Bob or Henry'll get him," he said, sitting down again. "What was it you asked?"

"About the one fight you've had outside the ring."

"It was in college," he said. "I was in the ROTC and this fella was my CO, and he'd chew on me. In military class he'd say how shaggy I looked, and he'd straighten my cap. He'd do that four or five times in one day, in front of everybody, and I'd just say, 'But I haven't touched my cap, sir, since you fixed it.' At first I thought it was a joke, but then he'd do it in civilian clothes, too.

"He was from Houston Heights, and a dignified dresser, and a lot of times I wore blue jeans, and he'd say how country I looked.

I didn't wear shoes until high school, and a lot of times I didn't wear 'em then. Well, this particular day I guess I was a little on the bad side and he met me on the campus. He said something about my clothes, and I swung on him with a right hand. He kinda ducked and it grazed him and spun him around, and I hit him a left hook over his eye and and split it and knocked him down. I kicked in a couple of his ribs, and I kicked him in the face. I skinned most of the hide off one side of his face and part off the other. There were some teachers came runnin', and some were hollerin' out of the windows, and they stopped it.

"If I'da had time to do a good job on him," he said, "I believe I'da made a friend of him. Half whippin' a man like that doesn't do any good. You just make an enemy, and I felt sorry about that. I really did. That was on a Saturday, and on Monday I came back and they called me before a board with three military men on it— a colonel, a major, and a captain. They kicked me out of school, but the student organizations threatened to go on srike. They wrote all kinds of deals and put them on the bulletin boards, so after a couple of days they let me back."

After lunch now Skipper Lofting and I got into his car to drive to the County Court House. A light rain was still falling, and he was backing the car out of the parking space.

"How good a fighter was Roy?" he said.

"He was good enough to beat Willie Pastrano, and later Willie won the light-heavyweight title," I said. "In the Patterson fight he had Floyd on the deck in the second round."

"I don't remember that fight," Skipper said.

"It was in Wrigley Field in Los Angeles and on theater TV," I said. "Patterson used to bob straight up and down, and in the second round, Roy caught him with the perfect combination—a left hook to the body, and when Floyd ducked straight down, a right uppercut under the chin dropped him. He got right up, and after that round it was all Floyd. Roy was cut over both eyes and his nose was bleeding and he was down four times when Big Henry, who was in the corner in a bright red shirt, and Bill Gore, who trained Roy for the fight, stopped it in the twelfth round. Patterson just punched too fast for him, and afterwards everybody wrote about Roy's guts."

In the nineteen years since I had been in Conroe the population of the county had more than tripled to about 125,000. Traffic was crawling over the wet streets, and we found what seemed to be the last parking space across from the white marble and white brick County Court House. We managed to become lost in the big building, but in the office of the County Clerk, one of the women at the more than a dozen desks behind a waist-high counter led us back to Roy's office.

"Well," I said, as we shook hands, "you still look like Roy Harris."

"Yeah, but a little heavier," he said, smiling. He was wearing a dark blue leisure suit and a blue-and-white-figured sports shirt, the collar open. His full head of glossy black hair was carefully groomed, his black eyebrows heavier than I remembered.

"You remember my wife, Jean?" he said.

She is dark-haired and had on a black pants suit. We shook hands and I introduced Skipper.

"We haven't had time for lunch," Roy said. "We thought we'd go across the street to the drugstore."

In Carter's Drugstore, on the corner of Main and Davis, we took the last booth on the left beyond the soda fountain. Roy and his wife ordered Coke floats, and Skipper a cup of coffee.

"How long have you been County Clerk?" I said.

"Ten years," he said. "I was workin' in real estate, and I'd always had an interest in law. My grandfather on my father's side was a lawyer."

"I remember about "Cussin' " Harris," I said.

They said he was three-quarters Indian, a six-foot-three-inch 200 pounder who thought it was a disgrace for a man to take money for fighting. He had been reading law and practicing it in Oklahoma, where he was a justice of the peace, before the day of bar exams and before he led the family south and into the Big Thicket. There he and his family raised their own crops and livestock, fished, shot game, and made moonshine whiskey, but he would emerge whenever one or more of the nesters ran afoul of the law.

"He cussed a lot," Roy had told me, "and whenever he defended anybody in court in Conroe they came from miles around just to listen to him. They crowded that courtroom, and I guess his greatest victory was when he defended himself. One night somebody hollered that the revenuers were comin', and Granny poured the whiskey down through the floor boards of the cabin and Uncle Bob threw the coil from the still out into the corn field and the dome into the creek. In court he convinced them that, with the equipment they had there as evidence, they couldn't prove it was a still. Then he got a court order forcin' them to return it and put it back together again."

"So I studied law," Roy was saying now. "I went to the University of Arkansas Law School in 1961, but I didn't go but one year. They have a lot of b.s. they put you through the first year, and it's all right for a kid, but I was a little older. I came home and studied in a law office for around three years and passed the bar exam and became a country lawyer.

"Then I figured the best way to learn about county government was to get into it. I didn't care to be a judge, but to be in a position to help other people and provide a service. I enjoy people, and I figured that county clerk would be the best position to be in."

"How long have you been in real estate?" I said.

"Around sixteen years," he said. "I paid $10 an acre for my first 1,000 acres in Arkansas, and it's layin' there now probably worth $250 an acre. Last year I bought land for $250 an acre that's probably worth $500 an acre now. I've got about 2,000 acres in Lawrence County, Arkansas and 440 in Randolph, and my father bought a place adjoining mine."

"Your dad doesn't live out in Cut and Shoot any more?"

"No," he said. "His place is still there, but the wells are dead now. He left, though, before they played out, because so many people moved in and it kinda messed up his life. He likes people, but he likes to be by himself, too."

"How is his health?"

"He's sixty-seven now, but his health is good. My Uncle Bob's not so good, though. He had a stroke, and his left arm and left leg don't mind him so good any more."

"They used to mind him very well," I said, "especially when they called him out onto the road that night."

"That's right," he said. "He used to be the strongest and fastest man ever lived. He used to turn flips frontwards and backwards."

"How's your brother Tobe?"

"Tobe's in Arkansas, too," he said. "He's married and workin' in real estate some and on the farm there. He had a lot of hard luck, but Tobe is smart. He always read easy, and he read a lot and made 140 in those I.Q. tests."

"When I was out here before," I said, "I got the impression that Tobe didn't think too highly of me."

"Oh?" Roy said. "I don't know."

"On the last day," I said, "I was saying good-by on the porch, and I shook hands with your dad. He said, 'Now the next time you come, don't stay in that hotel in Houston. Come stay with us.' I thanked him, and he said, 'You know, that first day you came out here you told those stories about Lew Jenkins. I always admired Lew Jenkins, and when I found out that you knew him and admired him, too, I knew you were all right.' Then I walked over to Tobe to shake hands and he looked me right in the eye and said, 'We've got a fella down the road with a bigger nose than you.'"

"Tobe said that?" Roy said now. "Heck, I've got a cousin would just really put you to shame. He lives in Arkansas now, too."

"How about Cousin Armadillo?" I said.

He was four years older than Roy, and not of the Harris clan, and one afternoon we drove by the shack in which he was living. It, too, stood on log pilings, and Cousin Armadillo had hollowed out the ground beneath it so that, on hot and humid nights, he could lie there on a quilt and benefit from any cooling breezes.

"About ten years ago," Roy had explained to me, "they had a bounty on armadillos here. They'd pay you ten cents for a pair of ears, and when we'd want to go fishin', all he wanted to do was hunt armadillos. He'd come in with thirty or forty pairs of ears, so we gave him the name."

Cousin Armadillo, according to J. T. Montgomery, had experienced great difficulty in mastering the intricacies of reading, writing, and arithmetic, and so in junior high school he had spent most of his time in the gym. One day he tied a can to a hound dog and sent it howling through the halls, and on another occasion, while the band played on the front steps in celebration of some historic event, Cousin Armadillo, from a high window, pelted the leader and the musicians with overripe tomatoes he had hauled to the top floor.

"Cousin Armadillo?" Roy said now. "He's in the penitentiary in Huntsville. He killed one of the neighbor boys, and I think they gave him twenty years. It's been several years ago, and they were old stealin' buddies. They went around and stole things in the oil fields, and Armadillo'd been sent up before on a deal. He felt the other fella had turned State's evidence, and he was kind of gunnin' for him.

"Armadillo had married a woman who had a little boy, and they were eating in a joint out in Cut and Shoot. This fella walked in, and the kid had on kind of a helmet, and he thumped the kid on the helmet. Armadillo said something, and the other fella drew his knife. Armadillo jumped up and pulled his pistol and shot him through the heart. The other fella sat down, and he said, 'You've been wantin' to do this for a long time, Armadillo.' And he died there.

"Armadillo ran to my daddy's house, and my daddy called the sheriff. Every time he got in trouble he ran to my daddy's house. A lot of people did that when they got in trouble, I guess because they thought he knew a lot about trouble and was always around it."

I looked over at Skipper Lofting, who was sitting across from me and next to Roy. He was sipping coffee and looking at me, and he raised his eyebrows.

"There's a fella over here," Roy said now, indicating a man standing at the counter to our left, "who was in college with me."

"When you did that job on that dude from Houston Heights?" I said.

"That's right," he said. "There's another, Charles Denman, who's a lawyer here in town now, and he and Dan Rather were among the student leaders who helped get me back in."

"Dan Rather, the CBS newsman?"

"That's right," he said. "I always liked Dan, and he was always fair."

"When you fought Patterson," I said, "and had him down, you must have thought at that moment that you could beat him and become the heavyweight champion of the world."

"I did," he said, "and I still do. Three weeks ahead of the fight

I knew I wasn't right. Lou Viscusi knew it when he came out there, that I was over my peak. I was young then, and I thought that the harder you work the better you get, but once you reach your peak you go down.

"I was readin' these stories about the boxing game, and I thought maybe my own people weren't on my side. Lou and Bill Gore wanted me to take a week off. If I'd listened to them I'da won the fight because of the way I handled him the first few rounds. Lew is a fine fella, just as straight as an arrow, just one hundred per cent, and Bill's gone now, but he was, too. I just didn't know."

When we left the drugstore and walked back across the street to the Court House, his wife got into her Cadillac to drive home. Roy and Skipper and I go into his, and we drove to his real estate office. It occupies a one-story brick building, painted white, and on a wall of the reception room he showed us an old, framed photograph of "Cussin'" Harris and Granny Harris riding a mule. He explained that this had been taken in Palestine, Texas, right after they had come out of Oklahoma Territory, and after he had signed some letters, we drove back to the Court House.

"You'd never believe this would happen in the United States of America," he was saying as we drove into the parking space beneath one wing of the building. "That's one of our sheriffs there, and he's gonna quit to take a job in private industry protection. You wouldn't believe that you'd have to protect everything."

On the wall behind his desk there were five shelves of bound volumes entitled *Texas Civil Statutes*. He check through some memos on his desk and made a phone call, and then he settled back in his chair.

"Driving in here," I said, "you remarked about what's happening to this country, about the need for private protection."

"That's right," he said. "I think we're being infiltrated by other countries tryin' to tear us down. They know they can't defeat us militarily, and nobody is goin' to drop the big bomb. They find a minority group, and they shove and agitate them and push 'em, and everybody feels a little sorry for himself anyway.

"They tell the Indians how bad they were treated, and the Nigra they tell how's he's been mistreated. Every minority they sell a bill of goods. You can't live in the past, and I don't think our government has put enough emphasis on braggin' on our country. Our country is the greatest country in the world. We've got the greatest people in the world. We've made more progress in two hundred years than the rest of the world in two thousand, done by people who didn't know it was impossible to do it. It's like an army charge up a hill. That happened in World War II and in Korea. The boys did it because they didn't know they couldn't do it.

"We don't have a democracy any more," he said. "We have a bureaucracy. When the population grows, they appoint people to do this or that so they won't have to shoulder the responsibility themselves. They turn it over to HUD and say, 'Well, that's the regulation.' There's no place for the individual to go for relief, and thousands of people get hurt for years before there's a public outcry.

"The other problem we've got," he said, "is too many people drivin' the wagon who don't help pushin'—people on relief and welfare with the right to vote and holdin' the balance of power. If they want to ride in the wagon, they should be content to ride where they're told to sit, and not be at the steerin' wheel and tellin' us where to go. They don't know how many of them can ride without breakin' it down.

"Only the productive people should be allowed to vote. I don't mean the old folks. I mean the total deadbeats, and we've got third and fourth generations of people who have been just ridin'. It's goin' to get so bad that the productive people will throw up their hands and say, 'I can't go any further.' And we may have a revolution.

"You take Viet Nam," he said. "Our leaders felt we should be over there. They may have been wrong, but if one is drawn to go, and they have been enjoyin' the goodies, they should have gone. Cassius Clay, people said, 'If he can do it, I can. If they don't do nothin' to him, what can they do to me?' I don't know all the answers, but I sure know all the problems."

He and his wife, Jean, have five children, three girls who were sixteen, eleven, and three, and two boys, who were fourteen and twelve at the time. The boys, he said, usually box late afternoons or early evenings at the open-air gym that had been erected, after my visit and before the Patterson fight, on the old Harris property in Cut and Shoot.

"I'd like to see that," I said, "if they're going to work out out today."

"My boys haven't got their growth yet," he said, "so I don't know what they'll be like. They didn't grow up like me."

"Maybe that's one of the problems of this country," I said.

"I do believe they've had it too easy," he said. "You worry about them some."

"Parents always have," I said, "and in many ways it's more difficult today. Is there a drug problem down here?"

"I guess it's everywhere," he said. "I guess it's fairly open. The children know about it. They don't talk too much about it, but it's even in the smallest towns, the most remote."

"That has to be a worry."

"I worry about it some, but not about mine," he said. "I hope I've raised them better than that, and I've got confidence in them. There's been parents who've been surprised I know, but I've spent a lot of time with them, and that's what they need—time, not money. People neglect their kids, and try to make up for it with money. Poverty isn't so bad if there's love that goes with it."

"So what do you think the answer to the drug problem is?"

"It's very simple," he said. "They could cure it in thirty days if they wanted to. They don't want to. If you want to cure it, you've got to make up your mind what you want to do, and whenever the people decide to do it, they can do it. When you go to cure it, you have to make the penalty hanging by the neck when they catch a drug pusher. If they started hangin' them on the court house steps, it'd be over in thirty days.

"I don't want to hurt anybody," he said, "but if a man gave drugs to one of my kids, I'd kill him. I'd cut his throat. If they hung them and gave it TV coverage, they could cure it easy in thirty days. That's cruel, but look at how cruel it is to destroy those kids, their minds.

"Does Skipper know about Roe Brown?" he said now, abruptly.

"No," Skipper said. "I don't believe I do."

"You didn't tell him about Roe Brown?" Roy said to me.

"No," I said, "but I remember him."

Roe had married Big Henry's sister Sibby. He was about five feet eight inches and weighed about ninety pounds and had a handlebar mustache.

"They claimed he was the champion storyteller in the county," I said, "but your dad said to me, 'He's the greatest in the world. They think Walt Disney is good, but they should get around Roe.'"

"That's right," Roy said, smiling.

"Your dad said, 'Once Roe gets started on a story, if you don't watch yourself you get soaked up in that stuff and you set there for twenty-four hours.' He said they used to have lying contests, and the people would bet on Roe—and he'd beat everybody."

"That's right," Roy said, and then to Skipper. "They brought this other fella in once, and they were supposed to tell fishin' stories. Roe, he went first, and he started off on how the weather was and the time of day, and how he'd catch these fish and haul them in. It took him several hours, and he'd always go 'huh-huh' so you couldn't interrupt him. He told about the kinds of trees and the way the branches were and the kinds of birds in the branches. Well, this other fella that they'd brought in and had bet Henry $10, he just paid Henry and left without even tellin' his story."

December darkness had fallen when we left the office at five o'clock. I got into Roy's car with him, and Skipper Lofting followed us in his. We drove through traffic over the black, rain-slicked pavement that reflected the car lights and the street lights and the glow from the store windows, and then he turned right onto Route 105, as Lou Viscusi had that first time almost two decades before.

"I saw Floyd Patterson not long ago," I said.

"Floyd?" Roy said. "How's Floyd doin'?"

"He's fine," I said. "He and his wife split up, and he married a white woman who was his secretary, and they have two little girls. He's concerned about the drug problem, too, and he's started a boxing club to try to combat it. He's also started taking piano lessons to encourage one of his daughters who is, I guess, as shy as he used to be. He believes, as you do, in spending time with his children."

"I'm glad to hear that," Roy said.

"He's miffed, though," I said, "about something you said about him and that, he felt, degraded him."

"Is that so?" he said. "I don't know what that was, and I like Floyd. I really do, and I'm sorry he feels that way. I think his problem was, though, that he had an inferiority complex. He never hurt anybody until they hurt him."

"He had too much compassion for a fighter."

"That's right," he said. "He did, and I'm glad he's all right."

Outside of town now only our headlights and those of oncoming cars broke the darkness. After several miles we turned into a driveway on the right and stopped in a pine and oak grove in front of a modern two-story natural wood and fieldstone house, and it was as if we were not in Cut and Shoot, Texas, but in the executive suburbs of upper Westchester Country, New York, or Fairfield County, Connecticut.

In the parking space there were two maroon Cadillacs of recent vintage, and a smaller car that, he said, belonged to his sixteen-year-old daughter. There was a large travel home and a pickup truck, and he led us into the house where he introduced us to his three daughters and two sons and showed us around. There were five bedrooms, two baths, a library with a baby grand piano in it, a play room, the kitchen and the living-dining area that rose two stories.

"How high is this ceiling?" Skipper Lofting said.

"Nineteen feet," he said. "My wife designed the house and we built it in 1966."

Against the long wall there was a huge fieldstone fireplace, its exposed chimney rising the full height. He said that the limestone hearth weighed three thousand pounds and the slab that formed the mantel eight hundred pounds, and over the mantel there was an oil painting, made from another old photograph, of two oxen pulling a buckboard through waist-high grass. "Cussin'" Harris was beside the oxen with a dog, and Granny Harris and five children were in the buckboard.

"That was when they were comin' out of Oklahoma," he said. "Three of their kids died there, and when they left, my granddad dug up their graves and put them in the wagon and brought them to Palestine and buried them there."

When I asked him later, he said that the house and its immediate acre would probably bring $150,000 on the current Cut and Shoot real estate market. The other thirty acres, at $5,000 an acre, would probably bring again as much.

"You all ready boys?" he said now. "Let's go."

The boys, slim, dark-haired, neat in their slacks and warm-up jackets and looking like prep-schoolers, got into the front seat of his Cadillac with him, and Skipper Lofting and I got into the back, and he backed out. We made several turns onto dark, paved, tree-lined roads and then onto another that was paved, but that I thought must be the one. Then he stopped the car, and I could see it, fifty feet ahead of us, illumined by the headlights.

"There is it," he said, even as Lou Viscusi had said it that first time. There were waist-high weeds and scrub bushes around it, and in front of it was a tree, bare of leaves now, but with a trunk about a foot across. The porch was cluttered with discarded furniture and appliances, including a couple of TV sets.

"I don't remember that tree there," I said.

"It's a walnut," he said. "I believe it was planted the year after you were here. My brother planted it."

"I'm trying to remember if you were born in this house."

"No," he said. "Tobe and I were born over there in a cabin they tore down for a well."

He turned left and drove about a hundred feet and stopped, the car lights playing through the mist now on the weathered white sideboards of the gym. Torn canvas, flapping in the wind, hung down from the eaves to the top of the chest-high sideboards, and we got out and waited, the headlights still on, while one of the boys went into the gym and turned on the two overhead naked light bulbs.

The ring was set up in the middle of the concrete floor, and there were two heavy punching bags suspended from the rafters. For fifteen minutes or so he had the boys, in their slacks and sports shirts and wearing bag-punching gloves, work out on the bags while he coached them.

"Kevin, you're puttin' no power behind it." . . . "Move fast on your feet, too, Robert." . . . "Put power in your right, Kevin." . . . "Turn your palm down on your right hand, Robert."

They put the big gloves on then, and he got into the ring first with one and then the other. With his open hands he picked off their punches, moving around and talking to them, and reminding me of Floyd Patterson who, half a continent away, was probably just finishing up with the members of the Huguenot Boxing Club in the gym in the white chicken barn outside New Paltz, New York.

"Here come the revenuers," I said to Skipper Lofting. "Let's get rid of the still."

The car lights were advancing on the gym over the uneven ground. The car pulled up, and the lights went out and two teen-agers in blue jeans and carrying their gloves, came in. They stripped to the waist, and while Skipper Lofting and I walked around with our coat collars up and our hands in our pockets and our breaths hanging on the damp air, they punched the bags and then boxed each other for three rounds while Roy moved around with them and coached them.

"Where the cabin was where you were born," one of the boys in the front seat said to him as we drove away, "is that well still there?"

"No," he said. "It's dry now, too."

"Did we get money from it?"

"No," he said. "Granny was married at fourteen, and she had sixteen children and she didn't have time to learn to read or write. She didn't hold onto all the mineral rights."

"It could have been a lot of money, couldn't it?" the boy said.

"It could have come to an easy million." Roy said.

When we got back to the house his wife, Jean, was in the kitchen. She had eaten with the children before we had left for the workout, but she served us chili and then fruit cake flavored with apricot brandy.

"Do you remember this out here?" she said.

"I'll never forget the way it was," I said, "but I can hardly rec-ognize it now."

"It's all changed now," she said. "We're just a part of Hous-ton."

"That's right," Roy said. "They built their airport out this way, and Lake Conroe and Lake Livingston are up here and it brings a lot of recreation. We have a lot of good timber, but recreation has become the big deal here."

Yes, I was thinking, and it always was for the people who lived as they wanted to and fished and hunted and fought dogs and chickens and raced horses for side bets on the clay and dirt roads. It was sporting to attend dances to which you were invited not to come, and there was the time your dad and Uncle Jack hung Uncle Bob head down in the 'gator well on the river bank so that he could slip a rope over one and drag it out just for the sport of it.

"It's all changing so fast now," his wife said. "We're becoming just a suburb."

When he walked us out to the car, a light rain was falling again. Dead oak leaves, wet and flattened by the rain, covered the ground and glistened in the yellow light from the house like burnished copper, and we shook hands there and he told us how to get back to town.

"Well," I said to Skipper Lofting as we drove back through the rain, "what do you think of Roy Harris and Cut and Shoot?"

"I'm impressed by him," he said, "considering his background and that he was a fighter. He's so well-mannered, and I noticed, that, even when he was talking to just the two of us, he never uses any crude language."

"And even," I said, "when he was proposing the violent remedy of hanging people on the court house steps and putting it on TV, his voice level never rose. It was all so matter of fact."

"I noticed that, too," Skipper said.

"When I saw how well he's doing, and that he had moved up into another social stratum," I said, "I thought he might be hesitant about my delving into the old days again and writing about them, but he's proud of his beginnings."

"That's right," Skipper said. "He sort of celebrates them."

"The Harrises have never worried about what other people would think," I said. "Right or wrong, he says what he believes, and it just seems to me that the rest of us, who don't want to offend and are afraid to stir up the waters, lose a little of our integrity every day of our lives."

"I know what you mean," Skipper said.

8

The Fireman

The Yankees beat the Dodgers in the Series because
I had an edge on Burt. I had DiMaggio and Page.
Gentlemen, I give you Joe DiMaggio . . . and Joe
Page.

Bucky Harris

We drove east out of Texas and across seven states and into western Pennsylvania. It took us three days, and I called him on the phone from South Hapeville, Georgia, and then from Beckley, West Virginia, to let him know where we were and when we might be in.

"How are you tonight?" I said the last night out, and when he answered his voice was flat and tired-sounding again.

"Oh, so-so, Billy," he said. It was what he had said two nights before.

"Only so-so?" I said.

"Yeah, Billy," he said. "When you coming in?"

"I figure we should be there early tomorrow afternoon," I said. "Will you be there then?"

"I'm here all the time," he said, the voice the same.

The address the Yankees had given me was in care of Joe Page's Rocky Lodge, Route 30, Laughlintown, Pennsylvania. Both times that I had called he had answered the phone himself and almost immediately, and so I had pictured him perhaps in a small office or maybe picking up a phone at the end of a bar.

"We'll need a couple of rooms for a night," I said. "What is Joe Page's Rocky Lodge?"

"It's a small inn," he said, "but I don't have any rooms. You won't have any trouble getting rooms in Ligonier, though, and that's only three miles. There's a couple of good motels there."

"Don't worry about it," I said. "I'll be there tomorrow."

"Sure, Billy," he said.

"He's not well," I said to Skipper Lofting after I had hung up. "He's real down, the same as the other night. I'm sure he's in poor health, and that makes me feel like a louse. I should know."

"How would you know?" Skipper said. "How many years is it?"

"It was 1950," I said, "and I said good-by to him in the Yankee clubhouse at the Stadium. The White Sox had just knocked him out of the box. I think it was Aaron Robinson who doubled in the winning run, and he used to catch Joe in the minors and on the Yankees before they traded him to Chicago. Two days later they sent Joe down to Kansas City, which was a Yankee farm club then."

"That was twenty-six years ago," Skipper said.

"That's what's wrong with this business," I said. "We're a lot of hustlers. We latch on to someone because he's in the public eye and we need to make a living. We plumb his background and pick his brain. We search out his motivations and his aspirations, and if he's a good guy, an association, even a friendship, forms. Then we say good-by and good luck, and if his luck runs out where are we? We're long gone, and on to somebody else."

"You can't be everybody's brother," Skipper said, "and besides, I'm getting hungry. When are you figuring to eat?"

When he had it, in '47 and '49, he was one of the great relief pitchers of all time. He was a fast-ball left-hander who, as the expression used to go, threw aspirins. Baseball, in New York at least, was reaching its peak of post-war popularity, and for the crucial games, and for those two World Series, of course, the Stadium would be packed. I can still see it the way it was in the late innings, the Yankee pitcher faltering with men on the bases, the conference on the mound, then Bucky Harris in '47 and Casey Stengel in '49 taking the ball from the pitcher and signaling with his left hand. In the stands 70,000 heads would turn and 70,000 pairs of eyes would fasten on the bullpen beyond right field.

"Now coming in to pitch for the Yankees," the voice of the public address announcer would sound, echoing, "Joe Page!"

It was like thunder, rolling, and it made a cave of the vast Stadium. They rose as one, all their shouts and screams one great roar, and the gate of the low chain-link fence would open, and he would come out, immaculate in those pin-stripes, walking with that sort of slow, shuffling gait, his warm-up jacket over his shoulder, a man on his way to work. In '47 he was in fifty-eight games, of which the Yankees won thirty-seven, including the seventh against the Dodgers in the Series. In '49 he appeared in sixty, forty-two of which the Yankees won, and in the Series he saved two, again against Brooklyn.

He was six feet three, perfectly proportioned at 215 pounds, and he was handsome. He had a smooth oval face, dark hair, blue eyes and a smile that, in those days, could have sold Ipana tooth paste. Of all the Yankees only Joe DiMaggio, his buddy and roommate on the road, surpassed him in popularity. After the '47 Series, a Mr. and Mrs. Bernard MacDougall, in Inverness, Nova Scotia, named their son Joe Page MacDougall after him.

He was the oldest of seven children, and his father had been a miner in the coal fields along the Allegheny just northeast of Pittsburgh, and he himself had worked in the mines for two years. As a rookie with the Yankees in 1944, he made the All Stars, but the night of the game his father died. A sister had been killed in an automobile accident earlier that year, and his mother had passed away the year before. He was married then to Katie Carrigan, whom he had known since they were children, and now he became the main support of three sisters and two brothers, the oldest eighteen and the youngest eleven.

"I had written a piece for *Cosmopolitan* called 'Fighter's Wife,'" I was telling Skipper Lofting, "about Rocky Graziano's wife, Norma. The night he fought Charley Fusari, when it started to come over the radio she ran out of the house, and I walked the streets with her and then waited with her until he came home. Then I got an assignment from *Life* to do 'Ballplayer's Wife' with Katie and Joe. When the Yankees would come off the road for a home stand, I'd sit with her in the wives' section, waiting for Joe to come in and save the game.

"I sat there with her for four weeks in all, and it was sad. In would come Joe, and he just didn't have it any more. When a speed-ball pitcher loses just that little bit off it, those hitters who have been standing there with their bats on their shoulders just love it. They tee off, and it is brutal. Sometimes we'd go to dinner afterwards, and I'd try to console them, but it wasn't any good.

"That last game he pitched for the Yankees, after he lost it, I left Katie and went down to the clubhouse to tell him she'd be waiting in their car. He always had the dressing stall next to DiMaggio, and he was sitting there with his head down. I said, 'Joe, tough luck.' He looked up at me, and he said, 'Billy, you're jinxin' me.'"

"Well," Skipper said, "you know how superstitious ballplayers are, or used to be."

"I know," I said, "but he meant it right then. He was grasping for anything. I said, 'You may be right, Joe, and I'm dropping the story.' I told him he'd probably get it back his next time out, and I wished him luck and shook hands, and I left. End of story."

"I guess you couldn't write about losing in those days," Skipper said.

"Only in literature," I said.

Now, after we had checked into the motel in Ligonier and had lunch, we drove southeast out of town on Route 30, the mid-December sun lowering behind us, and then through Laughlintown. Where the road started to rise toward a ridge, stands of hardwood crowded it on both sides, and then on the right we saw the blue sign with the white letters: Joe Page's Rocky Lodge. Set among the trees was a three-story building of fieldstone and wood, and the only vehicle in the parking space in front was a light blue pickup.

I got out of the car, and on the gravel of the shaded driveway there were patches of frost and on some of the dry, brown leaves a light sugaring of dry powder snow. Drapes had been drawn across the first floor windows of the building, and as I reached the door under the overhang, I heard the lock turn. I could hear the sounds of a football game on a television, and I knocked on the door.

"We're closed," a voice said.

"I'm Bill Heinz," I said. "Joe Page is expecting me."

"Oh," the voice said, and then the lock turned again and the door opened, and he said, "I'm his son Joe."

"And you look like him," I said, as we shook hands. He was in his late teens and wearing glasses with narrow steel rims, but it was there in the blue eyes.

"That's what people say," he said, smiling.

"I have a friend with me," I said. "I just want to go back to the car and bring him in."

He waited at the door, and I introduced Skipper to him. The barroom, deserted, was to the right, and he led us to the left into a long, darkened room, the only illumination coming from ceiling lights in the back. To the left, against the front wall, there was a juke box, and next to it the television. On the right a log fire was going in a fieldsone fireplace, dining room chairs and small tables were stacked against the other wall, and in an armchair his father was sitting. He got up slowly and walked toward me.

"You look good, Billy," he said putting out his hand. "A little heavier."

It was Joe Page, all right, but I knew it only by those eyes. That dark hair was gray now, and his mouth was shrunken. The left side of his jaw was hollow behind a gray beard of several days, his neck was thin, and that great left arm hung loosely at his side.

"How are you, Joe?" I said.

"Oh, so-so," he said.

I introduced Skipper to him, and he introduced his younger son Jon, who was seventeen, and two years younger than his brother, and Bryan Miller, a young friend of Jon's who had come in to watch on TV the Washington Redskins and the Minnesota Vikings in their National Football Conference play-off game. We found straight-back chairs, and he sat down slowly again in the armchair, as I tried to find a way to ask the question.

"Cancer of the throat," he said, while I was still groping. "It tears the hell out of you, the muscles all the way down. I can't shave. They took all my teeth, and just left me two, and I can't eat."

"When was that?" I said.

"In 1973," he said. "In August of 1970, I had the heart attack at the Old Timers Game. I walked up in the stands and started to sweat and couldn't talk. They sent me down to Lenox Hill Hospital, and then I come home and had the open heart at St. Francis in Pittsburgh."

"They've really been beating up on you," I said.

"That's what happened to my arm," he said, reaching across with his right and rubbing his left arm. "These fingers go numb. They want to give me a new jaw, but I don't know if I'll get it. They cut me enough, and I've got a hernia now, too."

I was groping again, but on the TV the announcer's voice and the crowd noise had risen, and his eyes went toward the set. In the backfield Fran Tarkenton was scrambling, with two big Redskin linemen lumbering after him, and then he released the ball and it fell short of a receiver who was coming back for it.

"How long have you had this place?" I said.

"Seventeen years ago I bought it," he said. "First I had one down in Irwin called 'The Bull Pen.' I closed up here about three months ago. I couldn't take that stuff at the bar any more. You ever see any of the guys?"

"No," I said. "I've been writing other things."

"I miss all you guys," he said. "It was a strange life, but once you're out of it there was nothing else like it. DiMag was here, though. They give me a testimonial, and he come in from Frisco. The same old Daig. When was that, Joe?"

"It was two years ago," young Joe said.

"They had Spec Shea here and Tommy Henrich," he said. "It was a nice party. Seven hundred people. The Daig was the same old Daig. He asked me about my back."

"I heard he had trouble with his back," Skipper Lofting said.

"That's right, Skip," he said. "I told him I had jammed up vertebrae and they opened it and straightened it out, and that's been fine ever since. You see him on that TV commercial? What's that thing he's doin'?"

"For the coffee maker?"

"Yeah," he said. "He sent me one. I got the filter, but not the maker."

"When I watch him on those commercials," I said, "I remember a story Frank Graham told. It was a couple of years after Joe came up to the Yankees, and he was still very shy and very quiet.

They were at Shor's—Frank and Toots and Joe and a couple of others at a table—and Lefty Gomez stopped by. He told some story, as he can, and made a couple of quips, and when he left, Joe said, 'Gee, I wish I could be like that.'"

"He's some Daig," he said. "When Joe wasn't hittin', you remember that Del Prado where we stayed in Chicago? They had those big mirrors on the doors, and at five o'clock in the morning I'd hear him, and he'd be up there in front of the mirror practicing hittin'."

"One year," I said, "the Giants and the Dodgers opened the season in Brooklyn the same day that you people opened at the Stadium. Joe had the bad heel then, and he wasn't playing, and the next day, when Jimmy Cannon and I walked into the clubhouse, he was taking a treatment. He asked us where we'd been the day before, and we told him we'd been to Ebbets Field. He said, 'Where was the wind?' Jimmy said, 'Behind the hitters.' Joe said, 'The same here. I was coming up here in the taxi and there's a flag on a building about four blocks away and I always look at that to see where the wind is. The wind was just right. It broke my heart.' He was probably the only guy on the ball club to check the wind before he got there, and he did it even when he wasn't playing."

"He's some Daig," Page said, "and Yogi's still goin' all right."

"He was another shy one," I said.

"Yeah," he said. "You're right."

When Yogi Berra came up to the Yankees to stay in 1947, they almost hazed him out of the league, the other Yankees among them. They mocked his squat, early primate appearance and quoted his malaprops, until Bucky Harris, who was managing them then, put a stop to it. In the seventeen years that Yogi caught for the Yankees, he played in fifteen All Star games and three times won the American League's Most Valuable Player Award, and in 1972 they elected him to the Hall of Fame.

"It was touch-and-go with Yogi for a while," I said now, "before Bucky straightened you guys out on him."

"Yeah," Page said. "We had a meeting and he told us to lay off. He told a few of the writers, too."

"I remember the day before the '47 series opened," I said.

"You people had worked out at the Stadium and several of us writers were hanging around the clubhouse. They had the table in the middle of the room, with the cartons of balls to be autographed, and Yogi and Spec Shea were sitting there and signing. One of us asked Shea how he felt as a rookie about to pitch, the next day, the opening game of the World Series, and he said something about it being just another ball game where you still just had to get twenty-seven outs."

"Yeah," Page said. "He would have said that. He was like that."

"So Yogi said, 'Yeah, but them shadows come awful early here this time of year.' He was worrying about those hits, with the ball coming out of the sunlight and then into the shadow of those three decks."

"That's the way it is there."

"Then one of the writers said, 'Come on, Yogi, stop worrying about it. You don't figure to get a hit, anyway.' With that, he and the others walked away. Yogi was sitting there with a ball in one hand, a pen in the other, and he said in that low voice, kind of to himself, 'Them writers think I'm kiddin', but they don't have to get up there and hit. They don't have to do nothin'.'"

"Yogi said that?"

"Yes," I said, "and it's a truth I have never forgotten, any time I have interviewed an athlete, or any time I have had to lay a critique on one."

"Yogi was the best receiver I ever pitched to," he said.

"And he could snap that bat," I said. "He had great wrists, so he could wait on the pitch. That's why he could get around on the breaking stuff, and even reach those bad balls."

"And he had a brain," he said.

"Which a lot of people found hard to believe at first," I said. "I remember that night game at the Stadium against the Red Sox—the game that made you. The bases were loaded, and you threw three balls to Rudy York, and Yogi came out from behind the plate and waddled up to you. As you two stood talking, somebody in the press box next to me said, 'This is ridiculous. What can he tell him?'"

It was May 26, 1947, and there were 74,000 in the stands that night, and all that Joe Page became and all that happened to him afterward stemmed from it. The Washington Senators had knocked him out in his first start that season, and several times he had failed in relief. In the third inning, with the Red Sox leading, 3–1, two men on base and nobody out, Bucky Harris brought him in for a last try. He got Ted Williams to ground to George McQuinn, a great glove man, but McQuinn bobbled it. Now the bases were loaded, and he threw those three balls to York and, as Yogi walked to the mound, Bucky Harris had one foot up on the dugout steps, and Joe Page was one pitch away from the minors.

"I forget what Yogi said," he said now.

York took two strikes, and then he swung at that fast ball and missed. The count went to 3 and 0 on Bobby Doerr, and again Harris was at the steps and again the future of Joe Page hung on the next pitch. He threw three strikes past Doerr, and got Eddie Pellagrini to lift an easy fly ball up into that rising thunder of sound for the third out. The Yankees won, 9–3, and Joe Page was on his way.

"Yogi knew baseball," he said now.

"I know," I said. "You guys won the opening game of that '47 Series, but Yogi had a terrible day. He went 0 for 4, and Burt Shotten had Peewee Reese and Jackie Robinson running. They each stole second, with Yogi bouncing the ball down there, and afterward he was sitting in his dressing stall, with his head down. I said to him, 'Yogi, forget it. You guys won, and you'll have a better day tomorrow.' He said, 'I guess I ain't very smart.' I said, 'Yogi, let me tell you something. I once asked you about last year when the Cardinals were in the Series and you were home in St. Louis. I asked you if you went to the games, and you said, 'No, I don't like to watch games.' I said, 'Why not?' You said, 'It makes me nervous, just to watch.' It makes you nervous to watch because you're always playing the game. Don't ever think that you're not smart enough, because you have a fine baseball brain. And Yogi said, 'I don't know. I don't know if you're right.'"

"Bucky knew it," he said now. "Bucky was the best manager I ever played for, but I was sorry when Stengel died. Rough to work for, you know? I'd come in, and Casey would come out talkin', but I never knew what the hell he was saying."

"You weren't the only one," I said.

"After I had the operation," he said, "I saw Yogi in New York at the Old Timers Game, and he didn't recognize me with this hollow neck. Jon said to him, 'It's my dad, Joe Page.'"

Young Joe had left the room. As he returned I watched him walk across in front of the television with its screen filled with a close-up of uniformed bodies and the sound voluming, and then sit down.

"He walks like you," I said. "When I watch him walk, I can see you coming in from that bull pen."

"The pup's got it, too," he said, nodding toward Jon. "I hope you get a chance to meet the wife. Mildred, but we call her Mitz. In 1954 I got married with Mitz. I think it was 1954. She's great. She's got her own insurance business, and I think she'll be back soon."

She came in a few minutes later. She is slim and dark-haired, and he introduced us to her. She took off her coat and she was wearing a denim jump suit. Skipper pulled up another straight back chair, and she sat down between him and Joe.

"What have you been talking about?" she said.

"The old days," Joe said.

"I can imagine," she said.

"Do you ever get people dropping in here," I said, "who see the sign outside and wonder if it's the real Joe Page?"

"Oh, yeah," he said. "Quite a few people. A guy would come in and say, 'Are you . . .?' And I'd say, 'Yeah.'"

"One guy came in," young Joe said, "and he said, 'I'm from New York, and I'd like to take Joe Page to dinner.'"

"Joe was in the hospital then," Mitz said. "I told the boys, 'If anybody comes in, don't tell them your dad's in the hospital.' So he told him, 'He's not in now, but if you want to see my mother, she's at work.' He came to the office, but I was at a restaurant, and when I came back to the office he'd gone.

"He came back here," she said, "and our other son here told him, 'My dad's in the hospital, and you can't see him.' I'd gone to the hospital by then, and this fellow came in. I told him he couldn't see Joe, and he said, 'I have to. When your husband was pitching, I was five years old. I sold newspapers, and one night I fell asleep where I was selling them. Your husband came along and he saw me there, and he woke me up and he said, 'You have to go home and sleep.' I said, 'I can't, until I sell these papers.' Your husband bought all my papers, and then he took me in and fed me. That's why I have to see him.'

"By now," she said, "he had the nurses and the doctor and me in tears. So we took him in to see Joe, and when we came out he told me, 'If there's anything you need, money or anything, just let me know.' He's a fine man."

"He must be," I said.

"He does hair replacement," she said, and then to young Joe, "Find that card he gave me."

On the business card was imprinted, "International Transitions Center." Under that, "Orange, Conn." Then, in the lower right corner, "George DeRosa, President."

"Where was it," I said to Page, "that you found him asleep and took him in to eat?"

"Patsy's," he said. "You remember we used to eat there? At 112th Street?"

"I remember," I said.

We went there a couple of times, after those bad ball games, when I was trying to console them. I would be trying to get their minds off the game, and so I would get him to talking about what it had been like growing up playing ball around Springdale. The field had been cleared of rocks and stumps, but it was uphill to first and second base, and downhill from third to home. They traveled in the Lockerman's Meat Market panel truck, but they had no money for tires, so they packed them with sod and wired them to the rims.

"I don't suppose," I said now, "that Lockerman is still in business with his meat market."

"Yeah," he said, "the sons are."

"Sam and Jim and Howard," young Joe said.

"They come up to see Joe once in a while," Mitz said.

"I was telling Skipper," I said now, "about the last time I saw you in '50, in the clubhouse right after the last time you pitched for the Yankees. I was working on that magazine piece that never came off, and you looked at me and you said, 'Billy, you're jinxin' me.' "

"I didn't mean it," he said now.

"I understood," I said. "You were reaching for anything. As I remember it, it was Aaron Robinson who'd got a double off you."

"I don't think so," he said. "Them left-hand hitters didn't hit me. After this throat, though, I couldn't remember nothin'."

"His memory was bad for a while," Mitz said.

"My back's givin' me hell now, too," he said.

"They took his lymph glands," she said.

She got up. She pushed her chair back and, standing behind his, began to knead his shoulder muscles.

"That feels good," he said.

"I think it was Aaron Robinson, though," I said, "because I was struck by the irony of it. He'd caught you on the way up, in Augusta and Newark and then on the Yankees, and it was his hit that sent you down to the minors."

"He was a hell of a catcher," he said. "He took a bottle of Seagram's to bed with him every night."

"He's dead," Mitz said.

"Yeah," he said, turning his head and touching the left side of his neck again. "Cancer."

"I'm sorry to hear that."

"You read what that Lopat said about me?" he said. Eddie Lopat was a left-hander who threw breaking stuff for the Yankees from 1948 to 1955.

"No," I said.

"That Lopat blasted me," he said. "It was in that book they wrote about Joe. They talked to people about Joe, and that Lopat was never in my apartment and he said I used to drink all night and come out the next day. He said I was lushed up every night, so how could I be ready sixty times a year?"

"I don't know," I said. "I didn't read the book."

There was that time, though, in '46, I was thinking, when Joe McCarthy let you have it out on the team plane two days before he quit managing the club. He figured you couldn't find the plate during the day because you'd touched too many bases the night before.

"Then a couple of days after I left you that last time," I said, "they sent you down to Kansas City."

"Casey never called me in the clubhouse," he said. "He saw me in the dugout, and he said, 'I've got your pink slip.' I said, 'Where am I goin'?' He said, 'Kansas City.'"

"What was that like?"

"Bad," he said. "That was more like a rest home. Johnny Mize was there with something wrong with him. Then I went to Frisco under Lefty O'Doul. That was bad, too. Cold, nobody in the stands and all that goddamn dampness. I never worked for a ball club like I did here."

He came back up to pitch in seven games for Pittsburgh in 1954. His record that year was 0 and 0, and that was the end of it.

"The Old Man," he said, meaning Branch Rickey, who was trying to rebuild the Pirates then with youth, "had kids. They had kids from all around, and we called them 'Rickey dinks.'"

While we had been talking, the game on television had finished, the Vikings winning on their way to the Super Bowl. Jon stood up and said he would be going out for a while, and he and his friend shook hands with Skipper and me and left.

"The buck's a good football player," Joe said. "They call him 'The Monster.'"

"He's got a lot of schools looking at him," young Joe said.

"What does he play?"

"Linebacker and fullback," Page said, and he got up out of the chair. He walked slowly to the front door and opened it and went out.

"Where's he going?" Mitz said.

"To get wood," young Joe said.

"You should get it," she said.

When he came back in he was carrying two splits of log. He bent over and put them on the fire.

"They didn't call him 'The Fireman' for nothing," she said, as he sat down. "You watched him pitch. He was always arrogant, and that's the way our youngest son is."

But that was just the pose, I was thinking. When he used to walk in there, he told me once, with those men on base and the thousands screaming, he could feel his heart pumping, and he said it seemed as if his stomach and all its contents were coming up into his throat.

"There was a fellow here from Bethany College, who was watching Jon," she said. "He said, 'You know, I don't think you'll ever make it in football.' Jon said to me, 'You know, Mom, I told him, 'I don't know about football, but I'm gonna make it somewhere.' He's just like his father."

As he walked from that bullpen, Tommy Henrich, in right field, would say to him, "Joe, you stop them, and we'll win it for you." Frank Crosetti, who was coaching then, told him, "If you knew how scared they are of that fast ball, Joe, you wouldn't worry about anything." When his control would begin to go and he would start to miss the plate, "Snuffy" Stirnweiss would come trotting over to the mound from second, and he'd say, "You're not bearing down on the left leg again, Joe." It would get him out of it.

"That was sad about Stirnweiss," I said now.

"Snuff?" he said. "Yeah, I read about it. Sad."

One morning in September 1958, three cars of a commuter train out of New Jersey plunged through an open liftbridge into Newark Bay, and Stirnweiss was one of the more than two dozen who drowned in the cars. He had been a fine baseball and football player at the University of North Carolina, and he played for the Yankees from 1942 until 1950, once winning the American League batting championship, once setting a major league fielding record for second baseman, and twice, with his speed, leading the league in stolen bases.

"What struck me when I read about it," I said, "was that the speed that made him such a great athlete cost him his life. Someone, who had seen him get on the train, said that when he arrived at the station it was pulling out and he ran to catch it."

"You remember," he said, "how the first thing he'd do when he'd get on the train was go to sleep? I thought of that."

"In the last game of the '47 Series," I said, "when you threw that spitter to Gil Hodges, did he pop it up to Stirnweiss?"

"No, I struck him out," he said, "but it wasn't a spitter. That was the oil, the graphite oil. I used to keep it inside my belt."

"You told me it was a spitter," I said. "In the clubhouse, during the celebration, I came over to see you and DiMag, and you said, 'Billy, don't write this, but I threw that Hodges a real hocker.' How could I, alone, write it? If I did, you and Joe would have denied it and clammed up on me forever."

"That Roe was throwin' it for them in '50," he said, meaning Preacher Roe of the Dodgers. "He later wrote about it. I used to load it up during a foul ball, when everybody looks up."

He got up now and walked slowly toward the barroom. When he came back he handed me his glove, still formed as it had been to fit his right hand, the dark brown, almost black leather cracked now.

"A Diz Trout model," he said.

"You ought to put oil on it," I said, as I handed it back.

"We're going to have it bronzed," Mitz said.

He sat down, and she stood up and began kneading his shoulders again.

"Them were good days in New York," he said. "We had a lot of fun."

"One day," she said, "he told Jon, 'Remember, if you're going to make it, you're going to have to work hard. And stay away from women.' Then we were going through some old things, and found a picture of Joe and Joe DiMaggio in Hawaii with these girls. So Jon took it to him, and said, 'What about this?'"

"I tortured a few in my day," he said.

"So you had your good days," she said, "and you should remember those."

"Yeah," he said, "and the young buck can play ball, too."

"Jon was playing over in Johnstown," she said, "and Joe used to tell this story of one he hit there."

"I hit one out 380 feet," he said.

"So Jon hit one out 440 feet," she said, "and Joe said, 'I'll never tell that story again.'"

"That was the end of that hit," he said.

"I have to get a loaf of bread," she said, walking out from behind the chair, "and where do I get a headlight? The low beam is out."

"In a garage," he said.

"But what one? The outside of the light is square."

"But the light is round," young Joe said. "Go to Mobil."

"I'll be back in a few minutes," she said.

"She don't know cars," Page said, "but she's got a hell of a brain. She works twelve, fourteen hours a day, Skip."

"She seems to be a fine woman," Skipper said.

"You can say that again," he said. "What beats me is that I can't hunt any more, and I've got them guns."

"What have you got?" Skipper said.

"I got a .320, a .406 and a .373 Magnum, and I can't use them."

"Didn't you once go on a bird hunting trip to Maine with Enos Slaughter and a couple of others?" I said.

"It was South Dakota," he said. "Huron. A guy had to be blind not to get fifty roosters."

"You were telling about it in the clubhouse one day," I said, "and Yogi was listening. You said, 'We were going after birds, and Slaughter had this cyst on his back, but it didn't make any difference to him. He went climbing through that brush and under those branches like it wasn't there.' And Yogi said, 'What the hell kind of a bird is a cyst?' "

"That's right," he said. "That was Yogi."

"With all you've been through," I said, "I've been thinking about that ballplayers' retirement plan. I've forgotten when that came in."

"We started it in '47," he said, "but it went back to '44. I know on the hospitalization they don't give you all of it, only 80 per cent."

"But that's a big help."

"Hell, yes," he said, bringing his hand over to his neck again. "This thing cost $19,000."

Young Joe had turned on the TV again, for the American Football Conference play-off. We talked about the game against Boston on the next to last day of the season in '49. The Red Sox led the Yankees by one game in the standings, and were ahead, 4–1, in the second inning when he came in and held them the rest of the way until Johnny Lindell won it with a home run. Then the Yankees beat them again, to win the pennant on the last day.

"The good old days," he said, as we got up to leave. "I'm glad you came, and that you're looking good."

"And I'll call you now and then," I said, "to hear that you're feeling better."

"I was fifty-nine in October," he said.

"I know," I said.

He walked us out, after we had said good-by to young Joe, and closed the door behind him and stood, watching, under the overhang while we walked to the car. Darkness had come by now, and another car, its lights on, drove in and Mitz got out. We walked over and shook hands.

"I'm really pleased you two came," she said. "It's done a lot for him."

"You've done a lot for him," Skipper said.

"It's been a long time," she said, "since he's talked that much or sounded so well, or moved so well."

"I'm glad," I said.

"So any time you're nearby," she said, "stop in to see him again."

"We'd like to," I said.

As Skipper backed the car around I looked back. He was still standing under the overhang, under the pale overhead light, waving good-by with his right hand.

"You know how pitchers are," Skipper said. "When they're talking, especially about pitching, they'll demonstrate with their pitching arm. He has to use his right arm."

"It was one of the great left arms," I said, "and it's a damn shame."

I had a terrible time trying to get to sleep that night. The Derry Sportsmen's Club was having its annual dinner dance in the ballroom of the motel, and it came up through the ventilating system and through the floor. The band must have played "Rock Around the Clock" a dozen times, but I would have had trouble sleeping anyway.

9

The Artist Supreme

It is not strength, but art obtains the prize.
Homer

"How did you get my number?" he said on the phone. I had called him one evening late in January at his home in Wethersfield, Connecticut.

"Come on, Willie," I said. "You're not unheard of."

"I'm a has-been," he said. "Nobody remembers me."

He was the greatest creative artist I ever saw in a ring. When I watched him box, it used to occur to me that, if I could just listen carefully enough, I would hear the music. He turned boxing contests into ballets, performances by a virtuoso in which the opponent, trying to punch him out, became an unwilling partner in a dance, the details of which were so exquisite that they evoked joy, and sometimes even laughter.

In 1940, when Guiglermo Papaleo—Willie Pep—turned professional after winning the Connecticut amateur flyweight and bantamweight championships, he was seventeen, still an adolescent. He won fifty-three fights in a row, and then at age twenty, beat Chalky Wright for the featherweight championship of the world. He won another eight before Sammy Angott, the former lightweight champion, a grabber and smotherer and too big for him, outpointed him. Then he won another seventy-three before Sandy Sadler knocked him out in the first of their four fights. In other words, of his first 135 fights, he won all but the one in which he was out-muscled and out-wrestled. In our time we never saw another like him.

"I'm on the Boxing Commission," he said. "It's in the State Building, so see me there. I'm there every day from eight until 4:30."

He gave me the directions, rapidly, for he always talked the way he boxed, the words spurting out. He told me what exit to take from the Interstate and what streets and how to get around the park and how to recognize the building. Hartford is a city I once knew and walked, but when I drove down the ramp off the elevated Interstate and got into the noontime traffic, I turned into the parking space of the high-rise motel and checked in. I had lunch, and I took a cab. At my age I wanted to have something left for Willie.

"Excuse me," I said. "I'm looking for Willie Pep."

I had found on the directory in the lobby "Athletic Division," under "Department of Consumer Protection." A middle-aged balding man, his jacket off, was sitting behind a desk on which there was a sign that read "Michael Boguslawski." On the door it had said that he was the assistant to Mary Heslin, the head of the department.

"Sure," he said. "You go out and take a left. Go down one flight of steps and go through the doors. Go straight ahead down the hall to the end. Take a right. It's the fifth door on the left, 31-A."

"I'm sorry," I said, "but will you give that to me again?"

"I'll give him a call," he said, picking up the phone and dialing, and then, "Sure he's here, and you're there, but come up and lead him down."

He came through the doorway quickly, sticking out his hand. He is five feet five, and he never had any trouble making the 126 pounds, but he was a little heavier now, his fifty-four years in his face, and he was wearing a glen plaid suit and a striped sports shirt open at the neck. He led me down, walking rapidly with those small, quick steps, thrusting the doors open, talking.

"It's a good job," he said. "Last year we had about thirty-five wrestling shows, twenty-three boxing shows. We supervise. We check to see a guy hasn't been knocked out in thirty days. If one guy's got forty fights and another's got ten, we don't allow. We go in before the fight and see that they bandage properly. Hugh

Devlin is the director. A good guy. I'm under him with Sal Giacobbe."

He led me into the office and introduced me to Devlin, a rather short, gray-haired, smiling man behind one of the gray metal desks. There were three desks, filing cabinets, a metal locker, a weigh-in scale, a sofa and armchair, and a coat rack.

"Hughie was the bantamweight champion of Massachusetts," he said, and then to Devlin, "How many fights you have?"

"I had 121," Devlin said, "and I won 113."

"He was a good fighter," Willie said.

"You weren't bad yourself," I said.

"Thank you," Willie said.

"The greatest I ever saw," Devlin said. "I can still see Willie's fights. I'll never forget them."

"He was a creative genius," I said to Devlin, "and he could do those things because he had the reflexes of a housefly."

"Thank you very much," Willie said, sitting down behind his desk. "That's very kind of you."

"I have to laugh at you, Willie," I said. "All we're doing is telling you the truth, and you think we're doing you a favor. You did us a favor being the fighter you were."

"That's nice of you to say that," he said, and that's the way he always was, slipping compliments the way he slipped punches while sticking out another jab.

"The last time I saw you in a ring," I said, "was in the Fifth Street Gym in Miami, about 1952. It was after the third Saddler fight, and you didn't have the title any more, and you were starting to hit the road."

"That's right," he said. "I fought in a lot of places."

He did, indeed. Once the really big pay nights were gone forever, he took what was left of his inimitable talents into Moncton, New Brunswick; Bennington, Vermont; Athol, Massachusetts; San Antonio, Texas; Lawton, Oklahoma; Florence, South Carolina; Presque Isle, Maine; Painesville, Georgia; and Caracas, Venezuela, among other places. In 1959 he retired, to come back six years later at the age of forty-two to add nine more wins to a record that reads 241 fights, 229 wins, one draw, and eleven losses.

"Tell Hughie," I said now, "about the time you fought the local boy in the town where the sheriff weighed you in."

"That's right," he said, and then to Devlin, "They didn't have no boxing commission, so the sheriff weighs you in with a gun on his hip. The fight's in the ball park, so when he calls us to the center of the ring . . ."

"Wait a minute, Willie," I said. "Tell him about the kid at the weigh-in."

"Oh, yeah," he said. "So at the weigh-in, the kid I'm gonna box comes up to me and says, 'Mr. Pep, can I have your autograph?' I looked at him, and I said, 'Get away from me, kid. There's people watchin' here. We're boxin' tonight, and what are they gonna think?' "

"You were his hero," I said.

"Yeah," he said. "So at the ball park they got a pretty good crowd, and the referee calls us to the center of the ring to give us the instructions. I look at the kid, and he's white. He's scared stiff. I'm thinking, 'Oh, boy, what kind of a fight can this be?' So the bell rings and we move around, and a lot of guys turn white, but this guy is startin' to turn purple. I figure I have to do something, so I threw a right hand over his shoulder, that would look good to the crowd but that would miss, and I stepped inside and grabbed him under the arms, and I said, 'Look, kid. Just relax. These people here paid their money, and we'll give them a show. We'll just box, and you won't get hurt. We'll have a nice evening, and everybody will like it.' That's exactly what I told him."

"And wait until you hear the ending," I said to Devlin.

"So I take my arms out from under his and let him go," Willie said, "and he falls right on his face and the referee counts him out."

"I love that," Devlin said, laughing. "That's a great story."

"That's the truth," Willie said.

"Then there was the time," I said to Devlin, "that Willie boxed Kid Campeche in Tampa. Frank Graham and Red Smith were covering the baseball training camps, and they were driving out of Tampa one afternoon on the Tamiami Trail starting back to Miami. Over the car radio they heard that Willie was boxing that night in Tampa so, without either of them saying anything, Red

just turned the car around and headed back. Willie pitched another shut-out, and in Campeche's dressing room afterward, either
Red or Frank said, 'Well, what was that like?' And Campeche
said, 'What was it like? Fighting Willie Pep is like trying to stamp
out a grass fire.' "

"Yeah, Kid Campeche," Willie said, nodding. "I remember
him."

"He'll never forget you," I said. "None of them will."

He picked up a pair of black-rimmed glasses from the top of his
desk, and put them on. He opened the desk drawer and took out a
photostat of a newspaper column by Don Riley and handed it to
me.

"He writes for the paper in Minneapolis," he said, "and it's all
in there. It's about when I boxed Jackie Graves there in '46."

Jackie Graves was a pretty good puncher out of Austin, Minnesota. He had had thirty-nine fights before he boxed Willie and had
won twenty by knockouts while losing two decisions, and Willie
knocked him out in the eighth round.

"It's all in there," he said. "Before the fight I told this Riley, 'In
the third round I'm not gonna throw a punch. Watch what happens.' So in the third round I did like I told him. I moved around,
feinted, picked off punches, made him miss, and I never threw a
punch, and all three officials gave me the round. Riley never forgot it."

"How could he?" I said. "And another fight I'll never forget
was your one with Famechon."

Ray Famechon was the European featherweight champion. Lew
Burston, of the International Boxing Club, had talked him into
coming over to box Willie in the Garden for the championship of
the world.

"The afternoon of the fight," I said, "I stopped by the Garden
to pick up my ticket, and Lew Burston grabbed me. He said, 'You
weren't at the weigh-in. You should have been there.' I said,
'Why?' He said, 'Why? Because, Eddie Eagan was explaining our
rules. He was telling Famechon that you can't spin a man, and
Famechon just reached across in front of him and grabbed Pep by
the elbow and spun him and said, *'Comme ça?'* "

"Yeah," Willie said now. "He was kind of fresh at the weigh-in.

He grabbed me, so I figured I can't fight him here, so I'll see what I can do in the ring."

"So then," I said, "Burston said to me, 'Why shouldn't he treat Pep like that? Who is Willie Pep to him? Famechon has had hundreds of amateur fights and sixty pro fights. He's boxed all over Europe, and fought every style there is and . . .' And I said, 'Wait a minute, Lew. He's fought every style there is except Willie Pep's style, and unfortunately he has to fight that style tonight.' "

"He was a tough guy, and he boxed everybody in Europe," Willie said now. "If he thought I was gonna stand there and trade punch for punch, maybe that's the way they do it in Europe, but not over here. He'd get set, and I'd jab him and move."

"I remember that fight," Devlin said. "Great."

"I'll never forget it," I said. "I never saw another fighter who was as frustrated as Famechon was that night. He was punching at air, and a couple of times Willie was actually behind him, tapping him on the shoulder to let him know where he was."

"Yeah," Willie said, "the guy wanted to punch me, and I didn't like to get punched."

"But what Willie probably doesn't know," I said, "is that the fight was supposed to have economic implications in France. Coca-Cola was starting to sell big over there, and the wine growers were up in arms. French kids for centuries had been brought up to drink wine, and now they were drinking Cokes. The agency that had the Coca-Cola account must have figured that Famechon would lick Willie, and they were ready. They had a case of Cokes in Famechon's dressing room, and the idea was that, after he won, there'd be pictures on the front pages of papers all over France of the new world champion celebrating with a Coke."

"I didn't know that," Willie said.

"So in the dressing room later," I said, "there was Famechon sitting with his head down, and saying in French, 'I couldn't hit him because I couldn't find him.' There were the agency guys like mourners at a wake, and there was the case of Cokes over in a corner unopened."

"Is that so?" Willie said. "Well, you know how it was. After the weigh-in, I knew what the guy had in mind, but I didn't have the same idea in my mind."

"That was obvious once the fight started," I said.

"But Willie's greatest was the second Saddler fight," Devlin said. "Great."

Willie's record in *The Ring Record Book and Encyclopedia* is a gallery of great art, from the meticulous miniatures that went only a few rounds to the masterpieces that went the distance. Of the latter, the second Saddler fight in the Garden was the greatest boxing exhibition I ever saw, for Saddler had knocked him out in their first fight and had the height and reach and punch on him. He hurt him the second time, too, cut him under both eyes and over the right, and rocked him time and again, but it was Willie's fight from the first round on when he jabbed Saddler thirty-seven times in succession without a return. There were times when he had Saddler so befuddled that he could stop the dancing and stand right there and rock him back and, though battered and cut and bruised, he won it big on everybody's card to send the sell-out crowd out into the streets still buzzing, still carrying the electrical charge of it.

"Willie sold a lot of TV sets that night," I was saying now. "In those days, you remember, boxing and Milton Berle sold TVs. Guys who didn't have sets gathered in bars or in the homes of others who had sets to watch the fights, and I'll bet Willie sold a lot that night."

"I'll bet you're right," Devlin said.

"Who knows?" Willie said.

"Another one I remember," I said, "was when you defended against Sal Bartolo. There was a loud-mouth there who was hollering, 'Walk in on him, Sal! He can't punch! Walk in! He can't hurt ya!' After you flattened Bartolo, the guy was hollering, 'Fake! Fake!' Bartolo's jaw was broken in three places."

"I got lucky," Willie said. "I boxed him twice before and never knocked him down, and in the first fight he knocked me down for the first time. He was a good fighter."

"I was thinking of you a couple of months ago," I said. "I was out in Cut and Shoot, Texas, outside of Houston. You remember. You were training in Houston and . . ."

"Yeah, I remember that fighter fought Patterson. What was his name?"

"Roy Harris."

"Yeah," Willie said, and then to Devlin, "He came from out in the woods there. They used to cut and shoot people, and they wanted me to go out there and I said, 'Look, I don't want to go. They're probably nice people, but I'm a city fella and I don't understand that stuff.' I wouldn't go."

"So Willie was training in Houston," I said to Devlin, "and Bill Gore had just attached Willie's speed bag into the overhead socket. Roy Harris has a brother named Tobe, who'd been a fighter, and he walked up and he teed off and hit the bag a smash with his right . . ."

"Yeah," Willie said, nodding. "That's right."

"Well, that was like some country fiddler grabbing Jascha Heifetz's violin. Bill Gore said to this Tobe, 'Don't do that. That's Willie's bag.' And this Tobe, he squared off against Bill."

"That's right," Willie said. "He wanted to belt old Bill Gore. Somebody stepped between them, but I didn't want nothin' to do with that Cut and Shoot place."

"And last fall I went up to see Carmen Basilio in Syracuse," I said. "He also says you were the greatest boxer he ever saw."

"That's nice of him," Willie said. "What's he doin'?"

"He's teaching in a college there."

"He teaching in a college?" Willie said. "How can he be teachin' in a college, when he can't even speak English."

"Come on, Willie," I said, "he speaks as well as we do."

"Yeah, I know," he said, "but, I mean, how can he be teachin' in a college?"

"He teaches physical education."

"Oh," Willie said. "Well, he could do that."

"He told me you wouldn't agree with me."

"He told you what?"

"He told me that you wouldn't agree with me. He says that everything he says, you disagree with."

"He's wrong," Willie said.

"You see?" I said. "That's exactly what he said."

"Every time he sees me," Willie said, "he grabs me in a headlock. Why does he do that?"

"I don't know," I said. "He likes you, I guess."

"That's enough," Devlin said, laughing and standing up. "I could sit around here all afternoon listening to these stories, but I have things to do."

He shook hands with me, and put on his coat and hat and left. Willie was sitting back, his hands clasped behind his head.

"So what do you want to know?" he said.

"How are things with you," I said. "I'm presuming you're presently married."

I had lost track of Willie's marriages. The first was to a girl from around Hartford, the second was to a model, the third to an exotic dancer, the fourth to a hat check girl and part-time actress. That's where some of the money went. Some went into a home for his parents, and some went at the race track, and some into Chilean oil wells, two night clubs, and a tavern.

"This is the fifth time," he said. "I'm happily married nine years to this girl—Geraldine. Her father was an All-American basketball player at Manhattan College—Nat Volpe—and he used to referee games in the Garden. When I first met my wife she didn't know Willie Pep from a hole in the wall. I got a seven-year old daughter—Melissa—a cat, two dogs, and a fenced in yard, and that's it."

"I remember a little kid, a boy about knee-high, who used to be around the gym here with you."

"I got a thirty-three-year-old daughter. I got two boys. One guy is thirty-one and the other is twenty-four. I run away the first time. We were both twenty years old, and she said, 'Willie, we ought to get married.' I said, 'I can't, until I'm champion of the world.' So two months later we got married. My first two are dead now, and the third and fourth—I don't know what happened to them once we got divorced. I did well by them, though."

"I recall somebody telling me," I said, "that a father of one of your wives told you before the marriage, 'Willie, don't marry my daughter. She's no good, and you're too nice a guy.' I thought that was quite a noble act by a father."

"But that's not so," he said. "Why would the guy tell me that?

I was champion of the world, and his daughter was gonna live in style. The wives and me, we couldn't get along, and if you can't get along, it's no good."

The door had opened, and a man in a windbreaker had walked in. He was standing in front of Willie's desk.

"How are you Willie?" he said.

"Fine," Willie said, looking up at him.

"You want to buy a TV set?"

"I already got a TV set," Willie said.

"How about a 19-inch black and white?"

"I already got a 19-inch black and white," Willie said.

"I know," the other said, "I'm the guy who's fixin' it for you."

"Oh, yeah," Willie said, "I forgot. Where is it?"

"I got it out in the car," the other said. "You want to come out, and I'll put it in your car?"

"Good," Willie said, and then to me, "Excuse me a minute. All right?"

With those quick steps he went over to the coat rack and put on a topcoat and he followed the other out. In about five minutes he was back, hanging up his topcoat and hurrying over to his desk.

"You see," he said, "I give the set to one guy to fix, and he gave it to this guy. That's why I didn't recognize this guy. I got to call my wife."

He dialed, and I could hear the ringing sound at the other end. Then the sound stopped.

"Hey!" he said into the phone. "The guy just brought the TV back. I'll bring it home tonight. What? All I know is what the guy said. He said he fixed it. There may be a few lines in it yet, but he did the best he could. What? What do I know about a TV? I don't know nothin'. All I know is the guy . . . Hey, wait a minute!"

He took the phone away from his head and held it out from himself. What I heard sounded like a recording tape being run rapidly through the player, and Willie was looking at me and shaking his head and laughing.

"Wait! Wait!" he was saying into the phone now. "Hold it! Listen to me. Oh, boy. Hey, put Missy on. Let me talk to Missy. Please?"

He waited, looking at me and shaking his head and raising his eyes and laughing.

"Hello, Missy?" he said now. "How was school? What? Yeah, I got it. What? Look, how do I know? All I know is the man said he fixed it the best . . . Hey! You sound just like your mother."

He held the phone away from himself again. This time the pitch was higher, as if the tape was being run even more rapidly through the player, perhaps even backward.

"Missy?" he was saying into the phone again now. "Listen. Hey! Never mind. Look. I got it in the car, and I'll be home with it about five o'clock. All right? Good. Good. I'll see you."

He put the phone back on its cradle. He shook his head, and he was still smiling.

"That was my daughter," he said. "I get a couple weeks vacation, and this year I'm thinkin' of taking her to Disney World."

"She'll like that," I said, "so you'll enjoy it, too."

"I live within 120 miles of six race tracks," he said. "We also got dog tracks and jai alai, and I can't go. You lose a hundred, and what are you gonna do?"

"Willie," I said, "I'm going to try something on you again. You were a great artist, and . . ."

"Thank you," he said.

". . . and the rest of us are always yearning to learn how the great artist does it. Can't you recall where you learned this move or that move?"

I had tried it on him many years before, but to no avail. It is what Hans Hofmann, the late abstract expressionist painter and teacher once said, "The painterly instincts are stronger than will. In teaching, it is just the opposite. I must account for every line. One is forced to explain the inexplicable."

"Styles are funny," Willie said. "One's guy's candy is another guy's poison."

"That's why no one else could really box Willie Pep's style."

"I don't know," he said. "My father wasn't athletic. He came from the old country, and he worked on construction in Middletown, but he liked sports. On the East Side I was a little kid, and I used to get whacked around."

"And run," I said.

"Right, and the Old Man said, 'Don't come home cryin', or I'll whack you around, too.' I didn't win any fights on the street, that's for sure. Then one guy, some older kid, said, 'Why don't you go to the gym? You're gettin' beat up, and you can get paid for it.'

"I got $3 in Danbury, Connecticut, in 1937. I got $5 all together, but it was $2 for the license. In Norwich, Connecticut, I weighed 107, and a tall black guy from the Salem AC gets on and he's 126. I said to the guy who was managing me, 'What about this guy?' He said, 'He ain't no good, or he wouldn't be fightin' you.'"

"Ray Robinson."

"Yeah. He boxed me under the name of Ray Roberts."

"And he says that, after he got the decision, they threw him in jail overnight, because they couldn't believe an amateur could beat Willie Pep."

"But he's wrong," Willie said. "I was a nobody then, so why would they throw him in jail for beatin' me?"

"I don't know," I said, "but did you learn anything in that fight, or any fight?"

"I can't say," he said. "You see, with me, guys were always trying to hit me, and I didn't like to get hit. I didn't like to get punched, and I was very fortunate. I think I won thirty or forty straight rounds without losing a round. It just came to me. The other guy was missing, and I was punching. Instinct. I just did it. I jabbed a guy, and then I made him miss, and then I was behind him. I was blessed with a lot of things.

"Then Bill Gore came along," he said, and Bill Gore was his trainer. "I'd come back to the corner, and Bill would be the most relaxed guy. He'd wipe me off, and give me water. He was calm and he made me calm."

"How nervous were you before a fight, say in the dressing room?"

"I was nervous," he said. "I sat. I walked. I wanted to get in there and get it over with. I was scared in every fight in a way, I guess."

"Can you recall anything that Bill Gore taught you?"

"He told me once, 'You jab, and you push your hand out and

you step to the side and you leave your hand there.' I fought a guy in Phoenix—you could look it up—and I kept doin' that, and after the fight he was complainin', 'I don't know what's the matter with my neck. It's stiff, and it hurts.'

"Bill Gore," he said, "he told me, 'The way you talk now, you're gonna talk when you quit.' He wouldn't let me get hurt. Against Saddler, the third time, my left eye was shut tight. Bill Gore said to the referee, 'He can't continue.' I said, 'Thank you.' He died in '75 in Tampa, and they buried him in Providence, Rhode Island, and I went to the wake. He was one of the greatest trainers of all time. If he was around New York he woulda been known as the greatest."

"So how did you finally decide, after 241 fights, to finally call it quits?"

"In January of 1966," he said, "in Richmond, Virginia, they told me, 'Come down here and box an exhibition, four rounds.' The day of the fight, Bill Brennan, the commissioner of Virginia, says, 'You're boxing six rounds.' I said, 'It's supposed to be an exhibition.' He told the other guy, Calvin Woodland, 'If you don't fight, I'll suspend you.' He told me, 'I'll have you suspended everywhere.' I stayed at the Admiral Sims, in Richmond, a real nice hotel, and I was there three days and I had a big tab, so I fought the guy, and he licked me in six rounds and I packed it in."

"And then what did you do?"

"I worked for a brewery for a while, and for a car radio company for a while. Rocky Marciano was instrumental in gettin' me that job in Brockton. I was a good-will man, and then I got a job as a Tax Marshal for Connecticut, but I couldn't stand that."

"Why not?"

"I couldn't make any money, and the stories ruined me. Basically, I'm a very soft guy. I'm a sucker for a touch, and a sob story makes me cry. The job was to collect unpaid taxes, and I got paid only if I collected the taxes—six per cent. After the Tax Marshall says, 'No funds.' they leave the guy alone, and I was always saying, 'No funds.' No money for me. This one guy had a gas station outside of town here, and he owed $3,000 in taxes. I knew the guy, but I hadn't seen him in fifteen years. The guy was married, with a kid, and dead broke, and he couldn't pay his bills, so I ended up loaning him ninety bucks. That was no job for me."

"Do you miss the way it used to be, Willie?"

"They told me I grossed close to a million," he said, "but I used to get cut fifty per cent. My father told me, 'Don't ever take anything that don't belong to you.' He couldn't read or write, but he knew right or wrong. I never hurt anybody. Maybe I did—I don't know—but I didn't mean to."

"But do you miss being in the ring?" I said. "You know, being able to box so beautifully and thrilling people and hearing the cheers and the praise."

"I don't think about it too much," he said, "because I'll never have it to do again. I made a lot of mistakes, but I'm very fortunate. I came out of them."

When it was coming up 4:30, I asked him to call a cab for me, but he said he would drive me to where I could cross the street to the motel. We walked out to the parking space, and the TV set was on the passenger's side of the front seat. I got in the back, and Willie seemed small, peering out over the wheel. City-soiled snow, sand mixed into it, was banked along the curb where a half dozen cars were backed up at the stop light.

"Now don't cross here," he said to me, as I started to get out. "Cross at the corner. I don't want to see you get hurt."

"I never wanted to see you get hurt, either," I said.

"Thank you," he said. "Good luck."

As I approached the corner, the light changed and the cars began to move. When he passed me he waved quickly, just once, and then turned back to the wheel, and that was the last I saw of the great artist, the like of whom I'm sure I shall never see again.

10

The Uncrowned Champ

He was as good as a fighter can be without being
a hell of a fighter.

A. J. Liebling, *The Sweet Science*

When he would come out of Stillman's Gym and walk down
Eighth Avenue he looked as if he should be over on Fifth. He was
given to good clothes and an occasional manicure, and except for
a small scar on the bridge of his Roman nose, there were no
marks on him. In 126 fights over fifteen years he was never off his
feet, and one night in Madison Square Garden, with the title on
the line, he licked the welterweight champion of the world, and
emerged uncrowned.

The science precedes the art, for the art is based on it, but with
the great ones it is instinctive. The rest of us are at best profes-
sionals, the science acquired by study and effort, by imitation and
adaptation, always waiting for and expecting the art to emerge
and transcend the science. It never does, and Billy Graham, the
consummate professional, was one of the rest of us. I think I was
attracted to him because he seemed to me to be the symbol of the
rest of us as he waited for the masterpiece that never emerged.

"When you started to box," I said to him the first time I ever
sat down to talk with him, "did you want to be a champion?"

"Sure," he said. "When I was a little kid, I wanted to be heavyweight champion of the world. When I was eleven years old,
though, I weighed sixty-five pounds, so I decided I'd like to be
middleweight champion. As it turns out, I'm a welterweight, you
know?"

We were sitting on one of the benches behind the rings at Still-man's Gym. He was in his ring clothes, bandaging his hands while he waited to get into the ring. By then he had been boxing for eight years. He had had eighty-five fights and had won all but the three he had lost by decision.

"And you'd still like to be champion?"

"Sure," he said, "but you know how it is. You have to pick your spots."

"You have one of the best records in boxing," I said. "Have you ever wondered why you don't receive more acclaim?"

"I think I understand that," he said. "A friend of mine said to me, 'You know, I enjoy seeing you box. You're a good boxer, but watching you, I don't get excited.'"

"I know what he means," I said.

"Teddy Brenner was talking to me about it once," he said. Teddy Brenner was a matchmaker then, and later the direc-tor of boxing at Madison Square Garden. "Teddy said, 'You're such a good boxer that you always make it look too easy. The people don't like that.'"

He was never one of those runners who, Jack Hurley used to say, should have been in track and field. He had mastered the sci-ence of punching distances and angles, so he was always there where the danger should have been but seldom was, and boxing divorced from danger is devoid of excitement and the emotion that is, of course, the quintessence of the art.

"Do you ever get mad in the ring?" I said to him, for suppressed anger, under control until released perhaps in a single punch, has always been in all the great ones.

"No," he said, "I fight best after I've been hit hard, but I know what I want to do. I want to be the boss in there, and I don't fight harder because I get mad, but because I want to show that I'm the boss."

"How are you in the dressing room?" I said. "Are you excited before a fight?"

"A little," he said, and then to be sure I understood, "but not afraid. There's nothing to be afraid of. I can handle whatever the the other guy tries, so I know I won't get hurt. I can smother a lead, but what I'm nervous about is that maybe I won't fight my

best fight. I'm a little nervous that I won't give my best performance."

"Works of art," Rainer Maria Rilke wrote, "are indeed always
products of having-been-in-danger, of having-gone-to-the-very-
end in an experience, to where man can go no further."

So the Himalayan peaks are scaled by those who dare, while the
rest of us frequent the foothills. We, too, have the desire to stand
atop the world, but there is something in the psyche that saps the
will, a timidity that tethers us to what we know, and so our work
is never the product of having gone to that very end in that experience.

One night Billy Graham went to the end. It was August 29,
1951 in the Garden. He and Gerardo Gonzalez, out of Cuba and
called "Kid Gavilan," had split two earlier fights, Billy winning
the first and Gavilan the second, but now Gavilan was the welterweight champion of the world. Over the fifteen rounds, all of them
close, it was a boxing contest and Billy Graham was never behind.
He outjabbed Gavilan, waiting for his leads, and when they came
he picked off the hooks and turned from the right hands and stepped inside the swings. He had the better of it inside and, late
in the fight and chancing right hands as he never had with as good
a fighter before, he rocked the champion. I had him winning it
nine rounds to six, and Red Smith gave it to him eleven rounds to
four in the press rows that were unanimous for Graham.

As Johnny Addie announced the decision, an angry roar thun-
dered down from the balconies and rose from the floor. One judge
gave it to Graham by a single round, the other and the referee
gave it to Gavilan. In the ring Billy Graham, unbelieving and bewildered, held his gloved hands out in supplication, and out of
their seats and into the aisles they came, waving their fists and
shouting, their faces contorted by their anger, as the Garden
ushers and security men and the city cops struggled to restrain
them into islands. In the passageway under the seats on the Fiftieth Street side there was a fight, and in his dressing room Billy
Graham sat, still unbelieving, while they tried to console him.

"You're still the champ," one of them was saying over the
heads of the others. "You're still the champ, and when you walk
into a joint they'll call you 'Champ.' "

Billy Graham knew the truth, though, and so did we. He had

gone to very end of his experience, beyond where he had ever been before, and he had won—but he had lost. They might call him "Champ," but it would never be there in *The Ring Record Book,* in the histories of the game, in the purses he would command, and in whatever use of the title he might be able to make in the years to come outside the ring.

That is the price the professional must pay when he performs within an art form. There are no goal lines to cross, no home plates to touch, no scoreboard to record his victories. In the decision contests of boxing, as in painting and writing and piano competitions, the judgments of honest men, who cannot totally explain them, are subjective, and so they differ.

It was two years later that I went into camp with him for the better part of three weeks as he prepared to fight Joey Giardello in a twelve-rounder in the Garden. In Havana, five months before, he had gone against Gavilan again, but his moment had passed, and he was out-pointed. Now he was thirty-one years old, his chance for a title gone, married and with two small children, a journeyman fighter making a living even as you and I. We so seldom celebrate them, those who are just honest workers, and yet it is they, and not the champions, who best represent and reflect us. That was why I wanted to do the magazine piece about him, about the way he lived and learned his trade and practiced it.

He picked me up with his car at midafternoon in early March at the Fiftieth Street entrance to the Garden. We drove through the Lincoln Tunnel and then, through the gray, damp gathering dusk, over the wide, flat concrete highways of New Jersey to the Long Pond Inn.

"You have too many distractions at home," he was saying. "My wife understands, but take like this morning. At 7:30 the kids wake me. They wake me at 8:30. At 9:30 they wake me again. I said to Lorraine, 'Look, can't you keep these kids away from me? I gotta get my sleep.' She said, 'You slept enough, didn't you?'"

"Every once in a while," he said, "Lorraine talks about me giving it up. It's tough on a wife. At first there's some glamour to it. You go out and you're recognized, but you're keeping in shape, so you can't go out a lot. She's alone—like now, for three weeks— and it's rough. So I tell her, 'Sure, I'll quit, but what else am I gonna do? Do you want to live on sixty a week? Let me work something out.'"

That morning he had driven her to the supermarket to load up with the groceries for the three weeks. Then they had driven to a toy store to buy a red wagon for young Billy's third birthday, two days away, and that he would miss.

"With me," he was saying, "it's a case of winning every fight now. If you don't have the big punch—you know, the glamour— you have to win for your bargaining power. All you have is your record."

This fight would be his attempt to rewrite that record. Three months before, he had lost in the Garden another of those split decisions. He had boxed Joey Giardello, and again, when the scoring of the three officials was announced, another near riot had followed. At ringside, within minutes, the New York State Athletic Commission had changed the card of one of the judges to give Billy Graham the fight, an act that was later to be reversed by the State Supreme Court.

"Did you ever try to build up your punch?" I said as we drove north. By now he had won ninety-nine fights, but only twenty-five by knockouts. He had fought eight draws and had ten losses, eight by split decisions, and whatever your art form is you want to make the definitive statement that overpowers subjective judgment, and in boxing it is the knockout.

"A punch is something you're born with," he said. "Either you have it or you don't. I gave it a try. I thought punching the heavy bag would do it. In 1946 I knocked out Pat Scanlon in five. I knocked out Frankie Carto in nine and sent him to the hospital. When I fought Tony Pellone he just managed to keep his balance, and I had Ruby Kessler on the deck. The papers were starting to write that I was becoming a puncher, and then I fought Tippy Larkin in the Garden, and I was looking to kayo him too. He won it big. After that I forgot about the big punch."

He was born and grew up on Manhattan's East Side, but not in the tenement section thirty blocks to the south that spawned Rocky Graziano and so many other street toughs who peopled boxing in those days and fought in the Garden ring. The neighborhood was starting to run down, but it was better than tenement. And Billy's father owned a candy store where he also sold some sporting goods, until after Prohibition went out, and he opened a saloon at Thirty-sixth Street and Second Avenue.

"Did you ever have any street fights?" I asked him, driving out.

"Lots of them," he said. "We had the candy store, and the park was across the street. My mother would come out and see a whole bunch of kids scrambling around, and I'd be in the middle of it. At least I've been told this, that my father said, 'Where can I send this kid to be taught how to fight before he gets killed?' He got up on a ladder and took these Everlast gloves down and said, 'Come with me.' He took me to the Catholic Boys' Club on Thirty-seventh, and I used to go there every night."

"Those street fights," I said. "You're so mild-mannered that it's hard for me to imagine you being in them. Did you have a temper?"

"I don't think I had a temper," he said. "I don't remember starting a fight, but maybe I did."

He weighed sixty-five pounds then, when he started to box for the club, and in more than eighty fights, of which he won all but two or three, he learned the rudiments. His hero was Walter "Popeye" Woods, who was out of the neighborhood and who, they used to say in boxing, could have been the middleweight champion of the world if he had just worked harder at it and lived right.

"I'd see him hanging around the corner or at the Boys' Club," Billy said. "I'd say, 'What round are you gonna knock him out in?' When he fought at one of the clubs in town I'd save up. A seat was seventy-five cents upstairs, and to get there I'd sneak on the subway or hitch on a bus or a taxi or any car that stopped for the light.

"He used to bust guys up with his jab. Once he told me something I never forgot. He said, 'You can watch a bum, and he may do one thing you can use.' I never forgot that."

For me the almost three weeks in camp were as pleasant an experience as I have known in sports. My own fight, the writing, would not have to be done until Billy fought his, and it was reassuring and rewarding just to watch a professional prepare at his own pace and in his own way, knowing always what he wanted to do and why he wanted to do it.

Greenwood Lake extends north and south across the line that separates New Jersey from New York State. A two-lane concrete highway runs along the west shore of the lake, and the camp, only the burned ruins of which remain now, was near the New York end. It stood, a long, low cement-block-and-wood building painted white with green trim, between the highway and the lake where the shore drops down to the water. At the highway level were the gym and the dressing rooms and the rooms where the fighters slept, and at the south end steps led down from the parking space to the bar and dining room and kitchen at the lake level.

The establishment was owned by Johnny Dee, Ollie Cromwell, and Eddie McDonald and his wife, Catherine. She did the cooking, assisted by her husband, who walked around, often in a butcher's apron and with a cigarette, the ash long on it, hanging from his mouth. He was a talker, and when he was at a loss for something to say, he would call on Skipper, a brown-and-white part-beagle that, after repeated commands, would emit a low guttural sound that Eddie McDonald insisted was talking.

"Here, Skipper!" Eddie said to the dog after we had come into the dining room late that afternoon. "Say hello to Billy. Say 'Mama.'"

We had shaken hands with Eddie, with Roland LaStarza, the heavyweight who was finishing his training to meet Rex Layne in the Garden, and Walter Cartier, the middleweight who was preparing to box Randy Turpin in England. The dog was squatting now at McDonald's feet.

"Speak, Skipper!" McDonald said. "Say hello to Billy. Say 'Mama.'"

"But why would he say 'Mama' to Billy?" I said, as we waited while the dog remained silent.

"Because he's a smart dog," McDonald said, "and he likes Billy. He'll talk to him later."

The first couple of days Billy slept late, ate well and, after his meals, took long walks along the side of the highway. I walked with him, and we talked about fights and fighters and their styles, interrupting our progress to demonstrate, as we squared off and made tentative leads and went through the motions of countering.

When Whitey Bimstein, who trained him, came up, he would get Billy up at 8:30, and Billy and Walter Cartier would do their roadwork. They would start out from the camp, running easy along the left side of the road north and into the town of Greenwood Lake, then off to the right along the shore of the lake by the white cottages with the rowboats turned bottoms up on the lawns. Then they would make the circuit back through the town again and down the highway to the camp, in all a distance of 3.3 miles.

When they would come off the road they would go to Billy's room. Whitey would bring them hot tea and lemon, and they would sit there with towels around their necks, sipping tea and sweating and talking. Then Walter Cartier would go into his room to read and listen to a disc jockey on his radio. He was reading William F. Buckley's *God and Man at Yale,* and Billy would lie down on his bed and cool out and listen to the radio through the wall.

On the fourth day Johnny Noel, the sparring partner, came into camp and Billy went into the gym. The gym was immaculate, with knotty-pine planking on the walls and the ring set over by the windows that looked down and out onto the lake. While Billy boxed, Whitey Bimstein would stand on the ring apron, never taking his eyes off him, every now and then calling to him and, at the end of each round, telling it to him again.

"Inside more," he would say. "Under the lead and to the body. "Stick. Stick. Slip the lead and the combinations to the body. You gotta do that."

"Sure, Whitey," Billy would say. "Relax. I know."

In the evenings, after we would walk on the road, Billy would shoot pool with Ollie Cromwell on the table beyond the bar. Then we would sit around and listen to Eddie McDonald argue fights with Whitey and talk to the dog.

"Watch this, Billy," Eddie would say. "Listen to Skipper now. Skipper is a real smart dog, and he likes you, Billy."

There would be the same songs, over and over again, on the juke box. Someone, who had dropped in for a drink at the bar, would plunk a coin into the juke box and out would come once more "Don't Let the Stars Get in Your Eyes" or "Blues in the Night" or "Glow Worm."

"Billy will lick this guy," Eddie McDonald would say, "Billy will lick him, but good. He will make mincemeat of Mr. Giardello."

He had a genuine affection for Billy, but it also seemed to me that he took a proprietary interest in the fighters who trained at his place. I think he regarded them, when they climbed into a ring, as advertisements for the Long Pond, and when, at the end of it, we drove into New York for the fight, he and his wife were in the car with Billy, Whitey, Johnny Dee, and me.

"You'll lick him good," he said to Billy, when we dropped him and his wife off in mid-Manhattan on our way down to the offices of the New York State Athletic Commission for the weigh-in. "You'll put lumps on him. You'll see."

"Sure," Billy said, smiling. "Don't worry about it, Eddie."

That was the way he was at the weigh-in too. When the photographers positioned them, stripped to the waist and facing each other in the fighting poses, Giardello's fists were trembling, while Billy's were motionless.

After the weigh-in, we drove up to the Shelton Hotel on Lexington Avenue and Whitey and Billy checked into a room there. Then we went into the dining room, and while Billy was having his breakfast, his mother came in. She was a small woman—four feet ten—with wide blue eyes, and Billy got up and kissed her and she sat down. She didn't say much, just sitting there and watching Billy until he finished and got up to go upstairs and rest.

"Good luck, chicken," she said when he bent down to kiss her again, and then she turned to Whitey and said, "I hate to think of it. I don't even watch on TV."

"Don't worry about it, Mom," Billy said. "There's nothing to worry about."

At three o'clock we walked to the Scribes Restaurant where Billy knew the bartender and where he had the meal on which he would fight, the steak and green vegetables and tea. After he had finished, and the bartender and the waiter had wished him luck, we stepped out onto the sidewalk.

"I got to get over to the Garden sometime," Whitey Bimstein said. "I got to pick up some tickets."

"Go now," I said. "I'll walk with Billy."

We walked back toward the hotel, the afternoon air gray and damp and laden with traffic exhaust fumes, and then up fourteen blocks and across one block and then back. Along the way they kept popping out of the crowd to wish him luck, and at one place one of them came out of a bar to drag him in to meet a couple of others.

"It's television," Billy said when he came out. "The last couple of years everybody recognizes you."

"Excuse me," another said, facing us on the sidewalk. "I've been thinking of you for three months."

He was short and slim, in a camel's hair coat and wearing a gray fedora. He had a small blond mustache with the ends neatly pulled to points.

"I was gonna write you," he said. "When you throw the right hand, step in with the right foot. You gotta do that. You see, I used to fight. I fought Young Corbett, Frankie Neil. I fought champions. I was no good, but I had Young Corbett on the deck."

"Is that right?" Billy said.

"Sure," he said, "and like I said, when you throw the right, step in with it. I'd have written you, but you might never have read it. All right?"

"All right," Billy said, nodding. "And thanks."

"And good luck," the other said.

"Of course we know he's right," I said, as we walked on.

"Sure," Billy said, "but when you've been doing it the other way for all these years and it's not your style, it's not gonna work, so forget it."

I know, I was thinking. We start out as initiators and adapters of other's styles, and then we become imitators and prisoners of our own.

In the dressing room he was as he had been throughout the three weeks and at the weigh-in. Irving Cohen and Jack Reilly, who managed him, came in, and as he sat there in his ring trunks and his robe on the bench against the wall and listening, Jack Reilly lectured him.

"There are three things you've got to remember," Jack Reilly was telling him while Irving Cohen stood there nodding. "On the break you have to get off fast, because he likes to sneak you there. Second, he's gonna look to throw the right over your jab, so after you jab you've got to weave. Third, you must go to his body, and slow him down. He don't like it in the body. Will you remember that?"

"Sure," Billy said. "Don't worry, Jack."

That was the way he fought the fight. Giardello came out as they had known he would. He dropped the right over Billy's jab and when he tried it again, Billy tried to weave under it and his nose banged against Giardello's head. When he came up, there was a cut across the bridge with the blood smearing his nose and his cheeks, and a shout went up.

Blood always looks bad to the crowd, and when Billy lost the first two rounds they probably thought he was in for it. In the corner, Whitey Bimstein did a good job closing the cut, and from the third round on Billy started to be the boss. Giardello made a fight of it though, and when he won the tenth round it was still close.

"Now forget the first ten rounds," Irving Cohen was saying in the corner. "You must win these next two."

"Sure, Irving," Billy said again, looking up at him. "Don't worry about it."

He turned it on in the last two. Giardello was swinging instead of punching now, his arms pulling his body after them, while Billy, still on a straight line, kept moving inside the swings to punch to the body and then rock the head back with hooks and straight right hands. Now he could do the things they had worked on in camp because the pace and the distance were too much for Giardello, still young then and just in there now on heart.

"And the winner by unanimous decision," Johnny Addie, the announcer, said, "Billy Graham!"

Back in the dressing room, Dr. Vincent Nardiello, the Commission physician, put five stitches across the nose. Billy just lay down on the rubbing table with a couple of towels under his head, and the doctor trimmed the edges of the cut and put in the thread, and Billy never moved.

"You don't need an anesthetic," he was explaining to them later. "You're still worked up from the fight, and you don't even feel it. You didn't see me move, did you? I'd move if it hurt."

It was an hour after the fight, and he was standing on the sidewalk outside his father's bar. The crowd had overflowed into the street, and they were shaking his hand and slapping him on the back when his wife came out. He threw his arms around her and kissed her, and together they walked into the crowded, smoky bar and into the cheers.

"These," his brother Robbie said to me, "are his fans. These are the guys who bought the tickets for the four-rounders and the six-rounders and the eight rounds at the Broadway and the Ridgewood and the St. Nick's, and they've been with him ever since. These are the most important guys in the world."

He retired two years later, after 126 fights, of which he won 102, with nine draws and fifteen losses by decision. In non-title fights he had out-pointed, at one time or another, three who went on to become champions—Gavilan, Giardello, and Carmen Basilio—and I would see him occasionally at fights in the Garden. I knew he was a sales representative for a national distiller, and that he and his wife and their now four children lived on Long Island. I hadn't seen him or talked with him, though, for a dozen years when I called him on the phone one January night.

"You live up there?" he said. "We're coming up that way in February, to go skiing with Douglas. He's sixteen, and our youngest."

"You ski?" I said.

"Not much," he said. "I kind of fool around with it, but Lorraine and I go along with Douglas. He's crazy about it, and we bought this five-day package at a place called Dostal's. You ever hear of it?"

"Sure," I said. "It's at Magic Mountain, about forty minutes from us. I'll tell you what to do. You three come up a day early, and stay overnight with us. You and I can talk about the old days, and then it'll be an easy drive over to Dostal's."

It was about a month later when they came up. It was just before six o'clock in the evening when he called, as I had suggested the night before on the phone, from a gas station six miles down the road. I told him I would meet him in town, in front of the inn and across from the general store, and I parked there against the banks of snow piled by the town plows.

When the lights of a car came around the corner, I got out and the car stopped. I opened the door on the passenger's side, and under the overhead light I could recognize him at the wheel. He had on one of those houndstooth Sherlock Holmes hats and a fawn-colored suede jacket, and he was wearing steel-rimmed glasses. Their son Douglas was on the passenger's side and Lorraine was in the back. They had been on the road for more than five hours, and as we shook hands they looked at me with glassy eyes.

I led them out of town and up the mountain, and that night, during dinner and later in front of the fire, while Douglas watched TV, we adults talked about family things, raising children and the struggle to keep ahead of inflation, about the changes in the New York we used to know, and about getting older. He was fifty-six now, his blond-brown hair grayed and thinning, and with just a little extra weight on his upper body. We did not talk much about boxing and his work now, as I was saving that, and the next morning I led him into my study.

"This is a nice room here," he said.

"I guess so," I said. "Each time we've moved, I've set up one of these rooms as I've wanted to. Each time I've thought, 'This is nice. It'll be a good place to work.' In no time at all it becomes just another chamber of horrors."

"I guess writing's not easy," he said.

"You can say that again."

"I guess writing's like fighting," he said. "When you're young and you start out, it's all you want to do. Then it becomes just a job."

"That's the shame of it," I said, "but a writer's not like a fighter. He's hooked for life. Tell me how you made up your mind to retire."

"To retire?" he said. "You think it's gonna go on forever. I never thought about it, until I lost a fight to Chris Christensen. One day in Stillman's, Irving Cohen pointed out Christensen. He said, 'What do you think of him?' I said, 'Why?' He said, 'He's the welterweight champion of Denmark.' I said, 'He must be the only welterweight in Denmark.' Irving said, 'I just made him with you for the Eastern Parkway.' I thought, 'Oh, boy. I'll do a number on this guy.'

"I had had my appendix out two or three months before, and every fighter gets tired around the fourth round, but that's in the head, and your condition gets you through. I had that feeling in the second round. I took the fight too soon, and he beat me.

"I took some time off, and then I started to train, and we went to the West Coast to fight Raymond Fuentes. To me he was just a rough, tough guy—muscled—and I didn't think he had too much then. I had it in my head that I could walk through him—you know?—and I didn't have to do much work. I guess I got to the point where I didn't want to do too much work, the least possible. I guess it happens to everybody. You get bored. You get disenchanted.

"Then after the Fuentes fight, which I lost, I was okay moneywise, and I took the rest of the year off. I boxed Chico Vejar in the early part of March in the Garden. I went up to the Long Pond, and every morning Whitey would get me up to go on the road, and he thought I was the kind of guy he didn't have to watch. You know?"

"I know very well."

"So I'd go out on the road," he said, "and I'd turn right and go north. I'd go about like four city blocks and down the hill and, where the road turned to the left, I'd go into Pat's place. I'd run in and have a cup of coffee and make a little small talk. Then I'd get a glass of water, and under my peaked cap I'd spray the water with my fingers like I was perspiring, and Whitey would be watching for me when I'd come in."

"I'm smiling," I said, "and I almost have to laugh. To me you were always the complete pro."

"Yeah," he said, "and it was stupid. When the bell rings, Whitey leaves me and I'm there."

"I didn't see the Vejar fight," I said.

"I felt I could handle anything he could do," he said, "but you're not gonna win the fight because you can't do what *you* want to do. I hated that roadwork because you do that alone."

"You used to run with Walter Cartier when I was in camp with you."

"That's right," he said, "but every fighter runs differently, and Cartier ran like a reindeer, one pace and a long, long way. When I ran with Marciano, he wanted to run up a mountain. I said, 'Hey, wait a minute. This is not for me.' I liked to run three minutes as fast as I could, then walk a minute like the rest period between rounds, and then three minutes again."

"How was the fight?"

"I dropped the decision," he said. "Jimmy Cannon came into the dressing room, and he said, 'What do you think?' I said, 'I guess it wasn't one of my best fights.' He said, 'I mean, what do you think of the decision?' I said, 'I thought maybe a draw would be all right.' And he said, 'I had you winning it by a round, but I gave the decision to Vejar.' I said, 'What's that mean?' He said, 'If Billy Graham can't do any better than that, you'd better quit.'

"Just before the guys came in, though, Irving had said, 'You've had a long career. When the newspaper men come in, I'll tell them you're going to retire.' I said, 'Let's wait a day or so.' Billy Brown was the matchmaker then, and he came in and said, 'You can have him back one month from tonight in Syracuse.' Irving said, 'I'll let you know.'

"So a day or two later, I said to Irving, 'Let me fight him again. If I don't beat him, I promise I'll pack it in.' "

"Did you train any differently?"

"No," he said. "I figured I had ten rounds under my belt, and I was right back in training again, so I still don't have to do roadwork, just long walks. I was all right, but up here in the head I couldn't bring myself to drive like when I was a kid."

"How was that fight?"

"It was close. I guess he won it. He was just a little speedier, had a little more hustle. Irving said, 'You said you would.' I said, 'Let's think about it, and see what comes up.' Nothing came up, moneywise. I laid off, and the summer was coming on, and I told Irving, 'Let's call it off.' He said, 'Good, and I'll talk to the press.' They got it in the papers, which was nice."

"So then?"

"So then, what do I do now? Do I go to an employment agency

and fill out an application? Education? That would be great. Two
years in high school, but a non-participant. I was in the Para-
mount Theater more than in school. I was a big-band buff."

"Benny Goodman?" I said.

"Yeah," he said, nodding, "and the Dorseys."

"Charlie Barnett?"

"And Glen Gray. Harry James. All of them."

"So?"

"I couldn't see doing that, so I used to get dressed every day,
just like I was going to work. I'd stop in my father's bar, and then
go to the West Side to Toots Shor's. I'd talk to some guys, maybe
somebody'd have something. Then I got a call from Frances
Hogan at the Garden."

She was stout and middle-aged and always smiling, and she ran
the boxing switchboard. She should have been with the FBI, because on request, and working those plugs in and out of that
board, she could find anybody anywhere.

"Frances told me," he was saying, "that she had a call from a
secretary, Miss Lynch. She was secretary to Mr. Ohlandt, vice-
president of National Distillers. I called Miss Lynch back. 'When
can I come in?' 'Tomorrow.' He was a great fight fan, and we sat
and talked and got around to the whiskey business. I told him I
had worked the bar and did my father's liquor stock when I was
in school. He asked me some brands, and I named some of his
and some of Schenley, and some of Seagram's and some of Hiram
Walker, and he hired me.

"The job was that you're a distiller's representative. It's a
straight salary, and expense account and a car. They gave me a
list of key restaurants and bars, and it's to get better distribution
of their brands. Ingratiate yourself. Know the product. You
know?"

"Were you nervous starting out?" I said.

"The first couple of times," he said, "I was a little apprehensive
of asking them, of trying to sell them something they don't have.
You try to get as many of your brands as you can on the back
bar. The idea was to get one of each category—your Bourbons,
your gins, your blends, your scotches."

"And what are the hours?"

"In the whisky business, there's no time clock. You can see a guy at eight o'clock in the morning, or nine o'clock at night, stores as well as bars, private clubs, anyone who has a license to sell liquor."

"And do you have to have a drink at every bar?"

"If you drink at every place you're in," he said, "you'd get boiled every day, so you have to judge where to have a drink, and where not."

"Did you ever get loaded?"

"At the beginning," he said, "you're trying to be a good guy, and you're happy they gave you an order. It's like being a fighter. You have to learn to pace yourself. You can't go all out and throw everything in the first couple of rounds and save nothing for the later rounds. You'd blow your wad in the first couple of bars.

"I'm not saying I never got high," he said. "That would be ridiculous. But I got to handle it okay. I stayed with National for thirteen years, and then the president of Calvert Distillers, Arthur Murphy, he and I were acquaintances and we used to make small talk, and he said, 'Let's have lunch.' I was with them for six years, and then I moved over to where I am now at Seagrams."

"And when you go into these places, do they still remember you as a fighter?"

"The name like rings a bell," he said. "I was in a bar about a week ago, and there was a change of management. The new guy said, 'You wouldn't be the fighter, would you?' I said, 'Yes, I am.' It's some time ago now, but one night I was in P. J. Clarke's, and there was this guy at the bar, a super star. Women were getting his autograph, and I figured I'd like to meet him. On the way back from the men's room, I stopped and I said, 'I'd just like to shake hands with a great actor.' He said, 'And what's your name?' When I told him, he said, 'Billy Graham, the fighter? When I was a busted actor, I won $800 on you when you fought Art Aragon.' We talked for hours. It was Richard Boone, and he'd had, I think, about fourteen fights."

"Billy Graham, the fighter," I said. "Growing up, that's what you wanted to be known as. You wanted to be like Popeye Woods. I remember you telling me that after you'd beaten some other little kid at some club tournament you put tape over your eye before you went to school the next day. You weren't cut, but you wanted to look like a fighter."

"That's right," he said. "That was when I beat Robinson."

"I'd forgotten that was the time you beat Sugar Ray."

"His name was Walker Smith then," he said, "but I never tell anybody that now. We weighed ninety pounds then, and that's not my claim to fame."

"Whatever became of Popeye Woods?"

"I never called him that," he said. "I called him Walter. He's around Queens, a steam-fitter. I was fighting Sammy Mastrean, and Walter was up in the gym, at Stillman's, and he said, 'Billy, look what you're doin' in there.' I said, 'What?' He said, 'When you knock that jab aside with your left, you're moving the guy over here. You'd have to square around to hit him with your right. Look. Take a jab, slip the next one, and he's movin' into your right hand. Practice it.' So I practiced it and tried it in the gym and practiced it some more, and I said to myself, 'Aw, I can't do it. Forget it.'

"So I fought this Sammy Mastrean, and at the end of the sixth round I'm ahead, but it's getting tough. At the start of the seventh round, Whitey is sayin', 'Do this, do that, you Irish this.' I said, 'Listen, you. I know what I'm doin'.' I'm not even listening to him. I said, 'Just wash out the mouthpiece, and put it back in.'

"The next round he comes out storming, and I figure I've got to do something here. He hit me a jab—bang—on the forehead. When he started the next one, I slipped it and threw the right and down he went. When he got up he was wobbling, and the referee is wiping his gloves under his arms and trying to see if he's all right, and he's dragging the referee around with him. When he motioned me to come back I figured I got to do it now, and I laid it on him—boom, boom, boom—and down he went and out."

"What is it like," I said, "for that kid who put tape over his eye because he wanted to be known as a fighter? When that recognition comes, is it as good as he thought it would be?"

"I remember I was boxing in the Broadway Arena," he said. "I was fightin' a guy named Al Guido, and on the way in I was carrying my own bag. When you become a star, Whitey carries the bag, so this guy stops me. He says, 'You're Billy Graham?' I said,

'Yes.' He said, 'Can I have your autograph?' The first time it's impressive, and then it became a part of your everyday life. The recognition makes you feel good, but it happens so often that you don't think about it."

"Other fighters have told me," I said, "that, right after they retired, they'd see a couple of other guys fighting in the ring—say in the Garden—and they'd think, 'Gee, I could take them. I could do better than that.' Did you ever have that feeling?"

"It always happens," he said. "Even today I see fights, and I think I could have handled them. Some guys would have given me trouble, but not too many, but once I finished I never really thought of it. I quit in May and went to work for National in July, and there was never any way I could do better than I did."

"But don't you ever miss it, ever wish you were young and back in it again?"

"It's a feeling you can't reproduce in any other field," he said. "Not a lot, but two or three times a year, I'll find myself driving into the city, and what comes to my mind are not the big fights, but those smaller fights in that scramble to get to a main event. That's where it's all at.

"You're in with fellas who are trying to get a $100 fight, and you're trying to get a $100 fight, and that guy is gonna fight harder than the guy who's gonna get fifteen or twenty thousand. I think, 'How did I ever do it for $100?' I used to go in with all those tough guys, and one day at the racetrack I said to George Cobb, who used to promote out in New Jersey, 'I never got more than $90 from you.' He laughed, and he said, 'But look at the education you got.'

"They had no showers. You had to take a bucket of water, and put one foot in and wash yourself. Elizabeth, New Jersey, $35, six rounds, and $37.50 the second time, and I had Irving and Whitey and myself. Today I'm not sure I'd want to go through all that again."

"Today no one would," I said. "Our world has changed, and I'm not sure it's all to the better."

"Today the attitudes are bad," he said. "When I was a fighter, I wanted to give them their money's worth, whether they were for me or against me, and today they don't put the effort in. No matter what I did, I put the effort in, or I wouldn't feel right about it. Today, when I get an order for a case, it makes me feel good. It spurs me, because I'm earning my way. I want to find some new bodies, guys who don't have it in, or get them to take more. I got to go see 'em. A lot of salesmen do it by phone. I may call a few personal friends, but I go around. I put the effort in."

"I don't want to open an old wound," I said, "but in your dressing room after you licked Gavilan for the title and didn't get it . . ."

"That's all right," he said, smiling. "It's a lot of years since then."

"I know," I said. "There was this guy in your dressing room, and he was saying, 'You're still the champ, and when you walk into a joint they'll call you "Champ."' You walk into joints now every day on your job. Do they call you 'Champ'?"

"Less frequently than years ago," he said. "A few people still remember that fight, but you know how it is."

"I'm afraid so," I said.

"Every old fighter," he said, "is called 'Champ.'"

More snow had started to fall by midafternoon, and it was coming on dusk as they prepared to leave. There were about four inches of new powder on top of the old, and the air was thick with it when my wife and I walked them to their car.

"Now, the driving is going to be hazardous," I said, "so you'd better put it in second going down this hill. Then, as you get near Bromley, the wind always whips across the flat there, so you'd better take it real slow."

"Don't worry about it," he said, the same Billy Graham. "Relax. We'll make it all right."

We waited while he backed the car out of the driveway, and they started on the road, the red tail lights showing through the falling snow. We went inside and watched out of the window, the headlights searching ahead into the white curtain as the car slowly made the turn to start down the hill.

"They're really a nice family," my wife said.

"And he really licked Gavilan that night," I said, "and it's still a damn shame."

11

The Coach, Relived

In Willie Davis we got a great one.
Vince Lombardi

It was the first week of July 1962, and we were starting to put a book together in Green Bay. It was to be Vince Lombardi's first, and he had a respect for good books, and so, at the beginning, he was caught up in that romance of being an author. For the two weeks before the Packer training camp opened at St. Norbert College across the Fox River in West DePere, I was living with him and Marie and young Vincent and Susan in their new ranch house at 667 Sunset Circle. Each morning, after he had come back from eight o'clock Mass at St. Willebrord's and we had had breakfast, we would go down into the rec room, and I would get out the notebook. We would put in three hours, and then after lunch we would get in two or three more.

"How are we doing?" he said, at the end of the third afternoon.

"We're doing all right," I said, because you hoped never to have to tell him that you were doing otherwise.

"Are we almost done?" he said.

"Almost done?" I said. "I'm only on my second notebook."

"The second notebook?" he said. "How many notebooks are there going to be?"

"Oh, I don't know," I said. "That's hard to say."

"Three? Or four?"

"Five or six."

"Six notebooks?" he said, those eyes burning into my head and that voice thrown like a spear. "Six notebooks? How am I gonna do six notebooks? Six notebooks? I've got paper work to do at the office! I've got players I haven't even signed yet! I've gotta play golf! Once training camp starts I can't play again until the end of the season! Six notebooks? How are we ever gonna do six notebooks?"

"I don't know, coach," I said, "but we'll find a way."

"You guys didn't tell me it was going to be this much work," he said.

"You didn't ask."

"Well, we'll have to do some of it in camp," he said. "We'll be living in the dean's suite, and we can get in an hour or two a day there."

"Relax, coach," I said. "I said we'll find a way."

I meant that I would find a way, and in the month I spent in camp the dream of working in the dean's suite dissolved, as I had suspected it would, into a total of an hour and a half. Before we went into camp I rode miles in golf carts, following him and his companions around the eighteen holes of the Oneida Golf Club, and then spent hours at the bar listening to replays of hole after hole. While he drove down to Fond du Lac to watch Susan in a horse show, I made notes in the car. We talked over drinks before dinner at home, and in restaurants, and I wedged my way amid the paper work at the Packer office that then occupied the old two story, flat-roofed, red-brick corner building at 349 South Washington Street in downtown Green Bay.

"I think I've found a way to simplify this," I said to him late one morning, sitting across from him at his desk, and it'll save some time."

"Good," he said.

"I'm going to start naming players," I said. "When I give you a name, you tell me the first thing that comes to your mind about him, not as a player—we'll get to that another time—but as a person. Do you understand what I mean?"

"Of course I understand," he said. "Let's get started."

"Right, coach," I said. "Bart Starr."

"Tense by nature, because he's a perfectionist. I've never seen him display emotion outside of nervousness. Modest. Tends to be self-effacing, which is usually a sign of lack of ego. You never hear him in the locker room telling 'I' stories. He calls me 'sir.'

Seems shy, but he's not. He's just a gentleman. You don't criticize him in front of others. When I came here he lacked confidence and support. He still lacks daring, and he's not as creative as I'd like him to be, but a great student of the game."

"Paul Hornung."

"Can take criticism in public or anywhere. You have to whip him a little. He had a hell-with-you attitude, a defensive perimeter he built around himself when he didn't start out well here. As soon as he had success he changed. He's still exuberant, likes to play around, but serious on the field. Always looks you straight in the eye. Great competitor who rises to heights."

"Jerry Kramer."

"Nothing upsets him, so you can bawl him out any time. He's been near death, but he's happy-go-lucky, like a big kid. Takes a loss quite badly, though."

"Ray Nitschke."

"The rowdy on the team. Big, fun-loving, rough, belligerent. Like a child. Never gives you an argument, but he'll turn around and do the same thing over again. He's the whipping boy, but he can take it. Criticism just runs off his back. You don't improve him. He improves himself."

"Forrest Gregg."

"Intelligent and, like Marie says, a picture-perfect player. Gives you a hundred per cent effort, a team player. Quick temper. I've seen him go at teammates in practice. Has all the emotions, from laughter to tears. Can take criticism anywhere, if it's constructive."

"Jimmy Taylor."

"Uses jive talk that I can't understand. Has a lot of desire, because he wants to be the best football player the NFL has ever seen. He likes to knock people down, and he'll go out of his way to do it. You have to keep after him, though."

"Henry Jordan."

"All-Pro, all-everything, but don't ever flatter him. He needs public criticism. He thinks he's the greatest and tends to be satisfied. Strangely, he's easily upset, but he needs to be upset to perform. In reviewing pictures I'll make him a target, not to impress somebody else as you do with some of them, but to help him."

In that hour or so I named off all thirty-six Packers, and out of their instant personality profiles there also emerged a profile of the man often described now as the greatest of all football coaches. In the month in camp and a week during the season, I heard the tongue-lashings. I saw men, grown beyond the size of most of us —some of them fathers—cringe, and I heard others swear under their breaths. They knew, however, and if they didn't they soon learned, what I knew after that morning in the office. He knew them, not just as football players but as distinct individuals, each of whom he was determined to make into a better player than that man had ever thought he could be, in Vince Lombardi's obsession to create, out of all the parts, one entity greater than any team that had ever been.

"Willie Davis," I said.

"Traded to Cleveland for him," he said. "A hell of a young man. Very excitable under game conditions. A worrier. Before a game he's got that worried look, so I try to bolster his confidence. He's not worried about the team losing—he's got confidence in the team—but he's worried about how Willie Davis will perform . . . about not letting the team down. Fine brain, too. In Willie Davis we got a great one."

Fourteen years later, on our way out to Jim Tescher's in North Dakota, my wife and I stopped off at Green Bay for three days. On that Sunday the Packers would be opening another season— under Bart Starr now—and I wanted to visit with old acquaintances. I hoped to find, in one or another, what still lived of Vince Lombardi six years after cancer took him on September 3, 1970, in Georgetown University Hospital.

"Willie Davis is coming in from California," Tom Miller said. He played end during the mid-Forties for the Eagles, Redskins, and the Packers, and he is the Packer's general business manager. "Willie's doing very well. He has a big Schlitz distributorship in L.A., and he's on the board of directors of the Schlitz Brewing Company. You remember Willie, of course.

"Of course," I said. "I remember him very well."

I remember that great smile flashing, and how the others called him "Doctor Feelgood," and I remember that worried look that Lombardi had described and that would shroud Willie Davis in front of his locker before a game. During the week he would be the outward optimist, but he was unable to eat before a game and until the morning after, and once, during that month in camp in '62, we sat in one of those dormitory rooms in Sensenbrenner Hall at St. Norbert, and he told me about his beginnings.

He was born in Lisbon, Louisiana, the oldest of three children of a broken family. He grew up in Texarkana, Arkansas, where his mother cooked at a country club, did catering and took in laundry. At Grambling College, which has sent so many football players to the pros, he captained the team for two years.

"When I was drafted by the Browns," he said that day, "I was the seventeenth choice when they picked thirty, and I was concerned. I was from a small Negro school, and there were guys with bigger names picked later. Then in camp you find a guy from Notre Dame or Michigan State whom you've read about."

"Well, they didn't run you off the field," I said.

"No," he said, "and pro football has been the difference between me being just another guy and having something today. In fact, I sometimes shake when I think I might not have finished college and not made a pro club."

"There are a lot of guys," I said, "who are lucky enough to be able to play this game but to whom that thought has never occurred."

"Well," he said, "I think the responsibility I had growing up of looking after the young ones helped me. I've never smoked, and I'm not considered a drinker."

"And the coach tells me you're a worrier, always worried about Willie Davis doing his best."

"That's right," he said. "I constantly replay situations where I could have played better. During the off-season I think of them over and over, and I come back thinking, 'I'm not gonna do that again.' What it is, I guess, is that I try to play so that I can live with myself."

He became the Packer's defensive captain, and on those Packer teams that won five NFL championships in seven years and the first two Super Bowls, he was one of the finest defensive ends ever to play the game. He made All Pro five times, and he retired at the end of the 1969 season.

On the morning after Tom Miller had talked about him, I met Willie, the high forehead a little higher but the smile just the same, at the Packer offices at Lambeau Field on what, in 1968, they renamed Lombardi Avenue. He drove me in his car over to the Midway Motel, and for an hour or so we talked in his room.

"Are you the first black on the Schlitz board of directors?" I said.

"That's right," he said, smiling. "In fact, I'm the second non-family member."

"How did that come about?" I said.

"Well," he said, "long before I quit playing I had started to put together for the day when I could no longer live up to Willie Davis's standards. I wanted to avoid that situation where some coach walks up to you and taps you on the shoulder and says, 'We can't use you any more.' The most fearful thing to me was the day when I couldn't play the game any more.

"My first year in Cleveland I subbed in the school system, but by the second year of subbing I just didn't feel I wanted to be a teacher. I caught on in sales with a brewery out of Pittsburgh, and when I came back to Green Bay the next year I approached the people in Schlitz. I moved to Chicago to work that area, and I enrolled at the University of Chicago, in the business school, and in four years I got my masters in business administration, in marketing. Then, any time the situation warranted, I could leave football."

"And how did you know when it was time to leave?"

"I came back in '69 because of Coach Bengtson," he said. Phil Bengtson, who had coached the Packer defense under Vince Lombardi, had succeeded him. "Coach Bengston had meant a great deal to me, and I wanted to see him have a winning season. I played that '69 season and when, with four games to go, we were mathematically eliminated, it was the first time since grade school that I walked out onto a field and had trouble scrambling for reasons to play.

"After that game—I believe it was against Minnesota—I said to myself, 'There's no need of me kidding myself. There's no way I'm gonna play.' On the twenty-first of December, Forrest Gregg and I walked out onto the field for our last game, and he said, 'Willie, we've broken a lot of huddles together, and we'll never do it again.' Later, Sid Gilman called me from San Diego, and he said, 'We've studied films, and you can play three or four years.' I told Sid, 'When I walked off that field in Green Bay I walked off a field for the last time. I'm never gonna play again.' A week later I got a call from Schlitz to buy out the company operation in Los Angeles.

"I'd been offered a few coaching jobs, five or six," he said, and only later would I learn that one of them had been at Harvard, "but I said to myself, 'I'm going into the heart of Watts, where I want to be an example.' I mean, I see so many basketballs bouncing in Watts. A kid can identify with that, but why can't I impress them that there's another avenue where maybe they can make it?

"You take the Willie Davis Distributing Company. Maybe people say, 'The guy isn't short of ego.' I didn't name the company a minute on ego. If I say that, I may be kidding myself to some degree, but there's a fine line between ego and pride. If the kids get a chance to see me on parade, maybe that'll help them to reach too. In the evenings, when I get ready to leave the place, many times I don't have to open the gate. Sure, maybe some want a dime or a quarter, but we have a relationship."

He was, he said, president of the Los Angeles Urban League, had been on the board of the West Adams Community Hospital, had served on a public commission to study county government and come up with recommendations to go on the ballot. He worked for the United Way, with Explorer Scouts, with the Watts Festival in Black, and on a career task force with junior high and high schools, and during his first four years there he averaged a speech a week.

"What I'd like to do," I said, "is come out and see you in your environment. Then we can talk at length about you and about the old coach."

"I give one man almost ninety per cent credit for whatever I am," he said. "I give Paul Brown credit for two years at Cleveland. I give my college coach, Eddie Robinson, credit for motivation and his approach to education, but right today I have a daughter and a fifteen-year-old son who is playing football, and the one sad thing is that he will never have a chance to play for Vince Lombardi."

In early March I flew out to Los Angeles, and checked into a motel near the airport. It was midafternoon when I called his office.

"Oh, he's out of town for the day," his secretary said.

"What time will he be in tomorrow?" I said.

"Oh, 7:30," she said. "He's usually here by then."

The next morning, after we spoke on the phone, he sent his younger brother Al out to pick me up. Al looks like Willie, tall and high waisted, and he has the same walk. On the way out, we talked about some of the great Packer games and, when we got into Watts, where whole city blocks, although cleared of rubble, remain vacant and weed-grown, we talked of the riots in 1965. We talked of promises unkept and dreams left still unfulfilled by a nation that, it seems to me, too often functions as if it is a battalion aid station that has neither the time nor the resources to do more than stop the bleeding.

At the plant he drove through the gate of the eight-foot chain link fence with the barbed wire on top, and up to the entrance to the two-story, modern red-brick office section that fronts the warehouse. He took me through the warehouse, high-ceilinged and immaculate, the cases stacked in perfect alignment, a white truck, spotless and with the name on the doors, being loaded.

"We usually have 150,000 cases in here," he said, "but we're down to about 120,000 right now."

While I was still trying to imagine 150,000 cases of beer being consumed, all that heisting of bottles and cans and the aftermath, he opened the door of the refrigerator room, the cold air hitting us. We stepped into an aisle between the stacked aluminum kegs.

"We have the Coliseum," he said, "and the Forum and the Sports Arena, so we move a lot of draft beer."

Back in the office reception room, he led me up a flight of stairs. There were two carpenters working, putting up the studding for new walls, and he said that Willie had just bought an FM radio station that would broadcast from there.

"KACE FM," he said. "It'll be 103.9 on the dial."

Willie's office is on the ground floor, a windowless interior room, walnut-paneled, on the wall behind the dark oak desk a black-tinted, gold-specked mirror; the carpeting tomato-red. On the wall to the left of the desk there was an oil portrait of Lombardi in the dark green Packer coaching jacket and holding a football. On the other walls there were two full-color Packer team photographs, award plaques, and framed certificates.

"I was very sorry to read about Henry Jordan," I was saying.

Willie was sitting behind the desk in a brown leather swivel chair. He had on a gray shirt, open at the neck, a dark green tie and dark green trousers. On his left ring finger was the Packer ring with the three diamonds denoting the successive championships in '65, '66, and '67.

"It was a shock to me," he said. "I've been affected. I've been moved."

Ten days before, at the Milwaukee Athletic Club where he had been jogging, Henry Jordan had died of a heart attack. He had been a five-time All Pro defensive tackle on those teams with Willie, and he was forty-two.

"I went to the funeral," Willie was saying, "and I was one of the pallbearers."

" 'I saw the picture in the paper," I said, "of you and Bart and Hawg Hanner and Bob Skoronsky and . . .'"

"Ron Kostelnik and Lionel Aldridge," he said. "After the service they slide the casket out, and you take a hold and you feel this weight. I thought, 'I've lifted tables and I've lifted cases of beer, but this is my friend that I played football with for eleven years.'

"That's a weight," he said, and he leaned back and put his hands behind his head, "and it makes you think. Henry was six months younger than I am, and how much time do any of us have to enjoy life?"

"Never enough, I guess," I said, "and I'm sorry to tell you that you'll have this feeling more often from now on."

"There's so much a man wants to do, and that he can do," he said, "and Henry's passing made me realize again that you have to get about the business of doing it."

"Lombardi got both Henry and you from Cleveland," I said. "I remember how, before Lombardi turned everything around, they used to say in the league that being traded to Green Bay was like being sent to Siberia. What was it like when they told you in Cleveland that you'd been traded?"

"By then the Packers had had their first winning season under Lombardi," he said, "but it was sort of—well—disturbing. I was subbing in the school system on the west side of Cleveland, and that evening I heard it on a sports flash on the car radio."

"What a nice way to be informed," I said.

"Yeah," he said, smiling. "I had started ten ball games for Cleveland as a rookie and played three games both ways, as an offensive tackle and a defensive end. I was in Cleveland last year, and a trivia question there was, 'Who was the last Cleveland player to play a complete game both ways?' I was kind of shocked by the answer: Willie Davis.

"The next year, I'd just signed three weeks before and been told I'd graded out second best to Jim Ray Smith, and I was to start in the old Lou Groza spot. Being traded I was probably as confused as any person could be, but I drove to Green Bay, with just a couple of rest stops, and when I got near I was kind of bug-eyed. I thought I could see what seemed like hay coming across a field toward the road on some kind of a conveyor. I thought it was an optical illusion, but it was a big wagon of hay being pulled by a tractor, and the guy came up and right across Highway 57 in front of me.

"I went off the road, and I thought, 'Where am I going? I get up here, and I darn near lose my life.' When I got in, they said the coach wanted to see me, and you know that Coach Lombardi, with all the meanness and toughness that's been written about, had that smile that could melt an iceberg. He said, 'Willie, I want you to know one thing. We really wanted to make this trade. When I was the offensive coach in New York we took advantage of you because it was the defense you were forced to play. I was impressed by your quickness and aggressiveness. If you play like that for us, you'll make it big.' Then he said, 'What were you making in Cleveland?' Now, he knew, and before I could say anything, he said, 'We're increasing it by $1,000.' Well, I was ready to be shown the practice field, and I started behind there for one week and I moved up and started for the next ten years."

"I heard him jump on any number of people," I said, "but never you. Did he ever abuse you?"

"Yeah," Willie said, smiling. "Henry Jordan told about it once. We were in training camp, and nothing seemed to be in Lombardi's style. He'd been after Jordan because he'd come in heavy, and in that seven-o'clock meeting he went up and down Henry, and he finally said, 'But Jordan is not a one-man team, so there have to be some other contributors.' I'm sitting there, thinking I'm having my best camp, when he jumped on me and he said, 'Davis, what about you? When are you gonna get with this game?'

"Well, I was shocked, and I almost thought he was kidding. That night, like around midnight if he'd been on the premises, I think I'd have told him, 'I quit.' The next morning Henry went to Bengtson and he handed in his playbook, and he actually wanted to quit. When Lombardi saw me that morning he said, 'I've got to prove nobody's beyond chewing out.' I said, 'Yeah, coach, but give me some warning.'

"The worse game I ever played in my life was the Sunday we played the Forty-Niners after the Kennedy assassination. Such an attitude pervaded the whole team, but Lombardi hardly said a word. He realized that that thing had taken a lot of starch out of everybody, including himself."

"He had met Jack Kennedy, and he greatly admired him."

"Then, after a Minnesota game he got on me in a deserving way. The frustrations of Fran Tarkenton just left me bewildered. At one of the pro bowls I told Fran, 'I went a whole season saying that, if I ever catch up with you, you're gonna be in a world of trouble.' So Lombardi got on me then, but once Max McGee said, 'This had to be a tough day. He even got on Willie.'

"What he would do was, he would never hit you when you expected it. When we'd win by 40, he'd take us apart. We'd lose by 17–14, and he would make a point of why we'd win again. He could walk you out of a defeat, and the next week you'd be absolutely convinced you were gonna win again. He'd pick out two or three essentials, and he'd say, 'If you get back to these basics, it's never gonna happen again.' When we were at the fatigue point, he'd sympathize, but when he thought we were ready to win and we didn't, he took us to task."

"To put it mildly," I said.

"The man knew us," he said. "He told me once, 'Not that I can ever be black, but I can understand. When you reach out, I can understand the reach.' Forrest Gregg was another one he never had to get on."

"Well," I said, "Forrest and you were a lot alike. You were both dedicated guys."

"For ten years," he said, "Forrest and I lined up across from each other day after day, and it was like a . . . a . . . ."

"A mirror?"

"Yeah," he said, smiling. "A black and white mirror."

"Speaking of black and white," I said, "I would judge, from walking around the plant and office with Al, that you've got an integrated company here."

"Is that right?" he said, laughing. "Since my favorite color is green, I really don't know. When I came here, there was one black in the office and one black truck driver and a few as salesmen. We're near fifty-fifty now, although I guess there are more black."

"Can you remember," I said, "when, growing up, you first became conscious of the difference between black and white?"

"Growing up in the South," he said, "you're segregated by so many patterns that the sight of a white person denotes the difference. My first real, believe it or not, experience in a black and white situation was when I worked at the club where my mother worked. You really felt like an object. It was the haves and the have-nots, and nothing distresses me more now than going into a restaurant and seeing a guy who has money giving a waiter or a waitress, regardless of color, a hard time.

"When I got up with Cleveland, it was the first time I was functioning as a peer, working with a white guy on the same level. In Cleveland we worked it out, and that made me appreciate Paul Brown, as I did Lombardi."

"But when you went to Green Bay," I said, "there was no real black community, and only two or three other blacks on the ball club. What was that like?"

"My wife was teaching school in Cleveland then," he said, "and the whole thing there was so interesting for both of us that my pre-disposed instinct was not to go. Being accepted by the Packers, though, was like being accepted into a family, and as to the people, they looked at you on the street kind of in awe. I'm not sure they looked at me as a Packer, or as a black Packer."

"You never found any prejudice?"

"The closest I came," he said, "was my second year, and I was looking for an apartment for the season. I saw something in the paper and I called on the phone, and it was still available. I went by, and it had just been rented. I left, and I had a friend call and it was available again.

"There was an emptiness in me. I thought, 'How can they see

you on the street and make you feel so good, and turn around and they won't rent to you?' Then I said to myself, 'That's one person. It's a population of 80,000, and let's multiply that person a few times and you're still going to have a chance to meet mostly good people.'

"I went to a service station there and I mentioned it to this guy, Paul, and he got so interested that he got on the phone and turned something up. Then, two years later, I met Fabian Redman, a builder in Green Bay, and he kept an apartment open for me, and I had that every year. I'm sure he missed the income, renting only between times, and in Green Bay I saw people who almost dealt with you with kid gloves. You had to turn down invitations to dinner.

"When I went to Green Bay I went with a lot of resentment on being traded, but I would say right now that, even taking the success and having it someplace else, I honestly enjoyed myself there as much as any place I could be, with the ease in getting to the ball park and the closeness. In Cleveland we saw each other at practice, and then there was a mad exodus. In Green Bay, even if you didn't go out socially with that guy, if you went out you saw him there, anyway.

"When you lost," he said, "some woman would come up to you and say, 'That's all right. You guys will get 'em next week.' You would look at the disappointment on their faces, and it was so strong that you had to win the next time."

His phone had rung, and he picked it up.

"I'll be right out," he said into it, and then to me, "It's my insurance man. I'll be back in a few minutes. I've got some problems with the guy about claims."

On his desk there was a copy of *The Wall Street Journal.* On the coffee table in front of the sofa there were copies of *Nation's Business, Business Week,* and *Black Enterprise,* and I looked through those until he came back with the insurance man, whom he introduced as Hector Rexton.

"But look," Rexton said, sitting down, and obviously picking up their previous conversation, "I'm sure that they're all indoctrinated, but what happens between the indoctrination and the execution that results in these claims?"

"Well," Willie said, leaning back in his chair behind the desk, "let me say this. You send a man out with a truck and fifty cases, and he makes stops and unloads. If, somehow, you can motivate each man so that he is accident-proof, then I'm telling you that you're 'Man of the Year' every year."

"I recognize your point," Rexton said, "but if you have another year this year like last year, your premium will be four times what it is now."

"But what are we talking about?" Willie said. "Sixteen cases, but it's only those two. I think you people have to get tough. If you fight these claims, not the legitimate ones but these ones that you and I understand, maybe it would stop.

"The saddest thing in this country," he said, "is that there's not a desire to work, but to get hurt working. It almost makes you ill when you see a guy come to work, and you almost know he's going to figure a way to make a claim."

They talked a few more minutes about coverages, percentages, and alternate plans. Rexton reeled off numbers, Willie nodding, and then he handed Willie some papers in a folder and shook hands and left.

"It's a problem," Willie said. "You hungry? Do you want me to send out for some sandwiches?"

"This problem," I said, after he had phoned the order, "it's not just those few who are looking to cop injury claims. It seems to me, and a lot of other people who remember another time, that there's a growing reluctance everywhere to do a hard day's work, a lack of pride in personal performance."

"You deal with what you see in this country," Willie said, "and you end up with opinions you've heard, as well as your own. You hear about minorities being shiftless, that they don't want to work, but you're being insulting when you generalize. There is a work-ethic problem in this country. To say that every guy should want to be gainfully employed is probably an unrealistic expectation. Today a lot of guys just don't believe they can get a decent job in which they can take pride.

"The problem, if you're the employer, is to impart pride, but that's not easy with some guys. When you tell a guy that, hey, he's not doing the job and he'd better start cuttin' it, he lights up. He's going on unemployment insurance. That's the problem."

"So what do you do about it?"

"With some there's nothing you can do," he said, "but what I try to do here is what Lombardi did at Green Bay, instill pride in the organization. When a new guy walked in there, he got caught up. Chuck Mercein, Ben Wilson, Anderson, the tight end, it was almost like they were saying, 'Hey, you guys really expect to win!' When I set up an incentive, it's how well are we going to do it? I try to make a guy grow in his own position, but always remembering that you can't compare some guy who just doesn't have it with a Dave Robinson. The ability is just not there, but I have brought salesmen in here who have said, 'I can't believe the attitude you guys have.' It's what Coach Lombardi used to say, 'Success is contagious. It breeds.' "

"Seeing you here," I said, "running a sizeable operation, and knowing that you sit on the board of the parent company, I have to make an adjustment. I had the same feeling at Green Bay last fall, watching Bart Starr on the practice field ordering people around. I remember you all just taking orders, subservient and day after day just following commands."

"Yeah," he said, smiling. "I can see what you mean."

"I recall, too, something Jerry Kramer once told me. He said, 'I often think, What am I doing? Here I am, a grown man, with a wife and three kids, and I'm rolling around on the ground like a kid myself.' "

"You know, it is a child's game," Willie said, "but all the years I played, and when I was getting older, I maintained my enthusiasm for it. Only in my last year, in those last four games did I say, 'What am I doing here?' "

"A fine athlete," I said, "expresses himself in his sport as he can in nothing else, regardless of whatever success he has later in some other endeavor."

"That's right," he said.

"Do you ever miss that moment when you would break through the block and make the perfect tackle, knowing that feeling you can never reproduce in anything else?"

"Yes," he said. "That's right. I do."

"Is that an idea I've just put in your mind?"

"No," he said, "I've thought of that, but what I really miss is being one of the guys."

"As a boss?"

"Right. People look at you in a different way. You want to say, 'Hey! I'm me!' You know?"

"Yes," I said. "I would imagine that maybe there's a sort of fraternity here of, say, drivers. They share experiences."

"Exactly," he said. "I go out, and I see them laughing and talking, and I walk up and something happens. It changes. On the Packers I was kind of a fun guy, a laughing guy. Now I see them standing around, and one guy is telling a story and laughing and they're all listening, and I walk up and I can see the guy's eyes change, and he goes on with the story, but it goes flat. I remember I'd be telling something and laughing, and Coach Lombardi would come up, and it was like it just wasn't that funny any more."

We talked, over the sandwiches and coffee, and between phone calls that he accepted and made, of the changes in professional football. We spoke of players' agents and the rocketing salaries and bonuses in all team sports.

"As long as the money is there," I said, "I'm for it going to the athletes. After all, who would pay to see Wellington Mara kick a football around with Edward Bennett Williams or Art Modell?"

"That's right," he said. "People ask me, 'Don't you really wish you were playing now? Wouldn't you like all that money?' I wouldn't trade my years for anything, though. I played in a period when football reached its maturity in this country, and I'm still so pleased that I'll take my period, the people who played with me, and what it meant to me. That's why it's hard to put away a Henry Jordan.

"Every time I get back to Green Bay it warms my heart all over, because the people reach out and bring me back to left end. They say, 'If you were at left end, this Packer team would have what it needs.' I chuckle, but that's unfair to the guy out there."

"You look like you could almost step in there," I said. "You haven't put on much weight."

"I'm 255," he said, "and I played last at 247. I jog in the morning, and there are days when I wake up and I don't feel like getting up and crawling into the office. I say to myself that I own the Willie Davis Distributing Company, and today I'm going to exercise my prerogative and not go in. Then I think, 'What would Lombardi do?' I get up and out of bed. It's six o'clock, and I throw on my sweats and drive here and I jog and do a few wind sprints. They get harder to do. I think that today maybe I'll do six, and then I say to myself, 'Why don't I do two extra?' So I do, and then I take my shower."

"The Lombardi syndrome," I said. "During those terrible grass drills—up and down, up and down—when you guys were ready to collapse, he'd call for more. You remember how Bill Quinlan was always trying to cheat on them, and Lombardi would jump him?"

"Yeah," Willie said, smiling.

"One day Quinlan said to me, 'When I give up this game and start to miss it, I'll have it solved. I've got a film of this grass drill, and I'll run that and sit back and say, 'The hell with it!' "

"The Lombardi syndrome is everywhere," Willie said. "Jerry Kramer and Bob Skoronski and people like that—we'll sit down and share experiences. I'm involved in the school supply business with Bob, and we'll compare notes on motivational speakers at conferences. You not only find that there are those Lombardi principles that work, but you can't believe the admiration they had for the man. Whether the speaker is from IBM, or whatever, you hear them throw back at you again dedication, effort, pride . . ."

"And the importance of winning," I said.

"I've made it a point to clarify that statement," he said. "When Lombardi said that winning is the only thing, it was so expressive in my own mind. If you knew the man, you knew it was the pursuit, and you don't prepare to lose. I say that I hope we never reach the point where we're planning to lose, and that's all Lombardi meant."

"He caught a lot of flak for that," I said, "and he caught some more when we did a couple of pieces in *Look,* and got onto the subject of competitive animosity and the need, each week, to build up a hate for the opponent. Of course, it dissolves the moment the game is over."

"That's right," Willie said. "Gale Sayers lived in the next block from me in Chicago, and he's one of the nicest human beings. We'd have dinner together, but when I'd see him in that Bear uniform, I could take him on with determination and hostility. That's what Lombardi meant."

It was shortly after five o'clock when Willie had finished with phone calls and office appointments and the signing of letters. He said he would drive me back to my motel, and we walked out into the parking space where, although I had failed to notice it coming in, there was an old double-decker London bus. It was painted a dark red, and a sign on it advertised a firm of accountants specializing in preparing income tax returns.

"We just got it today," Willie said. "We're going to have the engine reconditioned and have it reupholstered and repainted, and take it around for the radio station."

"As a sort of mobile unit?"

"That's right," he said. "To take it to the people."

He opened the door and I followed him in, and we climbed to the upper deck. Mounted in front and in back to face into frames were the black scrolls with the white letters that had revealed to those inherently patient and polite British who had queued up at stops 6,000 miles away, even amid the rubble of the London Blitz, the destinations: Oxford Circus . . . Regent Street . . . Picadilly Circus . . . Trafalgar Square.

"I've been meaning to ask you," I said, as we got out, "about your plans for the station."

"Well," he said, "I have felt for some time that one of the most important involvements I could have would be in the community where I'm selling my product. All my life I'd heard, especially in minority communities, of selling products and then going home every night regardless of the quality of life of the people. One thing I knew was that I was going to be able to sleep at night, and so I've worked with the Urban League and those other things, and the radio station can provide me with another opportunity.

"My greatest commitment with the station will be to serve the people. Equal to my profit motive is my motive to provide an outlet for the citizens within the coverage area. KACE will be a station of credibility."

"That's fine," I said, "but how do you accomplish that?"

"We did a survey," he said, "and found crime and unemployment were what were troubling people. You expect that, but I personally went out and I said, 'If you had a station, what would it address itself to? What do you like and dislike?' Now, this is not some computer-derived survey. Maybe we haven't gone through all that I went through at the University of Chicago. I don't care about the randomness or the statistical reliability. I talked with the people, and music and our public service will be what it's about.

Music transcends all racial backgrounds, and I want this to be a station that anybody can listen to and one that's sensitive enough to address itself to issues with meaningfulness and impact."

We got into his car. It was a new light-gray Cadillac Seville, and he backed it out of the parking space.

"This is the first Cadillac I've ever had," he said. "It's the smaller model, though."

"You don't have to apologize," I said. "You've earned it."

"I don't know if I should say this," he said, "or how you can put it in the written word."

"Try me," I said.

"When I go to white banquets—and I mean basically white motivated—people come up and say, 'I'd like an autograph for my kid.' When I go to a black dinner, nobody comes up. Now, I don't mean that I'm disappointed for myself, that I need that."

"I understand."

"I've wondered about this. I've thought that the black kid is maybe being deprived of the incentive that maybe the white father is trying to stimulate when he takes the autograph home, like, 'Hey! See what you might achieve.'"

"Maybe," I said, "it's because the black community still is not a community of achievers."

"Hey, that could be it," he said. "I don't know."

"It might be something," I said, "that your station might address itself to."

"It might," he said. "I'll think about that."

The decor of the cocktail lounge in the motel was American Anthracite, black banquettes, black tabletops, dark walls and carpeting. Candles were flickering in globes on the tables, and when we ordered, Willie asked for a glass of white wine.

"When you think back over the years," I said, "what games keep coming back?"

We had one of the banquettes. Willie was leaning back, his arms spread along the top, his eyes following the traffic between the tables.

"I know two or three experiences," he said, "maybe four. I know what the first championship meant in '61, when we beat the Giants, 37–0. I don't think any football team in the world could have beaten us that day. Then I think of the first Super Bowl, how uncomfortable it was to represent the NFL against the new kid down the block. How impressive, how convincing would we be? Would we convince the AFL fans?

"One thing Coach Lombardi said to us was, 'If there is any doubt you have about this Kansas City team being good, look at their roster. Look at the All-Americans—Dawson, McClinton.'"

"Did you have a fear of losing?"

"Oh, yeah," he said. "There was the reason to fear we might get beat. It was very uncomfortable for me. I didn't want to get hit by Mike Garrett on a quick trap. I didn't want Curtis McClinton busting one up the middle. That was the reason we played the first half so conservative."

With both CBS and NBC carrying it on television and radio and the press building it for weeks, that first Super Bowl had become the Game of Games, the pride of the old league against the precocity of the new. At the half, the Packers led only 14–10, and then they came out again and turned it into a 35–10 rout.

"When Lombardi huddled everybody for the second half," Willie was saying, "he said, 'Look. I'll tell you what. You went out and played thirty minutes where you adjusted to Kansas City. Now I want you to go out and make Kansas City adjust to you.' The man was so right."

"What about the two Dallas games?" I said.

They were for the NFL title in '66 and '67 and for the right to meet Kansas City in the first Super Bowl and Oakland in the second. They were playing, as it turned out, for winners' shares that added up to $23,000 per player that first year, and $24,700 the second.

"The Dallas games were important," Willie was saying, "in that they made the Packers, and in the same sense they didn't make the Cowboys. Even in preseason we didn't want the Cowboys to think they could beat us."

In '66 in the Cotton Bowl in Dallas, with time running out, and the Packers leading 34–27, Dallas had a fourth down on the Packer 2-yard line when Don Meredith, with Willie Davis chasing him and Dave Robinson hanging on to him, lofted the pass that Tom Brown, the Packer left safety, intercepted in the end zone. In '67, in that ice bowl at Green Bay, with time for only one more play and the Packers behind by 17–14, Bart Starr sneaked the ball in from the 1-yard line and the Packers won, 21–17.

"In that second game," I said, "what was it like on the side line? When Bart came trotting over, and it was all coming down to one single play, were you close enough to hear what he and Vince were saying?"

"I heard," he said, "but I couldn't understand what the play was. As Bart trotted back out, I thought of all the possibilities. You know, a bad snap, whatever? I said to myself, 'Aw, hell.' I turned my head. I didn't want to see it. I waited, until I heard the crowd reaction. When I looked up, it was just a mass of bodies out there. I didn't know that Bart had run a sneak.

"I think of other games, though," he said. "The Rams play-off in Milwaukee in '67. That was our challenge game, and you didn't challenge us, really—but they did. We'd already won our division, and they beat us out here on a blocked punt in the last minute, and then we started to read all about how they'd broken the Packer mystique and whatnot. Lombardi had those clips on the bulletin board, and he played it low all week."

"In other words," I said, "the Rams and the press dealt him a pair of aces."

"Right," he said. "He didn't have his Wednesday speech, and if he had put his Sunday morning talk, the one he gave us then, on Wednesday, we'd have just bubbled out by game time. He always had great respect for the Rams—Merlin Olsen and trying to handle their inside men—and in the dressing room he said, 'This is the game I wish I could play myself. If I could, I'd be sure how it could be played, but I have to trust it to you guys.'

"Then he got into it. He said, 'There are 50,000 people out there, waiting for you to come out of this dressing room. They're all your family and your friends. They didn't come here to see the Rams. They came here to see you, and any time you let a team sit in California and say how they've broken your magic and what they're going to do to you, they're challenging you, and if they get away with it, it will be something you'll have to live with the rest of your lives. It's like a guy calling you out before your family and saying, 'I'm gonna whip you.' "

"Well, Nitschke was growling, and Boyd Dowler ran to the bathroom and threw up. This man had aroused our emotions so much, the guys were so mad that when they ran out, they were running heavy. You could hear their feet pounding, and the first two series, I couldn't adjust, I was so fired up."

"And you clobbered them," I said, for the Packers won that one, 28–7.

"Yeah," Willie said, "and we might have beaten them anyway, but I don't know that. I say it was the man."

We ordered another round, Willie staying with the white wine. We went on talking about the man, his perfectionism, the fear of him that pervaded practices, his temper tantrums, and his tears.

"I remember," I said, "that Lions game in Green Bay in '62, when they had you, 7–6, with less than two minutes to go, and Herb Adderley intercepted the pass and Hornung kicked the field goal with thirty-three seconds left and you won it, 9–7. In the locker room, Vince tried to say something and his voice broke and I looked at him, and his eyes were filling."

"I think I was the last Packer to see him," Willie said. "Norb Hecker was an assistant coach with the Giants then, and I was in San Diego when they were there. He told me, 'The coach is real bad, and he's going.' So I flew from San Diego to Washington, and I called Marie, and we went to the hospital.

"Coach Lombardi must have been down to 150 pounds. I said, 'Coach, if you'll come back to Green Bay and coach again, I'll come out of retirement.' He smiled, you know?"

"As you said, it would melt an iceberg."

"Yeah," Willie said. "He tried to smile, and the tears started to come out of his eyes and he said, 'Willie, you're a hell of a man.' Then he said, 'Get out of here.' And we left—Marie, too—and we weren't in there for more than a minute-and-a-half. Since then I've wondered if maybe I shouldn't have gone. He cried."

12

The Greatest,
Pound for Pound

It is when we try to grapple with another man's intimate need that we perceive how incomprehensible, wavering and misty are the beings that share with us the sight of the stars and the warmth of the sun.

Joseph Conrad, *Lord Jim*

"When I am old," I wrote more than twenty years ago, "I shall tell them about Ray Robinson. When I was young, I used to hear the old men talk of Joe Gans and Terry McGovern and Kid McCoy. They told of the original Joe Walcott and Sam Langford, of Stanley Ketchel and Mickey Walker and Benny Leonard. How well any of them really knew those men I'm not sure, but it seemed to me that some of the greatness of those fighters rubbed off on these others just because they lived at the same time.

"That is the way," I wrote, "I plan to use Sugar Ray. When the young assault me with their atomic miracles and reject my Crosby records and find comical the movies that once moved me, I shall entice them into talking about fighters. Robinson will be a form of social security for me, because they will have seen nothing like him, and I am convinced that they never will."

I am still sure today that they will never be able to match Robinson because of the social changes that were altering life in this country while he fought. The prejudice that drove the black—as before him it drove the Irish, the Jew, and then the Italian—to the ring in desperation is becoming a part of our past. In an age of reason fewer men are forced to fight with their fists, the amateurs are not what they used to be, the bootleg circuit, where Robinson received his intermediate schooling, is long gone, and the professional game has been on the decline for twenty-five years.

Ray Robinson—and Archie Moore, the venerable Sage of San Diego and the greatest ring mechanic I ever saw—were the last of the old-fashioned fighters because they fought from the end of one era through the beginning of another, and because they were the products of poverty as well as prejudice. Robinson was eight years old when his mother brought him and his two older sisters from Detroit to New York, and tried to support them on the fifteen dollars a week she made working in a laundry. Robinson sold firewood he gathered in a wagon under the West Side Highway and as far south as the Bowery. On Saturdays and Sundays he shined shoes, and at night he danced for coins on the sidewalks off Broadway. For him, as for all those others of that time, the fight game was a court of last resort.

"You may find this hard to believe," he told me a couple of times, "but I've never loved fightin'. I really dislike it. I don't believe I watch more than two fights a year, and then it has to be some friend of mine fightin'.

"Fightin', to me, seems barbaric," he said. "It seems to me like the barbarous days when men fought in a pit and people threw money down to them. I really don't like it."

"But at the same time," I said, "I must believe that fighting has given you the most satisfying experiences you have ever known."

"That's right," he said. "I enjoy out-thinkin' another man and out-maneuverin' him, but I still don't like to fight."

I believed him then, and I still do, because of something else he once told me and that one of his sisters confirmed. On the streets of Detroit and New York he ran from fights.

"I would avoid fightin'," he said, "even if I had to take the short end. I'd even apologize when I knew I was right. I got to be known as a coward, and my sisters used to fight for me. They used to remark that they hoped that some day I'd be able to take care of myself."

How able he became is in the record. He began fighting when he was fifteen, and he had 160 amateur and bootleg-amateur fights before he turned pro. As a professional he not only won the welterweight championship of the world, but he won the middleweight title for the fifth time when he was thirty-seven and he went fifteen rounds trying for it again when he was forty. He was forty-five when he finally retired in 1965, and in 362 fights, amateur and pro, over thirty years, he failed to finish only once. On that June night in 1952, when he boxed Joey Maxim for the light-heavyweight title, giving away fifteen pounds, it was 104 degrees under the Yankee Stadium ring lights, so brutally hot and humid that Ruby Goldstein, the referee, had to be replaced in the eleventh round. Robinson was giving Maxim a boxing lesson, and seemed on his way to winning yet another title, when he collapsed in his corner at the end of the thirteenth.

While Willie Pep was the greatest creative artist I ever saw in a ring, Sugar Ray Robinson remains the greatest fighter, pound-for-pound and punch-for-punch, of more than a half century, or since Benny Leonard retired with the lightweight title in 1924. Perhaps it is foolish to try to compare them, for Pep was a poet, often implying, with his feints and his footwork, more than he said, as that night when he won a round without even throwing a punch. Robinson was the master of polished prose, structuring his sentences, never wasting a word, and, as he often did, taking the other out with a single punch. That was the Robinson, however, that most Americans, enthralled by him as they were but who came to follow boxing on television, never saw. His talent had peaked between 1947 and 1950, before the era of TV boxing and before it saddened me to watch him years later on the screen struggling with fighters like Gene Fullmer and Paul Pender whom once he would have handled with ease.

"The public don't know it," he told me when I brought it up as far back as 1950, fifteen years before he retired, "but I do. The fighter himself is the first one to know."

"And how does he know it?" I said.

"You find you have to think your punches," he said. "The punches you used to throw without thinkin', you now have to reason."

It is something that happens to all of us, once the instinctive inventions and discoveries have been made. Then we reach back into the library of our experience, and what was once the product of inspiration is now merely the result of reason.

"How are you, old buddy?" he said on the phone, when I called him before flying out to Los Angeles. "When are you comin' out?"

"I'm fine," I said, "and I want to come out next week if you'll be there. How about next Friday?"

"Let me check that," he said, and then, "I'll be here. I'll be lookin' for you, because you're my man."

In his 202 professional fights, he hit fifty or more towns, and I imagine that in most, if not in all, there are still writers today whom he annointed as his "man." He was as smooth outside the ring as he was in it, and under pressing interrogation he was as elusive, but until you found that out he was a charmer.

I met him first in the spring of 1946. Already unquestionably the best welterweight in the world, he was unable to get a shot at the title, and he had hired a press agent named Pete Vaccare. We were sitting, late one morning, in Vaccare's office in the old Brill Building on Broadway, waiting for Robinson as, I was to find out, one almost inevitably did, when we heard singing out in the hall. Then the door opened, and they came in, Robinson and Junius ("June") Clark, whom he called his secretary, both of them in heavy road clothes topped off by red knitted skating caps, for they had been running on the Harlem Speedway, and they finished the song. It was "The Very Thought of You," with Robinson carrying the melody and Clark improvising, and they ended it with a soft-shoe step and a hand flourish, and amid the laughter, we were introduced. We talked, with Robinson telling how he once stole so much from a grocery store that the owner gave him a job as a delivery boy to protect his stock, and how the minister who caught him in a crap game on the steps of the Salem Methodist Episcopal Church took him inside and introduced him to boxing.

"I've just met Ray Robinson," I said to Wilbur Wood when I got back to the office that afternoon. "He's quite a guy."

"Oh, no," Wilbur said. "He conned you too."

"What do you mean, conned me?" I said.

"Hang around the fight game a little longer," Wilbur said, "and you'll find out."

In the fight game they like fighters who will fight anybody anywhere at any time and leave the business end to their managers. After he won the welterweight title, with George Gainford doing the dickering, Robinson made his own deals, and I knew a New York boxing writer who had collected two dozen complaints against him from promoters around the country.

"The trouble with Robinson," another one told me one day at lunch in Lindy's, "is that every time I get ready to bomb him, he shows up at some hospital or at the bedside of some sick kid. He's always one move ahead of you."

"As he is in the ring," I said.

There was about him an air of humble superiority, a contrariety that annoyed and frustrated those who tried to come to know him. He would plead humility and reserve a pew in church for Easter Sunday. At big fights, when other notables gathered for their introductions in the ring before the main event, Robinson would wait beyond the ringside rows and receive his applause apart as he came down the aisle and, all grace, vaulted through the ropes. He was a man who was trying to find something he had lost even before he turned professional.

"The biggest thrill I ever got," he told me once, "was when I won the Golden Gloves and they streamed that light down on me in Madison Square Garden and said, 'The Golden Gloves featherweight champion, Sugar Ray Robinson!' I bought the papers. I read about it over and over. It was more of a thrill than when I won the welterweight championship of the world.

"Once I read," he said—and he even read law, fascinated by its contradictions—"something that King Solomon said. He said, 'The wiser a man gets the less beauty he finds in life.' If I try to explain that to people they don't understand. It's like the first time you go to Coney Island and you ride the chute-the-chute and you get a big thrill. The second time it isn't so much."

Few fighters have been as disliked within their profession and by its press as was Robinson while he was struggling to make his way, and the fight game was, in part, responsible for that. In this country, from the turn of the century on, boxing gave the black man, because it needed him, a better break than he received in any other sport, but it only gave him what it had to. For years, while Mike Jacobs ran big-time boxing, he refused Robinson that chance at the welterweight title.

"Mike explained that to me," Robinson told me once. "He explained that I'd kill the division. He said, 'I got to have two or three guys fightin' for the title. You'd darken the class.' I understand that. That's good business."

I am sure he understood it, but he did not have to like it. In his early days, in order to get fights, he had to take less money than the opponents he knocked out. Once, after he had trained three weeks for a fight, the promoter ran out. A couple of years later, Jacobs promised him $2,000 beyond his small purse if he would box for a Boston promoter to whom Jacobs owed a favor. When, after the fight, Robinson showed up for his money, Jacobs ridiculed him.

"You didn't think I'd go into my own kick," Mike said, "for some other guy's fight."

They tried to do it to him in the ring too. There was the story that Duke Stefano, then a manager of fighters, was telling me one afternoon in Stillman's Gym.

"I remember Robinson one night when he was just starting out as a pro," Duke said. "Just before the fight, Robinson complained that he had a bad ear, and he didn't want to go through with the fight. It was his left ear, and they looked in it, and you could see it was red and swollen.

"The other guy's manager—he was from New Jersey—looked at it and he said, 'Look, my guy is just an opponent. Go through with the fight, and I promise you he won't touch the ear.' Robinson said, 'Okay, long as he stays away from the ear.' Well, the bell rang, and the other guy came out of his corner and winged a right hand at the ear. Robinson just turned his head and looked at the corner. The guy did it a second time, and Robinson looked at the manager again. The third time the guy tried it, Robinson stepped in with a hook and flattened him.

"The manager," Duke said, "turned right around and went back to New Jersey. He didn't even second another kid he had in the next bout."

Fritzie Zivic did it to him too, as he did to many others. He was the recently dethroned welterweight champion of the world when Robinson, in only his second year as a pro, outpointed him over ten rounds in Madison Square Garden. Ten weeks later he would knock Zivic out in ten.

"Fritzie Zivic," Robinson told me once, "taught me more than anybody I ever fought."

"What did he teach you?" I said.

"He taught me that a man can make you butt open your own eye," he said, and I appreciated the phrasing. He was one of the cleanest of fighters, and what he had learned from Zivic was not something that you did to another man, but that he could do to you.

"And how does a man do that?" I said.

"He slipped one of my jabs," Robinson said, "and reached his right glove around behind my head and pulled my head down on his."

Young Otto, who boxed the best lightweights during the first two decades of this century and was a great student of the science, refereed that first fight. One day in Stillman's I asked him about it.

"In the sixth round," he said, "Robinson said to me, 'He's stickin' his thumbs in my eyes.' I said, 'You ain't no cripple.' After that he give it back to Zivic better than Zivic was givin' it to him. I said to myself then, 'This kid is gonna be a great fighter.' "

So they tried to use him and abuse him, and sometimes succeeded, in and out of the ring. When, in self-defense, he retaliated, he acquired the reputation that provoked *The Saturday Evening Post* to ask me to do a piece they were to entitle, "Why Don't They Like Ray Robinson?"

"This is a tough assignment for me," I said to him.

"How's that?" he said.

We were sitting in his office at Ray Robinson Enterprises, Inc., in Harlem, and he had his feet up on his triangular glass-topped desk. He owned most of the block on the west side of Seventh Avenue from 123rd to 124th streets, and he had $250,000 tied up in the five-story apartment house, Sugar Ray's Bar and Restaurant, Edna Mae's Lingerie Shop, and Sugar Ray's Quality Cleaners, with its five outlets.

"I have to ask you the tough questions," I said.

"That's all right," he said. "Go ahead."

"I will," I said, "but I want to explain something first. I think this piece can do you a lot of good. You're unquestionably the greatest fighter since Benny Leonard, and there are some old-timers who say you may be the best since Joe Gans, who died ten years before you were born."

"They say that?" he said, as if he hadn't known. "I appreciate that."

"My point is," I said, "that you should be the most popular fighter of your time, but you're not. There are raps against you in the fight game, and they keep bringing up your Army record and you've never made the money that you should. A fighter like Graziano, who's a beginner compared to you and has a dishonorable discharge from the Army while you have an honorable one, has made twice as much as you have."

"That's right," he said.

"Part of that is style," I said. "All his fights are wars, and that's what the public likes, but it's style outside the ring, too. He's open and frank, and you're not, really. What I want to do is explain you. I want you to tell me what it's like to have a fine mind and great physical talents, to be a great artist but to be colored and to have that used against you in the fight game and out of it. It can explain a lot about you, and I'll understand. If I understand, I can make the readers understand, and as I said, that can mean a lot to you, if you'll level with me."

I really believed it. I believed it for about five minutes.

"If you can do that," he said, "I'll appreciate it. Nobody's ever done that for me before. You just ask me the questions, what you want to know."

"All right," I said. "Let's get the Army thing out of the way first."

It wasn't any good. We went around and around, as in a ring, and when Robinson couldn't counter my leads or even slip them, he professed only astonishment that I should hold such documented assertions to be facts.

There was something to be celebrated in his Army record. He had been a member of Casual Detachment 7, known as "The Joe Louis Troupe." Joe and he and four other fighters spent seven months touring camps in this country and putting on boxing exhibitions. In Florida, Robinson refused to box unless black troops were allowed to attend, and he, an enlisted man, faced down a general. At Camp Sibert, Alabama, a white M.P. saw Louis emerge from a phone booth in so-called white territory, and he threatened to club Joe. Robinson took him on, the two rolling on the ground, and there was rioting by black troops before apologies were made to the two fighters.

It was a matter of Army record and common knowledge, however, that when the troupe sailed for Europe, from Pier 90, New York, on March 31, 1944, Robinson was not aboard. It was also in the record that he had previously declared his intention not to go, and that the Articles of War as they applied to the punishment for desertion had been explained to him.

"But why would a man say such a thing?" he said when I had read to him from the affidavit.

"He not only said it," I said, "but he swore to it."

"I can't understand that," Robinson said. "I never met that officer, and he never read me such things."

Years later, in his autobiography, he would state that he had been suffering from amnesia following a fall, and had been hospitalized for that before his honorable discharge as a sergeant on June 3, 1944. It was a book he had wanted me to write after he had retired for the first time in 1952. Because he preferred to avoid using elevators, as he also preferred not to fly, we had met late one afternoon with my agent and another, not in my agent's office on the twentieth floor of the Mutual of New York Building, but in the cocktail lounge of the Park Sheraton.

"I just can't do it, Ray," I said, after we had talked for a while, the others listening, and I had tried again. "There are those conflicting versions of those events in your life, in and out of boxing, and we tried two years ago in your office and we've tried again now, and we still can't resolve them. I'm sorry, but I just can't do the book."

"That's all right, old buddy," he said. "I understand."

I doubt that he did—why couldn't we just put it all down the way he said, and possibly even believed it had been, and ignore the conflicts? And when I would see him after that it would always be in camp before his fights and I would be with others. Now I had heard that he was heading up a youth project in Los Angeles, and at ten o'clock on that Friday morning the taxi driver and I found it, finally, on West Adams Boulevard with the sign— Sugar Ray's Youth Foundation—fronting the one-story building.

"He's in conference with Mr. Fillmore right now," the woman said across the counter, and I had missed her name when she had introduced herself. "I don't think he'll be long, though."

"That's all right, " I said. "I have plenty of time."

"Maybe while you're waiting," she said, "you'd like to look at some of our material."

"That would be fine," I said.

She introduced me then to Mel Zolkover, who had arisen from behind one of the desks beyond the counter. He is a middle-aged retired mechanical engineer and the foundation's administrative director, and we shook hands.

She went back to a desk, and while I waited I could hear the even tones of Robinson's voice, still familiar after all the years, in an office on the left. When she came back she handed me the several sheets of publicity and a folder from the 1976–77 "Miss Sugar Ray Teen Pageant." From a photograph I identified her as Thelma Smith, the executive secretary, and elsewhere I noted that Bob Hope is the foundation's honorary chairman, Robinson the chairman, and Wright Fillmore the president. I read about arts and crafts projects, costume making, karate instruction, talent shows, art classes, and workshops in beauty and personal development, drama, band and combo repertory, and dance.

"Old buddy!" he said, smiling and his face fuller and shaking hands across the counter. "How's my old buddy?"

"Fine," I said. "And you?"

"Just fine," he said. "Come on in here and sit down and we'll talk."

I followed him to the middle desk at the back. He was wearing a blue leisure suit, the jacket over a dark blue-and-fuschia sports shirt. Once I had checked his wardrobe. He owned thirty-four suits, twenty-six pairs of shoes, nine sports jackets and as many pairs of slacks, six overcoats and four topcoats, most of which apparel he said he had never worn even once.

"You've gained some weight," I said.

As a fighter he was one of the most lithe and handsome of men. He moved with such grace and rhythm, in the ring and out, that watching him made me think of rubbing silk or satin between one's hands. During his first retirement, in fact, he tried it as a dancer, opening at the French Casino in New York for $15,000 a week. After that, it was downhill.

"Robinson was a good dancer, for a fighter," a Broadway booking agent told me, after Robinson had come back to knock out Bobo Olson and win the middleweight title the second time. "Maybe no other fighter ever danced as well, but the feature of his act was his change of clothes. He looked good in everything he put on."

He was leaning back now in the high-backed desk chair. Not only was his face fuller, but at fifty-six he was a lot heavier across the shoulders and chest and at the waist.

"Yeah, I'm heavier," he said now. "You see, I sit here with something on my mind, and I don't get the exercise I should. Every day, though, I try to take a five-mile walk."

"How heavy are you?"

"Oh, 183–84," he said, and he fought best at 147. "You see, you've got a certain ego about having been a champion, and you'd like to keep like that, but it's so difficult. There are temptations, and it takes will power. When you're fightin' you have to live by the rules, because when that bell rings condition is the name of the game. Even then, in camp, Joe Louis and I would go out in the boat and have quarts of ice cream and our trainers would get mad."

He reached into a desk drawer, and he brought out a package of Danish pastries. He tore one end off the transparent wrapper and took out one and, leaning back again, began eating.

"My breakfast," he said. "You know, the most important meal is breakfast."

"And that's your breakfast?"

"That's right," he said, "and Jack Blackburn used to get after Joe and me."

Blackburn was Louis's discoverer, teacher, and trainer. He developed Louis so precisely in the image of what he himself had been as a fighter that Louis had the same flaw that Blackburn had of dropping the left arm after a jab. It was what made Louis vulnerable to a straight right counter over the jab.

"Blackburn," Robinson was saying, "used to tell us, 'You got to eat breakfast.' Then they used to squeeze blood from the meat, and I'd drink that. From Monday through Friday I'd drink it. You have to get that from a slaughter house, and they put this blood in a can and I used to go down there and get it. I'll tell you, that's the most potent thing there is."

"I remember that you used to do that," I said. "Do you ever drink it now?"

"Every now and then I think I'll do it," he said, "but I don't."

He had finished the pastry and folded over the end of the package. He put the package back in the desk drawer.

"What brought you out here to California?" I said.

"My wife is from out here," he said. When he was fighting he was married to Edna Mae Holly. She had been a dancer and they had two sons, and I had not known he had remarried. "Joe Louis was goin' with a girl out here, and I met Millie through the recommendation of this other girl. You know, like a dog. You see something, and the ears go bong! We were married in 1965, and that's how I met Mr. Fillmore, and we started this foundation."

"Tell me about that."

"We went to London," he said, "and she was having her thirty-third or thirty-fourth birthday party, and . . ."

"Who was?" I said.

"Queen Elizabeth," he said. "Millie and I, we were invited and we went to the party. It was a wonderful ceremony, and Prince Phillip and I were talkin'. You remember those strikes?"

"What strikes?"

"I think it started in Berkeley," he said.

"The student protests?"

"That's right," he said. "We were talkin', and he said, 'Sugar, I believe you could help that.' I said, 'What do you mean?' He said, 'Youngsters look up to you, and I've got an idea.' I had met Mr. Fillmore, and of all the people I've met—all the Popes and all—I never met a man who believes in God and lives it more than Mr. Fillmore. You never hear the guy say a harsh word, even a loud word, and I want you to meet him."

"I'd like to," I said.

"I came back to New York," he said, "and I was goin' with my present wife. She lived upstairs out here and Mr. Fillmore lived downstairs. I talked with him, and we went to the Council of Churches and asked them to help us, and they gave us money. The county saw the potential and funded us. Now we hope to have the State Junior Olympics, and Jimmy Carter was out and I met with him, and he's a nice guy and likes what we're doing, and we hope for Federal funding. We work with the Board of Education and the Department of Parks and Recreation, and there has never been a paid member of the board of trustees. Every dollar goes in, and I'm about the poorest cat on the board."

"What happened to all that property you owned in Harlem?"

"I sold that even at a loss," he said, "just to get out. I fell in love with my wife out here, and Harlem was goin' down hill so bad, and now if you see a white face there, you know it's a cop."

"Did you get clipped?"

One day, sitting in his office in Harlem, he had told me that he felt he was destined to make a great success in business. It was that afternoon in 1950, when he spoke of how he knew his ring skills were starting to decline.

"After a man attains all the things he likes," he had said then, "he has to find some other form of happiness. I feel I'm gonna find that in business. I'm not cocky within myself. I'm an extreme Christian within myself. I just believe. My faith is so strong that I know that someday I'm gonna be the head of some real big business. I thank God for the success I've had, and the investments I've made."

"Yeah, I got clipped," he said now. "It happened to Joe, too, but that's a part of life. I didn't get out with too much, but I didn't lose too much, either."

"As you say," I said, "it happened to Joe, too, and it happens so often. They talk about the dirty fight game, but a fighter makes a fortune in it, and when he gets out into the nice clean world of American business they take it all from him."

"You're so right," he said. "What other fighters are you seeing for the book?"

"I just saw Willie Pep last month."

"He was a great one," he said. "When I beat him in the amateurs in Connecticut, they took me to the police station."

"I remember that story," I said. "Willie's all right. He's working for the Athletic Commission in Connecticut, and he's married for the fifth time."

"You know how that is," he said, smiling. "When Joe was the

champion and I used to go to the airport, they came off that plane like it was a parade."

"And I saw Billy Graham," I said. "He's doing fine, working for Seagram's."

"Billy Graham?" he said. "He's my man. He beat me in the first fight I lost."

"When you were ninety-pound kids," I said.

He had reached into the desk drawer again. He brought out the Danish, and started on another one.

"There are so many of your fights I remember," I said. "The night you won the middleweight title from Jake LaMotta in Chicago . . ."

"Jake wasn't smart," he said, "but he was in condition. He was 'The Bull.'"

"I know," I said. "I remember that, after your first fight with him, you were passing blood for days."

"That's right," he said.

"When you fought him in Chicago for the title in '51," I said, "I watched it at a neighbor's house on TV. Ted Husing was announcing the fight, and in the early rounds he was filled with LaMotta. He kept saying that we were seeing an upset, that LaMotta was running the fight."

"He said that?"

"Yes, and I said to my neighbor, 'Husing doesn't know what he's talking about. Watch what Robinson does the next time the referee breaks them, or Robinson backs off from an exchange.' You would back off so far that sometimes you went out of the camera range, right off the screen. I said, 'LaMotta had trouble making the weight, and Robinson is walking the legs off him. When he gets ready to turn it on, Jake won't have much left.' In the thirteenth round you turned it on, and the referee had to stop it."

"That's right," he said, nodding. "That's exactly what I did. You remember that?"

"Another fight I remember," I said, "was the one with 'Flash' Sebastian, and that one scared me."

"That scared me, too," he said.

On June 24, 1947, Robinson knocked out Jimmy Doyle in the

eighth round in Cleveland, and the next day Doyle died of brain injury. At the coroner's inquest, Robinson was asked, "Couldn't you tell from the look on Doyle's face that he had been hurt?" Robinson said, "Mister, that's what my business is, to hurt people." Because he was absolutely frank, he caught the criticism. He set up a $10,000 trust fund for Doyle's mother, and two months later he took little more than his expenses to fight Sebastian, the welterweight champion of the Philippines, on an American Legion show in Madison Square Garden.

"It was right after that Doyle fight," I said now.

"I know," he said. "The night before the Doyle fight I dreamed what was gonna happen, and I got up the next day and I called the commission and I told them. They said that they'd sold all the tickets, and they went so far as to get a Catholic priest to talk to me."

"In that Sebastian fight," I said, "you came out of your corner for the first round and he threw a wide hook, and you brought your right glove up and blocked it. He backed off, and came in again and did the same thing. This time you threw the right hand inside the hook and followed it with a hook of your own, and he went back on his head. Then he tried to get up, and he fell forward on his face, and the photographers at ringside were hollering, 'Get this! Get this! This guy may die, too!' "

"I know," he said. "I said, 'Oh, Lord, don't let it happen again.' "

"In the dressing room later," I said, "Sebastian was hysterical. Whitey Bimstein had seconded him, and he took a towel and soaked it in ice water and snapped it in Sebastian's face to bring him out of it. I said to Whitey, 'What kind of a fighter is this they brought all the way from the Philippines to almost be killed?' Whitey said, 'I never saw him before tonight, but they asked me to work with him. After I got him taped, I told him to warm up. He threw one punch, and I stopped him. I said, "Look, fella. When you throw that hook, don't raise your head. You're fightin' Ray Robinson. You do that with him, and he'll take your head right off your shoulders." ' "

"Then sometime later I was talking with Ruby Goldstein. You remember Ruby was the referee that night, and Ruby said, 'That Sebastian threw that first hook, and Robinson brushed it away. I was just thinkin' to myself that if he did that again Robinson would cross a right. The next thing I knew he did, and I was saying, 'One . . . two . . . three.' "

"I was lucky that night," Robinson said now.

"And Sebastian was, too," I said, "and I'll tell you another night when you were lucky."

"When was that?" he said.

"When you got the title back from Randy Turpin."

In August of 1950 Robinson carried Charley Fusari over fifteen rounds of what was ostensibly a fight for Robinson's welterweight title but was, on Robinson's part, just one of the greatest boxing exhibitions I have ever seen. He gave his entire purse to the Damon Runyan Cancer Fund, of which Dan Parker, the sports editor and columnist of the *New York Daily Mirror,* was president. This act of charity had the effect, however unintended, of silencing Parker who, whenever the word got out that Robinson intended to go to Europe, would recall that he had missed that opportunity when he had failed to sail with the "Joe Louis Troupe."

The following May, Robinson left for Paris—Parker merely pointing out that it was "by boat"—and took along his fuschia Cadillac and George Gainford's black one. Included in the party of eleven were Robinson's golf pro, and his barber, and in Paris they acquired an Arabian midget who spoke five languages. They occupied most of one floor of the Claridge, and seldom left to eat in restaurants. There was an almost constant flow of room-service waiters through the suites, and the bill at the end was staggering.

"You know how the French are," Lew Burston, who had lived for many years in Paris and ran the foreign affairs of the Mike Jacobs boxing empire, said to me one day following Robinson's return. "In the old days they used to see the maharajas arrive with their retinues, and they basically believe that another man's business is his own. At the end of Robinson's stay, though, even the French were somewhat stunned."

Robinson fought a half-dozen times in Europe, in Paris and elsewhere, and on July 10 in London he defended his middleweight title against Randy Turpin, the British and European champion. Turpin out-pointed him over the fifteen rounds in an upset so startling that in the fight game on this side of the ocean they found it hard to believe.

"You may remember," I was saying to him now, "what Lew Burston said after the first Turpin fight. He said, 'Robinson had Paris in his legs.'"

"That was one of the few fights," he said, nodding, "where I took a chance. Remember what I told you—about temptation and will power? Then he had one of the most unorthodox styles, too. You remember the second fight?"

Two months after the London fight they met again in the Polo Grounds in New York. Robinson won the early rounds, but then Turpin, awkward, sometimes punching off the wrong foot, lunging with his jab, chopping with his right in close and eight years younger, began to come on. By the tenth round, Robinson seemed spent, and then a wide cut opened over his left eye and, obviously fearful that the fight might be stopped and with the blood gushing out of the cut, he took the big gamble. He walked in with both hands going. He shook Turpin with a right, pushed him off and dropped him in the middle of the ring with another right. When Turpin got up at nine, Robinson drove him to the ropes, and there he must have thrown forty punches. Turpin, reeling now and trying to cover, was half sitting on the middle rope, and there were 61,000 people there, and it sounded as if they were all screaming.

"Of course I remember the fight," I was saying now, "and, as I said, you were lucky that night. When you had him on the ropes and he didn't go down, you reached out with your left, put your glove behind his head and tried to pull him forward. There were only eight seconds left in the round, so if you had pulled him off the ropes and he had gone down, the count would have killed the rest of the round. You had that cut and you were exhausted, and you would never have survived the next five rounds."

"You're right," he said.

"And I'll tell you a night," I said, "when you did out-smart yourself."

"What night was that?" he said.

"That night in the Yankee Stadium when you fought Maxim and it was 104 degrees in there. You were not only licking him, but you were licking him so easily that you made a show of it, dancing around in and out, throwing unnecessary punches. That's why, in that heat, you collapsed at the end of the thirteenth."

"You're right, old buddy," he said. "That was a mistake. I was incoherent all the next day. I never remembered when Goldstein fell out. I had a premonition the night before that fight too. I had a premonition that I would die."

He had finished the pastry and reclosed the package again, and he returned it to the desk drawer.

"There's this Sugar Ray Leonard," I said, "who won a gold medal in the Olympics. There was another one—Sugar Ray Seales. How do you feel about these kids calling themselves Sugar Ray?"

"Bill, you know," he said, sitting back and smiling, "it's a good feeling to think that the kids think that much of me."

It was different when he was a fighter. There was another welterweight at that time named George Costner, and in Chicago in 1945 Robinson knocked him out in two minutes and fifty-five seconds of the first round. Five years later they were matched again, this time for Philadelphia, and in the days leading up to the fight, the other, by then known as George ("Sugar") Costner, was quoted on the sports pages as disparaging Robinson.

"Listen, boy," Robinson said to him at the weigh-in, "I've been readin' what you've been sayin' in the papers about what you're gonna do to me."

"Why, there are no hard feelings, are there, Ray?" Costner said. "I just did that to boost the gate."

"That may be all right," Robinson said, "but when I boost the gate I do it by praisin' my opponent."

The logic of publicity, revolving as it does around the build-up of the underdog, was all on Costner's side, but this time Robinson knocked him out in two minutes and forty-nine seconds. While it was succinct, this was, in its scientific precision, one of Robinson's finest performances.

"There's only one 'Sugar,'" Robinson was quoted as saying right after the fight, but I remember another aftermath. It involved still another welterweight who was asked by his manager if he would fight Sugar Costner.

"No thanks," the fighter said.

"But you can lick Costner," the manager said. "Robinson flattened him twice inside of one round."

"I don't want to fight anybody named Sugar," the fighter said.

"I've been remembering," I said to Robinson now, "the first

time I ever met you. It was in Pete Vaccare's office in the Brill Building, and we heard you singing out in the hall, and you and June Clark came in wearing road clothes and harmonizing 'The Very Thought of You.' You two did it very well."

"Yeah," Robinson said, smiling. "June Clark, he was a musician—Armstrong was in his band—and he, too, was a believer in God."

"That was a long time ago," I said. "It was in March of 1946."

"Are you sure?" Robinson said. "Didn't we meet before then?"

"I'm certain," I said, "because I didn't start to write sports until I came back from the war."

"You were in the war?" Robinson said.

"Yes," I said, "but only as a war correspondent."

"Where were you?" Robinson said.

"All through northern Europe," I said.

"In the ETO?" he said. "Then how come we didn't meet over there?"

"I don't know," I said. It was as if I had just been stunned by a sucker punch, one you never expect the other to throw, and I was sparring for time.

"We were over there," Robinson was saying now. "Joe Louis and I we had a troupe, and we boxed in the ETO and everything."

I still didn't know what to say. There were the others at their desks—Thelma Smith and Mel Zolkover and a secretary—who could have heard us, and I didn't want to challenge it there. I am quite sure that, if we had been alone, I would have, just to try again after so many years to understand him, but as I have thought about it since, I believe it was better that I let it ride. He is a man who has his own illusions about his life, as do we all, about the way he wishes it had been, and there is little if any harm, although some sadness, in that now. I shall send him a copy of this book, however, and when he reads this chapter I hope he understands that, as a reporter, my responsibility, as pompous as this may sound, is to draw as accurate and honest a portrait as I can.

"I want you to meet Mr. Fillmore," he was saying now. "Mr. Fillmore can tell you a lot about the foundation."

"I'd like to meet him," I said, and he led me into Fillmore's office and introduced us.

Fillmore, a slim, immaculate man, bald and wearing dark glasses, said that he would be seventy-eight in a couple of months. He had worked, he said, for the Southern Pacific Railroad for forty years, as a waiter and then as an instructor, and he had been retired for seven years when Robinson and he started the foundation in 1969.

"The first time I met Ray personally," he said, "was through his present wife. She was rooming with us, and he was going with her, and then he finally married. We got to talking and got to be buddies, and one day I got a telegram from London that he wanted to see me.

"I wondered, with all the people he knew, why he wanted to see me. I waited, and he and his wife flew in and, it being hot, we sat in the back yard. I asked him what was so important, and he said he'd always wanted to do something for youth. I said, 'What do you want me to do about it, Ray? With all the people you know, you want me to put together something for children? I'm retired.' He said, 'No. You have just started working.' I told him, 'We need money, and we need children. If you can get the money, I can get the children.'

"From the back step we moved to Millie's kitchen, then to the church, and when it got too big for there, we moved here. Since 1969 there's no black mark on this organization, and I challenge anybody to go to the IRS or wherever.

"The Southern Pacific," he said, "had given me a three-year course in human relations, and what we try to do here is make good citizens, not only a Sugar Ray Robinson or a Sandy Koufax. We had these fellas here, and they called themselves 'The Young Black Panthers.' They knew every way to do wrong. There was 'One-Legged Joe' and there was 'Bluefish,' and the one was fourteen and the other was fifteen, and we gained their confidence.

"The news came out one time that a hamburger stand had been held up, and it sounded to me like 'One-Legged Joe' and 'Bluefish,' so I called in Tony, one of the lesser lights. I said to him, 'Where were you on such-and-such a night?' He said, 'I know what you want, but I wasn't in it.' I said, 'I know, but if I could find out where it was and I could find the pistol, I could help out.

"He told me where it was, where to find the pistol, and it was a toy. 'One-Legged Joe' went to UCLA and stayed there three years and got a job. 'Bluefish' joined the Navy, and that was what Ray Robinson had in mind, and what we try to do."

When I came out of Fillmore's office, Robinson was at his desk, finishing another Danish, and he suggested that we go over to the foundation's annex. We walked up the sidewalk, then through the blacktopped parking area of a shopping center, and at the far side, into what had been a store and was now partitioned into several rooms. He led me into a conference room, and we sat down with Zolkover, and with Richard Jackman, a then thirty-two-year-old law graduate who is the program director, and his assistant, Scott McCreary, then twenty-six and a graduate of the University of California at Santa Barbara.

"Tell Bill," Robinson said, at the head of the long table, "what we do here."

"Well, take our baseball program," Zolkover said. "We kind of take the place of the YMCA and the Little League for kids six to sixteen in the lower socio-economic areas where they can't afford those others. The children are not allowed to pay, and when you think of it, when Ray was a kid his mother couldn't afford it."

"We're not trying to build a Sugar Ray," Jackman said.

"That's right," Robinson said, "and the last thing, that we're just goin' to start now, is the boxing. I didn't want people to think we're a boxing organization."

"At the same time," Jackman said, "it's Mr. Robinson's charisma that makes it go. He has friends all over the world, and if we get the Junior Olympics started here it could include ten to fifteen cities, and we could expand to Europe, too."

"He can open any door," Zolkover said, nodding toward Robinson. "One day the question was, where could we get readership? I said, *'The Reader's Digest.'* I looked up the chairman of the board, and Ray called, and it was, 'Hey, Ray!'

"You see," he said, "we're like a church. We pay no money, so we have to have people with dedication like Ray."

"When he was boxing," Scott said, "they called him the greatest fighter, pound-for-pound. We say that, pound-for-pound, we get the greatest distance out of our money."

When Robinson and I left them a few minutes later, we stood for a moment on the sidewalk edging the parking area, looking out over the quadrangle of parked cars. The California climate, unlike that of the Northeast where I abide, is conducive to keeping cars clean, and I was struck by how they glistened, older models as well as new, in the sunlight.

"Are you still on the Cadillac kick?" I said to him.

"No," he said. "No more."

"I remember you turned that chartreuse one in for the fuschia one."

"The car I drive now," he said, and then pointing, "is that little red Pinto over there."

"That's your car?"

"Yeah," he said, and then, smiling, "but I've been there."

"I'll say you have," I said.

We walked slowly across the parking area. We were dawdling in the warm sunlight.

"While you were fighting," I said, "did you take out any annuities?"

"Nope," he said.

"Did you buy any stocks?"

"A few, and I sold those."

"When you had all those investments in Harlem," I said, "I was always afraid you were going to get clipped."

"That's right," he said.

"So how do you get along now?"

"I've got friends," he said. "I borrow five grand, and I pay back three. I borrow three, and pay two. Then something drops in, and I pay everybody. People say to me about this foundation, 'What are you gettin'?' They can't understand doing something for kids. I've always been a Christian believer in God. I was gifted with a talent that helped introduce me to people, and all that was in preparation for what I'm doin' now."

"And I celebrate it," I said.

When we got back to the office I called for a cab. While I was waiting for it, he said he thought he would take his five-mile walk, and we shook hands and wished each other well. He went out the door and, through the wide front window, I saw him start up the sidewalk, the greatest fighter I ever saw, the one I wanted so much to know.

13

G.I. Lew

. . . tens of thousands of young men fighting for . . .
for . . . well, at least for each other.

Ernie Pyle, *Brave Men*

"Bill, this is Lupie," his wife said on the phone when I called from
Los Angeles. It was just after ten o'clock in the evening.

"How are you?" I said. "And how's Lew?"

"I'm fine," she said, "and Lew's in bed. I'll see if he's still
awake."

"Don't wake him," I said. "I just called to say that I'll be there
tomorrow."

"He's asleep," she said when she came back to the phone. "I
have to wake him up at eleven o'clock, though, to give him a pill,
and I'll tell him then."

"How is he?"

"He's all right," she said. "He's coming along fine."

Jack Fiske had found him for me. Jack covers sports for the
San Francisco Chronicle, and he had written to ask if I could find
him a copy of a boxing anthology I edited and that went out of
print about a decade ago. I didn't find the book, but he found Lew
Jenkins living in Concord, just outside of Oakland, and he had
written that Lew had had a heart attack some three years before.

"We'll be delighted to pick you up," Lupie was saying on the
phone now. "I'll have to drive Lew."

"Then don't do it," I said. "I'll rent a car and . . ."

"Oh, no," she said. "I do anything that has to be done for Lew, and he'll want to pick you up. He'll insist, and he's been so excited since you told him that you were coming."

"Well," I said, "you know that he's a hero of mine."

"I just know," she said, "that, whatever it is, you two really have something together."

"Yes," I said, "we do."

We do, indeed. No athlete of our time, perhaps of any time, lived more wildly than this man who disgraced the title he held of lightweight champion of the world. During his days in the ring, before I knew him, he was the epitome of the anti-hero, the antithesis of all I had grown up to admire in sports and in life, and yet when I came to know him we came to know something together that goes deeper than life styles.

During the summer of 1952 I was trying to put together a magazine piece on what it takes to be a great combat infantryman. At Fort Benning, Georgia, the captain who was in charge of public relations took me in to meet the commandant, a major general named Robert N. Young. The general was just back from the war they called a police action that was going on in Korea, and he had commanded the Second Infantry Division there.

"I brought two fine combat men back with me," he said. "I had places for a staff, but I didn't have a staff, so I picked two good combat sergeants. I brought back a sergeant named Adams and a sergeant named Jenkins."

"I know the sergeant named Jenkins," I said. I knew it was Lew, because I had seen the AP story out of Korea when he had been awarded the Silver Star.

"He's a great combat soldier," the general said. "He's famous up and down the front."

He was famous up and down Broadway and on the main streets and side streets of so many of those towns in which he boxed, or tried to when he was coming off those drunks that lasted for days and sometimes weeks, and more than once they put whiskey in his water bottle to keep him from falling on his face in the middle of a round. He was jailed in half a dozen towns, and they wrote about that and about him, but they didn't know the half of it, and they didn't know him. I came to know him because of when and where I met him.

It was that summer of 1944, and it was one of those blue and pink evenings they were getting then off the Channel coast of France. We were tied up with a Coast Guard LST several hundred yards off the beach, waiting to get in, and it was quiet and the air was soft and the water was almost flat and had in it those same pastel colors of the sky.

The Army had pushed inland, breaking through now toward Paris, and I was coming back from England, trying to get with the Army. I was sitting in the jeep among the other jeeps on the forward deck, reading, when I heard them talking off to the right.

"You know who's on this tub tied up with us?" the first one said, in the high voice of a kid.

"Sure," the second one said. "Betty Grable."

"Lew Jenkins," the first one said. "He was the lightweight champion of the world."

All I had to do was step from our ship to his and ask for him, and there he was. He had on a pair of dirty blue jeans and a faded blue shirt and a dirty white cap stuck on the back of that wild bush of reddish hair. There he was, a skinny little guy with the heavy brows of a fighter and those pale blue, sunken eyes, and we sat on a deck housing and we talked.

He had put the First Division ashore at Sicily and the Thirty-sixth Division ashore at Salerno. He had put the British ashore behind the Japanese lines in Burma, and he had put them ashore again here in Normandy on D-Day. He had been up and down many beaches in the small boats, bombed and strafed and shelled, and now he was saying that that wasn't fighting.

"Lew," I had said, "how's the Coast Guard?"

"I guess it's all right," he said, in that Texas drawl. "But I don't like it."

"Why?"

"I don't want to knock the Coast Guard or the Navy either," he said, "but we don't fight."

"Don't fight?" I said.

"Sure the Coast Guard and the Navy been in there," he said, looking at me in that sad, matter-of-fact way of his. "We ain't always had it easy, but we take the Army in there and then we go away and leave 'em. It ain't the same as the Army.

"When I say the Army," he said, "I mean the soldier. I mean

like the First Division. Before we took 'em in, I talked with them, and when I talked with them I knew this was the greatest Army in the world. Then I took 'em in and seen them get killed, and you know what I'd do now if I had a house?"

Of course, he didn't have a house. When he was fighting Henry Armstrong in the Polo Grounds, loading up on the booze until three or four o'clock every morning and making $25,000 in one night, more than four times what most men made then in a year, he had two houses. He had one in Sweetwater, Texas, where he came from, and one in Florida, but while he was running those LCVPs up on those beaches and his only home was that tired old LST, they sold him out of both houses.

"If I had a house," he said, "and a soldier didn't have a house, I'd give it to him. If I didn't, I'd be stealin', because he earned it. There ain't nothin' they shouldn't give a soldier if he's a soldier like in the First Division or the Thirty-Sixth or one of them."

"I know what you mean." I said.

"I see sometimes that a landing was easy," he said. "Sometimes they say that a landing was easy, and I remember some poor soldier I saw get killed. I think about how, back home, some person is goin' to be just as miserable as if our whole Army got killed. I think about that a long time."

"I know," I said. "Many times I've thought the same thing."

"When they told us we were takin' the British in here," he said, "my heart wasn't in it. You know where my heart was?"

"No."

"My heart was with the First Division here. I wanted to be with them I knew. Then I saw the Limies get killed, and then I liked them, too."

"There's no difference between any of them, Lew," I said.

"You know what got me?" he said.

"No."

"When I put the Thirty-Sixth Division in at Salerno," he said. "That's the Texas Division, and it was two or three in the mornin' and I put them on the beach and they were just mowin' 'em down. Just everybody was gettin' killed, and I'd walk up there to see who wanted to go back and they were just piled up.

"My mind and my soul was with the soldiers on the beach, and they'd load me up with wounded and I'd go from ship to ship and the medics would say, 'Take 'em away. We can't handle any more here.' There'd be men with their legs blown off and there'd be men with their sides blown open, and they wouldn't say a word. There wasn't one of 'em let out a moan, and I hid my head in my hands and I cried.

"I never did go for cryin' as a kid or nothin'," he said, "but I wanted to go and fight with them and help them, but I was afraid if I did I'd get court-martialed. I felt so cheap. My own state's men were dyin', and I felt so ashamed bein' off the beach."

He looked at me and I looked at him.

"I just prayed," he said. "I just prayed for another war to start, for me to be a front-line soldier."

I suppose it seems uncivilized, even barbarous, now that a man should pray for the catastrophe of war. Even generals who, in their secret hearts, may long for the opportunity to express and distinguish themselves in the science to which they have devoted their lives, would be loathe to admit it. Lew admitted it, and I understood when he said it and I understand now. He was not a man seeking distinction, but the expression of something else, and what that was I shall try to explain.

Then we came back off that war, and for a while I used to follow in the papers what was left of his career. He was broke, and he took a couple of small fights in New England. Then he went back to Texas, and every now and then I would see in the agate fight results at the bottom of the sports pages that he was fighting out there.

Then, one day in the winter of 1946 there was several of us out at Brown's Hotel at the New Jersey end of Greenwood Lake. Lee Oma was there getting ready to fight Gus Lesnevich in the Garden, and we were standing around there where the ring was set up next to the bar, waiting for Oma to work out, when Al Buck came off the phone. He was writing boxing for the *New York Post,* and he had been talking to his office.

"Do you want a laugh?" he said.

"What?" I said.

"My desk just told," he said. "Lew Jenkins has enlisted in the Army."

"What is it?" somebody said. "Is he going for that bonus they get, or is it a gag?"

I didn't try to explain it to them. There wasn't a war going on then, and they all knew him and liked him, but there were some of them who had written when Lew was champion and Freddie "Red" Cochrane knocked him down five times in a non-title fight in the Garden, that he was not only a disgrace to himself and the title he held but to the whole fight game.

They didn't know that he had three broken vertebrae in his neck after piling his motorcycle into a traffic circle in New Jersey, blind drunk at three o'clock one morning less than three weeks before the fight. They knew a lot about Lew and they put it in the papers, but what did they know?

"Here were two youngsters," Caswell Adams wrote in the *New York Herald Tribune* when Lew fought a fierce draw in the Garden with Fritzie Zivic who was the welterweight champ, "in perfect condition and with the sole idea of knocking the other fellow out."

Lew was in perfect condition all right, but for a drunk act. At 3 A.M. on the day of the fight he was loading up in a bar on Broadway with some Texans he had met, and he had been loaded every night for a week.

"You know something, Lew?" I said to him down at Benning, after the general had called him in, and Lew and I had walked over to the EM canteen to sit and talk. "They say in the fight game that Harry Greb was the greatest liver anybody ever saw."

While I was with him down there, he and I would sit in that canteen and drink two or three iced teas one right after the other, trying to get cool on those hot, muggy Georgia summer afternoons.

"Even Greb," I said, "couldn't have lived like you."

"People who knew Greb," Lew said, "say he was a junior compared to me."

He didn't say it as a boast but as a matter of fact, and a rather sad one at that. Lew could be very funny too, but even when he would come out with a line that would bring a laugh there was only that weak smile around his mouth, and then it would go away and there would be just that sad, puzzled expression with those deep eyes seeming to be trying to find an answer somewhere off in the distance.

There was the night he fought Joey Zodda outdoors in the Meadowbrook Bowl in Newark, New Jersey. In the third round he hit Zodda with that straight right, and down went Zodda in his own corner. As he lay there, one of his seconds reached up with the smelling salts and held it under Zodda's nose. Zodda got up, and when he did Lew moved in with another right and, as Zodda went down and out, Lew just turned and walked to his corner.

"Willie," he said, to Willie Ketchum, who trained him, or tried to, "he can give him all the smellin' salts he wants now. The man's gone."

Willie said he had to laugh. Then there was the night Lew fought Tippy Larkin in the Garden. Larkin was a picture boxer with a beautiful left hand, and his fight was to move around Lew and stab him, make him miss and tie him up inside.

"You know what I'm gonna do to that man tonight?" Lew said to Willie in the dressing room.

"What?" Willie said.

"I'm gonna knock him out," Lew said, "and pick him up by his legs and drag him to his corner."

"Listen," Willie said, "don't get heated up. With this Larkin everything has to go his own smooth way. You go out there and you jab him."

"Jab him?" Lew said. "Why do I want to jab him? I wanta knock him out."

"Jab him," Willie said, "because he won't be looking for it. He thinks he's gonna jab you."

"I think that's crazy," Lew said.

He walked out and he jabbed Larkin, though. He hit him three stiff jabs, and Larkin backed off. Lew jabbed him again, and Larkin just stood there, trying to decide what to do. Then Lew threw that right hand, on a straight line from the shoulder, and it hit Larkin on the chin. Larkin stiffened and then he shuddered, and as he started to go Lew hit him with a hook, a right and another hook, and Larkin landed on his face underneath the ropes.

When the referee started the count, Willie started up the steps. He said he was afraid that Lew would pick Larkin up by the feet and try to drag him to his corner.

"You know something?" Lew said, sitting on the rubbing table in the dressing room. "That man was the most convinced knocked-out man I ever knocked out."

The newspaper men, crowding around him, laughed. That was

another of those times, though, when he didn't mean it for a laugh. It was just that there was so much about people and about life that saddened Lew, because he was born into sadness.

"Nobody," he told me, sitting in that canteen, "really knows the poor people of Texas in my time."

The way he felt about the poor of Texas was the way he felt about the poor of the infantry, and he came from one and he joined the other. In between he was champion of the world and he made enough money to retire on, but all of that and his title he threw away because he had no understanding of it and it meant nothing to him. All he understood was trouble.

"The poor old private," he was saying down at Benning. "The only time he's first is when they say, 'Take that objective there.' I stand back with 'em at shows. I eat with privates. The noncoms eat together in a circle, but I eat with the privates. I always wanted to be with the underdog. They hold up."

It was that way with Lew when he was a fighter. He made his greatest fights when no one believed in him and he was the underdog, and his worst when he was the favorite. When he was a 4–1 underdog he won the title from Lou Ambers because only then did fighting have some meaning.

I am sure, you see, that he didn't enlist for Korea to win a war or save a world, but just to be a part of that misery that is the private property of the front-line soldier. He became a great front-line soldier because he came into the world in misery and because, when he was making that money and had a chance to rise above it, he felt like a stranger and was not at home in success—and so he sought his level.

"Where are you?" he was saying now on the phone, after I had flown into Oakland and checked into the motel at noon.

"I'm in the Holiday Inn near the airport," I said. "It's not far from the Coliseum."

"I know where it is," he said. "When I was drivin' the truck for the linen supply, I used to deliver there. We'll pick you up."

"I'll be in the lobby at 1:30," I said. "I guess we'll recognize each other."

"Yeah," he said, "but it's been a long time."

It had been twenty-five years, and after I left him at Benning I heard, a couple of weeks later, that he had malaria and that, while he had been running a fever of 105.6 he had been delirious and shouting that he had to get back to Korea. After that I would hear from him occasionally, the cryptic notes complaining that what he was doing wasn't really soldiering. Sometimes they would be typewritten on Army requisition forms and at other times they would be handwritten on lined pages torn from a looseleaf notebook, and they came from Hawaii and from Germany and then from Fort Ord in California, just before he got out of the Army in 1963.

"It ain't the same, old pal," he wrote once from Germany. "If you could see what's happening to our Army now it would make you sick, but I just mind my own business and I do my job until I can get out."

I was in the lobby of the motel now at 1:30, and when I didn't see him there I walked outside to stand in front and to meet them as they drove up. I had been waiting there for about ten minutes when behind me the glass door from the lobby opened and he walked out.

"I'm sorry we missed each other," I said, after we had shaken hands. "I didn't see you inside."

He was thin and looked older, of course, and with that same fighter's face. He had on a light gray suit and a dark blue knitted sports shirt buttoned at the neck and one of those narrow-brimmed, checkered plaid hats that Bing Crosby used to wear.

"I been out in back visitin' with them nigra maids in the housekeeping department," he said. "I know 'em all from when I used to deliver the linen here, and they're all my friends."

"Where's Lupie?" I said.

In 1947 he had met and married Lupie Galarza at Camp Stoneman, California. At Benning I had met her and their then four-year-old son, and I used to get Christmas cards signed by her, "Lupie, Lew, and Lew II."

"She's back in here somewhere," he said.

We found her in the lobby, dark-haired, oval-faced, and smiling, and we exchanged greetings and walked out to the car. I got into the back, and Lupie started to back the car out.

"Before we go," Lew said, "drive around here to the housekeeping department."

"The housekeeping department?" Lupie said. "Why do you want to go there?"

"So you can meet my friends," Lew said. "I want to introduce 'em to you and Bill."

"Must we?" Lupie said.

"Yeah," Lew said.

He led us into the linen room, and introduced us. Several of them seemed embarrassed, even bewildered, shaking our hands, but a couple of them smiled and kidded with Lew and seemed to understand.

"Them nigra gals are all right," Lew said when we got back in the car. "They like me, and I like them."

"You shouldn't call them nigras," Lupie said. "Nobody uses that word any more."

"Yeah, I know," Lew said, "but what difference does it make what I call 'em? I like them."

"It was the same way in the Army," Lupie said. "Your friends in the Army were colored, too."

"Yeah," Lew said.

They live in a condominium, stucco with redwood trim, in a newer residential area where the roads curve between landscaped and well-kept lawns. Lupie parked in the carport, and after they had led me in Lew took off his jacket and we sat down.

"You want a drink?" he said. "There's a bottle out there in the kitchen."

"It's still too early in the afternoon for me," I said. "Are you drinking?"

"I had a beer about a year ago, I guess," he said.

"There was a time," I said, "when that would have brought a big laugh."

"Yeah," Lew said, his face impassive as he thought about it. "Nobody would believe it then, and they'd hardly believe it now."

The night he knocked out Ambers and won the lightweight championship was the last time he was ever in shape for a fight. He won the title on May 10, 1940, and two months later they put him into the Polo Grounds against Henry Armstrong. Armstrong was one of the greatest ever of the smaller men, and once he held the featherweight, lightweight, and welterweight titles at the same time. He was still the welterweight champion, and going in they had him 9–5 over Lew. If they had known that Lew had been drinking until four o'clock every morning, Armstrong would have been 90–1, with no takers.

Lew was down seven times in the six rounds. Arthur Donovan was the referee, and at the end of the sixth he took a look at Lew gasping in his corner, and he walked out to the center of the ring and he threw his hands out, palms down.

"How'm I doin'?" Lew kept asking in the dressing room. "What round did I get him in?"

"You didn't," Hymie Caplan, who managed him, said.

"You're crazy," Lew said, his eyes firing up. "I wasn't knocked out. I wasn't hurt."

"Donovan stopped it," Hymie said.

"You mean I couldn't get up?" Lew said, and then he started to ramble. "Get me another fight. Get me another shot at him. Say, listen. Where am I?"

Two months later he fought Bob Montgomery in Shibe Park in Philadelphia. Montgomery was enough of a fighter so that, four years later, he would win the lightweight championship, but this one was over-the-weight, and Lew's title was not on the line. The fight was postponed once when one of Lew's sisters called him and told him that their mother was dying in Stillwater. Lew was sitting there in the bedroom and looking at his mother, who was unable to recognize anyone by then, when he got a phone call telling him that if he didn't come back and fight he would be fined and suspended.

Lew had a new convertible, with less than 3,000 miles on it, and he and Eddie Carroll, a welterweight, started back. They took turns driving around the clock, and in Sparta, Tennessee, Lew fell asleep in the back seat when they went off the side of a mountain. The car rolled down the slope and wedged against a tree and Lew was thrown out.

"When I come to," he was telling me, sitting in that canteen in Benning and drinking that iced tea, "Eddie was pinned behind the motor and he was bleedin' and moanin'. There was this little old Brownie camera in the car, and I grabbed that and he was moanin' and I said to him, 'Wait a minute, you sonofabitch. Hold still. This'll make a hell of a picture.'"

"But there was something wrong with the camera," Lew said, and this was Lew Jenkins. "The camera wouldn't work, but wouldn't that make a hell of a picture?"

"Yes," I said. "It would."

Lew had a cut on the top of his head and a cut on one knee and there was something wrong with his hip. The next day he took a used-car dealer out to look at the car.

"Ain't that a wreck?" Lew said.

"It sure is," the other said. "I'll give you two-fifty for it."

"Make it three hundred," Lew said, "and you can have the tree, too."

When Lew got to Philadelphia he ached all over, so he reasoned that there was no sense in trying to train. He and Willie had a suite in a good hotel where there was one of those business men's gyms, and Lew was supposed to work out in the gym. He tried to go two rounds, but he couldn't, and Willie told me later that he thought that Herman Taylor, who was promoting the fight, was going out of his mind.

"He's a disgrace," he kept saying to Willie.

"I know," Willie said, "but what can I do?"

Willie was living in the big suite alone. He found a doctor to treat Lew's hip, but he couldn't find Lew. The fight was on a Monday, and on Friday afternoon Lew showed up, stewed. He flopped into bed and he slept until Saturday morning.

"I'll tell you what we'll do," he said to Willie when he woke up. "Let's go on the road."

They went down and Willie called a cab and they rode out to Fairmount Park. Lew got out of the cab and he disappeared. He was gone for an hour and a half.

"Where is he?" the cab driver kept asking Willie.

"I don't know," Willie said. "Maybe he fell in the lake."

Finally they saw Lew coming down the road. Willie said Lew's arms and legs were going, and he was flying. He got in the cab and they went back to the hotel. He had a meal, flopped into bed and that afternoon he worked a couple of rounds in the gym. He had another meal, and he slept until Sunday morning when they went to the park again and he disappeared for another hour and a half. Then he ate, went back to bed, woke up at midnight, ate and then slept again until it was almost time to go to the weigh-in.

"Man," he said when he got up and stretched. "I feel good."

"You must," Willie said, looking at him. "How good can you feel?"

Hymie Caplan had come in from New York. He waited until Lew went into the bathroom.

"Willie," he said, "what kind of shape is he in?"

"What shape can he be in?" Willie said. "He's lucky if he can clumb up the steps to the ring."

In the third round Lew was on the floor. He had just belted Montgomery with a right to the body and Montgomery had hit him with a long right on the chin, and he was face down on the canvas.

"Well," Willie said, turning to Hymie in the corner, "That's two in a row."

"But look!" Hymie said. "He's gettin' up!"

He got up at nine, punching. He hurt Montgomery with a right hand, and Montgomery went into a shell. While he was in the shell he kept walking to Lew, and Willie said that if Montgomery had just walked away, Lew would have fallen on his face.

"Lew," Willie said to him after the ninth round, "it's the last round. That guy just about got to his corner."

"I know," Lew said, gasping, "but I can't get off this stool."

Willie lifted him off and pushed him out. Halfway through the round Lew was bleeding from the mouth and nose, but he kept throwing punches, and they wrote on the sports pages later that this was the most savage fight in Philadelphia since Lew Tendler and Willie Jackson, fifteen years before.

"At the end," Willie was telling me, "the referee walks over and he lifts Lew's hand and he says, 'The winner, Lew Jenkins!' I just stood there and I said to myself, 'Did I see this thing? Can it be true, with his hip and his knee, and the way he's living?' "

"How could I do that?" Lew was asking me at Benning. "How could I even stand up for ten rounds in those fights with good men, the shape I was in?"

"I don't know, Lew," I said. "Don't ask me."

"When did you decide," I said to him now, "to call it quits on the booze?"

"I stopped about twenty-five years ago," he said. "I just had to quit. I was just bein' crazy. I said to myself, 'I can't go on. I got a son and a wonderful wife, and my wife and son are doin' without.' I used to drink days, weeks, months at a time."

"I know," I said.

The day after the Montgomery fight in Philadelphia, Lew went back to Sweetwater, and he got there just as his mother died. After the funeral he bought a new Cadillac in Dallas and he drove it back to New York. He put it in a parking lot, and he took a plane to Miami.

He was married then to Katie, and they had had another of their rows. When they first met, Katie was a stock car racer in Dallas, and theirs was a marriage that should have been made in a carnival booth. It was a Punch-and-Judy show, and in Miami they had another go-round and Lew walked out. He was ambling along the street when, in a store window, he saw a display of new motorcycles.

"How do you turn one of these things on," he asked the salesman, "and how do you turn it off?"

The salesman explained it to him, took $500 from Lew and fixed up the license. Lew wheeled the motorcycle out onto the street, ran it once around the block, and started off for New York.

"Man," he was telling me, "you fall off a motorcycle about ten times goin' sixty miles an hour and it raises hell with your insides. I was near shook to death by the time I got to New York."

They matched Lew to defend his title against Pete Lello in the Garden on November 22, 1940. Lello had stopped Lew in seven rounds in Chicago the year before, and Lew was supposed to be training at Pompton Lakes, New Jersey. He trained there, if you want to call it training, for a number of fights after that, and it was always the same.

"He'd disappear," Allie Stolz was telling several of us in the boxing office at the Garden one afternoon, and Allie was a good lightweight. "He'd be gone three or four days. Then he'd call me up and say, 'Where have you been?' I'd say, 'Me? Where have *you* been?' He'd say, 'Don't go away. I'll be right out.' Sometimes he'd come out that day. Sometimes it would be another three or four days.

"After a while," Allie said, "he had three motorcycles. He had one for straight speeding and one for hill climbing, and one that, so help me, ran in curves and circles."

I remembered Lew telling me that evening on the LST off Normandy about the last cycle he owned. He said that Katie was trying to find it, but that he had it locked up in a garage at Pompton Lakes where, he said, the New Jersey State Troopers were guarding it.

"One day," Allie was saying, "he was missing from camp, and just about when it was time for him to box we heard a terrific clatter out on the road that runs past the camp, and there he was at the head of about fifty guys on motorcycles, waving to us as they roared past."

Lew also had a guitar and a phonograph and a stack of cowboy records. He would play them over and over, and then take the guitar and strum it and sing.

"Don't I sound like him?" he'd say.

"No," Allie would say.

He would write a couple of songs a day. Allie said that no matter what the words were, the tune was always the same.

"Listen to this one," he would say, and then he would start strumming and singing again.

"I heard that one yesterday," Allie would say.

"No you didn't," Lew would say. "I just wrote it. I hear fellas get a lot of money for writin' songs. I'm gonna write some more and sell 'em and make a lot of money."

On the afternoon of the Lello fight the police picked up Hymie Caplan. Hymie was out of New York's Lower East Side, short and pasty-faced, blue-eyed and blond, and he had a brother who was known as "Kid Dropper." Kid Dropper was what they used to call a torpedo or trigger man, meaning a gun-for-hire, and that was the way he died. Hymie also had a brother who taught in the New York school system and another who worked for the United States Customs, and I leave that to the child psychologists, family counselors, and sociologists.

Hymie was one of five the police rounded up, and Bill O'Dwyer, who was the District Attorney of Kings County then, before he became Mayor of New York and Ambassador to Mexico, described it as a $4,000,000 marked-card swindle. A real estate dealer was taken for $150,000 and a Park Avenue doctor for $18,000. Two manufacturers from Philadelphia had lost $40,000 and $25,000 apiece, a jeweler went for $75,000, and a yarn manufacturer for $100,000. There were thirty-eight other business men who said they had lost $700,000 in two years, and O'Dwyer said Hymie was the godfather who had been putting up the money for the expensive establishments.

Hymie went to Sing Sing, but it was always around New York that he took the fall for somebody else. When he was dying of cancer in 1949, Irving Rudd and I went over to see him in the hospital in Brooklyn, and I wanted to ask him then about it, but I never did.

"I'll get him off," Lew said, when he heard they had Hymie.

They were holding Hymie in a Brooklyn hotel, and when Lew got on the phone with the detectives, he knew he was not going to get Hymie off. He pleaded with them to bring Hymie to the fight so that he could see it, and when they told him that they couldn't do that, he asked them to put Hymie on the phone.

"Listen, Hymie," he told him on the phone, "when you hear the building shake, that's Lello hittin' the floor."

Lello hit the floor in the second round. They were coming out of a clinch and Lew threw a hook and Lello started down. Lew was on top of him, and he came back with a right as Lello was going. Lello rolled over on the canvas and got up at nine. When he did, Arthur Donovan moved in to wipe Lello's gloves, and as he lifted them Lew belted Lello with another right and he went down again. He was down three more times and was on his knees in Lew's corner, about to pitch forward on his face, when Donovan stopped it.

"Did you miss Hymie," one of the newspaper men asked Lew in the dressing room.

"I missed Hymie," Lew said, "but I didn't miss Lello."

"Against Lello," Dan Parker wrote in the *New York Daily Mirror,* "Jenkins looked like a great champion. Certainly no lightweight within the memory of this present generation of fans could hit like this bag of bones."

It was a month after the Lello fight when they put Lew and

Fritzie Zivic together in the Garden. Zivic had just won the welter-weight title from Henry Armstrong, and it would have been a tough fight for Lew, even if he had bothered to get in shape. The fight was on a Friday night, and Lew and Willie were out at Pompton Lakes when Lew disappeared on the Saturday before the fight. He showed up on Monday and they decided to finish training in New York. He was out every night, though, and at three o'clock on the morning of the fight, Willie left him and the Texans on Broadway. The weigh-in was at noon and at 10:30 Willie was in the lobby of the hotel, waiting for Lew.

"You waiting for Lew Jenkins?" a bellhop said to Willie finally, at eleven.

"Sure," Willie said.

"He's gone an hour and a half ago," the bellhop said.

"Are you kidding?" Willie said.

"No," the bellhop said. "I saw him go out with a pair of ice skates."

Willie went down to the Boxing Commission. Zivic was there waiting and so were the newspaper men. When Lew finally walked in, it was one o'clock.

"I got lost on the subway," Lew said.

He was never very good with a lie, though. It seemed as if he always had to get it off his chest.

"You know, Willie," he said when they were alone later, "I didn't get lost in the subway."

"I know," Willie said.

"I went ice skatin'," Lew said.

"Why?" Willie said. "Why on the day of a fight?"

"Well," Lew said, "somebody told me it's good for your legs."

After the weigh-in Willie took Lew to eat, and then they went up to the suite in the Astor. Lew took a cigarette—he always smoked three or four in the dressing room waiting to get into the ring—and he fell back on the bed with his hat and coat and his shoes on, and he went to sleep. Willie took the cigarette out of Lew's hand, and he said there must have been twenty others in the suite, smoking cigars and shouting to be heard. Every now and then the phone would ring in the bedroom, but Lew slept until seven o'clock when Willie woke him.

"Man, I feel good," he said, stretching, and that was the night he and Zivic fought that great draw and Cas Adams wrote about the two finely conditioned athletes.

"Lew had that heart attack you know," Lupie was saying now.

"So Jack Fiske told me," I said. "When was that?"

"In April of 1973," Lew said. "I felt somethin' here in my left arm, and I laid down on the bed and I kinda blacked out, like when I fought Primo Flores in the Bronx and I was down five times, but I knocked him out and I didn't know it."

"And in the dressing room," I said, "Lester Bromberg told you that you'd won."

"That's right," Lew said.

"I got on the phone," Lupie was saying, "and the Fire Department came."

"They took me over to San Francisco," Lew said, "and with that electric shock a couple of times, they like to knock my goddamn head off."

"The side of his heart broke open," Lupie said, "but it healed itself. It was what they call a myocardial infarction."

"I was in San Francisco three weeks," Lew said, "and in John Muir here. That cost sixteen or seventeen thousand dollars."

"Did you have Army insurance that covered some of that?" I said.

"Yeah, I had some insurance," he said, "but I had to pay practically all. It left me with nothin'."

"We're still paying it off," Lupie said, "but I'd live in a tent if we had to."

"I got about eight pills a day," Lew said. "I weighed 119 pounds when I come out of that hospital. I stuttered and I stumbled all over the place, and it was three months before I could talk. A rough, tough guy like me and starvin' to death with that diet, and I thought I'd jump under a car a few times, but I didn't have the courage."

"You know," Lupie said, "Lew types and exercises his hand. He taught himself to touch-type, but he can't make the 'a,' and before he had the heart attack he was a terrific speaker. He used to tell about his cotton-picking days, and they were fascinated. Some people would come up and say, 'I lived like that, but I was ashamed to say so.'"

"Yeah," Lew said. "They were ashamed of bein' poor and workin'."

He was born Elmer Verlin Jenkins in Milburn, Texas, on December 4, 1916, one of seven kids. For a while his father was a blacksmith in Brownwood, and then he tried running a second-hand clothing store. He could never make a go of anything, and each time that he tapped out he would load the family in an old covered wagon and hitch up the two mules and they would push off in hope, while they really knew that it would never be any different. In all, over those years, they hit twenty-two towns.

"I come from a poor, ridiculous family," he once said to Jimmy Cannon, and Jimmy said that about told it all.

The whole family would pick cotton. They would go out in the fields at sunup, and they would still be out there at sundown.

"We'd pick fourteen hours," he said, "and no ten-minute break or nothin'. We'd get to the end of a row and my dad would say, 'Come on!' In cold weather your hands would chap and the burrs would prick 'em. That's the way it was with the poor people of Texas in my time."

When Lew was sixteen they were living in Sweetwater, and he fought Mexican kids in an alley that ran along the side of a pie shop and the winner got a pie. The following year his father died, and Lew hooked up with the T. J. Tidwell carnival, boxing all comers.

"They weren't fighters," he said, "but neither was I. I only weighed 120 pounds, and some of them were heavyweights."

When the carnival folded in January of 1936, Lew went to Mesa, Arizona, to pick cotton. He and a couple of others cleaned out an old chicken house and were living in that when he read in a paper that Jim Braddock, who was then the heavyweight champion of the world, was to box Jack McCarthy, his sparring partner, in Phoenix.

"I never seen a champion or been close to one," Lew told the others. "I'm gonna get me a fight on that card."

With one of the others he bummed into Phoenix, and the promoter gave him a dollar in advance of the five he was to get for boxing four rounds. The fight was a week off, and Lew's buddy starved out and hopped a freight, but Lew lived on oatmeal and water and won his fight. He picked up the four dollars and bummed to Dallas and lived for a week on doughnuts and coffee waiting for another fight.

"You could get doughnuts and coffee for a nickel," he told me, "and after I licked the guy, he told them I won because I had a big steak. I could have killed him, because I had to lay back between rounds because I was exhausted and the referee had to tell me I was winnin' to keep on. Why would that guy lie that I had a steak?"

"I don't know, Lew," I said. "I don't know why."

"But why would he lie?" Lew said, sitting there in Benning and still hurt by just the thought of it after sixteen years and all he had been through since then.

After the fight in Dallas, he caught a freight for El Paso and enlisted in the cavalry at Fort Bliss. He was not yet twenty. What he was to see of man and feel for man in war was still years away, and he enlisted because he was hungry and tired of sleeping out.

"They think more of a horse in the cavalry than they do of a man," he told me. "Horses cost a lot of money, and they could get all the men they wanted for $21 a month."

He weighed only 136 pounds, but he was the welterweight champion of Fort Bliss, and he fought pro in El Paso and Silver City. When his two years were up, he boxed in Dallas and then drifted to California and Chicago and Mexico. In Mexico he put together enough of a stake to start for New York, and when he hit the city in July of 1939 he and Katie had eight dollars between them.

"When he first came into Stillman's," Willie Ketchum told me, "he didn't look like anything."

"Jenkins," Joe Williams was to write in the *New York World Telegram,* "looks about as much like a fighter as a Bohemian free-verse writer. A starved cannibal wouldn't take a second look at him. He has a hatchet face, and a head of wild, stringy hair, and deep, sunken eyes that seem to be continuously startled. Where he gets his punching power is baffling."

Somebody described him, undernourished and bony-thin at 129 pounds and with that bush of hair, as a floor mop walking on its stick end. They said, though, that you had to go back to Willie Jackson and Richey Mitchell and Charley White and Benny Leonard to remember any lightweights who could punch like him.

They were amazed by the way he could punch with a straight right hand, and he was born with that, and he had it in the alley in Sweetwater and when he got to the Garden in New York.

Lew won seven fights in a row in the smaller clubs around New York before they put him in the Garden, and every fight was a brawl. By now Hymie Caplan had moved in to manage Lew, but although he had handled three other champions—Ben Jeby and Lou Salica and Solly Krieger—he couldn't handle Lew. Johnny Attell was making matches for Mike Jacobs at the Garden then, and without telling Hymie, he went up to the hotel where Lew and Katie were living and signed Lew to fight Billy Marquart. Jack Hurley had Marquart, who was another of those hands-down, walk-in left hookers like all of Jack's fighters, and he could hit.

"Are you out of your mind?" Hymie screamed at Lew when he heard about it. "This guy is a murderous puncher. He'll kill you."

"I'll kill *him,*" Lew said. "This is gonna be a short trip. I'll knock this guy out so they'll have to give me a fight for the title."

"You're crazy," Hymie said.

Hymie tried to get out of the match. The contract had Lew's signature on it, though, and the night of the fight Marquart was another 9–5 favorite over Lew.

"Never mind," Hymie said to Lew in the dressing room. "Don't worry if he knocks you out, because we'll start building you up again."

"Ain't this awful?" Lew said, and he looked around the room. "There ain't anybody here believes in me. I'm the lone man who believes."

Eddie Joseph was the referee that night, and once he had to pull Lew off Marquart while Marquart was through the ropes and going down. It ended in the third with Joseph holding Lew off with one hand and counting Marquart out with the other.

When they matched Lew with Ambers for the lighweight championship of the world, no one could see him winning it. Ambers had fought all the good men and licked Armstrong and Zivic and Tony Canzoneri, and as it was, Lew almost walked out on the fight.

He was training at the Long Pond Inn at Greenwood Lake, and one day they brought a half dozen sportswriters up from New

York to watch him work twelve rounds in that pine-paneled gym overlooking the lake. Hymie Caplan was there too, and when Lew started to work, Hymie started to shout.

"Jab!" Hymie was hollering. "Cross! One-two! Turn 'em off!"

Willie Ketchum told me later that he could see what was going to happen, and he was standing across the ring and he was trying to flag Hymie down. Nobody could flag Hymie down, though, and at the end of the fourth round Lew climbed through the ropes, ripped off his headgear and gloves and headed into the dressing room.

"What's the matter with him?" Hymie said to Willie.

"I told you," Willie said. "He don't like that stuff. With all these newspaper men here, he thinks you're trying to show him up."

Hymie took the newspaper men down to the bar, and then he saw them off. A few minutes later he ran up to Willie's room.

"Quick," he said, "he's puttin his suitcases in his car and he's leavin'!"

When Willie ran out, Lew was pulling out onto the road in his black Ford. Willie ran to Hymie's car and he got in and he chased Lew until he squeezed him off the road in Suffern, New York, about twenty-five miles from camp.

"What are you doing?" he said to Lew.

"I'm goin' back to Texas," Lew said.

"But you can't," Willie said. "You're fighting for the lightweight championship of the world."

"I don't care," Lew said. "I can knock that man out, so I don't care."

It took Willie a half hour to convince Lew to come back. Finally, Lew said he'd turn around if Hymie would stay away from him and if he could train in New York. Hymie was with Lew the night of the fight, though. Two hours before Lew climbed through the ropes for the biggest night he would ever know as a fighter, Hymie was showing him off in the restaurants around Broadway. Two hours before a fight a fighter is in a hotel room, resting in a bed, and the sportswriters never forgot Lew walking around in an old rumpled suit and a flannel shirt, with that seamed, drawn leathery face and that hair sticking up, shaking hands and smiling that small, sad smile when somebody asked him how he thought he would do with Ambers.

"You would have thought," Frank Graham wrote later in the *New York Journal-American,* "he was going to fight some stumblebum in an out-of-the-way fight club, for all the tension he showed."

Lew had Ambers on the floor before the fight was a minute old. In the second round Ambers came back and started to take the lead when Lew dumped him with a left hook. Just as the bell sounded, Lew hit him a right on the chin and then he belted him two more before Billy Cavanaugh, the referee, could pull him off. In the third, Lew was on top of him and knocked him down for seven. Ambers got up groggy, and Lew piled in, and that was the end. He was the lightweight champion of the world.

"But how about hitting him after the bell at the end of the second round?" one of the newspaper men asked Lew in the dressing room, with everybody crowding around and the noise and the photographers taking pictures.

"I didn't hear any bell," Lew said.

When the cops finally cleared everybody out, Lew sat there on the rubbing table for a minute, not saying anything. Then he looked up at Willie.

"Willie," he said, "you know damn well I heard that bell."

"I know," Willie said.

"But when they start to go," Lew said in that sad way, "they got to go."

"On December fourth," Lupie was saying now, "Lew was so pleased. He said, 'Imagine, I'm sixty.'"

"I never imagined I'd make it," Lew said. "I was thrilled. Our son said, 'I never thought you'd make it.' People around New York never thought I'd make it either."

"That's right," I said.

After he won the title they matched him with Ambers again in the Garden, over-the-weight. Lew had Al Dunbar, a welterweight, with him out at Pompton Lakes, and early one morning, with Lew driving, they hit the bridge going into Paterson on Route 4.

"He's been in an auto accident," Mike Jacobs said, calling

Willie on the phone and getting him out of bed. "They think he's dead."

He didn't have a scratch on him, but that afternoon he was back in New York and riding in a cab when it hit the back of another. Lew pitched forward and came out with a bad knee.

"You see?" Lew said to Willie. "I smash that car to pieces, and nobody would think I would come out of it alive. Now I'm ridin' in a cab and mindin' my own business and I hurt my knee. It don't pay to mind your own business."

Two weeks before the Ambers fight Lew came down with the grippe. For seven days he was running a fever and in bed, but Willie said it won the fight for him.

"This is one guy," Willie said, "that the grippe helped. He rested for seven days."

When they came in from Pompton for the weigh-in it was snowing. About two o'clock in the afternoon, after Lew had had his big meal and they were still sitting in Lindy's, Lew said he had some tickets to deliver.

"Lew, it's bad weather," Willie said. "Let me deliver them."

"No," Lew said. "These are personal friends, and I got to deliver 'em myself."

Willie went to the suite in the Astor to wait. At eight o'clock they were supposed to be at the Garden, and at 8:15 Lew walked in.

"Whatta ya know?" he said, and there was a big smile on his face.

"Oh-oh," Willie said. "You're drunk."

"Willie," Lew said, "I like you. You're a man."

The blizzard had closed down all the cabs, and they walked the eight blocks to the Garden through the deep snow. They had to sneak Lew into the dressing room, past the boxing commission inspectors, and Willie sent out for mouthwash to get rid of the alcohol on Lew's breath.

It took Lew four rounds to sweat the drink out. In the sixth he had Ambers going, and in the seventh he finished him.

"Willie," Lew said in the dressing room, "how come I didn't knock him out as quick as I did the last time?"

"I don't know," Willie said. "I can't imagine."

After that Ambers fight, Lew fought Montgomery again in the Garden, and Montgomery gave him an awful cuffing around. They had to put twenty stitches over Lew's eyes and across his nose. Before he fought Cleo McNeill in Minneapolis, he developed an abscess in his throat, and he had trouble swallowing, and he was unable to eat.

"So I took him to a doctor," Willie was telling me, "and he lanced it. Lew just swallowed and he said, 'That's fine. I'm hungry.'"

Lew knocked McNeill out in the third round. He hit him so hard that McNeill's cheek and upper lip opened as if they had been cut with a knife—and that was the way Lew could punch.

Lew was to fight Freddie "Red" Cochrane in the Garden three weeks later, and he had driven his car to Minneapolis for the McNeill fight. Willie didn't want him bouncing back in the car, so he sent Lew by train and he drove the car back. On the way he stopped off at Pittsburgh to see Harry Bobo fight Bill Poland, and that morning he turned on the radio in his motel room to listen to the news while he was shaving.

"Lew Jenkins," he heard the voice say, "the lightweight champion of the world, is in critical condition in a New Jersey hospital as the result of a motorcycle crash."

At that time Benny Goodman was playing at Frank Daley's Meadowbrook in New Jersey, and Peggy Lee was singing with the band. Lew used to ride his cycle over to the club from Pompton Lakes, and he would sit in the back with the band after they came off the stand and he would drink. About three o'clock in the morning he got on his cycle to find an all-night spot, and he hit a traffic circle.

He woke up in a hospital three hours later. They had his arms and back and neck taped, and two hours after he came to, he had them carry him back to camp, and he stripped the bandages off.

"I had to train," he told me, "but I couldn't even wash my own face."

Cochrane had him down five times, and that was when they wrote in the papers that Lew was a disgrace to the title he held. After the fight Lew went back to Texas, and it was in a clinic in Fort Worth that they found he had the three broken vertebrae in his neck. They put a cast on, and Lew went out the back door while the newspaper men were waiting at the front door because he was matched to defend his title a month later against Sammy Angott in the Garden. Then he took the cast off. He never told Willie what was wrong with him, and Angot won fourteen of the fifteen rounds.

Nineteen months after he had won the lightweight title, he had lost it. Starting with the Cochrane fight, he had lost nine in a row and eleven out of twelve before he enlisted in the Coast Guard in 1943. The last time Willie ever worked with him was when Lew fought Al Tribuani in Wilmington, Delaware. The week of the fight Lew was drunk on Broadway, and he got into a bar fight with a couple of sailors. He grabbed a glass and cut his left hand across the palm, and it took thirteen stitches to close it.

"This will heal all right," the doctor told Lew and Willie, "but I've got bad news for you."

"What?" Lew said.

"You'll never be able to close the index finger of that hand."

"Then how can I punch?" Lew said. "How can I make a fist?"

"I don't know," the doctor said. "I'm afraid you can't."

Willie told me that, when they walked out of the doctor's office together, Lew didn't say anything for a while. Then suddenly he stopped.

"Don't worry, Willie," he said. "I know what we'll do."

"What?" Willie said.

"We'll cut it off," Lew said, "and we'll make it even with the knuckles."

"You're out of your mind, Lew," Willie said. "Don't even talk about it."

"But you have to, Willie," Lew said. "Please, Willie. You got to cut it off."

"All right," Willie told him. "I'll cut it off."

Lew was training at Stillman's with one hand, and after another doctor took the stitches out, the cut reopened. Willie bandaged it, and the day before the fight he sent Lew and a sparring partner to Wilmington with Artie Rose, who worked in the corner with Willie. At midnight Artie called Willie at his apartment in New York.

"You got to come out here quick, Willie," Artie said. "They're drunk, and they're breaking up the town."

"I thought you were gonna keep an eye on him," Willie said.

"I did," Artie said, "but they went into the diner on the train, and when they came back they were drunk."

"Forget it," Willie said. "There's nothing you can do. Go back to sleep."

Lew and the sparring partner had had a pint of gin apiece on them when they went in to eat. Lew was still high when Willie got to Wilmington the next day, and he was just starting to come out of it in the dressing room.

"Get me in there," he kept saying. "I'm gonna die."

Willie sent Artie out to get a bottle of whiskey. That got Lew back on the track, and then it was time for Willie to bandage Lew's hands.

"Now we got to face it," Willie said. "I can't bandage you, Lew, with this stiff finger."

"Give it to me," Lew said. "I'll fix it."

Willie told me that Lew walked up to a wall with his finger sticking straight out. Willie said that Lew put the finger against the wall and he pushed against it, and Willie said that he couldn't watch. He said he felt himself getting sick, but Lew pushed until he closed the finger.

"You see?" he said, showing Willie his fist. "There it is."

Willie bandaged him, and he put a sponge in the left glove to keep the blood from running down Lew's arm from the cut that Willie knew would reopen when Lew punched. Lew was good and high now with the whiskey, and as they started to leave the dressing room, he hit the door with his right fist and Willie said he split it as if it had been hit with an ax.

"I'm ready," he said.

It took Tribuani three rounds to discover that Lew wasn't ready, and he knocked Lew down six times in the next seven rounds. The crowd was booing and calling Lew a bum, and when Lew and Artie and Willie got back to the dressing room Willie called it quits.

"Lew, you got to quit," Willie said, and Lew told me later that the tears were in Willie's eys and starting to run down his cheeks. "If you don't quit, I'm through, anyway. I can't stand to see a great fighter like you gettin' licked by guys like this. I can't stand it."

"Imagine that," Lew was saying at Benning. "Willie was cryin'.'"

"When you got out of the Army," I was saying to him now, "did you have your twenty years in?"

"Yeah, with the Coast Guard included," he said. "I couldn't stand it any more, what was happenin' to the Army. When they sent me back to Korea in 1954 the war was over, and oh, it was disgusting. It was the same everywhere. Even little Lew, when he was in, said, 'Oh, Pop, you'd kill yourself in this kind of an Army.' My whole heart, as far as the Army, is gone now, but at least I still stand at attention when they have the 'Stars and Stripes.'"

"So what did you do about a job?"

"I took any goddamn thing I could get," he said.

"You couldn't get a job without belonging to a union," Lupie said, "and you couldn't belong to a union without a job. His first job was selling cars, but Lew was such a horrible salesman. He felt sorry for the people paying all that money for those cars."

"That's right," he said.

"But at the same time," she said, turning to him now, "you weren't thinking of us, the family, and we didn't have the money."

"I stayed a month," Lew said. "I told 'em, 'You're all a bunch of goddamn thieves.' And I left the place. Some poor old farmer with no money would come in with his family in an old truck, and I was supposed to sell him what I knew was another piece of junk. I could have done it, but I didn't have the heart for it. I told 'em, 'You're all a bunch of sorry bastards.' I walked out."

"Then what did you do?"

"I was a greenskeeper," he said. "I worked almost five years on a golf course out here. Then I went to the linen supply as a driver, and I worked there about five years."

"Until he had the heart attack," Lupie said.

"After I was out of the Army three months," he said, "I'da gone back as a corporal if they'da had me."

He got up out of the armchair and took several steps and he held out his hands. Disgust and anger were in his face.

"Look at these friggin' bums hangin' around in civilian life on the corner like this," he said, dropping his jaw and hanging his head. "Long hair, beards, dirty. It's such a shock. We went up to San Francisco a couple of years ago, and Lupie had to hold me. I said, 'Look at these goddamn bums.' I like to cried. It's so far gone now, nobody can save it.

"You go to a shopping center here, and they talk about things bein' high, and there's all that money. There's no honesty in anything, and there's no faith in anything anymore. You go to a store and see bums like me loaded up and their kids with everything.

"Lupie and me," he said, "we go down there and look at it. I said to Lupie, 'I'm gonna get in this food stamp line.' Lupie said, 'Get out of there.' The guy told me, 'You can't have 'em.' I said, 'Whatta you mean? These people have more money than I have.' Ain't that awful?"

"I don't know the answer, Lew," I said. "I guess we just have to ride with the punches."

"That's right," he said, sitting down again, "and it's comin', and the Man upstairs better say somethin'."

While he had been talking, the phone had rung. Lupie had picked it up in the dinette, and now she was walking back and smiling.

"Little Lew is coming over," she said.

"Good," I said. "When I last saw him it was at Benning, and he was about hip high. We three were watching a review on the parade ground with him, and Lew said to him, 'Come on, take a boxin' stance.' Little Lew said, 'I don't wanna.' Lew said, 'Come on, let's see your stance.' Little Lew took the pose, and Lew said to me, 'Look at that. Don't he look better than those bums you see fightin' on the TV now?' "

"That's right," Lew said now. "He did."

"When he was born," Lupie said, "the headline said, 'No Boxing Career for Lew Jenkins' Son.' He was never interested."

"He was in the ROTC," Lew said, "and when he got his bars I was the first one to get a salute from him. Hell, he's so far ahead of the rest of the world it's sad."

"But you brag too much about him," Lupie said. "It embarrasses him."

"Hell," Lew said.

"He'll be thirty this December 27," Lupie said.

"And what business is he in?" I said.

"He went to San Jose State and got his engineering degree," Lupie said. "In the ROTC he was a distinguished military student. Then he went to Fort Bliss in missile training, thirty years after Lew was there as a horse-shoer."

"From horses to missiles in one generation," I said.

"He set up computers in the Army," Lew said.

"Did you read about that black market in Korea?" Lupie said. "My little Lew stopped that. He set up the system to catch everybody. Colonels and everybody was scared of him. Now he sets up computers for businesses, and he's in business for himself and he's married and they have two little ones. He's like his father. He doesn't know how to go around and connive."

When he came in, his wife, Linda, and their two children, Jimmy, five, and Stephanie, two, were with him. He is six feet, nicely built, a handsome young man with his mother's facial features and his father's coloration, and after the introductions and we were all seated, there was that pause that precedes the start of a new conversation.

"Well," he said, smiling, "would you believe all this domesticity?"

"I believe it because I see it," I said, "but there are some others who remember your dad who won't."

"When I register at a motel," he said, "they say to me, 'You've got a famous namesake.' I say, 'That's my father.' They say, 'A wild man.' I don't know if they believe it, but I say, 'He's changed now.'"

"They're always picking up guys who say they're Lew Jenkins," Lupie said.

"There were a couple of guys out here," Lew said, "and one in Pontiac, Michigan, and one in New York. Big stories come out that I'd been picked up stealin' here or there, and drunk everywhere."

"A couple of years ago," Lupie said, "Lew signed the register in a motel in Greenfield, and the fella said, 'Yeah, and I'm Jack Dempsey.'"

"They were always pickin' me up," Lew said. "It started in Dallas. They throwed me in jail for no reason at all. I was in my damn car, and I went to Forth Worth to see Ernest Tubb, the hillbilly singer, and I got thrown in jail there and in Arlington and in

Dallas again and in jail everywhere. I wasn't doin' anything. The cops just picked me up.

"Did you ever see a guy in jail who never did anything?" he said. "That was me."

I looked over at young Lew. He was smiling and shaking his head slowly.

"A couple of years later," Lew was saying, "I fought in Arkansas, and after I fought I was standin' on the damn corner and they put me in jail. I was goin' to Pittsburgh to fight Fritzie Zivic, and they put me in jail in St. Louis. They beat the hell out of me in St. Louis for no reason. I was in the railroad station, and I'm layin' on an old bench, and I woke up and the cops are just beatin' up on me. They knew I was gonna fight Fritzie Zivic in Pittsburgh.

"Imagine me fightin'," he said, and he seemed small and frail, sitting there in the armchair. "The next morning I paid the $10 fine, and they wished me luck."

"The cops should see Grandpa now," I said to young Lew.

"They wouldn't believe it either," he said, smiling.

"I was in Miami," Lew said, "and I was tryin' to get across the street to this bar. Maxie Rosenbloom run it, and they put me in the damn jail. There was three of us drunks, and the other two made it across the street and I didn't."

"Maybe they were on a point system," I said, "and they got extra points for picking up Lew Jenkins."

"Yeah," Lew said. "Somethin' like that."

We talked for another twenty minutes or so, about young Lew's business and about children, and then young Lew said they had to leave. He is a ham radio operator, and his club was involved in a contest, the point of which, as I understood it, was to try to reach as many other operators as possible around the world. He said that, starting at five o'clock, he had to man the apparatus throughout the night.

"He's a fine young man with a fine family," I said, after they had left.

"When Lew and I were married," Lupie said, "I was working in the finance office at Camp Stoneman. We were only going together two days when we decided to get married."

"That's right," Lew said.

"So I quit," Lupie said. "In the old days, when you got married you quit your job. Then I took my three-months old son to show him off to the people I worked with, and the colonel said, 'Come back to work.' I said, 'He's a lot of work, and I'd rather be with him.' The colonel said, 'We can get a little cradle, and you can rock it with your foot.' I said, 'No, thanks.' I took care of my family for thirty years."

"I was comin' back from Japan in 1948," Lew said, "and little Lew was ten months old and . . ."

"He was walking by himself at seven months," Lupie said, "and at the Presidio at San Francisco, Lew was on the ship. As an enlisted man he couldn't get off right away, but he wanted to jump off and get down to his baby, and he threw his duffle bag onto the dock."

"That's right," Lew said.

"When he got off," Lupie said, "I let the baby walk to his father. He had on a little blue snowsuit, with a little bit of red hair coming out and his little nose sticking out. He went right to his father, and Lew said, 'Is this little Lew?' I wondered who he thought it was."

At about 5:30 we got into the car to drive back to Oakland and have dinner. When we joined the traffic it was moving well and in the lanes, and then a motorcyclist, helmeted, passed us on the right and cut in ahead of us.

"Look at that guy," Lew said, sitting in the front with Lupie.

"Do you ever get the urge," I said, "to get on one of those things again?"

"No more," he said. "Hell no."

The story about Lew and his motorcycles that became a classic around New York involved Mike Jacobs. There was a good advance sale for Lew's second fight with Bob Montgomery in the Garden, and a couple of days before the fight Mike came out of the Brill Building, where he had his office then, to cross Broadway and have lunch at Lindy's. He was about to step off the curb when he heard the noise, and there was Lew on his cycle swinging into Broadway from Fiftieth Street.

"Hey, Mike!" Lew hollered. "Look! No hands!"

"Did you take your pill?" Lupie was saying to Lew now.

"No," he said.

"You were supposed to take it at five o'clock."

"I'll take it at the restaurant," he said, and then, turning back to me, "I smoked all my life. I used to smoke with a towel over my head during the rest period. I smoked and drank and frigged around, and people said when I had the heart attack that boxing done that. Hell, boxin' had nothin' to do with it."

The restaurant specializes in sea food, and it is on an inlet off the bay. We got a table after only a short wait, and from where we sat I could look across the band of water at a pleasure-boat dock. The sun had gone down by now and the air was clear and the sky cloudless and again, as on that evening when I had first met him off the beaches of France thirty-three years before, there were those same pastel colors of pink and blue in the placid water as in the sky.

"Sitting here," I said to him, "and seeing the pinks and blues in the sky and water, I'm remembering that evening when I first met you on that LST off Normandy."

"The sacrifices," he said. "The sacrifices were so great that I can't even think of it. I'll break down."

"I know," I said.

I knew what it was in Europe, but he knew what it was in Korea, too. He told me about it, sitting in that EM canteen at Benning.

"You remember," he said, "how they were all sayin' in 1946 that we were gonna fight the Russians. I read about all that in the papers, and I went right to Baltimore to enlist and told them I wanted to be in it."

At the time they were talking about putting Lew in with Charlie Fusari in Jersey City. Fusari was a Jersey boy, and the fight figured to draw a good gate, and they were going to guarantee Lew $6,000.

"I got a chance to make this six thousand," Lew told the colonel at the enlistment center. "If I sign up now, can I get off to make that fight?"

"No," the colonel said. "I'm afraid you can't. When you're in the Army, you're in. Why don't you fight that fight and get the six thousand, and then come back and enlist?"

"No," Lew said. "I'm afraid if I wait I might talk myself out of it. You better give me that paper. I'll sign it now."

He signed it, but no war came. At the end of 1948 he was discharged after two years in Japan, married to Lupie now and the father of young Lew. He fought around Philadelphia, training by playing the guitar in a night club called "Big Bills," and singing songs like "I'm a Plain Old Country Boy," and "Take an Old Cold Tater and Wait." Then came the invasion of Korea, and Lew stood up to what he told me that evening off Normandy about praying for another war.

"There's nobody can know what it's like," he was saying at Benning. "There's nobody but the front-line soldier knows, with the shellin' and the woundin' and goin' without food and bein' so tired that you want to die. The poor front-line soldier he knows, but nobody knows if they ain't been there.

"I ain't so young any more," Lew was telling me—and he was thirty-five then, "and my legs ain't so good. I'd get to the top of a hill and I'd be so tired I'd holler, 'Dig in! Dig in, everybody!' Then I'd just turn around and I'd holler, 'Kill me, you sons-abitches! Kill me! I'm so tired I don't care.' I was too tired to dig in, but there was only one fella ever beat me to the top of a hill, and he was twenty-two years old and from Philadelphia and a squad sergeant. I just had to do it, and you know why?"

"No," I said.

"I had my pride," he said sadly, again in that way of his. "I was Lew Jenkins, and the rest of 'em were kids and they looked up to me. We'd take a hill and I'd be scared, but they'd all be watchin' me, so I'd make up a rhyme about the hill bein' so rough but we'll get them gooks sure enough. Then they'd all holler, "Listen to old Lew, he's singin'! There he goes!' Then they'd all follow me, and we'd take that hill."

On August 17, 1951, they set up a road block and they held it for ten days against the Chinese Reds. Only sixty-eight out of a company of two hundred eventually got out, and Lew said he would have gone back to the battalion with the rest of them, but he was too tired to make it.

"They were shootin' 'em down all around me," he said. "It was rainin' and I lay in a creek bottom and I didn't care if I got killed, and I could see 'em takin' prisoners and killin' our guys. I remember one kid was nineteen years old and with his leg blown off, and when they started to take him out they went by me and he said, 'So long, Lew. I'll see you.'

"I had a kid in my platoon, one of those screw-off kids you give details to. He got it through the leg and the arm when it was man-eat-man, and this kid was about seventeen and he come limpin' out two or three miles in the rain. Then I got a letter from him later from the hospital, and it was signed, 'Your Buddy, the Detail Kid.' He wanted to know who got out and who got killed, and that shows you he was a real man.

"When they had us surrounded there was another kid I could see was breakin'. I told an officer about him and he said, 'He's fine. He's bigger and stronger than I am.' The kid wasn't even in my platoon, but he used to come to me. This second day he come to me he started to scream. He was hollerin', 'We'll all get killed! They'll kill us all!' I patted him on the shoulder and I told him tanks were comin' up to get us, and they were gonna give us artillery for support.

"Hell," Lew said, "none of that was gonna happen, but I had to tell him somethin'. Then I saw him walk over to some trees, and I heard a shot and I walked over to the trees. There was the kid, and he had put his rifle under his chin and he pulled the trigger. I looked at him with the blood runnin' all over and his face blown, and I got sick and I threw up right there."

In the ten days at the road block Lew formed a company of Americans and some remnants of the 36th ROK Regiment, and they sent another company down to him. That is what they gave him the Silver Star for, and the citation said that George Company and Fox Company were being withdrawn when Lew took his Fourth Platoon up a draw and held there and saved what was left of the battalion.

Over dinner now we talked about the efforts that over the years I and several others had made to get someone in Hollywood to make a motion picture of Lew's life. Lupie said she couldn't understand why, with the pictures they have made and are making about prize fighters' lives, they wouldn't want to make one about Lew. I said I couldn't understand either, and when we got back to the motel and I got out of the car Lew got out too.

"Now stay well," I said as we shook hands.

"Yeah, and you too," he said.

"And I'm sorry," I said, "about what we see happening in this country, but I guess it's true that the problems of peace are more difficult than the problems of war."

"I just don't understand it," he said. "I don't understand it at all."

"I don't either," I said, "but I've often thought how in war—as they say, the most evil of man's inventions—the good in man, his willingness to sacrifice himself for others, comes out. That's still there in man, but we can't seem to find it in peace."

"I don't know," Lew said. "I sure as hell don't know."

"Anyway," I said, "what I'm trying to do is thank you. I mean thank you for all you did in two wars."

"Hell, what I did was nothin'," he said, "compared to all them that got killed. They gave their lives, and it's such a goddamn shame."

On my way up to my room and then in my room I thought about all he had seen and all he had done. Then I remembered the day I spent in early December of 1944 with a graves registration unit in the Huertgen Forest while they picked up American dead. It was raining and we went out in a jeep hauling a trailer, and we made several trips. They would pick them up, every one of them a mother's son, and lay them in a trailer, one on top of another, and when the trailer was full they would tie the tarpaulin down over the mound of them and then, with the rain beating down on the tarpaulin and running off it, they would haul them back to the regimental collection point. They had a small radio in the jeep tuned to the Armed Forces Network, and on one of our trips back we could hear the play-by-play of the Army-Navy football game being played in Baltimore.

14

The Smallest Titan of Them All

> I think no virtue goes with size;
> The reason of all cowardice
> Is, that men are overgrown,
> And, to be valiant, must come down
> To the titmouse dimension.
> Ralph Waldo Emerson,
> *The Titmouse*

"Little guys," he said once, "usually don't have it their own way."

His mother was sixteen when he was born, and he weighed three pounds. She told me that for two months the doctor who had delivered him came to the house daily to bathe him in warm water with whiskey in it. She said she didn't know why that was, and until he was four months old her own mother used to wrap him cotton flannel strips, and they called him "the shoe box baby."

"The only thing I ever hungered for as a kid," he said, "was the size to play baseball. Those other kids didn't want me. I was always the one left over."

For the month of August of 1955 I was tailing him around Saratoga where, for those four weeks, New York thoroughbred racing moves each year as it has since 1863. Tailing is the right word, for I never took on as elusive a single subject as Eddie Arcaro when he was this country's greatest jockey, or one who, when I could corner him and sit him down, was more of a delight with that quick mind, that frankness, his ability to paint word pictures, and his sophisticated knowledge of his calling.

"On the streets," I asked him once, "did the other kids beat up on you?"

"Hell, no," he said. "I was too small to fight."

"What about that temper of yours?" I said.

"That's an odd thing," he said. "I've asked my mother about that, and she says I was kind of a nice, mild-mannered kid. The temper was what racing did to me."

He came into racing before the day of the film patrols that record every foot of a race and on tracks where rough riding—sawing off an opponent, fighting your way through jams, leg-locking, and holding saddle cloths—were the style of survival. On the backs of those 1,000-pound animals and in the heat of those races, that temper of his ignited and he was fined or suspended more than thirty times, once for a year. Over his career he himself survived more than forty falls.

"Even when I caddied," he said, "I didn't weigh seventy pounds, and I couldn't carry doubles like the big kids. I had all I could do to lug singles. Racing was the only thing I ever found where I could be a competitor."

A competitor he was, and more than that. He never grew taller than five feet three, and he rode best at 108 pounds, but in what he did he was as big as the other giants of his time—Joe DiMaggio, Ted Williams, Sammy Baugh, Joe Louis, Ben Hogan—and one for all time. He was the first to win five Kentucky Derbies—Bill Hartack would tie him in that—and the only one to win twice the Triple Crown—the Derby, the Preakness, and the Belmont. When the best of the ballplayers aspired to make $100,000 a year he was making $150,000 and more.

"I'll get into Miami late Thursday afternoon," I was saying on the phone now. "Let's get together on Friday."

"But how much time will this take?" he said.

It was that way in 1955. We had signed a contract with *Look* to do two articles, and I tailed him not only during that month at Saratoga but for another month at Belmont and elsewhere on Long Island, where he and his wife, Ruth, and their young daughter and son lived. There was always somebody who had just got into town or someone with whom he had to discuss a business deal, or there was a date that he and his wife had for dinner.

"I'll make it as painless as I can," I said. "How about lunch Friday?"

"Lunch?" he said. "We'll probably be done by two o'clock, and that's too late to play golf. What am I going to do the rest of the afternoon?"

I don't know, Eddie, I was thinking. Read a book, perhaps? No, I don't ever recall you mentioning a book, and with all that nervous energy, reading wouldn't be the answer. I don't know the answer, because I've never been able to put myself in your place.

"I'll tell you what I'll do," I said. "I'll call you on Friday morning."

"Good," he said.

Then he would surprise me. After the articles had been accepted by the magazine, I phoned him one night at his home.

"Eddie, I hate to ask you this," I said, "but the editors at the magazine want to meet you. You don't have to do it, because they've already bought the pieces."

"What the hell," he said. "They're paying that money, so if they want to meet me I'll come over."

We had lunch at Toots Shor's, and while we were having a drink I got him talking again about riding tactics. On that white tablecloth, before the food came, he started moving the silverware around, demonstrating a blind switch—three horses strung out from the rail and his horse pocketed behind—and how you know the capabilities of all of them and at what point one figures to come up empty and leave the opening. I was getting it from the master, and that is the bonus of the business I am in.

When we finished lunch we still had a few minutes to kill before the appointed hour for the hand-shaking, so walking him east toward the *Look* building on Madison Avenue, I led him south a block to Rockefeller Plaza. It was early November, and down on the ice rink in front of the gilded Prometheus statue the skaters were circling.

"What the hell is that?" he said.

"It's a skating rink," I said.

"How long has that been there?" he said.

"For more than twenty years," I said.

"I never knew this," he said. "I've got to bring the kids over here."

He was a man of the world, but of his own world. It was the world of the race tracks across this country, of jockey rooms and racing's millionaires, of fashionable resorts and eating places, of celebrities and hangers-on, and high stakes races and honors, and oil wells coming in and stocks paying off. It was a world I would never know any more than he would know mine.

He and his wife live now at the Jockey Club on Biscayne Boulevard in North Miami. It is an elegant, white, balconied high-rise with gate house, and if you can pass muster, they will relieve you of a hundred dollars a night.

"Hell, if you're on your own, as I presume you are," he had said on the phone, "I'd stay at the Holiday Inn across the street for thirty a night."

"I'll do that," I said.

At the motel on Friday morning I called his apartment at nine o'clock. His wife said that he had left for Boca Raton, and to check back later. I called at one and left my phone number, at five, at six and from a restaurant at seven.

"I haven't heard from him," his wife said. "I don't know where he is, but I know this. When he gets in we're not going to eat dinner here."

"So when you finally get him on the phone," my good and long time friend Bard Lindeman, who was then the medical writer of the *Miami Herald,* said at dinner, "straighten him out. Tell him you've come all the way down here, and you've got a job to do and a living to make and . . ."

"Come on, Bard," I said. "You've been in this business of ours long enough to know what the basic relationships really are. The subject doesn't need the writer. The writer needs the subject. Eddie Arcaro never needed me."

"I suppose that's right," he said.

"In fact," I said, "I'll never forget the first time I met him."

It was at the old Aqueduct track before they were to tear it down to build the Big A. It was in the jockey room between races, and changing silks he was washing his face from a pail of water that stood on the wooden bench in front of the row of metal lockers. *Cosmopolitan* had asked me to do a piece about a day in the life of a jockey from the time he gets up at six o'clock in the morning to work horses until he has ridden his last race of the day. They said they wanted Eddie Arcaro, and I explained it to him. "I don't want it," he said. "It's not for me."

"But it would be good public relations," I said, "not only for you but for racing."

"You mean publicity?" he said, the towel in his hand and his face wet and turning to me. "You know what publicity does for me? It makes an 8–5 shot even money, and when it behaves like an 8–5 shot and I don't bring it in, they boo my butt off."

I understood that. He was so good and so prominent that they believed he could win on almost anything he rode. When he didn't they booed him unmercifully, abused him with filthy language and, in letters, threatened his life and his family. Racing crowds are the most avaricious and vicious of the audiences of sport, and for a while the Pinkertons guarded him at the track and he seriously considered giving up riding.

"I called you last night," he was saying on the phone now, when I finally got him at nine o'clock on Saturday morning. "You weren't in."

"I finally went to dinner."

"I've got it right here," he said. "It's 893-4110, room 419."

"Right. Now when do we meet?"

"Well," he said, "I don't know exactly what you want."

"Come on, Eddie," I said. "I want to ask some questions, and they won't be stupid questions."

"Hell, I know that, Bill," he said. "I mean I have to get my day straightened out, so how long will this take?"

"Let's say an hour."

"Okay," he said, "but let me finish my breakfast and get my day straight, and I'll call you back."

"I'll be waiting by this phone," I said.

I waited, reading the paper and working on and finishing the crossword puzzle, and it was 1955, at Saratoga and Belmont and around Long Island, all over again. When I would finally sit him down, though, in the house he and his wife rented at Saratoga and at their home in Garden City, the flavor and aura of racing would fill the room and my notebooks. I thought of Sherwood Anderson and the way he wrote "I'm a Fool" and the other stories in *Horses and Men*.

He was born in Cincinnati on February 19, 1916, and started to grow up there and across the Ohio River in Southgate, Kentucky. He really grew up around the tracks, though, because he quit school when he was thirteen and came to racing by one of those accidents by which most of us come to do what we do.

"There was some fella I caddied for," he was telling once. "I never remember his name, but he was a good stake. He'd give me $1.25 when them other kids were only getting that to carry doubles, and he had some connection with the race track. He used to kid me about being a jock, and he'd introduce me to his friends as 'my jockey.' He put the bug in my head."

When he threatened to leave home on his own and change his name, his father took him one day to Latonia. There was a porch there off the jockey room, and he said he stood there for two or three hours just watching the jocks in their colors.

"Then when I heard how they traveled," he said, "and the big races they won, I had to have it."

For three months he kept nagging until one morning his father took him back to Latonia. He introduced him to Rome Respess and Roscoe Goose, who trained horses.

"Rome," he said, "was an old, hard, chew-tobaccy guy, and he looked at my hands and feet and said I'd grow too big to be a jockey. Roscoe just said he'd like to have me, but he already had two boys he was starting. Then we went out by the gap at the five-eighths pole and we watched the horses working, and my old man had a hell of a time getting me away. I know that going home I was a really dejected little man."

"Had you ever been around horses before?" I said.

"I'd seen milk-wagon horses," he said.

"I mean race horses," I said. "Standing there by the rail and watching them go by you so big and with the jockeys on them so small, didn't the thought of riding them scare you?"

"Hell, no," he said. "I was so damned elated how fast they went by that I couldn't wait to get up on them."

He would wait for some time. His father got him a job with the stable of T. H. McCaffrey, and each morning he would leave home at six o'clock to take the three trolleys that would get him to Latonia where he would walk hots, rub horses, fill the buckets, and clean tack.

"The first day," he said, "I bought a pair of boots and then my old man sent me over to Cincinnati to have a pair of English whipcord riding pants made. I was the best-dressed kid walking hots you ever saw, and I was in those things from morning till night. Right now I'd be embarrassed to get on a streetcar with boots and riding pants on, but then it was a thrill just copying somebody who could do something."

McCaffrey had two exercise boys, and they showed him how to saddle and knot the reins and set the stirrups and how to tread the saddle, which off the track is called posting. They put him up on the stable pony and he rode that around the stable area, and then Odie Clelland, who had been a rider and trained for McCaffrey, started to make improvements on him. He pulled the stirrups so Eddie said he felt as if he had no perch at all, and he got him off the horse's back so the weight would be on the withers and he would get more purchase. He used to emphasize getting a deep seat, to be low, and he was the first to start him out of a gate, teaching him how to leave his hold long so that, if the horse bobs, you can give with it. Once a filly ran off two miles with him, with Eddie afraid only of what Odie would say.

"That second winter," he said, "Odie took me to Florida, and any time I'd gallop a horse he'd be with me, and we always worked two at a time, head and head. I lived with him and his wife in a cottage they rented, and Odie would bring home jock's boots and pants and I'd try them on at night. McCaffrey wouldn't go for it, though. When we got back to Latonia he told my old man I should go back to school. He said, 'If your boy ever makes a rider, we'll have a snowy day in July.' After I won a couple of Derbies my mother saw him, and she said, 'Well, Mr. McCaffrey, we've been having a lot of snow in July.'"

He hooked up with Paul Youkilus, who had a three-horse stable, and at Bainbridge, Ohio, he rode his first race. He was fifteen, and he had to borrow the equipment from the other riders. He was all over the horse and lost his cap and finished sixth with the tails of his silks hanging out of his pants. He would ride in forty-five races before he would win one.

Youkilus had A. W. Booker training for him, and when they shipped to Agua Caliente in Mexico, Booker's brother and Eddie went along with them. There were a dozen horses from another stable in the horse car, and the railroad allowed one man to take care of three horses. That man was Booker's brother, so Eddie was stowing away.

"In that car," he said, "there must have been six of us who shouldn't have been on, and they had straw piled up and bales of hay, and when you'd feel that train slow down at any time of day or night we'd be in our holes in the hay. The only schedule we had was to feed the horses at five and eleven in the morning and at five or six at night, so we'd just sleep when we were sleepy. We never got out of our clothes, and while we were still in the cold part of the country we'd have the horse blankets over us. It was amazing, too, how everybody kept clean, washing and shaving in a pail.

"Being only fifteen," he said, "I was all ears. The rest of them would sit around and tell stories and reminisce over races, and Booker's brother had me captured. He was kind of an old man, and he'd tell me about great riders and great races, and whether he was conning me or not he sure was entertaining me. When we got to the desert where it was hot, those people had a knack of opening the door a little and setting up the bales of hay for the air to bounce off. I sat there and looked out at that sand and cactus and listened to their talk by the hour.

"At Caliente," he said, "until Booker and his wife got there and we moved in with them, Booker's brother and I lived at the stable. The tack room was fixed up with a couple of cots, and we used to eat at the track kitchen or make our own breakfast or our own stews over the open fires they used for the water boilers. We'd get up at 4:30 or five to water and feed the horses, and I can still remember the smell of that bacon frying and the coffee boiling with the grounds right in the pot."

I can see it all again now, that trip West and the life around the track, and that is what I mean. When I could get him off that merry-go-round that was his life, it made all the tailing, all the waiting worthwhile.

At Caliente, on Eagle Bird, one of the three that Youkilus had, he finally won his first race. It was a long meeting though—107 days that ran right through Christmas and New Years—and he had no money and he was homesick.

"Booker was supposed to pay me," he said, "but he had no money himself. He was a game little guy, though, and he had the grocery and the feed man on the cuff. I used to just look at those mountains and wonder if I'd ever get back over them again, and many a night I used to cry. When Booker got out of there he had to leave Eagle Bird and another horse to cover the feed bills."

"How did you feel about leaving Eagle Bird?" I said.

"I don't suppose anybody ever forgets the horse he broke his maiden on," he said, "so when I hitchhiked out of there for Tanforan I had to be sad about Eagle Bird. They probably raced him around Mexico until he broke down, and then they destroyed him, because he never showed on an American track again. If he had, I'd have known it."

At Caliente he had talked Clarence Davison into taking him. Davison carried between twenty and thirty horses, and Eddie said that it seemed that every time he looked up Davison's colors—yellow with blue hoops on the arms and body—were coming down on top.

"Davison and his wife," he said, "were kind of farmerlike people, with their own sense of humor, and not much of it at that, but I'd never have made it without him. I don't know who elects a guy to meet those kind of people in your life, and there's been many a time since when I wished I still had them around.

"When I was a kid at home, everybody was sort of a half-baked hoodlum, seeing who could live the fastest. I'd never had anybody boss me before, and with him there was no staying up until twelve. It was a training proposition, and you worked hard. It gave me a sense of responsibility, and there was no lying, no matter how bad it was. Threre was no sulking either, and whenever I'd get depressed I'd have to sit down and talk it out with Davison to find the meaning. He'd say, 'I'm the one who's puttin' up the money. You got nothin' to lose. If a lot of people around me start sulking I'll start to sulk, and I don't want to.'"

When Eddie first went with him, Davison used to rig reins onto a bucket in the barn, and he would have Eddie sit on a bale of hay, whipping and practicing how to switch the whip while passing the reins from hand to hand at the same time. Eddie said that some of the prominent jocks, and he named them, still couldn't do it without putting the whip in their mouths while they switched the reins.

"In the mornings," he said, "he was very exact about time, and he was the first one to make me time conscious. If he told you to work a mile in forty-one, he didn't want you coming down in forty-two."

That is a minute and forty-one seconds, and what they mean when they say a jockey "has a clock in his head." They used to say and write that about Eddie, and I told him that I couldn't understand how, not only during the morning works but during the heat of a race, he could keep track of the time within a second.

"Night after night," he said, "Davison would sit me down with that stop watch. He'd flip the watch and start talking to me, and then he'd say, 'How much?'"

"But I still don't understand how you can do it," I said.

"You break time down into twelves," he said, "because if a horse runs an eighth of a mile in twelve seconds, he's going pretty good. People who can't do it think it's quite a thing to be able to come within two-fifths of a second, but actually it's four-fifths, because it's two-fifths either side of the second, and not as hard as it seems."

"It would be for me," I said.

"I never rode a race for Davison," he said, "that he didn't tell me everything I did, whether I sawed on his mouth or pulled him up too short. He and his wife watched me from the time I left the paddock until I got back, and now when I see jocks kidding and laughing going to the gate I think of those days. Davison had better not catch me laughing on one of his. I was a solid citizen."

Davison was the first to teach him how to place a horse, how you shouldn't make your run all in an eighth of a mile but gradually, unless it is to save ground. He said that Davison was bugs on saving ground.

"He made me rail conscious," he said. "He had me always looking at that rail first, and if I went around when there was room to come through on the rail, he'd scream, 'I can't run a horse that much the best! You gotta save something on any horse I ever run!' At first he made me lose more races than he helped me win, because he tried to ride every race for me. I rode almost that whole apprentice year and couldn't grasp it, because mentally I didn't know management. I was trying to be a robot for Davison, and he was shouting me into some awful scrapes."

From Tanforan they had moved to Chicago, and Davison also had ten horses stabled up at Devonshire and Kenilworth in Windsor, Canada, just across the border from Detroit. Eddie and Lefoy Cunningham, Davison's other rider, would ride in Chicago and then they would get into Davison's car, and while Davison drove they would sleep in the back seat. The next day they would ride at one of those Windsor tracks.

"That first year I had twelve or fourteen falls," he said, "and I was picking up fines and suspensions at every meeting. Davison would holler, 'Don't get beat no noses on any of my horses!' He was so desperate that if you were on number 8, he'd say, 'Number 6 is the favorite. Now don't give him any of the best of it.' When you put that in a kid's mind you're playing with dynamite. Davison was all for shutting horses off, and when one of his would get beat a head or a nose he'd be so goddamn mad I'd be scared to bring the animal back. He'd holler, 'Why didn't you get ahold of him?'

"It was nothing," he said, "to grab a saddle cloth. The other boy could hardly tell, and if he turned around you just let loose. Riding with your toe in you'd leg lock, hooking your heel in front of his toe. At those Canadian tracks the rail was made of pipe, and where it was joined together there were couplings. You'd get another horse against the rail, and you could hear that fence sing until the jock's boot would hit one of those couplings. There was many a rider got a broken foot up there that way."

One day, while Eddie was trying to take his horse around the leader, the boy on him—a jock named Sielaff—grabbed Eddie's leg. They were about seventy yards from the finish, and Eddie just dropped the reins and grabbed Sielaff by the throat, and that was the way they went across the line with Eddie choking him.

"I won it," he said, "but they disqualified the horse and fined me $50, and that was a horrible trip back to Chicago that night. I'd just get to sleep in the back seat when Davison would go at me again. 'But have you got any idea why you did it?' he'd say over and over. 'You know how bad-legged that poor old horse is, and you just tossed that race off him. Why did you do it?' Who was thinking of that horse? I was just thinking of choking Sielaff, but Davison had a piece of that rough riding and that temper trouble of mine.

"One day he put me up on a filly, and Joe Guerra, the jock from Cuba, threw me against the fence. When Davison came down he wanted to kill Guerra, and the next day he had five horses entered and he put me on all five. He said, 'I'm gonna give you a fair chance. If Guerra don't go down, home you go.'

"At first I didn't pay any attention. The first two races I didn't get near Guerra, but in the third race he put me on a real speedy filly. He said, 'Here's your chance. You haven't been anywhere near Guerra all day. I don't care how this filly finishes. I want Guerra on the ground.' I nailed him. I threw two horses in that race. I threw Guerra, and some poor innocent guy who was in the middle went down too. I got fined $50 again and came near getting Davison's filly all cut up, but that satisfied Davison."

Waiting for him now in that motel room, I turned on the television. There was a game show in progress, and two losers had just walked off, winners of more than $3,000 each, when the phone rang.

"Bill?" he said. "What the hell kind of a place is this?"

"It's a motel," I said.

"I know that," he said, "but they don't answer the goddamn switchboard. I've been calling for the last half hour but nobody answers, so I came over. I'm down in the lobby."

"So come on up," I said. "Turn right after you get off the elevator. I'm in 419."

I opened the door and waited for him. He came striding down the hall, that little man, and he was wearing a light brown, summer-weight suit and a dark brown sports shirt open at the neck. Around his neck there was a small-linked gold chain with whatever was on it hidden beneath the shirt. That swarthy face was more lined now, but there was that prominent nose and those big dark eyes as quick as ever as he looked around the room and we sat down.

"So what can I tell you?" he said.

"Oh," I said, "about how you're living these days."

"We've got a two-bedroom apartment over there," he said, "and it's nice for Ruth and I. When we moved in nine years ago we had to cut down on a lot of furniture and the trophies and things. Ruth gave a lot to the museums at Saratoga and Lexington. There was a whole trunk—one of them steamer trunks—with articles and scrapbooks and stuff.

"The last race I rode, in Australia in January of '62, when I came back I just had that bag with the saddle and the whip and the boots and pants. I put it in a closet, and I've never been able to find it. I've hunted all over the Jockey Club. The place was new then, and they were moving stuff around, and maybe somebody stole it."

Out of a jacket pocket he had taken an emery board. He was starting to work on his nails.

"I don't have time to get a haircut or a manicure," he said.

"What takes up all your time?" I said. "I see you occasionally on TV doing the commentary on a big race. I've seen you on that RCA commercial in the silks and talking about the colors."

"I just did one for Buick," he said. "I don't know if it'll play up your way or not, but I say, 'I rode 250 races before I rode a winner, and this is a winner.'

"Don't tell me you say that," I said. "We had it in those two articles we did for *Look,* how many races you rode before you broke your maiden."

"We did?" he said. "I don't know if I ever read those things."

"Of course you did," I said. "You had to approve them before the magazine would accept them."

"I remember at Saratoga you were on my tail for the whole month," he said, "but I don't remember reading the articles."

"After Saratoga," I said, "and when I got back to the city, I spent four hours one afternoon in the library at the *Morning Tele-graph*. I got down the chart books and I checked every race at every track you were at when you were breaking in. They'd been writing for years that you'd ridden over 200, and I figured that, if I never did anything else in my life as a reporter, I would at least establish how many races Eddie Arcaro rode before he had a win-ner."

"How many was it?"

"When you won on Eagle Bird at Caliente, it was your forty-fifth race."

"When I did that Buick thing," he said, "the guy in the truck said, 'You rode 250 before you won?' I said, 'I never rode that many. I couldn't have, but I sure as hell don't know how many it was.'"

"You know now," I said. "So tell me what it was like when you quit."

"I thought I'd go fishing and play golf," he said, "but that be-came old hat in a hurry. I'd doodle around, and then I got into a couple of businesses and I lost my butt, but I had to keep busy."

In '55 I asked him one evening if he was a millionaire. I never forgot his answer, "To tell you the truth, I don't know. I've never sat down to figure it out."

"I got in a trap with an electric burglar alarm," he was saying now, "and I lost four hundred thousand on that thing."

That's a lot of money to drop, I was thinking, no matter how you make it. When you make it riding, that's an awful lot of races over a lot of years and an awful lot of risks.

"I never got into any serious financial problems," he was say-ing, "where it curtailed my way of living, and then I got into the horse insurance business and I lost there, but not a lot. I jumped our premiums from three hundred thousand to three million in three-and-a-half years, but you can't make money insuring thor-oughbreds. In insurance you hold a claim for a year and make a profit where it's millions of dollars, but you can't do that with horses. I lost a couple of years of my life."

"Speaking of your life," I said, "I was worried when you had that open heart operation. I heard about it on the morning news on the radio."

"I didn't know I had anything the matter with me," he said. "One evening I was going over some claims to evaluate horses, and Julie Fink came in and he said, 'You don't look good.' I said, 'Man, I don't feel good.' He ran me down to his doctor, and the guy took a cardiogram and told me I had angina. I got out of the insurance business—if that was affecting my health—and I was hitting golf balls one day when the thing hit me.

"Dr. Richard Elias—a hell of a guy—looked at me and took an arteriogram, and he said, 'You need an operation.' He showed Ruth and I the pictures on a TV set like the one there."

"Did that scare you?"

"No. You go to the Heart Institute here and see the people they've done it on, people up to seventy-five, and the loss ratio is so small. I've been operated on from ankles to head, so I've never had that fear. Then the Heart Institute is like living at the Waldorf. I've been on the board there for four or five years, and you've got to see it to believe it.

"They give you a menu, and the night before, the Doc said, 'What do you want for dinner?' I said, 'A Martini and a big steak.' He walked to the phone, and I said, 'You're kidding.' He said, 'No.' I said, 'What are my chances?' He said, 'You're chances are good, and you better bet on me. The only ones we lose are the ones we take a chance on when it's the only thing to do.'"

He reached for the gold chain around his neck and on it was a small, circular gold pillbox. He opened it, and in it were small pills, some green and some pink.

"I'm a nervous guy," he said, "and I take 9,000 pills a day to slow me down."

He snapped the pillbox shut and put it back inside the open collar of his shirt. He had been smoking, and he lit another cigarette.

"With all the bullets I dodged in my life," he said, and he meant all the jams and those more than forty spills on the track, "I'm not going to worry about lung cancer. All the races you ride, and you have a near miss every day."

At that winter meeting of 1931–32 at Caliente, where he finally rode his first winner, it was a rodeo every day. He was one with Sylvio Coucci and Hank Hills and Wayne Wright, whom they called "Cowboy Wright," and Georgie Wolf who, he said, used to holler at you and hit you with the whip at the same time.

"When you got half a length in front of a guy," he was telling me once, "you sawed him off. If a guy bothered you one day you didn't run to the stewards and complain, but you got him the next day. That sort of thing started a chain reaction that never stopped, and we had a couple of falls a week.

"One day Jackie Westrope's brother, Billy, was killed. It happened right after the finish, as he was pulling up at the seven-eighths pole, which was right in front of the jocks' room. The horse stumbled and Rope's brother landed on the point of his chin. We all saw it, but I don't believe it scared any of us, we were such a wild bunch of bastards."

The following year, at Washington Park, in Chicago, he had the fall that almost killed him. All he could remember when he came to in the hospital was leaving the gate and running into a jam.

"I was unconscious for three days," he said, "and when I came to I was still a little groggy and I saw my mom and my old man and my Aunt Libertina from Pittsburgh standing there. On the way up they'd heard I was dead. I had a fractured skull and a punctured lung and a broken nose, and it had me cross-eyed for a while.

"The family tried to talk me out of ever riding again, but I thought I really could ride now, and laying there I never thought I'd be scared. I came back at Hawthorne, and I'd been galloping horses mornings, and I thought I was fine until that first day when we went into a turn and I could see those bastards stepping all over me again. You just don't have any fear of those hoofs until one of them nails you.

"For five or six days I couldn't win a race. I was pulling them up, and a lot of times that's the worst thing you can do. They come together in front of you, and you hit their heels, and that's when you go down. You have to fight them in there, if you can make yourself do it.

"That Davison saved me again. He said, 'I've got to send you home. You've lost your nerve. You're just yellow, and you're no good to me or yourself, and you're gonna get yourself killed.' I know it hurt his wife to hear him bawl me out, and he'd holler, 'You're just yellow! I've got two more years on your contract, and if you pull another of my horses up I'm gonna set you down.'

"When I went to bed I cried all night. I was more scared of being sent home than I was of getting hurt, but I still couldn't do it until I went down on a filly of his named Printemps. There was a jam at the half-mile pole, and I was pulling up when I should have been going. I didn't get a scratch on me, and that cured me. After that, just to prove I wasn't scared, I'd put those sonsabitches up there where they had no chances. I'd put them up there running and just split the field open.

"It's an awful thing," he said, "being scared to ride and having to ride. Young kids laugh at that sort of thing, but they haven't had it. Nick Wall was laid up in a hospital once for fourteen months, between life and death. When he first came back he couldn't do it. He'd scream and holler in a spot where you could put a bunch in sideways. Johnny Gilbert went into the hospital black-haired and came out gray. Alfred Robertson had a fall at Jamaica and said, 'I quit.' Ralph Neves had a fall in California one year, and when they got him to the hospital there was no pulse or heart beat. They gave him adrenalin, but nothing happened. They pulled a sheet up over him, and after a while he pulled it off and said, 'I'm riding in the fourth race. What am I doin' here?'

"Gilbert Elston had two terrible falls. He was a nice-looking boy, real trim, until a horse stepped on his head and scalped him and popped his eyes. After that he was never exactly right. He never smoked or drank, but then he became an alcoholic and he tried suicide two or three times. I stopped him one night in a hotel in Chicago. I had him living with me, trying to get him to straighten out, and he was trying to get out the window. Then later he shot and killed himself."

"I'll always remember," I was saying now, "something you told me when we were doing those pieces. You said, 'Jockeys are the only athletes who, if you left them alone, would kill one another.' You said that, if it weren't for the stewards and patrol judges and film patrol, you could start out with twenty jocks and at the end of three months of racing there would be only one left, because that's what racing does to you."

"That was right," he said.

"Do you think that, left on their own, jocks would still be that way today?"

"More or less," he said. "It's the nature of the game, and I don't think that's changed, but people have changed."

"In what way?"

"You take Shoe," he said, meaning Willie Shoemaker, and since the day when they first became competitors they have been the best of friends. "I've seen Shoe time and again throw away the race rather than hurt somebody. People are more considerate. It's like you've got a gun on a guy and you pull the trigger.

"They tell me this Cauthen kid in New York," he said—Steve Cauthen was having his sensational apprentice year—"is like that. He'll give a little."

"Do you wish you were him, and starting all over again when you read about him?"

"Hell, no," he said. "I hardly remember riding. I go to the races occasionally because I still get a kick out of seeing a good horse run, and I can hardly conceive of doing what they're doing. He's an awful nice kid though, sixteen going on thirty mentally. He handles himself real well."

"You've met him?"

"I did that race on TV when he rode here. They told me, 'Go interview him. We want him on.' I said, 'Hell. Leave the kid alone. He just rode a race. The press has been bothering his butt off.' I didn't want to do it, but they insisted."

"I know," I said. "Now you're on my end of this business."

"He couldn't have been nicer. He was real nice to me."

"After all," I said, "you're Eddie Arcaro. You're probably a hero of his."

"I don't know about that," he said. "He's just a real nice kid. A fella interviewed me for the paper here. I wasn't derogatory. I just said that, like with all jocks, his butt has got to hit the ground, and if he's busted up you have to see how it bothers him. He wrote an awful article—that I said he's gonna get hurt and he may be chicken."

"The last spill you ever had," I said, "was it in that Belmont?"

It was the 1959 Belmont Stakes, and I was watching it on television at home. It had come up mud, and Eddie, on Black Hills, had started to make his move on the stretch turn when the horse and Eddie went down. Another fell over them, and after the finish a camera closed in on Eddie, lying there like a lifeless doll, face down in the ankle-deep mud just off the rail.

"That couldn't have been the last time I went down," he said. "I rode four or five years after that and, hell, you can't ride four or five years without falling. I wasn't really hurt."

"It scared *me*."

"A horse hit me in the back of the head, and I was unconscious for four hours and . . ."

"And that's not being really hurt?"

"And there was a photographer there who took a picture of me laying there in that slop. You saw that picture in *Life?*"

"I may have, but I remember it from TV."

"The guy who took the picture saved my life. After he took it he saw I didn't move, and he turned my head out of the slop. If he didn't, I would have suffocated. Then they took an encephalogram, and it would come to one spot and zero up. The Doc said, 'There's something wrong.' I had some torn ligament in my back here too, and finally I said, 'Doc, there's nothing the matter. I'm drinking a quart of whiskey a night and dancing.'

"I went fishing in Canada with my dad and my son, and I came back and he gave me another encephalograph. I said, 'It must be the machine.' He said, 'Let's start all over. Did you ever have a fractured skull?' I said, 'Yes, when I was eighteen.' He said, 'That's it.' I said, 'Yeah, That's just great.' I blew the Queen's Plate in Toronto. While we were fishing I heard on the radio what won it, and I said, 'What the hell am I doing here?' "

"Are your folks living and well?"

"My mother's not well now, and my old man is dead. He lived with us for eight years, and died in our house in Garden City. You know, he and my mother split, and when that happens it's hard to take, but when I got to know my old man I came to understand him."

"You told me something about your dad once," I said, "and you asked me never to write it as long as he was alive, and I never did."

"What was that?"

"About the bootlegging."

"You can write it now, if you want to."

His father had a paint store and a taxi business, and then he began buying up houses and putting couples to live in them. He would also put stills in them.

"When I was six, seven, and eight," Eddie had told me, "I remember sitting there at the dining room table and separating money. I'd separate the fives and tens, and we had a closet full. When I first came on the track as a kid, I had more money than the jocks did."

"Hell," he was saying now, "I was labeling whiskey when I was twelve. I was getting a hundred a week when people were in breadlines, and in that town it was like everybody did it. I had my own car when I was fourteen. Then later my dad had this place in Erlanger, called 'Arcaro's,' and one day Spencer Drayton called me in."

Spencer Drayton was the head of the Thoroughbred Racing Protective Bureau. They police racing and are concerned with the pedigrees and performances of both horses and people.

"Drayton said, 'You're a public figure. You know they're making book down there. I want you to talk to your father.' I said, 'Why don't you go out there and tell him?' I didn't want any part of telling my old man."

"He had that temper you inherited?"

"Hell, he had a boiling point at zero. So Drayton sent a guy out, and after he got done talking, my old man said, 'I'll tell you what you do, fella. You finish your drink and then get the hell out of here, and remember that my name was Arcaro before Eddie's was.'"

When Eddie's temper flared only Red Adair, the fireman of the oil field blowouts, could have capped it. In 1942 in the Cowdin Stakes at Aqueduct, it almost cost him his career. He was riding a horse named Occupation, and Vincent Nodarse, the Cuban jockey, was on one of the others.

"All Occupation's races had been in front," Eddie had told me, explaining it, "and they wanted somebody on him who could rate him. I said I'd take him back, and I told Nodarse in the gate that I wanted to take my horse back at the start, and to give me time.

You'll talk like that with other jocks, and when Occupation broke a neck on the field and I started to take him in, Nodarse got a half-length in front and sawed him off.

"I damn near went over his head, and by the time we hit the chute I didn't have a horse beat. I was on the outside, and I just lost my temper. Nodarse was in front, and I got Occupation gathered up and hit him, and he must have run the quarter in twenty-one seconds. Before we hit the turn I got a neck in front of Nodarse's horse and I nailed him. He saw me coming, and he knew what I was gonna do. He was hollering, "No could help, Eddie! No could help!' I hollered, 'I'll help you, you sonofabitch! I'll help you right now!'

"I just tried to put him over the fence, and it was lucky he didn't get killed. Even as bad as I rode Occupation, he finished second, but naturally the stewards claimed foul and I walked down that tunnel and up in the elevator. They were trying something new then. They had a microphone to record your claim of foul or your defense, and I sure gave it a great inauguration.

"Marshall Cassidy said to me, 'Eddie, did you do that on purpose?' I said, 'On purpose? I'd have killed the sonofabitch if I could!'"

From Eddie you got an honest answer, and he was grounded for a whole year. For a while he went on drunks for a day or two. He took up golf, and he said that the discipline in learning to control his nerves on the course helped to cure him.

"I'll always remember you," I was saying now, "coming back on the train from Baltimore after you won the Preakness on Citation."

Two weeks before, he had won his fourth Derby on him, and no other jock had ever won more than three. Now he had just won the Preakness, and he would win the Belmont and, with it, his second Triple Crown.

"Arthur Daley and Jimmy Cannon and I," I said, "were sitting in one of the parlor cars, and you came in and sat down. Daley was always carrying around a big Manila envelope. I never knew what he had in it, but I figured it was clippings pertaining to the event he was covering, because he often used other people's research in his columns. He used to make notes on those Manila envelopes, so he took out his pencil, and he said to you, 'What's it like, Eddie, riding Citation? It must be a thrill.' And you said, 'Actually, it isn't. It's like driving a Caddy. When you want the power it's there, and there's really not much of a thrill to it.'"

"That was right."

"So then Arthur, writing that down, said, 'But you must have got a thrill winning your fourth Derby on him.' And you said, 'Hell, if I'd had any luck, I'd have won a lot of those Derbies.' Arthur was stunned, and I had to laugh."

"That was right, too."

"I know," I said.

In 1942 he was riding for Greentree, and had the choice of Shut Out or Devil Diver. He picked Devil Diver and Shut Out won. In 1947 he was on Phalanx, the best of the three-year-olds, and was beaten a head by Jet Pilot, and he would tell me later that he bought the movie of that race and played it over and over and that he didn't sleep well for weeks.

"You don't think about those Derbies you've won," he told me. "You've already got those. The ones I think about are the ones I didn't win when I should have."

When I got him to thinking about them, the ones he won, though, there were stories. Four of his five Derby winners—Lawrin in 1938, Whirlaway in 1941, Citation in 1948, and Hill Gail in 1952—were trained by Ben Jones, and B.A., as he was known, starred in Eddie's stories.

"He knew that Louisville track," Eddie said, "better than he knew the back of his own hand, and he knew those horses better than he knew his own relatives."

On those Saturday mornings of the Larwin and Whirlaway Derbies, B.A. had Eddie come out to the stable early, and he made him walk the track. B.A. was on his stable pony, and Eddie hoofed it alongside while B.A. picked out the best footing and the spots where the track was bad.

"Stomp right there," B.A. would say. "That should be a little soft."

When they got back to the barn, B.A. had a chart of the course and they went over it again. In 1945, though, when Eddie won on Hoop, Jr., he rode him for Fred W. Hooper, and it had rained hard the night before the race. The track was a lake, but when they came out for the Derby, with the band playing "My Old Kentucky Home," Eddie spotted in front of the stands a dry spot about three-sixteenths of a mile long and about fifteen feet wide.

"I got Hoop, Jr. out good," he said, "and I went for that beach. It gave him a three-length lead, and that did it. He didn't get any of that slop thrown in his face, and led all the way and won by six."

He said that, just before he was to win his fifth Derby and set that record on Hill Gail, though, there was a moment in the paddock when he wouldn't have given anything for his chances.

"Hill Gail would usually run as kind as any horse you'll ever see," he said, "but in the paddock he was a wild sonofabitch. When they led him out to put me up he lunged into the stable pony, and when he did, B.A. just reared back and hit that horse a right-hand punch on the soft part of his nose. My eyes must have popped, because I mean that's a hell of a thing to see happen to a horse you're hoping to win the Derby on, but that slowed him, and when I got on him, he was fine."

I got him to tell me, of course, how he rode each one of them, how Lawrin's Derby was one of the roughest, and how he got knocked back to next to last at the start and then played the rail all the way, how the problem with Whirlaway was that once you got him in competition you couldn't hold him, and how Hill Gail, going into the turn coming off the back stretch, started for the outside rail and he had to spin him in mid-air and then let him open at ten-length lead because he was afraid to stop him. As he told me everything that had happened in those split parts of seconds in one race and then another, he said that thinking alone won't do it for a jockey, that it has to be instinct, and I knew what he meant.

"So what are your days like now?" I was saying.

"I'll be on the course in a little while," he said, "and I keep pretty occupied. I'd like to play golf and be a bum, but they won't let me. Next week I go to New York to do the TV on the Wood. I've got to go to Bermuda for a Buick meeting. I come back and I go to the Derby for Seagram's. I do public relations work for them, and then I've got seven more Buick commercials. I haven't done my OTB commercials, and I've got to do them because I've already been paid."

It is New York State's Off Track Betting. When he was starting to ride into the big money he used to bet $1,000 or $2,000 on a horse.

"At the end of a couple of years," he was telling me once, "I came up empty. My mother said to me one time, 'Eddie, why don't you give me some winners?' I said, 'Mom, if I could beat the races, I wouldn't have to ride.' I might ride a horse for a fella now and go for a story like any sucker and bet a hundred, but never enough to get hurt. I just don't think you can win. If you could, the bettin' jocks would be wealthy. It's the ones who don't bet who have all the money."

We got to talking now about the match race at Washington Park in Chicago, in early September 1955, between Nashua and Swaps. Swaps, with Willie Shoemaker on him, had beaten Nashua, with Eddie on him, a length and a half in the Derby. In the newspapers and on radio and television they made this rematch the equine battle of the century, between the western champion, owned and trained by two ex-cowboys, and the effete eastern challenger, owned by William Woodward, Jr. and trained by old Sunny Jim Fitzsimmons. It was also, of course, a contest between Shoe and Eddie.

They had Nashua in training at Saratoga, and when I wasn't tailing Eddie, I watched some of his works. When he shipped out for Chicago, I went down to the railroad siding to watch them load him, and so I had a subjective rooting interest that, because I was not covering the event, I had no reason to constrain.

"The day of the race," I was saying now, "I was in Philadelphia researching a magazine piece on Bert Bell, who was then the head of the National Football League. He was living at the Racquet Club, and we watched it there. There were a dozen or so others watching, too, and when you came out of that gate first, beating on that horse, and then took Shoe wide on that first turn, I came right up out of my chair. I must have been yelling through the whole thing, and when it was over and you'd come down on top I remember hollering. 'He stole it! He stole it!' There was this white-haired, dignified old gentleman there, and he came up to me and he stuck out his hand and he said, 'I don't know who you are, sir, but let me congratulate you. You've just ridden a great race.'"

"With Shoe," Eddie said now, "he was never jealous of me and I was never jealous of him. In a stakes, if one or the other of us won it, it was just the same. After that race in Chicago, though, he said, 'You'll only do that to me once, buddy.' And that's the way it was."

We talked about some great horses and about some people we both knew who are now gone. When I looked at my watch almost two hours had passed, and I said I would let him off the hook. We stood up and I walked him to the door.

"I've got to tell you something you said once," I said, "that couldn't have been more wrong."

"What was that?"

"Like a lot of other people at the time, I was asking you how long you figured to go on riding, and why you didn't quit right then. You had enough money to retire for the rest of your life. You'd won those five Derbies, and there had been great riders who had never won one. You said, 'But I want the next one, and besides I like being a celebrity. If any sonofabitch tells you he don't like it, you'd better look at his head.' Then you said, 'And when I retire I'll be just another little man.'"

"I said that?" he said, smiling.

"Yes, and when you said it I knew you were wrong."

"I didn't know it," he said, shaking my hand. "Listen, I've got to go."

15

The Primitive

There was nothing to do but what we were told.
All ten of us climbed under the ropes and allowed
ourselves to be blindfolded with broad bands of
white cloth . . . I was unused to darkness. It was
as though I had suddenly found myself in a dark
room filled with poisonous cottonmouths. I could
hear the bleary voices yelling insistently for the
battle royal to begin.

"Get going in there!"

"Let me at that big nigger!"

Ralph Ellison, *Invisible Man*.

"Put your name on a piece of paper," Chick Wergeles said to me.
"Then give it to Beau."

It was the first time I met Beau Jack, and Chick Wergeles managed him. It was in one of the dressing rooms at Stillman's, and
Beau had just finished his workout. He was still in his ring clothes,
and he was sitting on a stool next to the rubbing table. With those
high cheek bones in that broad face and those deep, dark eyes and
that coloration, he had the appearance of an Indian.

"But why should I give my name to Beau?" I said. I realized
later that I had fallen right into the common habit of talking
around Beau the way you talk around a small child.

"He's learnin' to read," Chick said. "He wants to take your
name home and study it. He does that with all the writers, so
when he sees them he'll know their names."

"Yeah," Beau said, smiling. "They all my friends."

I cannot conceive of his ever having an enemy. He was the most amiable and, it seemed to me, the happiest of human beings, a primitive in the most primitive of sports, and a man who found joy in all the training, in the comradeship, and even in the conflict itself, whether he won or lost. He exuded pleasure, and seemed able to filter it out of the most trying experiences of his life.

"How was the operation?" I said to him one day.

While he had been in training in Chicago to fight Willie Joyce his left knee had given way under him. Now it was four months later, and he was back in Stillman's again getting ready to box Tony Janiro in the Garden.

"The operation was great," Chick Wergeles said, talking around Beau again.

"How was it, Beau?" I said.

"Oh, fine," Beau said, smiling and slapping his knee. "I never felt better in my life."

"You felt good?" I said. "Did they put you to sleep?"

"That's right," Beau said, still grinning and slapping the knee again. "I never had such a sleep in my life. It didn't make me sick or nothin', and I never felt better in my life."

"Did you dream, Beau?" I said. "Were you dreaming when they put you to sleep?"

"Dreamin'?" he said. "I didn't dream nothin'. I just said, 'Do a good job, Doc.' After, they tells me that's all I said all the time, 'Do a good job, Doc.'"

"The guy does a great job," Chick Wergeles said.

"That doctor that fix that knee," Beau said, and he nodded toward Wergeles, "ain't no bigger than him, and he a great man. He my friend."

As devoid as Beau's world was of enemies, so was it filled with those he felt were his friends. Chick Wergeles, in addition to managing Beau, took care of the football press box for the New York Giants games at the Polo Grounds. He had the same duties in the hockey press box at the New York Rangers game at the Garden, handling the seating and providing programs, copy paper, and refreshments, and he used to take Beau to both places.

"Ask him about his favorite football player," Wergeles said to me another day in the dressing room at Stillman's. Again it was as if Beau were a child.

"You have a favorite football player, Beau?"

"My friend," he said smiling. "He number seven. He a tackle, I think."

"Number seven," I said, "is Mel Hein. He's a center, Beau."

"That's right," Beau said. "He fast, and he my friend."

"Ask him about his favorite hockey player," Wergeles said.

"You have a favorite hockey player too, Beau?"

"Yeah, number seven," he said.

"That's Phil Watson," I said.

"Yeah," Beau said. "He fast, and he my friend too."

"Has he met Mel Hein and Phil Watson?" I said to Wergeles. I should have asked Beau, but as I have said, that was the way it was around him, and it becomes almost instinctive for a reporter to try to belong.

"No," Wergeles said. "He never met them, but he likes the way they play. He thinks everybody he likes is his friend."

"That's right," Beau said, laughing and nodding his head.

His Maker was his friend too. He conceived of that relationship, however, as one in which he had a responsibility to protect his Friend.

"Chick tells me," I said to him once, "that you pray before every fight."

"That's right," he said, grinning.

"For what do you pray?"

"I pray that nobody get hurt," he said. "Then I pray that it be a good fight."

"Don't you ever pray to win?"

"No," he said, shaking his head. "I would never do that."

"Why not?" I said.

"Suppose I pray to win," he said. "The other boy, he pray to win, too. Then what God gonna do?"

In that Janiro fight, four months after the operation, the knee gave out again in the fourth round, and Beau fell to the canvas. He managed to rise and he tried to go on, but they had to stop it. After that, and after another operation, he fought for five more years, mostly outside of New York, but he was never again as good as he had been. In his last fight in the Garden, where he set the record of appearing in twenty-one main events, Tuzo Portuguez licked him, and I went back to the dressing room to see him.

"I'm sorry, Beau," I said.

He was sitting on a stool, his white terrycloth robe over him, the sweat still on him.

"Were it a good fight?" he said.

"Yes, it was a good fight," I said, and it had been.

"Did the people like it?" he said.

"Oh yes," I said. "They liked it."

"If the people like it," he said, smiling, "that's all that matter. That's good."

He was born Sidney Walker in Augusta, Georgia, and he fought in the battle royals. They would blindfold a half dozen or more blacks in a ring and sound the bell, and the survivor was the winner. It came in after bearbaiting went out, and he shined shoes at the Augusta National Golf Club. Bobby Jones and Jimmy Demaret and the others whose names could have floated a bond issue staked him to his boxing career. They sent him north, and somebody was supposed to be handling his money. Those twenty-one Garden fights drew a total of $1,578,000 at the gate. When he fought Bob Montgomery there on August 4, 1944, and admission was by purchase of United States War Bonds, the gross gate for that fight was $35,864,000, but where Beau's money went I could never find out.

He retired in 1955 after 112 fights and after twice holding the New York State version of the lightweight championship of the world. Some five years later I saw Chick Wergeles upstairs in the boxing office at the Garden, and I asked him what Beau was doing.

"He's down in Miami, shining shoes at the Fontainebleau," Wergeles said. "He's doin' fine."

"How fine can he be doing?" I said. "He started as a shoeshine boy, and now he's a shoehine boy again."

"But now when he shines shoes," Wergeles said, "he gets twenty bucks. Them guys with money, they want a former world's champion to shine their shoes, so they ask for Beau."

The cab driver dropped me off now at the south entrance, and I walked through the lobby looking for either a bellhop or the bell captain at his station. The lobby is Grand Central Terminal with foreign marble, furniture, and potted palms, and I found the station just inside the north doors.

"Excuse me," I said, "but can you tell me where I can find Beau Jack? In the barber shop?"

"Beau?" he said. "I'm not sure. There's a TV fight card on, and he may have gone to the weigh-in. Just a second."

He pushed open the nearest of the glass doors. Two couples were getting into a car at the foot of the broad steps, and a couple of carparks were standing off to the right, talking.

"Hey!" he shouted at the two. "Did you see the Beau go out? Did Beau go to the weigh-in?"

The two shrugged their shoulders and shouted back something I couldn't hear. He let the door swing back and turned back to me.

"I don't know if he went out or not," he said, "but you might find him in the barber shop."

"And how do I find that?"

"Take an elevator over there. Go down to the basement and turn left."

"Thank you," I said.

"Sure," he said.

It was just after ten o'clock in the morning and just into the start of the slow season in the temples of Ra along Collins Avenue. Back north again now the winter's sun worshippers would be contemplating their fading tans and confronting their credit card accounts, and when one of the elevators stopped on its way down, there was only one couple on it. They were in tennis clothes and carried racquets, and I rode to the basement with them, turned left and found the barber shop.

In one of the chairs a customer, his head back, his eyes closed and towelling around his neck, was being shaved by the lone barber. In front of her vanity, her back to it, the manicurist was sitting on a stool and reading a newspaper. In the far left corner, with three pairs of white shoes and one black shoe on the floor in front of him, Beau Jack was sitting on a chair, buffing the other black shoe. He had his head down, but I recognized that head with the small, tight curls of hair grayed now.

"Beau," I said. "I'm Bill Heinz."

He looked up. He put the shoe down on the floor beside the others and stood up, heavier now but the weight well distributed. He had on neat gray slacks and an immaculate white T-shirt with the logo of Don King, the boxing promoter, on it, and he smiled and took my hand.

"I used to be a sports writer in New York," I said, "when you were a fighter there."

"Sure," Beau said. "Sure."

I doubt that he remembered me for, starting with that day some thirty years before when I printed my name on that slip of paper so that he could study it, our conversations were always brief, and I was but one of many. He was still smiling at me now, though, as if he did remember.

"What I'm doing, Beau," I said, "is writing a book about athletes I remember, and . . ."

"Good," he said. "Good."

"—and, of course, I remember you. If you have a few minutes, now or later, I'd like to talk with you."

"Yes, sir," he said.

He turned and led me past the barber chairs to the small carpeted foyer just inside the glass door. He pulled one of the chairs away from the wall and turned it for me. Then he turned another so that, as we sat down, we faced each other.

"Beau," I said, "how are you doing?"

"Fine," he said, smiling. "Just fine."

"How long have you been here?"

"It's twenty-two years," he said. "Mr. Ben Novack, he's my friend. You know him?"

"No," I said, "but I know he runs this hotel."

When they built the Fontainebleau right after the war and it became the show place of Miami Beach, I would see his name often in what they used to call the Broadway columns. This singer or that comedian would be appearing there for Ben Novack.

"He's a fine man," Beau was saying, "and I get along just fine. All my friends come here. Joe Louis. Muhammed Ali and Willie Pep, they come by and say hello. My great friend Frank Sinatra and Sammy Davis and all his friends, they come by here. I know no man like Frank Sinatra and Sammy Davis and all his friends, and they pay me respects."

"That's good, Beau," I said.

"Rocky Marciano was my friend too," he said. "He was some man."

"That's right," I said.

"He was my best friend," he said, "and I went to his funeral, but they wouldn't let nobody see him, just maybe his family."

On August 31, 1969, on the eve of his forty-sixth birthday, Rocky Marciano died in the crash of a private plane in an Iowa cornfield. He was buried in Fort Lauderdale, Florida.

"They didn't open the casket," Beau was saying. "Just for his family and Joe Louis. I know they opened it for Joe."

On October 26, 1951, in Madison Square Garden and in his last fight, Joe Louis was knocked out by Rocky Marciano. Joe was thirty-seven years of age and he took a beating. In the eighth round, he stood helpless against the ropes, his eyes glazed and his arms hanging at his side, and Marciano landed a right to the jaw. Louis's head went back, and he was suspended there for the briefest of moments, the back of his neck against the top rope. Then he slumped through the ropes and onto the ring apron, and that was the end of the great career of the man for whom Beau Jack was telling me now, they would open his conqueror's coffin.

"Are you married now, Beau?" I said. I knew that he had been married while he had been fighting, and that there were a number of children.

"I been married twice," he said. "This time eleven years."

"How many children do you have?"

"I got all together fifteen. Ten and five, boys and girls."

"Any fighters among them?"

"No, they not fighters," he said. "Just to protect they own self and don't fight on the street. Maybe they want to be fighters, but they ain't gonna stick to it. Too much life otherwise."

"Yes," I said. "Life is easier now than it was when you were growing up."

It was different talking with just Beau now, without Chick Wergeles or someone else prompting him. I felt, though, that even if there had been someone else there, we would no longer be talking around Beau, for the manchild, more serious now, had grown up.

"My wife is strict," he said, "because you got to put the bell on 'em or otherwise you're gonna have a bad child somewhere. They respect her and me, and so far I got wonderful children."

"Some live up North?" I said.

"That's right," he said. "They live in New York, and every other Saturday they call me. One have two cabs in New Rochelle, New York, and the other boys have jobs on the dock and things, and they doin' fine for theirselves."

"I'm glad to hear that, Beau."

"Then I have one son here that goin' to college next year, and he gonna be a doctor. That's what he says."

"Well, I hope he makes it," I said. "That would be wonderful."

"Then the other younger boy he say he gonna be an arch-i-teck. He fourteen, and he say he gonna build houses that moves, and you don't have to have trucks to move 'em. When he just small he draw a round thing and he draw boxes around it. He say that's a house and those rooms, and I don't see how, but he got it up here in his mind."

"That would be truly wonderful," I said, "to have one son a doctor and another an architect."

"That's right," he said, smiling.

"You earned a lot of money as a fighter, Beau," I said. "Do you know where it went?"

"No, sir," he said. "I don't know and I don't care. The members of the Augusta Golf Club gave me enough to get started, and I enjoyed it and I thankful. I'd never got out of Augusta but for Bobby Jones, may he rest in peace, and them, and they give me the money."

"I never asked you how you started fighting," I said. "Was it on the streets, or did you start in the battle royals?"

"Some guys took my shoe shine polish," he said, "and I come home cryin' and my grandmother . . ."

"Excuse me," a woman said, standing just inside the door. "Can you tell me where the lost-and-found is?"

"Yes, ma'am," Beau said. "Right there to the left, and go down there and push the door."

"Thank you," the woman said.

"Yes, ma'am," Beau said.

"You came home," I said, when he turned back to me, "and your grandmother . . . ?"

"That's right," he said. "She said, 'You pull your clothes off.' Then she gave me a good spankin' and said, 'Don't you ever run.' She live to 112, and she plowed a mule like she nineteen. She worked a farm—that's what we had—and all that work and farmin' made me strong in my fights."

"What were the battle royals like?" I said.

"They used to put five, six guys in a ring at the same time," he said, "and they blindfold us, and when the bell ring you walk into a shot and you don't know where you are. I stay in my corner, and when I feel the wind I know to get goin'. One time it only my brother and me left and I knock him out. Yes, sir."

"Where were those fights held?"

"In Augusta, in an auditorium like a car place but the cars are gone, and the guy put in a ring, and it was a nice place."

"I never knew anyone else," I said, "who seemed to enjoy boxing as much as you did."

"That's right," he said, smiling. "I liked that."

"You'd be the first one into Stillman's, and about the last to leave. As long as there was sparring going on, you'd be there behind the rings watching."

"You remember that?" he said.

"Yes, I do."

"I watched 'em all," he said. "I love that, and sometimes a boy I lookin' at I was gonna meet him, and I know exactly what he's doin'. In my lifetime, though, I never want to hurt anybody, just that it be a good fight."

"I know," I said. "You used to ask me if it had been a good fight and if the crowd liked it."

"You remember that too?" he said. "That's right. I liked to see the crowd, and even when I losin' I could hear my name and the screamin' and that make me fight harder. I used to have so many ladies on the Forty-ninth Street side in the Garden, and I'd hear the screamin' and that make me fight harder, too."

"In your work here now, Beau," I said, "have you any idea how many pairs of shoes you'll shine in a day during the busy season?"

"No, sir, I don't," he said. "At the Master's in Augusta was the most I did, though. Oh, my goodness, I don't know how many I did there. That Jimmy Demaret he had all kinds of shoes. He had green shoes. He was a real sharp man."

"I know," I said. "What are your hours here?"

"I work kind of late," he said. "I here at eight until six, and then I go to the men's room upstairs until twelve. I give towels and soap, and you got to keep goin' when you got a lot of children and the food so high, but I don't mind workin'."

"Are you here five days a week?"

"Seven days," he said.

"Seven days a week?"

"That's right," he said, "but I come a little late on Sunday."

"That's a lot of work hours, Beau."

"My grandmother taught me how to live in the world," he said, "and everything she taught, it come true. 'If you want to live a long life like me,' she used to tell me."

"Well, you're fifty-six," I said, "so you're half way there."

"And I think I gonna make it," he said, grinning. "I don't smoke or drink, and I do thank God for lettin' me live."

"So, Beau," I said, getting up, "I'm glad to see you looking so well and doing so well, and I thank you for taking this time to talk to me."

"That's all right," he said, standing up and taking my hand, "And I want to thank you for all the time you took writin' about me when I fightin', and all the time you're takin' to write about me again now."

I thought about that, leaving Beau. The next morning I had packed my bag to leave for St. Petersburg, and I was checking the room. The *Miami Herald* was on the lamp table where I had left it, and I started to pick it up to put it into the waste basket. It was opened to the second section, and the banner headline across the page read: "Novack Said to Owe Hotel $3.3 Million."

"Hotelman Ben Novack," I read, "owes the Fontainebleau Hotel $3,394,000, according to bankruptcy court testimony made public for the first time Friday."

I know nothing about that beyond what I read. All I know is that, down in the basement of that hotel during the day, and then up in the men's room on the first floor at night, Beau Jack, who twice won the lightweight championship and set a record for appearances in Madison Square Garden, works more than a hundred hours a week, shining shoes and handing out soap and towels, paying his own way.

16

The Man They Padded the Walls for

He was the best I ever had, with the possible exception of Mays. At that, he was even faster than Willie.

Leo Durocher

"What times your plane leave?" he said, turning to me after I had settled myself into the cab. It was 1:20 in the afternoon.

"In forty minutes. It leaves at two."

"No problem," he said. "You from New York?"

"I used to be," I said.

"I can still tell," he said. "I'm from Rockaway myself."

"I remember Rockaway," I said, thinking that between the two of us, we've at least got the title. If you can write the music, I can write the words.

"Down on business?" he said, over his shoulder. He had the cab moving now.

"That's right," I said. No golf clubs, no tennis racket, and no tan.

"What business you in?"

I could have told him dry goods or hotel supplies or computer analysis, but I didn't. Even as a lot of cabbies play their passengers, writers, reaching too, often play cabbies.

"That so?" he said. "You ever write about the Dodgers?"

"Brooklyn, yes. Los Angeles, no."

"That's what I mean," he said. "That's what I'm talkin' about. The old Dodgers. Ebbets Field. You remember Furillo?"

"Of course. A great arm."

"How about Gil Hodges?"

"They brought him up as a catcher," I said, "and I saw him play his first game at first on a western trip in '48. He fielded it as if he'd been there all his life."

"Talkin' about fieldin'," he said, "how about Billy Cox?"

"Absolutely great. "I didn't see Pie Traynor, but at third base, Billy Cox was . . ."

"The best," he said.

"Talking about old Dodgers," I said, wondering what kind of a rise I would get from the cast, "I'm on my way to St. Pete to see one now."

"You are?" he said, glancing back at me. "Who?"

"You remember Pete Reiser?"

"Pete Reiser?" he said. "Pete Reiser?"

He had turned his body so that he was half-facing me and half-facing the road and the traffic ahead.

"Pete Reiser?" he said, his head turning back and forth. "Do I remember Pete Reiser? You got to be kiddin'. Just a great ball-player."

He was right. When Pete Reiser first came up to the majors they said and wrote that he might be the new Ty Cobb. The Cardinals grabbed him out of the St. Louis Municipal League when he was fifteen, and Branch Rickey, as astute about the game and ball-players as any man ever, said he was the greatest young ballplayer he had ever seen. After Judge Kenesaw Mountain Landis, the commissioner of baseball, freed Pete and seventy-two other ball-players from what was called "The Cardinal Chain Gang" and the Dodgers grabbed him, the Yankees offered $100,000 and five ballplayers for him before he had played his first major league regular season game.

"Pete Reiser?" the cabbie was saying again. "You know he like to almost kill himself playin' ball."

He was right again. In two and a half years in the minors, three seasons of Army ball, and ten years in the majors, Pete Reiser was carried off the field eleven times. Nine times he regained consciousness in the clubhouse or in the hospitals, and once at Ebbets Field they gave him the Last Rites of the Church. He broke a bone in his right elbow, throwing. He broke both ankles, tore a cartilage in his left knee, and ripped the muscles in his left leg, sliding. Seven times he crashed into outfield walls, dislocating his left shoulder or breaking his collar bone, and five times he ended up in an unconscious heap on the ground. Twice he was beaned and suffered concussions at the plate, and once he was operated on for a brain clot, and the ever-diminishing few who still remember him must still wonder today how great he might have been.

"Hell," the cabbie was saying now, "they put the padding on the walls there for Pete Reiser."

He was right once more. After the 1946 season the Brooklyn Dodgers, in a classic demonstration of a ball club's concern for the health and welfare of its employees, changed the walls at Ebbet's Field. They added boxes, cutting forty feet off left field and dropping center field from 420 to 390 feet. In a night game on the following June 5, the Dodgers were leading the Pirates by three runs with one out in the sixth inning when Cully Rickard hit one. Pete made his turn and ran. Where he thought he still had those thirty feet he didn't.

"The crowd," Al Laney wrote in the *New York Herald Tribune,* "which watched silently while Reiser was being carried away, did not know that he had held onto the ball . . . Rickard circled the bases, but Butch Henline, the umpire, who ran to Reiser, found the ball still in Reiser's glove. . . . Two outs were posted on the scoreboard after play was resumed. Then the crowd let out a tremendous roar."

It was at the end of that season that the Dodgers had the outfield walls at Ebbets Field covered with the one-inch rubber padding for Pete, but he never hit them again. He had headaches most of the time and played little, and in 1949 he was traded to Boston. In two seasons there he hit the wall a couple of times and twice his left shoulder came out while he was making diving catches. Pittsburgh picked him up in 1952, and the next year he played into July with Cleveland, and that was the end of it for him.

"So what's he doing in St. Pete?" the cabbie was saying now.

"He's with the Cubs," I said. "He's in charge of some rookies in training there."

"How about that?" he said. "Listen. Tell him you met a guy remembers him."

"I will."

"You're gonna see Pete Reiser," he said. "How about that?"

Most airports are cattleyards, but the one at Tampa was designed and built to accommodate people. I took the elevated that runs from the docking area to the main terminal and picked up my bag and walked out across the carpeting to a phone booth. Some weeks before, when I had phoned him at his home in Woodland Hills, California, he had said he would be staying in St. Petersburg with the Cubs and Mets rookies at something he named as the Downtowner Motel. In the directory I found a Downtowner Apartments, and I dialed the number.

"This is the operator," the voice said. "May I help you?"

"Yes. I'm calling the Downtowner Apartments."

"Just a moment, sir. I'm getting an intercept on that. Just a moment, sir. That phone has been disconnected."

"Thank you."

I wrote down the address and I walked out to the taxi station. There were three cabs in line, the cabbies standing and talking, and the starter walked up to me.

"You want a cab?"

"Yes," I said, "and I want a driver who knows St. Pete. We may have to do some riding around."

"He'll take you," he said.

"Where to?" the cabbie said.

I gave him the address and got in. He was young—I judged still in his twenties—and so I didn't try Pete Reiser on him. I told him we would probably draw a blank at the address I had given him, but that I had to find some young ballplayers and we might as well start there.

"Sure," he said, "we'll find them somewhere."

When, about twenty minutes later, he pulled up at the curb I could tell from the cab that there were no signs of current life. It was just beyond the sidewalk, what had probably once been a modest private home, and behind it were several cottages, everything painted white with red roofs and red trim. I got out and tried the jalousied front door and came back and got into the cab.

"Closed," I said, "but this can't be the place anyway. What do you suggest now?"

"Well," he said, "I'll tell you what we can do. The Hilton is right near here. Why don't you check in there, and then try to find them?"

"I thought we were going to drive around until we found them?" I said.

"You see," he said, "I'm not supposed to work the city here."

"All right," I said. "You win."

After I had signed for the room I gave the girl at the desk the problem. She listened and nodded and then thought a moment.

"You know what you might do?" she said. "When you get up to your room you might call the Edgewater Beach. Some ballplayers stay there."

I went up to the room and looked up the number and dialed it.

"Pete Reiser?" the woman's voice said. "There's nobody under the R's. I think he left yesterday."

"He's with the ballplayers," I said. "Do you have any ballplayers there?"

"Oh, no," she said. "They all left on March 26."

"I don't mean the major leaguers," I said. "He's with some Cubs and Mets minor leaguers."

"Oh," she said. "Well. Then you might call the Payson Complex. That's where they'd be. I can give you the number. It's 347-6138, but you'd better call in the morning, when they'll be there."

"Thank you," I said. "Thank you very much."

I dialed and waited, listening to the phone ringing at the other end. Then the ringing stopped and a male voice answered.

"Payson Complex."

"I'm trying to reach Pete Reiser."

"He's not here," the voice said. "He's in the hospital."

"What?" I said. "In the hospital?"

"That's right," he said. "He went in yesterday."

Oh, no, I was thinking, not again. The last time I had seen him, twenty years before, I had left him in another hospital—St. Luke's, in St. Louis. I had driven him there from Kokomo, Indiana, where he was managing a Class D ball club in the Dodgers' chain. I had gone out there to do a magazine piece about him and Class D ball, and when I arrived I had found him moving and talking slowly and suffering with chest pains, and he had just come from seeing a doctor.

"He says I should be in a hospital right now," he said, "because if I exert myself or even make a quick motion I might go—just like that."

He snapped his fingers.

"He scared me," he said. "I'll admit it. I'm scared."

"What are you planning to do?" I said.

"I'm going home to St. Louis," he said. "My wife works for a doctor there, and he'll know a good heart specialist."

"How will you get to St. Louis?" I said.

"It's about three hundred miles," he said. "The doctor says I shouldn't fly or go by train, because if anything happens to me they can't stop and help me. I guess I'll have to drive."

"I'll drive you," I said.

He had a seven-year-old Chevy, and it took us eight and a half hours, driving from midafternoon late into the night. I would ask how the pain in his chest was and he would say that it wasn't bad or it wasn't good, and I would get him to talking about this manager and that one and one ballplayer and another. The lights of the oncoming traffic flashed in our faces and trucks crowded us, and each time we left a town and its hospital behind I wondered if we would make the next one.

"What's wrong with him now?" I was saying on the phone.

"He had trouble breathing," the voice from the Payson Complex said. "He wanted to try to get home, but he's in St. Anthony's Hospital. That's all I know."

I looked up the number and I dialed it.

"Are you calling 894-2151?" the woman's voice said.

"Yes."

"You want 823-5111."

"Is that St. Anthony's Hospital?"

"Yes, it is."

"St. Anthony's Hospital," another woman's voice said, after I had dialed the second number. "May I help you?"

"Do you have a Pete Reiser there? That's R-e-i-s-e-r."

"Just a moment," the voice said, and then there was a wait and then another voice said, "Yes?"

"Do you have a Pete Reiser there?" I said, spelling it again.

"Just a moment. Is he a new patient today?"

"I believe he came in yesterday. He may be listed as Harold Patrick Reiser."

"Just a moment. Harold Reiser?"

"Yes."

"He's in room 632. Would you like me to ring it?"

"Please."

The phone rang three times.

"Hello?" the deep voice said, and I could hear the breathing, the breaths short but heavy.

"Pete?" I said. "This is Bill Heinz."

"Hello, Bill," he said, breathing it.

"What's going on?" I said. "I see you once every twenty years. I leave you in a hospital, and I find you in one."

"I know," he said.

"What's wrong, and how are you?"

"Not too good," he said, pausing. "I've got pneumonia and a heart murmur. I tried to get home, but I decided I'd better come in here."

"Well," I said, "I don't think we should try to drive home this time."

"No," he said. "It's much too far."

"I'll be over," I said. "Tonight? Tomorrow?"

"Tomorrow," he said, breathing it. "I'm a little rocky."

"Sure," I said. "Now, listen. I'm at the Hitlon, and if you need me just call."

"Yeah," he said. "Thanks."

His first full season with the Dodgers was 1941, and he was beaned twice and crashed his first wall and still hit .345 to be the first rookie and, at twenty-two, the youngest ballplayer to win the National League batting title. He led the league in triples, runs scored, total bases, and slugging average, and tied Johnny Mize with thirty-nine doubles.

He was beaned the first time at Ebbets Field five days after the season started when a sidearm fastball got away from Ike Pearson of the Phillies. Pete came to at 11:30 that night in Peck Memorial Hospital.

"I was lying in bed with my uniform on," he told me once, "and I couldn't figure it out. The room was dark, with just a little night light, and then I saw a mirror and I walked over to it and lit the light and I had a black eye and a black streak down the side of my nose. I said to myself, 'What happened to me?' Then I remembered.

"I took a shower and walked around the room, and the next morning the doctor came in. He looked me over, and he said, 'We'll keep you here five or six more days for observation.' I said, 'Why?' He said, 'You've had a serious head injury. If you tried to get out of bed right now you'd fall down.' I said, 'If I can get up and walk around this room, can I get out?' The doc said, 'All right, but you won't be able to do it.' "

He got out of bed, the doctor standing by ready to catch him. He walked around the room.

"I've been walking the floor all night," he said.

On the promise that he wouldn't play ball for a week, the doctor released him. He went right to the ball park. He got a seat behind the Brooklyn dugout, and Durocher spotted him.

"How do you feel?" Leo said.

"Not bad," Pete said.

"Get your uniform on," Leo said.

"I'm not supposed to play," Pete said.

"I'm not gonna play you," Leo said. "Just sit on the bench. It'll make our guys feel better to see that you're not hurt."

Pete suited up and went out and sat on the bench. In the eighth inning it was tied, 7–7. The Dodgers had the bases loaded, and there was Ike Pearson again, coming in to relieve.

"Pistol," Leo said to Pete, "get that bat."

On the two ball clubs and up in the press box they were watching Pete at that plate. After a beaning a man may shy up there, and many of them do. Pete hit Pearson's first pitch into the center-field stands, and Brooklyn won, 11–7.

"I could just barely trot around the bases," Pete said when I asked him about that. "I was sure dizzy."

Two weeks later they were playing the Cardinals, and Enos Slaughter hit one, and Pete turned in center field and started to run. He made the catch, but he hit his head and his tail bone on the corner near the exit gate. His head was cut, and when he came back to the bench there was blood coming through the seat of his pants. They took him into the clubhouse and pulled his pants down and put a metal clamp on the cut.

"Just don't slide," they told him. "You can get it sewed up after the game."

In August of that year big Paul Erickson was pitching for the Cubs and Pete took another one. Again he woke up in a hospital, but he walked out the next morning. The Dodgers were going to St. Louis, and he didn't want to be left in Chicago.

I waited in the hotel now in the event he should call. The next morning I phoned the hospital and asked for his room.

"How do you feel today?" I said. When he had answered his voice had still sounded heavy and his breathing still labored.

"A little rough," he said.

"Then I won't come over and bother you," I said.

"I hate to hang you up," he said.

"Forget it," I said. "You don't think I'd leave you now."

"I think tomorrow I'll be better," he said.

Pete always said that his second year up, 1942, was the beginning of his downfall. It was early in July, and Pete and the Dodgers were tearing the league apart. They opened a western trip in Cincinnati and went from there to Chicago, and in those two series Pete went 19 for 21. In a Sunday double-header against the Cubs he went 5 for 5 in the first game, walked 3 times in the second game and got a hit the one time they pitched to him. He was hitting .391, and they were writing in the papers that he might end up hitting .400.

When they came into St. Louis the Dodgers had a ten-and-a-half game lead. When they took off for Pittsburgh they left three games of that lead and Pete Reiser behind them. In the twelfth inning, with no score and two outs, Enos Slaughter had hit one off Whit Wyatt.

"It was over my head," Pete said once when I asked him about that one, "and I took off. I caught it and missed that flagpole by two inches and hit the wall and dropped the ball. That's the only one I ever dropped, but I had the instinct to throw it to Peewee Reese, and we just missed gettin' Slaughter at the plate, and they won, 1–0. I made one step to start off the field and I woke up the next morning in St. John's Hospital. My head was bandaged, and I had an awful headache."

"Look, Pete," Dr. Robert Hyland told him, "I'm your personal friend. I'm advising you not to play any more baseball this year."

After two days Pete took the bandage off his head and got up. The room, he said, started to spin, but he dressed and sneaked out past the nursing station. He took a train to Pittsburgh and went to the ball park.

"Leo saw me," he said, "and he said, 'Go get your uniform on, Pistol.' I said, 'Not tonight, Skipper.' Leo said, 'Aw, I'm not gonna let you hit. I want these guys to see you. It'll give 'em that little spark they need. Besides, it'll change the pitching plans on that other bench when they see you in uniform.'"

In the fourteenth inning the Dodgers had a runner on second and Ken Heintzelman, the left-hander, came in for the Pirates. He walked Johnny Rizzo, and Durocher had run out of pinch-hitters.

"Damn," he was saying, walking up and down in the dugout. "I want to win this one. Who can I use? Anybody here who can hit?"

Pete walked up to the bat rack. He pulled out his stick.

"You got yourself a hitter," he said to Leo.

He walked up there and hit a line drive over the second baseman's head that was good for three bases. The two runs scored and Pete rounded first base and collapsed.

"When I woke up I was in the hospital again," he told me. "I could just make out that somebody was standing there and then I saw it was Leo. He said, 'You awake?' I said, 'Yep.' He said, 'By God, we beat 'em! How do you feel?' I said, 'How do you think I feel?' He said, 'Aw, you're better with one leg and one eye than anybody else I've got.' I said, 'Yeah, and that's the way I'll end up —on one leg and with one eye."

He still hit .310 for the season, but he said he figured that he lost the pennant for the Dodgers that year, when the Cardinals beat them out on the last two days. He suffered with dizzy spells a lot of the time, and he had trouble judging fly balls. Once at Ebbets Field, when Mort Cooper was pitching for the Cardinals, Pete was seeing two baseballs coming up there, and Babe Pinelli, who was umpiring behind the plate, stopped the game twice to ask him if he was all right.

"How are you today?" I said on the phone now the second morning.

"Better," he said, and I could hear that a TV was on in his room.

"You sound it," I said, although I could still hear his breathing.

"Yeah," he said. "Why don't you come over in the afternoon?"

He had a small private room at the end of the hall. The head of the bed was elevated, and he was in one of those hospital gowns, a sheet up to his waist. He was bald and heavier under the sheet and the oval face was fuller and he needed a shave.

"Bronchial pneumonia they call it," he said, speaking as he exhaled. "I can't breathe. I had an attack in 1970. In Palm Springs. In spring training. I been getting them on and off once a year. Now three times a year. This is the third. They're worried because each time the heart murmur shows up. That time in Kokomo it was a strained heart muscle. In '64 I had a heart attack. I also got a hiatus hernia. I can't make quick moves any more."

Quick moves. In the outfield he was so quick that he seemed to get his start on the ball in that almost infinitesimal part of a second as it came off the bat. On the base paths he was a burner. In 1946 he led the league when he stole thirty-four bases, thirteen more than the runner-up, Johnny Hopp of the Braves. That year he also set a major league record when he stole home seven times.

"Eight times," he told me once. "In Chicago I stole home and Magerkurth hollered, 'You're out!' Then he dropped his voice and he said, 'I'll be a sonofabitch, I missed it.' He'd already had his thumb in the air. I had eight for eight."

Rod Carew tied that in 1969, but I doubt that anyone will ever tie or top the way Pete did it, because that was another year when he was in and out of Peck Memorial Hospital. He was knocked out making a diving catch. He ripped the muscles in his left leg beating out an infield hit. He broke his left leg sliding. He broke his collar bone, and he dislocated his left shoulder. With all that he led the league in stolen bases and set that record.

"We're playing the Cards," he told me once, "and Whitey Kurowski hit one in the seventh inning at Ebbets Field. "I dove for it and woke up in the clubhouse. I held the ball, but I was in

Peck Memorial for four days. It really didn't take much to knock me out in those days. I was coming apart all over. When I dislocated my left shoulder they popped it back in, and Leo said, 'You'll be all right. You don't throw with it anyway.'"

That was the year the Dodgers tied with the Cardinals for the pennant and lost the play-off. Pete wasn't there for those two games. He was in Peck Memorial again.

"I'd pulled a charley horse in my left leg," he told me. "It's the last two weeks of the season, and I'm out for four days. We're playing the Braves, and the winning run is on third with two out in the ninth, and Leo sends me up. He says, 'If you don't hit it good, don't hurt your leg.'

"The first pitch was a knockdown and, when I ducked, the ball hit the bat and went down the third base line, as beautiful a bunt as you've ever seen. Well, Ebbets Field is jammed. Leo has said, 'Don't run.' But this is a big game. I take off for first, and we win and I've ripped the muscles from my ankle to my hip. Leo says, 'You shouldn't have done it.'

"Now it's the last three days of the season, and we're ahead of the Cards and we're playing the Phillies in Brooklyn. Leo says to me, 'It's now or never. I don't think we can win it without you.' I said, 'I don't feel good, but I'll try.' The first two up are outs, and I single to right. There's Charley Dressen, coaching on third, with the steal sign. He knows I've got a bad leg. I start to get my lead, and a pitcher named Charley Schanz is working and he throws an ordinary lob over to first. My leg is stiff and I slide and my heel spike catches the bag and I hear it snap.

"Leo comes running out. He says, 'Come on. You're all right.' I said, 'I think it's broken.' He says, 'It ain't stickin' out.' They took me to Peck Memorial, and it was broken."

"I had a bit of a time finding you," I was telling him now. "When I talked with you on the phone, I got it that you were staying at something called the Downtowner Motel. There isn't any."

"It's the Uptowner," he said exhaling the words again, rasping them. "Downtowner. Uptowner. I thought I said Uptowner."

"That solves that," I said.

He had started to cough. He reached for a gauze wipe and coughed into that and dropped it into the waste basket with a plastic bag liner in it.

"I was supposed to have a breathing treatment at noon," he said, "and they're not here yet."

"Listen," I said. "If this is hard on you and you'd rather rest, I'll come back tomorrow. We don't have to talk now."

"That's all right," he said. "I'd rather talk."

I knew he had been a coach with the Dodgers, after they had moved to Los Angeles. Then he had been a coach with the Cubs, after Durocher had taken over as manager.

"The last thing I remember reading about you," I said, "was when you were carted off the field again after some kind of rhubarb."

"In '73," he said. "In Candlestick Park. There was a big scrap at home plate. I went up to separate Bonds and Hundley. Somebody gave me a karate shot. Broke my collar bone. Somebody hit me on the head. Knocked me out. I went down and got spiked. I think that's what broke up the fight. They saw I'm on the ground, and they're steppin' on me."

Just the thought of it made me uncomfortable, and I was aware that I was wincing. How, with his medical history, could he go near a scramble like that, even as a peacemaker? He never shied from a wall, though, or a pitched ball or anything that his instinct asked that once-remarkable body to do.

After that catch he made on Culley Rickard, when Butch Henline found the ball in his glove and in the clubhouse they called for the doctor who sent for the priest, he was in Peck Memorial for three weeks. For the first ten days he couldn't move, but when they let him out he made the next western trip with the Dodgers. In Pittsburgh he was working out in the outfield before the game when Clyde King, chasing a fungo, ran into him. He woke up in the clubhouse and he went back to the Hotel Schenley and lay down. He had dinner with Peewee Reese, and later they were sitting on the porch and he scratched his head and felt a lump there.

"Gosh," he said. "I don't think that's supposed to be like that."

"Hell, no," Reese said.

They flew him to Johns Hopkins in Baltimore, where they operated on him for the blood clot. They told him that if it had moved just a little more, he would have been gone. He was unable to hold even a pencil. He had double vision and when he tried to take a single step, became dizzy. He stayed for three weeks and then went home for almost a month.

"It was August," he told me, "and Brooklyn was fighting for another pennant. I thought if I could play the last two months it might make the difference, so I went back to Johns Hopkins. The doctor said, 'You've made a remarkable recovery.' I said, 'I want to play.' He said, 'I can't okay that. The slightest blow on the head can kill you.'"

Knowing that, he played. He worked out for four days, pinch hit a couple of times and then, in the Polo Grounds, made a diving catch in left field. They carried him off again, and in the clubhouse he was unable to recognize anyone.

He was still having dizzy spells when the Dodgers went into that 1947 World Series against the Yankees. In the third game he walked in the first inning, got the steal sign and, when he slid into second, he felt his right ankle snap. At the hospital they found it was broken.

"Just tape it, will you?" Pete said.

"I want to put a cast on it," the doctor said.

"If you do," Pete said, "they'll give me a dollar-a-year contract for next season."

The next day he was back on the bench at Ebbets Field. Bill Bevens was pitching for the Yankees, and Pete was to put a postscript onto one of the most memorable of World Series games. Bevens had given up a run on walks, but with two out in the ninth and the Yankees leading, 2–1, he was one out away from pitching what would have been the first no-hitter in World Series history.

"Aren't you going to volunteer to hit?" Burt Shotton, who was managing Brooklyn, said to Pete. He and Pete had never hit it off since the day in 1937 when Shotton was managing Springfield and he threw Pete out of camp. Shotton told him he would never be a ballplayer, and Pete was eighteen then, and he said the tears were rolling out of his eyes.

Al Gionfriddo was on second now, with another walk and a stolen base, and Bucky Harris, who was managing the Yankees, ordered Pete walked. Eddie Miksis ran for him, and when Cookie Lavagetto hit that double the two runs scored and Brooklyn won, 3–2. In a World Series game, in which not only a win but a no-hitter hung in the balance, a man with a broken ankle, who didn't dare confess it to his own ballclub because he knew they wouldn't credit him on his next contract for past favors, was intentionally walked for what became the winning run.

"I gave up coaching in the big leagues," he was saying now, "so I wouldn't have to travel so much. I have to be near home."

A nurse had come in. She handed him a pill and a paper cup of water and he sat up and, after he had popped the pill into his mouth and followed it with the water, she gave him a medicinal dose in a small bottle and he swallowed that. When she had left I asked him about the rookie program that had brought him to Florida.

"We get these high school and college kids we sign," he said, and I had to listen carefully to get the words. "We've got fifteen Cubs and fifteen Mets here. It's a forty-five-day extension of spring training. For the rookie league that starts in June. It's forty-five more games experience."

"What are these kids like who come up today?" I said.

"You get all kinds," he said.

"You don't think the world is going down the drain because of the younger generation?"

"Hell, no," he said, stopping for breath. "I see too many good ones. It's so much easier to write about kids doing bad things, than about kids doing good things for others."

He had paused again. I didn't think I should keep this going, but he seemed to want to talk.

"There's a lot of stinkers in the world," he said. "And it's a damn shame. I think if they'd put in some juvenile laws with teeth in them, so the police and parents can hit a few butts, it'd be better. Too many come in the third time, because they never served the first two times."

He started to cough into a gauze wipe again.

"This coughing tires you out," he said, pausing. "I was supposed to have a breathing treatment at noon. But she ain't here yet. I must have had the button on for three hours last night. I said, 'I'm sure glad I'm not dying.' She said, 'You're not the only patient on the floor.' One of them says, 'Aren't you keeping your record of your intake?' I said, 'I'm not supposed to write that down. You are.'"

"That oxygen there," I said, pointing to the tubing on the stand. "I'm not trying to play doctor, but does it work?"

"Yeah, if you can plug it into the wall there," he said. "I can hardly breathe."

I plugged it in and handed it to him. He put the nasal cannula into his nostrils and lay back, breathing from it. After a minute or so he handed it back to me.

"If I leave it in too long," he said, "my sinuses get worse."

I placed it back on the stand. He was breathing a little easier now.

"When I wrote about you managing in Kokomo," I said, "I told about the time one of your kids had made a bad throw. You asked him what he was thinking while the ball was coming to him, and he said, "I was thinking to myself that I hope I don't make a bad throw.""

"That's right," he said.

"Then you told him how, when you were playing, you used to be saying, 'Hit it to me. Just hit it to me. I'll make the catch. I'll make the throw. Give me the steal again. Give me the sign. I'll go!'"

"That's right," he said. "You have to think positive. I try to tell them that."

"So after the story ran," I said, "I got a letter from a father. He said he had sat his own kid down and he'd read that to him, and he thanked me. I wrote him back, saying that I appreciated his letter but that he shouldn't thank me. He should thank Pete Reiser."

"You try to tell these kids," he said, "and one of them said to me, 'I didn't know you played major league ball.'"

"That's awful," I said. "It hurts me to hear that."

"Any manager in the National League," Arthur Patterson wrote in the *New York Herald Tribune* during Pete's rookie year, "would give up his best man to obtain Pete Reiser. On every bench they're talking about him. Rival players watch him take his cuts during batting practice, announce when he's going to make a throw to the plate or third during outfield drill. They just whistle their amazement when he scoots down the first base line on an infield dribbler or a well-placed bunt."

"How many guys," Tom Meany, who wrote baseball for more

than three decades, said one day, watching Pete, "does God make like this?"

Not many. When he was with Elmira in '39 he made a throw and heard something pop. His arm was broken, and after they had cut into him and reset it at Johns Hopkins, he carried it in a cast for three months. A month later he played ten games as a left-handed outfielder until Dr. George Bennett, who had operated on him, heard about it and stopped him. That winter in St. Louis he bowled, using first one arm and then the other. In the back yard he practiced throwing a rubber ball left-handed against a wall, and then he went to Fairgrounds Park and worked on the long throw, left-handed, with a baseball. When he arrived at the Dodgers camp in Clearwater that spring he could throw as well with his left arm as he could with his right.

"Then you run into some kids," he was saying now, "who are hero-worshippers. They tell you everything about you until you wish they'd shut up."

"On the way to the airport in Miami the other day," I said, "I had a cabbie from Brooklyn who still remembers you. He said, 'Pete Reiser? They put the padding on the walls there for him.'"

"I still get quite a lot of mail from Brooklyn," he said. "People tell me their grandfathers talk about me. They send me some of the oldest looking pictures. I don't know·where they get 'em. Old pictures on newer type of paper. They must be selling them at the Mets stadium and Yankee Stadium."

He had paused again, breathing heavily.

"They send baseballs to be signed," he said. "I had one not long ago with the names of about thirty batting champions. That has to be a collector's item."

"Was it insured?" I said.

"It didn't come insured," he said. "It came in like an old burlap bag with the label on, and one inside to mail back. It was from eastern Connecticut or Pennsylvania. There's a guy in Pennsylvania you hear from twice a year. He's always got something for you to sign. He must spend a fortune. They send bats to sign. It's easy to get your address. There's an organization that sells 'em."

"When they send you the bats," I said, "are they Pete Reiser models?"

"Sure," he said. "They write to Louisville and get 'em."

"It's nice to be remembered," I said.

"Yeah," he said. "It sure is."

A nun, in white habit and wearing glasses, had come in.

"How are you this afternoon?" she said.

"So-so," Pete said.

"Have you seen a priest since you're here?" she said.

"Yep," Pete said.

She walked over to the stand and took the water carafe and carried it into the bathroom. We could hear her emptying it and refilling it, and she brought it back to the stand.

"I'll leave a little prayer here for you," she said.

"Thank you," Pete said.

On her way out she must have passed the maintenance man, because she had no sooner left than he was standing there. He was carrying a small aluminum step ladder, and he had on one of those wide leather belts with tools on it, worn gun-slinger fashion.

"There's something wrong with your air conditioning?" he said.

"Yeah," Pete said, nodding up at the circular vent in the middle of the ceiling. "It blows right down on you when you're in bed here."

"I can flatten the louvres," the other said.

"You do that," Pete said.

We watched him climb up on the ladder, and take the cover off and bend the louvres and replace the cover.

"I didn't close it all the way," he said, getting down. "Now the air is blowing to the side and not down on you."

"It's got to be better," Pete said. "Thanks."

"You're welcome," he said nodding and leaving.

"I don't know who the hell designs these hospitals," Pete said.

"It's not the patients," I said, "but you could."

"I've been in enough of them," he said.

In 1946 the Dodgers played an exhibition game in Springfield, Missouri. When they got off the train, there was a young radio announcer there, and he was grabbing them one at a time and asking them where they thought they would finish that year.

"In the first place," Peewee Reese and Hugh Casey and Dixie Walker and the rest were saying. "On top . . . We'll win it."

"And here comes Pistol Pete Reiser," the announcer said. "Where do you think you'll finish this season, Pete?"

"In Peck Memorial Hospital," Pete said, and with that left ankle he broke sliding back to first against the Phillies, he did.

A young black woman in the uniform of a nurses' aide had come in now. She had walked over to the stand and had picked up the water carafe to look into it. Now she put it down, and picked up a sheet of paper.

"How many glasses of water you drink honeybun?" she said.

"Today?" Pete said. "About three."

She wrote it down, and without saying anything more, left.

"This artificial turf," I said. "How do you think you'd have done playing on that?"

"I'd a loved it," he said. "I'd a played run-run, bounce-bounce all day."

In 1941 the Dodgers trained in Havana, and one day they clocked Pete at 9.8 for 100 yards. That was in baseball spikes and the loose, heavy flannel uniform, the garb that seemed so right then and that now, in the old photographs, seems so shockingly and sadly comical. Five years later the Cleveland Indians were bragging about George Case and the Washington Senators had Gil Coan. The Dodgers offered to bet that Pete was the fastest man in baseball, but there were no takers.

"As Mr. Rickey used to say," he was saying, breathing it again and pausing between the sentences, " 'It takes no talent to hustle. The easiest thing a man can do, outside of walking, is to run.' I believed him."

I heard the sound beside me, and when I turned a young woman was pushing in the wheeled apparatus with the glass tank on top. She was wearing a nurse's white pants suit, and she looked up from a piece of paper she had in her hand.

"Mr. Riser?" she said, giving it the German pronunciation.

"Ree-sir," I said, thinking that, if Pete weren't listening, in thirty seconds I could tell her who and what he was.

"I been waitin' for you," Pete said.

She was adjusting the two knobs on the front and checking the two dials, turning the apparatus on and off. She uncoiled the plastic tubing and handed the end to Pete. He put the orange plastic mouth-piece in, and there was the evenly spaced sound of the air and of Pete's breathing.

"What is this called?" I said to her as we watched Pete, his chest rising and falling.

"It's called an IPPB."

"What does that mean?"

"Intermittent Positive Pressure Breathing," she said, and then to Pete, "How's that feel? Too high, or too low? Okay?"

He nodded.

"It's hooked up to oxygen," she said to me, "and also has humidity."

Pete had taken the mouthpiece out and he was coughing into a gauze wipe.

"Are you productive at all?" she said.

"I wasn't then, but I have been," he said, putting the mouthpiece back in.

She took his pulse and walked over and examined some of the wipes in the wastebasket, making notes.

"Getting tired?" she said, and Pete shook his head. "Take a rest if you get tired."

I had clocked it, and after fifteen minutes she shut it off.

"When will I be gettin' another one?" he said.

"Every six hours," she said, smiling.

"Every six hours?" he said. "But every day it's a different six hours."

Pete sizes up hospitals and doctors the way he sizes up ball clubs and ballplayers, and he has his own views, which are sometimes contrary to prevailing opinion. In 1938 he was with Superior, Wisconsin, and three days before the season ended, in an exhibition game at Oslo, North Dakota, he was going into second base when he felt something snap in his left knee.

"An old country doctor came running out," he told me once, "and he popped it back in—one, two—and I near died. He said, 'That's what you've got to do, sonny. The longer it stays out the worse it is, and then they'll have to operate on you. You put an elastic bandage on and don't let anyone operate on you.'"

"MacPhail," he said, and Larry MacPhail was running the Dodgers organization, "heard about it, and he sent me to the Mayo Clinic. They wanted to cut me for a torn cartilage, but I kept hearing that old country doctor say, 'Don't let anyone operate on you. It'll heal itself.' I talked the doc into letting me go home, and in '41 I went back to Mayo with Durocher and Medwick for checkups. In came the doc. He said, 'You're the one I want to see. Let's see the results of that operation.' I said, 'I had no operation.' He checked me over and he said, 'Remarkable.' "

Now, about five minutes after the respiratory technician had wheeled her apparatus out, a nurse came in. She took his pulse and unwound her blood pressure cuff and put it around his arm. She pumped it up, checking the dial.

"I don't know who's attracting all these people," Pete said, looking over at me. "It must be you."

"Maybe they think I'm from the Health Department," I said.

"Yeah," he said. "I can lay here for hours and nobody comes in."

"Is there something you want?" the nurse said.

"Yeah," Pete said. "The doctor. I haven't seen him all day."

"He'll be in," the nurse said.

"Yeah," Pete said, and then, after she had left, "He came in and I thought the top of my head was gonna blow off. I said, 'My sinuses are killing me.' He said, 'How do you know?' I said, 'I've been treated for sinuses since I was five or six years old.' He said, 'What do you mean sinuses?' I said, 'If you don't know, I'm not gonna tell you. I've had them cleaned out five or six times, and when you've had that done you know it.' "

"Pete," I said, "what about these salaries ballplayers are getting now?"

When I read about a .276 hitter who is a lackadaisical fielder and laggardly base runner on balls hit to the infield but who signs a multiyear contract worth almost two million dollars, I think of Pete. When he was fifteen and the Cardinals found him in that St. Louis Municipal League, his father signed for him, and I asked him once what he and his dad got.

"A handshake," he said. "You felt honored if a scout even talked to you."

When Judge Landis freed Pete and those seventy-two others from the Cardinal chain and Pete signed with Brooklyn he got $100.

"I'm glad to see the ballplayers finally getting something," he said.

"I am too," I said, "but I often think . . ."

"You can't go back," he said, reading my mind, "and say what you should have got. When I played I guess there were guys who'd played before me who said they wished they were playing when I was, not that I ever got that much."

"That's the only way to look at it," I said, "and I'll never forget something you told me. I asked you if you ever thought that if you hadn't played the game as hard as you did, there would be no telling how great you might have been or how much money you might have made. You said, 'Never. It was my way of playing. If I hadn't played that way, I wouldn't even have been whatever I was.'"

"That's right," he said. "I may never have got there."

"You said, 'God gave me those legs and that speed, and when they took me into those walls that was the way it had to be. I couldn't play any other way.'"

"That's right," he said. "I had a good body, and I just wrecked it, that's all. It took a lot of beatin' to do it, but that's the way it was."

I didn't want to leave him on that, so I got to telling stories about some of the writers who covered the Dodgers in his time and what those who are left are doing now. We reminisced for twenty minutes or so, and then I said I would be going.

"So if you want anything," I said, "just call the Hilton."

"I'll be all right," he said. "As soon as I see that doc, I'm gonna get out."

The restaurant at the hotel is on the top floor, and the waitress, a middle-aged, semi-stout motherly type, led me between tables. At one of them, a man and a woman in their sixties were seated, and as I passed them he was speaking.

"So you married Frank," he was saying, "and I married Grace, and that's the way it was."

And that's the way Noel Coward would have written it too, I was thinking. A brief encounter forty years later.

"Is this all right?" the waitress was saying.

"It's fine," I said.

The table was at one of the picture windows, and I could look down at Al Lang Field where the old green-painted wooden stands have been replaced by a cantilevered concrete stadium. Dusk had descended and the lights were on in the towers, flooding what I could see of the field, and the two ball clubs—St. Pete and Tampa in the Florida State League—were getting ready to play.

"Would you care for a drink?" the waitress said.

"Yes," I said, giving her my order.

"While I'm getting it," she said, "you can watch the game."

When Pete appeared at the Dodgers' camp in Clearwater in 1939 he had never been in a major league camp before. He didn't know that at batting practice you hit in rotation, and he was grabbing any bat that was handy and cutting in ahead of Ernie Koy and Dolph Camilli and the others, and that impressed Durocher.

One day the Dodgers were to bus down and play the Cardinals here at St. Pete. Leo was still playing some shortstop, but he had a chest cold and besides, it was St. Patrick's Day and Pete's twentieth birthday, so he told Pete to start in his place. His first time up on that field below me now—the way it used to be with those wooden stands and not the way it is today—he hit a homer off Ken Raffensberger, and that was the beginning. In exhibition games that spring he was on base his first twelve times at bat, with three homers, five singles, and four walks. His first time against Detroit he homered off Tommy Bridges, and his first time up again on that field so changed below me now, he put one over the fence off Lefty Gomez.

"I thought I'd get my social security before I got this drink," the waitress was saying when she finally brought it. "You enjoying the game?"

I could see all of the stands, with about fifty people in them, home plate, and all of the infield within a line running from just beyond first base into shallow left field. When I leaned toward the window I could see second base.

"It's just about to start," I said.

"I don't know who they are," the waitress said.

"They're minor leaguers," I said, "all of them dreaming about someday being major leaguers."

"I guess that's so," she said.

"And I don't know that any of them will make it," I said.

"Well," she said, "they've got their dreams."

"Yes," I said.

"And it's keeping them out of trouble," she said.

Having another drink and then my dinner I watched the start of the game. The turf was very green under the lights and the base paths a clean tan, and Tampa got a run on a walk and a double to right that was out of my view. With one out, and that man on second, the man at bat hit a line drive and, leaning toward the window, I could see the second baseman, who apparently had been holding the runner near the bag, spear it and then just reach down and tag the runner trying to get back, to complete the double play.

Watching what I could see of it down there while I ate, I kept thinking, of course, of Pete and of the days he had there and all the other days elsewhere, and who was now, thirty-eight years later, lying in that hospital bed just across town, paying the price for trying too hard and now having trouble breathing. The next morning I phoned him.

"How are you today?" I said.

"Much better," he said.

"Did the doctor see you after I left yesterday?"

"No," he said. "I don't know where the hell he is, but I'm gettin' out."

"Don't leave before you see the doctor," I said.

"I can't," he said. "I've got my clothes here, but they've got my wallet and all my credit cards locked in the safe."

"Good," I said.

Two nights later, from my home and as I had said I would, I called his home in California. His wife answered and said he was feeling better and, when he got on, he said the same thing.

"Then take it a little easier," I said.

"Yeah," he said. "I guess from now on, with everything I got wrong with me, I'll have to."

"Maybe," I wrote once, and I will stay with it, "Pete Reiser was the purest ballplayer of all time. I don't know. There is no exact way of measuring such a thing, but when a man of incomparable skills, with full knowledge of what he is doing, destroys those skills and puts his life on the line in the pursuit of his endeavor as no other man in his game ever has, perhaps he is the truest of them all."

17

I Remember, Mom

My mother is the kind of woman who can't stand to
see suffering and wants to help everybody.

Rocky Marciano, 1955

They came from Italy, Pierino Marchegiano from Ripiatitina, near
the Adriatic coast, and Pasqualena Picciuto from San Bartolomeo
in the south central hill country. They met in Brockton, Massachusetts, where they worked in shoe factories and they were married in 1921. Their first child, a thirteen-pound boy, died at birth.
The second, a twelve-and-a-half-pound boy, to be christened
Rocco Francis, was born at one A.M. on September 1, 1923, and
as Rocky Marciano he became the heavyweight champion of the
world.

"I say to the doctor," Pasqualena Marchegiano told me once, "I
ask him, 'How much this cost?' He say 'Forty dollar.' I say, 'Well,
doctor, I give you cash.' He say, "Well, thirty-five dollar.'"

I went to see the doctor. His name was Josephat Phaneuf, and I
found him, invalided and gaunt, in a wheel chair in his own
ninety-four bed, red-brick Phaneuf Hospital.

"I remember a delivery at that time at 80 Brook Street," he
said. "I recall it was fairly difficult because of the size of the
baby."

This was in 1954, and he was sixty-six years old. As a general
practitioner in and around Brockton he had delivered 7,235 babies.

"Strangely," he said, "I have never seen him fight. A great

many of my patients talk about him, though, and when they do I say, 'I was the first one ever to hit him.'"

Six years before, I had stopped off one afternoon at the Catholic Youth Organization gym on West Seventeenth Street in New York to watch a fighter work out. I no longer remember who that fighter was, but there were a couple of heavyweights thumping each other in the ring. Charley Goldman was standing on the ring apron near one corner, leaning on the top rope and calling advice to the shorter of the two.

Charley was sixty-one years old. He had had an eighth-grade education and, as a bantamweight, more than four hundred fights. He was a little man, with a broken nose and one broken hand, and he was proud of his abdominal muscularity. Every now and then in one of the gyms or at a training camp he would get on the subject of conditioning, and he would take my right hand and press it there in front where the bottom of the rib cage meets the lower end of the sternum.

"Feel that?" he would say. "Hit me a punch there."

"Please, Charley," I would say. "I believe you."

"No," he would say. "Go ahead. Hit me."

Embarrassed, I would throw a right hand underneath, not really hard but harder than I would want anyone to throw one into me.

"Come on. Hit me harder," he would say and then, after I had complied, he would grin and say, "You see? Not bad for a fella my age."

He trained five world champions, four of them for an avaricious man named Al Weill, and he was a teacher. In fact, in my seventeen years of formal schooling I knew only four other teachers I would put up there in the same class with Charley.

"You watched that fella in the ring?" he said to me that afternoon at the CYO after the two heavyweights had finished pounding each other. He nodded over toward the corner where the shorter of the two was punching the heavy bag.

"Yes," I said.

"What do you think of him?"

"What do I think of him?" I said. "I don't know. From what I saw, I think he's just a strong, awkward kid."

"But he ain't a kid," Charley said. "He's twenty-five."

"Oh?" I said.

"Weill's got him," he said, "and he wants me to work with him. At my age, though, and startin' all over again with some guy who's twenty-five and all he don't know and has to be taught, I could be just wastin' my time."

"That's right," I said. "If you ask me, it's a real long shot."

"I'll tell you somethin', though," Charley said. "He can take a punch, and he can punch like hell. With the heavyweights we got around today, maybe that's all you need."

"Maybe," I said, "but I don't know, Charley."

"I'll introduce you," he said.

He walked over to where the fighter, wide-legged, was throwing heavy punches at the bag. He brought him back to me. The fighter's black curly hair and face and neck glistened with sweat, and it had soaked through his white T-shirt, graying it.

"This is Rocky Marciano," Charley said, "and this is Bill Heinz."

We shook hands, my right hand in his right glove, the fighter smiling.

"Bill's a sportswriter," Charley said.

"Is that so?" the fighter said, smiling again.

"Rocky and a buddy of his bum down from Brockton, Massachusetts, on the trucks," Charley said. "They stay in the 'Y' for $1.50 a night."

"That's right," the fighter said.

"Well, you're with a real good man here in Charley," I said.

"I know that," the fighter said.

"You listen to him," I said, "and do what he tells you."

"Oh, I do," the fighter said.

"Yeah, he does," Charley said, and then to the fighter, "You can go back to the bag now."

"I'm pleased to have met you," the fighter said.

"I'm pleased to have met you, too," I said, "and good luck."

"Thank you," he said.

We watched him walk back to the bag and set his feet and start punching again.

"Who knows?" Charley said.

I didn't. I saw a lot of the fighter and Charley after that, and one night four years later I sat in what was then called the Municipal Stadium in Philadelphia and I watched the fighter, with one right hand punch, knock out Jersey Joe Walcott in the thirteenth round in one of the greatest of all title fights and win the heavyweight championship of the world.

That was why I was talking with Dr. Josephat Phaneuf. I was putting together a magazine piece about the impact upon Brockton, twenty miles due south of Boston, of that right-hand punch. The year before, Brockton had exported 12,384,378 pairs of shoes, and I went into the shoe factories where, in the executive offices, salesmen told me that coming from a champion's town gave them access throughout the country to buyers whose doors had been closed to them before. I checked with television dealers whose sales had gone up since Marciano's fights had begun to be shown on TV, and with repair men whose clients demanded impossible guarantees that their sets would not malfunction during a fight. I visited loan offices where Marciano's supporters signed for monies they bet on his fights, and I traced the profits of some of those wagers to automobile salesmen who told me of customers who had started out with near wrecks and were now driving new Buicks, and Oldsmobiles, and even Cadillacs.

I went, of course, into the home of Pierino and Pasqualina Marchegiano at 168 Dover Street, where they had moved with their three sons and three daughters when Marciano was eleven. They lived in five immaculate rooms on the first floor of the two-family green-shingled house across the street from the James Edgar Playground where the fighter had played baseball and dreamed of some day being a big league catcher.

Allie Colombo took me there, as he led me elsewhere around Brockton. He had been a boyhood friend of Marciano's, the one who, as Charley Goldman had said that first day, used to bum to New York on trucks with the fighter, and he helped train him and he worked in his corner. I had come to know him in the training camps at the Long Pond Inn and then at Grossinger's as an intelligent, perceptive young man who found the consequences of his close friend's rise to the heavyweight championship not only gratifying but highly amusing.

"You know Pop," he said, driving me to the Marchegiano home then.

"Of course," I said.

I had seen him around the camps, a rather short, frail, bespectacled, quiet man in his late fifties, his close-cropped black hair turning gray. After he had come to this country in his teens and gone to work in the shoe factory, he had fought in World War I at Chateau-Thierry and elsewhere and been wounded by shrapnel and gassed.

"Have you met Mom?" Allie asked.

"No," I said.

"They're a great pair," Allie said, chuckling, "and you'll love Mom. After Rocky started knocking guys out in his fights in Providence, the press started to come around. Rock's built like Mom, you know, so they'd take a look at little Pop and they'd look at her, and you could see them thinking, 'Oh, she's the one. That's where Rocky gets it.' So they'd all talk to Mom.

"Then Rocky started training in camp, and Pop came along. Now the press was all interviewing Pop, and Mom would read it. So one day there was a phone call for Pop at the Long Pond and it was Mom."

He was chuckling again.

"She said, 'Hey! When you come home?' He said, 'I can't come home.' She said, 'What you mean, you can't come home? You a husband and a father, and you supposed to be home.' So Pop said, 'I gotta help Rocky.' She said, 'What you do to help Rocky?' Pop said, 'I carry the pail and I carry the towel.' She said, 'You carry the pail and you carry the towel? Rocky got Allie, and he got Charley Gold to carry the pail and carry the towel. You come home.' So Pop went home."

He parked the car, still savoring his story, in front of the house. As we got out a mailman, the bag suspended from his left shoulder, had turned off the sidewalk toward the house.

"Hey, Red!" Colombo said, and then to me, "You got to meet this guy. He was a good shortstop, and he and Rocky went South together when they tried to make it with the Cubs' farm team."

He introduced me to Red Gormley. Standing across the street from that James Edgar Playground where he, too, had dreamed of being a big leaguer, Gormley told how they had been released by the Fayetteville, North Carolina, farm club of the Cubs and then had gone to Goldsboro, where they were also let go.

"Our arms were gone," he said. "We couldn't throw. We were broke, and I guess we looked like a couple of bums, so we decided to come home. A guy picked us up in an old car. Rocky got in front and we were driving along and Rocky turned to me and he said, 'The heck with it. I'm through with baseball. I'm gonna get some fights, and you're gonna handle me.'

"There I was," Gormley said, "sitting right next to half the money in the world, and I didn't know it."

He hitched the mail sack higher on his shoulder and started up the steps of 168 Dover Street. To that address now it had become his duty six days a week to deliver some of the mail that a heavyweight champion gets from around the world.

"So what's the sense of talking it?" he said, turning back to us. "I've got a wife and three kids now."

Allie Colombo took the mail from Gormley and we went into the house. It was early afternoon, and Pop was in the living room. We shook hands and Mom came out of the kitchen, a robust, blackhaired woman in whom I, like all the others, could immediately see her son the fighter, and by whose warmth I was immediately engulfed.

"You hungry?" she said to Allie, and then turning to me. "I fix you something to eat?"

"Oh, no," Allie said. "We just had lunch."

"You sure?" she said to me.

"I'm sure, but thank you," I said. "I just want to talk with you and Pop."

"Sure, we talk," she said. "We tell you what you want to know."

"Do you ever go back to the shoe factory?" I said to Pop. "I mean, just to visit with some of the workers you know?"

"Sometimes I go back," he said. "Not much."

For years, with the nails in his mouth and using both hands and both feet, he had run a Number 5 bedlaster. It formed the toes and heels of the shoes, and Marciano had told me that the shoe workers claimed it took more out of a man than any other machine. Two years before, at the age of fifty-eight and suffering from a respiratory ailment attributed to his war experience, Pop had retired.

"Now I go back," he said, "and I see my old friends and everybody say, 'What a difference, Pete. Years ago you couldn't talk with the super, and now he take you around the shop.'"

"I'll bet," I said. "Now you're the father of the heavyweight champion of the world."

"In the shop they have the shoe," he said. "There's something wrong with the shoe. These are good shoe, but they don't try to sell these shoe because they have some little thing wrong. Every year they sell these shoe cheap to the worker. Every year I work there I go to old Lucey, and I tell him I want to buy a pair of these shoe."

"Luce," Mom said. "He manage the shop."

"And every year," Pop said, "old Lucey he tell me, 'We no got your size, Pete.'"

"That's right," Mom said.

"Now every time I go," Pop said, "you know what they do? They measure the feet!"

I looked over at Allie Colombo, and he was laughing. That got me to laughing too, and I looked at Pop and he was serious, just contemplating it.

"What I'd like to do, Pop," I said, "is see where you used to work. I don't want to put you out, but do you think you could take us to the factory and show us?"

"You want to go to the shop?" Pop said.

"Sure," Mom said. "You take Beel and Allie. Beel, he's a friend of Rocky now, too, and he wants to see where you used to work."

"So," Pop said.

He got up and left the room, and when he came back he was carrying an obviously new, light gray topcoat. When he started to put it on Colombo got up and helped him into it.

"You notice that?" Colombo said, turning to me, and he was chuckling again. "You see how Pop just shrugged his shoulders then, kind of hiked the coat up? After the Rock knocks those guys out, I climb up into the ring with the robe. After I help him into it, he shrugs just like Pop did, as if to say, 'Okay. Let's go.'"

"So when you come back from the shop," Mom said, "then you hungry. Then you eat with us. Yes?"

"Fine," I said. "I would like that."

He led us through the shop, and everywhere they turned from the machines to greet him and shake his hand and clap him on the back and ask him about Rocky. Then the word must have spread to the front office, because one of them came out and led us in there and introduced me to another. I no longer remember their names or the positions they held, but I told them what I was doing in Brockton.

"Well," one of them said, "we're not interested in any publicity or any advertising."

"Good," I said, the ire popping up in me like a cork, "because you're not going to get any from me. I'm not in publicity, and to get any advertising in the magazine you have to buy it. I'm a reporter, and all I'm interested in is Pete here, and where he used to work."

"Well," he said, "all we care about is Pete, too."

I know, I was thinking. In all those years he worked here you never could fit him with a pair of shoes, and his son, now the heavyweight champion of the world, once told me how, during the summer and on school holidays, he used to carry his father's lunch to the shop. He saw how his father had to work and he saw the money he brought home, and he told me he resolved then that he would never go into the shoe shops.

I have forgotten what we talked about for the next few minutes. As we were walking toward the car, though, Allie Colombo was chuckling again

"What's got to you now?" I said.

"You," he said. "I wish Rocky could have heard you lay that on them in there about the publicity and Pop."

"I hope I didn't embarrass Pop," I said.

"Pop's all right," Allie said. "Right, Pop?"

"What?" Pop said.

Allie let Pop and me out at the house, and we talked for a while in the living room while Mom prepared dinner. Peter, the youngest of their six children, was thirteen then, and it was while the four of us ate that Mom told, when I asked her, about the birth of the eldest son at 80 Brook Street and about Dr. Phaneuf.

"I'd like to go and see him," I said.

"He's not well," she said, "but you go see him. He remember, and he tell you. You see, I lose my first baby. The doctor say, 'You gonna have no more baby,' I cry. After a while I say, 'If God want me to have baby, and if God give me children, I gonna do the best I can.'

"All I want is to keep my house clean. I keep my children clean, I make my supper. Always at breakfast I tell my children, 'Now try your best in school.' I tell them the same like when they go to church.

"Now it's just sit in my heart," she said. "It's hard to say the beautiful thing that happen with Rocky. You feel happy, and you feel like crying when you think."

"A heavyweight champion," I said, "has an influence on the lives of a lot of people. All over this town I guess you meet people who have a special feeling for Rocky."

"I don't go downtown," Pop said. "Too much talk."

"I don't go but one day a week," Mom said. "Last week I went to post office and there is a big line and I wait, and a man I don't know say to me, 'How is our boy?' I say, 'Fine.' He say, 'You know, we're very proud of him down at the Cape.' Then he introduce his wife and his sister. Who is this man?

"I walk on the street and a woman come up to me. She say, 'God bless you, Mrs. Marchegiano. My son and my son-in-law they make a fortune on your boy. I tell no one, but I tell you because I want to thank you.' Who is this woman?

"I go in a store. In the store the man say, 'If you need credit, Mrs. Marchegiano, you get credit. Your son make a lot of money for us.' I go to Rocky's house and I see a letter there from someone who wants his picture. I bring it home and I look at the letter and I say that God been so good to my son to give this beautiful luck, why can't I give to people who like my son? So I send these poor people the picture. Sometimes I cry."

After dinner Peter and I helped clear the dining room table, but Mom said she would rather do the dishes alone.

"You talk," she said. "You sit and talk."

At the kitchen table Pop, with two saucers in front of him, was slowly and carefully peeling an apple. Peter and I sat down with him, watching him turning the apple in one hand, the peel curling over the knife in the other. He put the peels in one saucer, and then he cut a half dozen slices from the peeled apple and placed them in the other saucer and passed it first to me and then to Peter.

I asked Peter what it was like for him, being the brother of the heavyweight champion, and if he found it difficult to concentrate in school on a day when his brother would fight that night. He said that on the day of the second Marciano-Walcott fight, the science teacher had announced a test.

"Then he asked me," Peter said, "if I thought I could take it. I said, 'I'm afraid I can't today.' Then he let me take it the next day."

As the three of us talked, there were long pauses in our conversation. There was just the quiet in the room and throughout the house, with none of the conversational clatter that clutters so many American homes, and with just the sound of Mom doing the dishes. At one point there were no more apple slices on the saucer.

"Cut me another slice of apple, Pop," Peter said. "Please?"

"What's the matter?" Pop said. "You old enough now. You know how to cut the apple."

"I know," Peter said, smiling, "but I like the way you do it."

Pop said nothing, just nodding. He began to slice the apple again and when, fifteen years later, I heard on the radio that a small private plane had crashed in Iowa and Rocky Marciano was dead, that scene in that quiet kitchen and what Mom had said there earlier and all it conveyed to me came first to mind. Now another eight years had passed, and I called Peter at the sporting goods store he owns in Mansfield, just west of Brockton.

"You sound just like your brother," I said, startled by his voice. There was not only the same broad 'a', but the same cadence—the same level and the same rhythm—and it was as if I were talking to his brother.

"I know," he said. "Everybody says that."

"How are you and your folks?" I said.

"Pop died three years ago," he said, "but Mom is fine. She's living with my sister Alice now."

"I'm sorry to hear about Pop," I said. "He was a shy and quiet man and a good man."

"You're right, he was," he said. "He was seventy-nine when he went."

I told him that I wanted to visit with Mom and him again, and three days later I drove to Mansfield. It was early afternoon when I got into the town and found the store. It occupied a single-story red-brick building on a corner, and when he came out of the office in the back I was startled once more.

"You not only sound like your brother," I said, as we shook hands, "but you look like him, too."

He was wearing chinos and a white T-shirt, his build the same as that of his brother, and his face split into the same smile.

"That's right," he said, "but I'm a little heavy right now."

Not certain how long it would take me to drive to Mansfield, I had arrived more than an hour early. He said that he had some work to finish, and I went out and, following his directions, found a diner. When I returned he was still busy in the back room, and he introduced me to the two young women working with him and then I waited in the front of the store amid the baseball gloves and bats, the baseballs, basketballs, footballs, and soccer balls, the boxing gloves, track shoes, tennis rackets, fishing poles, and fishing lures.

Several times he came out to serve customers. One was a woman who wanted a baseball glove for her son, had no idea what position he played and said she would return another day. Two young men were comparison shopping for jogging shoes, and there was a father who led in his son seeking a baseball glove. The boy was about eight or nine, and it was as if he were silenced by finding himself in a shrine. The father tried to bring the boy into it, asking him his opinion of one glove after another as they tried them on him, but the boy was elevated beyond opinions. When the father finally settled on one, the boy walked out ahead of him, the new glove on his left hand, and on his face a small smile and a faraway look that, I presumed, was now reaching as far as Fenway Park.

"Gee, I'm sorry," Peter said, after the two had left. "I didn't know I was going to be so tied-up."

"That's all right," I said. "I'm in no hurry."

"My sister Alice is bringing Mom over to our place for dinner, and we can talk then. I have to deliver some bats at the high school in Brockton, though."

"That's fine," I said.

I followed him in my car and parked it in front of his split level in one of Brockton's newer residential areas. I got into his station wagon and we started for the high school.

"How's the business going?" I said.

"Real good," he said, "I started it in '73 and I sell Brown University, and I've probably got a hundred schools and colleges."

"Do I remember that you played some professional baseball?"

"Right," he said. "Three years in the Milwaukee Braves farm system, but I didn't make it."

"That was a big disappointment?"

"Very much so," he said. "Like a ton of bricks. You feel as though you're as good as anybody there, but you look around and see guys who can run faster than you, hit the ball better than you, and do everything better than you. The one thing that kept me going was the love of baseball, like Rocky must have loved boxing.

"I said to myself, 'Should I go home and tell everybody?' I wanted to lie about it, but I figured if I told the truth, I'd be better off in the long run. My dad always told me, 'Tell the truth, and you can't go bad.' Rocky was one in a million, because he never had to make excuses. How do you follow forty-nine straight fights and never lose a fight? It's very difficult."

"But Rocky didn't make it in baseball either," I said. "Boxing saved him. Did you ever want to be a fighter?"

"I boxed in college," he said. "At the University of Miami. I was successful. I loved it next to baseball, and I won a championship. I knocked out two of my opponents in college, but I don't know, I didn't go into it."

"You had a college education, and you didn't have the economic hunger your brother had."

"That's it," he said. "I didn't have to do it. Rocky's answer was that you always have to be hungry."

The Brockton High School is an example of architectural cubism, a huge gray-white rectangular block, the upper stories overhanging the first, and we drove down off the road and around one side of it. He parked the car and got out and opened a rear door and picked up the half dozen bats that were on the back seat.

"I'll be back in a couple of minutes," he said.

Beyond, and down a slight slope, I could see part of the stadium, the back of the concrete stand, and part of the field and the running track bordering it. There were two yellow school buses in the parking space near the stand, some students standing by them.

"When was all this built?" I asked him when he came back.

"In 1970," he said, "right after Rocky died. Armond Colombo, a cousin of Allie's, is married to my sister Betty, and he coaches football here. In '70, when they named the field Rocky Marciano Stadium, they won every game they played. It was like someone was directing the show."

He had started the car, and he drove slowly around the side of the school and back onto the road. He stopped at the side of the road where we could look down the length of the field, with the concrete stand on one side and, across the football field, the wooden bleachers. There were some runners in warm-up clothes jogging around the track bordering the field and clusters of others here and there. Facing the road was the sign: ROCKY MARCIANO STADIUM. Centered under the sign, resting on the turf, was a large boulder.

"You see the rock there?" he said. "The teams are now called the Boxers, and the mascot is a boxer dog, Rocky. They also have a Rocky Marciano room in the city museum."

"It's an impressive memorial," I said.

"Yes, it is," he said.

"When he went," I said, "I naturally thought immediately of your folks and of you. How did you hear about it?"

"I'm glad you asked that now," he said. "When we get to the house I'd rather that you didn't ask Mom. She took it real hard."

"I presumed that," I said. "That's why I asked now. What was he doing in a private plane in Iowa at night?"

"It was sort of a business-pleasure thing," he said, "He was flying from Chicago to Des Moines. The next day was his birthday, September first."

"I had forgotten that."

"He was going to be forty-six. They crashed about 10:30. I was woke up by Mom, who was home alone with my Dad. It was about 1:30 or 2 A.M. She woke me up screaming on the phone. She kept repeating, *'Figlio mio, cuore di mama!'* I understood what she was saying, but immediately I thought of my dad, because it's a kind of idiom in the Italian language. It means, 'My son, heart of my life.' I still had my dad in mind, though, because he wasn't well.

"I said, 'Mom, please settle down.' But she kept repeating, *'Figlio mio, cuore di mama!'* I said, 'Mom, what's happened there?" She said, 'Your brother was killed in a plane crash!' I have another brother—Louis."

"I know."

"I jumped in my car and this close friend, Henry Tartaglia, came up. He said. 'Do you know what's happening? Have you heard anything? I heard that Rocky Marciano or Rocky Graziano was killed in a plane crash.' I said, 'I hope it's Graziano.' Hank drove me over and we went into the house, and then the phone calls started coming and the reporters and so on."

"I hope this isn't going to upset Mom," I said. "I mean my coming back after all these years and reviving memories of Rocky."

"Oh, no," he said. "Mom's all right now, and she'll be glad to see you."

He put the car in drive, and we started along the road.

"As you know," I said, "when Rocky was training at Grossinger's, Mom would be there some of the time, and she called it 'The Grossinge.' She didn't eat her desserts, so she'd carry them over to the cottage and she kept them in the refrigerator. She'd say, 'Beel, you get hungry tonight you come over and you have a piece of pie, piece of cake.'"

"That sounds like Mom," he said.

"Her heart was always going out to the acts that appeared in the night club on the lower level there. There was this dance team that I think she wanted to adopt. She said to me one night, 'Oh, Beel, they such a lovely young couple. They dance so nice, and they have this lovely baby. It's so hard for them to make a living. Why don't you write something about them, Beel?'"

"That's Mom all right," he said.

"Your mom and Rocky and Allie Colombo used to tease your pop about Charley Goldman. You know what a gnarled, little old guy Charley was, and your mom would say to your pop, 'You go to bed tonight, because I have a date with the Charley Gold. We go to the club and we dance.' Allie used to chuckle about that as he did about so many things. There was so much that amused him in life."

"I know," he said.

"At the time that I spent about a week here in Brockton," I said, "Allie was starting another heavyweight. One night he had him on a fight card in a place over a pool hall somewhere here in town."

"I know the place."

"I went along, and Allie's guy knocked out the other guy in a couple of rounds or so, but he was just a strong earnest beginner. As we walked out in the dark to the car Allie was chuckling again. I said, 'What are you laughing at now?' He said, 'I was just thinking that this guy may go all the way, too.' I had to laugh, too, because it was ridiculous. He'd had only one other fighter in his life, but that one went all the way, and now Allie thought that lightning would strike twice."

"That was the way Allie was."

"Of course, your brother didn't look like anything either when he started."

"That's what everybody thought."

"That's what I thought, and I as much as told Charley Goldman that in the CYO gym in New York. Charley wouldn't train Rocky in Stillman's because Rocky was so awkward that Charley was afraid people would laugh at him and discourage him."

"They'd never discourage Rocky," Peter said.

"I know," I said, "but anyway, a few months after I'd met your brother at the CYO I saw Charley one afternoon in Stillman's, and I said to him, 'How's that fella who bums down on the trucks from Brockton doing?' Charley said, 'He's knockin' out guys, but he scares me.' I said, 'Why?' He said, 'Because of his stance. The way his stance is, he gets hit with too many punches, but I'm afraid if I change his feet I might take something off his own punch.' "

"Charley said that?"

"He did," I said, "and that's where Rocky was so lucky. He could have fallen into the hands of any one of dozens of guys who call themselves trainers, but who would have changed his stance and ruined him. Charley altered it gradually without taking anything off the punch."

"That's interesting."

I could have told him, but I didn't, about an afternoon at the Long Pond Inn when Charley had Marciano sparring with Nino Valdez, the big Cuban. Marciano was forcing the going, as he always did, and Valdez was just moving around, sticking out his left hand, and with his right glove high, he was blocking Marciano's left hooks.

"Look, Rock," Charley said to him at the end of one round. "You got to learn to move both ways. You got to practice moving to the right the same way you move to your left. Work on it."

Marciano nodded and turned and started walking the ring, waiting for the next round to start. Charley turned to me.

"Watch what happens," he said. "He'll throw a punch off that move, and he'll land with it."

The next round started, and Marciano began to work on it. Suddenly, after a move to his right, he leaned back to his left and he threw the left hook, and it landed on the big Cuban's jaw, inside his high right hand, and it shook him.

"Time!" Charley shouted and then, feigning excitement, he said to Marciano, "You see what you did, Rock? You just discovered somethin'. When you punch off that move to your right you can get that hook inside the glove. That's great, Rock."

The two went back to sparring, with Charley watching them. Then he turned to me again.

"You see?" he said. "If I told him how to do that, he'd forget it.

If I showed him, he might remember it. Now he thinks he discovered something new, all by himself, and he'll never forget it."

There is an ancient Chinese proverb but, of course, Charley had never heard of it, "I hear and I forget. I see and I remember. I do and I understand."

Several months later, in Yankee Stadium, I watched Marciano throw that hook off that move and knock out Harry Kid Matthews, my old friend Jack Hurley's fighter. Off that fight they matched Marciano with Walcott for the heavyweight championship of the world.

"So Rocky was lucky when Allie took him to Al Weill," I was saying to Peter now. "Nobody ever said Al Weill was a nice guy, but he had Charley training for him, and he knew how to move a fighter. There were a few other good teachers still around then—Ray Arcel and Whitey Bimstein and Jack Hurley—but he needed Weill, and his connections in the fight game too."

"You're probably right," he said.

"So Charley died the year before Rocky," I said. "Then Allie went, and when Weill died I realized that the whole corner had gone, all within a few years."

"Allie was killed just before Rocky," he said.

"Oh?" I said. "It was in a car accident, wasn't it?"

"No," he said. "After Rocky retired, Allie had some hard times, and he was working nights at a warehouse. He was walking along by the loading platform when a truck backed up and crushed him."

I could feel myself cringing.

"That's awful," I said. "Terrible."

"And Barbara's gone," he was saying. "She died three years ago of cancer."

Barbara Cousins was the daughter of a Brockton policeman. Al Weill, trying to possess the fighter totally, had opposed Marciano's marriage to her, and with the fighter away in camp and on personal appearance tours so much of the time, it was never an easy one.

"And their daughter?" I said.

"Mary Anne?" he said. "She lives in Florida."

"I remember her when she was about four years old," I said.

"There was a swing in the yard of the house they had here, and one afternoon I must have pushed her on that swing for an hour, waiting for Rocky."

"She's about twenty-four now," he said, "and we've been in touch with her, trying to find Rocky's money."

"Trying to what?" I said.

"Trying to find his money," he said. "We don't know what he did with all his money."

The total of Marciano's purses as a fighter came close to $1,500,000. Weill's end and expenses must have cut that in half, and there were the taxes. After the fighter retired, though, there was the $80,000 I got him for his life story, and there was the $1,500 here and the $2,000 there that he picked up regularly for personal appearances.

"You mean that no one knows where the money is?" I said. "He was the closest guy with a buck I ever knew. He never spent anything."

"I know," he said. "That's the thing. We figure that it's got to be somewhere, but Rocky was a very mysterious guy. He never trusted attorneys, banks, or anyone with his money but himself."

"You mean you think he kept it all in cash?"

"That's right," he said. "You see the two families—Barbara's and ours—were never very close. After Rocky died and there wasn't any money, I guess they thought we knew where it was and we kind of thought they knew. After Barbara died, Mary Anne was sort of suspicious of us at first, but she trusts us now, trying to find it."

"This amazes me," I said.

"Mom used to ask him about the money," he said. "He'd always say, 'Don't worry, Mom.' Some may have been stolen by some lawyer, but we think that Rocky literally buried his money."

He had slowed the car slightly, and he nodded across the road. A man, his head bald in back, was raking leaves in the sideyard of a frame house.

"You see that fella there?" he said. "He set a precedent in the United States. He was brought to court as a male prostitute, and it went all the way to the Supreme Court. It was what they call a . . . a . . ."

"Landmark case?"

"Right," he said.

"But you think the money may actually be buried?" I said.

"In the soil somewhere," he said, "but we don't know where to look."

"And it's a big country," I said.

"Right," he said. "We've tried to figure out everywhere he went and where he stayed in people's houses and where he may have hidden it."

"That's amazing," I said, because I couldn't think of what else to say.

He had pulled up in front of the house and we went in. His wife, Linda, slim and blonde and blue-eyed, met us in the living room and he introduced me and then led me into the kitchen where Mom was standing at the range, stirring something in a pot.

"Mom," he said, "you remember Bill."

She turned, at seventy-five the same sturdy woman. She was wearing a black, short-sleeved dress, glasses with hexagonal frames, and her hair had only partially grayed. She was searching my face as we shook hands.

"Oh, now I remember your face," she said. "Now I remember you, Bill."

"You used to call me Beel," I said.

"That's right," she said, smiling. "Bill."

We each remarked how well the other looked. She said we would be eating soon, and Peter made a drink for me and one for himself. I met the children, three boys then ten, seven, and five, and the girl then eight, and Peter and I sat down in the living room.

"On the way here," I said, "we were agreeing how close Rocky was with his money. Shortly before he retired I drove him from here into Boston one afternoon. I forget why we went, but the next day he was going to appear at the opening of a supermarket in Rochester, New York, and we had planned to drive back here again for the night. Around six o'clock he said he wanted to drop in at Somerset Hotel. There were five or six guys there who, he said, were well-to-do business men or contractors or whatever. He said they called themselves 'The Jolly Ps.'"

Peter was nodding, indicating that he had heard of them.

"Rocky said that once a month they'd do something together. Maybe it would be just a night in Boston or maybe it would be a weekend hunting or fishing trip, and we dropped in on them in a suite at the Somerset. They had plates of hors d'oeuvres and drinks, and we sat around with them for a while. Then Rocky and I went to dinner at some restaurant where the owner knew him. From there we went to another place where we picked up Frank Fontaine, the comedian, and from there we went to another spot where there was a show. Wherever we went we were on the house. Rocky wasn't springing, and he wouldn't let me."

"That's the way he was," Peter said, smiling and nodding.

"About midnight I told him we either had to start back for Brockton or get a room, so we decided to get a room. We went into a hotel—I've forgotten the name—and walked up to the desk and I told the clerk what we wanted. He turned the register around for me and handed me a pen. I was just about to sign us in when your brother said, 'Wait. Don't sign that. I know where we can get a room for free. It won't cost us anything. We can go back to the Somerset, and those guys will be leaving soon and we can sleep there.' I said, 'Look, Rock. I'll pay for it, so let's stay here.' 'No,' he said, and he took the pen out of my hand and handed it back to the desk clerk.

"When we got back to the suite the guys were still there. The place was full of cigar smoke, the ash trays were full and what was left of the hors d'oeuvres looked like animal leavings."

Peter was laughing now.

"So Rocky said to them, 'You fellas won't be using the beds in there, so do you mind if Bill and I sack out?' They said it was all right with them, so we went into the bedroom. Your brother went right to sleep, but I lay there listening to the laughter in the sitting room and finding it hard to believe I was in a situation like this with the heavyweight champion of the world.

"Finally, about two or three in the morning, I heard our hosts leaving and the door slam. Rocky had left a call for eight o'clock, but when we got up and I walked into the bathroom, there weren't any clean towels. All of them, bath towels and all, had been used and most of them were on the floor. After we washed, we dried our faces and hands with toilet paper."

Peter was laughing again.

"Now we go out to the car, figuring we'll get breakfast at the airport. I remember it was a beautiful sunny morning, and we're just about to get into the car when we hear a voice hollering, 'Hey Rock!' We look up at the hotel and your brother says, 'It's Ted! It's Ted Williams! We can get breakfast with him. Let's go up.'

"Up we go. Ted asked if he could order breakfast for us, and I was so embarrassed that I declined. Rocky had orange juice, a couple of eggs, toast and coffee, and he had no sooner finished that when he asked Ted if he could use his razor. Ted told him to go right ahead, so he shaved with Ted Williams' razor, and I drove him to the airport where he took off to open the supermarket at noon in Rochester, New York."

"That's the way he was," Peter said. "In a way he was peculiar, because he was different with all kinds of people."

"I can believe that," I said. "In fact, I know it."

"He never wanted to offend anybody."

"How well I know," I said. "One night in Boston, he and Allie and I drove out to the airport to pick up someone. Allie said, 'You don't want this guy, Rock.' Rocky said, 'I know.' So Allie said, 'Then tell him.' Rocky said, 'I don't want to hurt his feelings.' Allie said, 'The hell with his feelings.' And Rocky said, 'You see, I don't mind knocking a guy out in the ring, but I don't like to hurt anyone's feelings.'"

Peter was nodding again.

"You know how he was in the ring," I said. "He was a destroyer, and they used to say that you'd have to kill him to get him out of there. After he became champ, and he was in camp or traveling around the country, he used to send post cards to guys he'd knocked out on the way up. They were house painters or carpenters or whatever now, and he'd inquire how they were and wish them well, and some of them corresponded with him."

"I know that," Peter said.

Mom called us to dinner. The children had already eaten and we four sat down.

"So eat now the *pasta e piselli*," Mom said to me. We had the spaghetti and peas, meat loaf, and tossed salad. We had red wine, and I complimented Linda and Mom.

"My father was a real good cook," Peter said. He was looking at me and he winked, and then he looked at Mom.

"Sure, but I teach him," Mom said.

"Come on," Peter said, winking at me again. "Pa told me he taught *you*. He said you couldn't boil water."

"What you say?" Mom said, looking at Peter and then getting it. "You just talk."

"I know Mom's a great cook," I said, "because I had dinner one night at 168 Dover Street. Pop was good at peeling apples, though. After dinner, at the kitchen table, he peeled an apple and cut it up for us."

"That's right," Peter said. "I always liked when he did that."

"Too many memories in that house," Mom said to me, "through Rocky's career and in that park. For four years after Rocky pass away I no good. I give too much trouble my kids. After four years, with my faith, I even had to go to psychiatrist, and then my husband pass away. Fifty-two years together. It took me four years get over my Rocky, and my husband I over in one year, but I love him very much."

"I know," I said.

"A lot of people they miss Rocky," she said. "Some people call me regular. Steve Melchiore, the Rock's bodyguard from Philadelphia. He say, 'How are you, Mom?' They all miss Rocky, but I miss my husband, too. People used to say, 'Rocky, he look like his mother.' But I say, 'Look at the hands, like his father. The same frame.'

"When Rocky became champ, my husband he very shy, and Barbara she shy, too. When Rocky train in the Grossinger, and it be a big fight and I pray he no get hurt, all the people come. He come out and sweat, and he wants to get the shower. He say to the people, 'Why don't you go over there? My father tell you where I born and everything.' My husband see and walk away and I say, 'Somebody got to do the talking.' I did, and my daughter Alice and Peter."

I was remembering Allie Colombo's story of the press and Mom and Pop.

"My daughter Alice," Mom was saying, "for twenty-two years she answer all the letter, and in Italian I answer to Italy. I send the picture and make Rocky autograph it. I was going to be school teacher. My father wanted me to be, but I didn't want to go, and my father he was very upset. You talk about this letter answer in Italian, and in Italy I very small and in reading I understand very well, in writing not so good."

"How old were you when you came to this country?" I said.

"Maybe you can't write this, Bill," she said, "because he did a wrong thing, my father. My father say I sixteen when I fifteen. He was here, and when he send for me he wrote my mother to say that. On a Saturday me and my sister we land, and on Monday I have job in Millburn, New Jersey. I got a lot of people there from the old country."

"And what was the job?" I said.

"Making flannel nightgown," she said. "I used to make the buttonhole and then I make the puff. You know, the powder puff, and we make by hands. Then we went to New Rochelle, and we stay a little bit."

"What work did you do there?" I said.

"What I used to do there?" she said. "Wait a minute. The same thing. The nightgown in the factory. We move to Bridgeport, and we live over there about three years. I work in the bullets factory, and I don't know if you know. Was a big machine like this table. It go around, and it was a nice job."

"Was it at Remington Arms?" I said.

"That's right," she said. "Then I work where they make the corsets. Then I work in another factory, and a lot of people used to die. In this factory they used to carry this steel and they put it here and carry over there, and they call it The Butch Shop because so many people die. I had good job with this steel. All men and very few women. I had big surprise, when they give back pay. It was war time. You know?"

"World War One."

"Yes, and when I get $200, I don't know. It was so much

money and I give to my father. One time I open envelope to take ten cents, and he almost kill me. He send all the money to Italy, and then he send here my mother and one girl and three boys. We were six in family.

"Then there was electric factory, making all equipment for electricity. We used to make, what they call the mantles. You know?"

"Gas mantles?" I said, and then demonstrating, for I remember them. "A kind of mesh hood like this that, if you had gas lights, you lighted?"

"Yes," she said. "Gas, electricity, I don't know. It was combination. With the piece work I make the most, the fastest. The boss, he like me so much he bring the other girl, and I show what to do. Then we have accident in my family. It took my mother two months to come here. The boat almost sink with the many under water, and then my brother was eleven and he used to go on the tricycle."

"Scooter," Peter said.

"Yes," she said. "This big truck, it get my poor little brother. My mother couldn't talk English, and I had to go to St. Vincent Hospital in Bridgeport. He live three-four days. His name was Nicky—Peter Nicholas—and I name my Peter for him."

"I only mention this," Peter's wife, Linda, said, "because it ties in with the name, but I had a brother Richard who was killed in an accident."

"And now Peter's oldest boy is named Peter Richard," Mom said. "So right after the accident my father, my mother were broken-hearted, and we came away to here because they didn't want to live there no more."

"And then you went to work here?"

"Oh, yes, in shoe factory. They put the little ribbon around, especially the pumps, and I used to put it around, and they liked my work very much. We moved here in March, and in July I meet my husband."

"She never worked after they were married," Peter said.

"Oh, I work when I marry," she said. "Even when I have you I had night job. I nurse my kids all, and with Peter I go to work and only nurse seven months."

"You worked when you had the others too?" Peter said.

"Off and on, so my husband could be home with kids. And then in the war I make bullets in Hingham."

"Hingham, Massachusetts, in World War Two?" I said.

"Yes. Was good money there. There was danger. The powder they put in bullets, there was poison in. You used to break on the skin. In all my hair and my skin it broke out. I had to go to skin doctor, and for fifty-two week I got seventy dollar. They pay me good because they think I poisoned.

"Then Pop was working in shoe shop, and he was getting twenty-one dollar, twenty-five dollar and thirty-five dollars the most. At war time he made fifty, sixty dollars, but everything was cheap."

"And the work was hard," I said, "I'll always remember something Rocky told me one afternoon at Grossinger's, after he had won the title. We were sitting by the pool, and he said he had just made an appearance at a convention of shoe manufacturers in Boston. He said, 'When they introduced me I had to say something, and I don't know if I said the right thing or not, but I told them I used to go into the factory where my father worked and I saw how hard he had to work, and then I saw the pay he brought home. I said, 'One thing I was sure of was that I was never gonna go into the shoe factories, so I became a fighter, and you men are responsible for me being heavyweight champion of the world.' He asked me if that was all right. I said, 'All right? That was great!' "

"Everybody used to tell me when Rocky become champ," Mom said, "that it gonna hurt Peter, but I don't think so."

"Of course not," I said, looking across the table at Peter. "You have a fine son in Peter."

"When I was playing in Duluth," Peter said, "I was a good catcher—not a Johnny Bench—but I remember one foul-mouthed guy who said, 'It's Rocky's brother, but he's not an inch of his brother.' If I was John Smith's brother it would never have happened. You don't compete with a Rocky Marciano."

"When Rocky first started to fight," I said to Peter, "you were quite young. Do you have any early memories of what it was like having a brother who was starting out to be a fighter?"

"I sure have," he said, "in the kitchen at 168 Dover Street, when Rocky lost a fight to Coley Wallace in the amateurs. It was like a bad, bad dream in that kitchen. Mom was in church. She used to go before every fight he had."

"I remember," I said to Mom, "that later, on the nights when Rocky fought, a doctor used to pick you up and drive you around until the fight was over."

"That's right," she said.

"I had to be seven, eight years old," Peter was saying, "and it was the first time I knew Rocky was a fighter. Somebody said, 'Rocky lost the fight.' It was like the end of the world, and when Mom came in I told her that Rocky lost the fight, and she said, 'He may have lost, but he didn't get hurt.'"

"Always he shouldn't get hurt," Mom said.

"Were you in Philadelphia for the Walcott fight?" I asked Peter.

"I sure was," he said.

"It was some fight," I said. "Some sportswriters, who had seen them all, said it was the greatest heavyweight championship fight since Dempsey and Firpo, and some time later I said to Rocky, 'When Walcott knocked you down with that left hook in the first round, it was the first time you were ever down. What were you thinking when you found yourself on the deck?' He said, 'I was thinking, 'Boy, this guy can really hit. This is gonna be some fight.' And it was."

"I was sitting with a priest in the tenth row ringside," Peter said. "Father McKenzie, and how many times he's been in my house. Father kept saying, 'Keep praying, Peter.' I said, 'No, I got to leave. I don't want to see my brother get beat up.' I left one time, and he brought me back."

Mom was silent. She was just sitting there, looking at her hands folded on the table.

"You tired, Mom?" Peter said. "Do you want to go home?"

"No," she said, straightening up. "I want to talk with Bill."

"Okay," Peter said, smiling. "I just don't want you to get tired."

"When Rocky ten, eleven year old," she said, "he come home from school. I used to make my own bread. He look, and I said, 'What you look?' He said, 'You work all the time.' I say, 'Why don't you help? Wash the dish.' So he took the cloth and he go like this. He make one slap with it and put it down, and I said,

'What you do?' He said, 'You got the daughter. When they come home from school, let them wash the dish.'

"Then he say, 'What be your wish if I make a lot of money?' I say, 'Rocky, we got nice home, not big but clean.' He say, 'What you like if I make a lot of money? What? You see my arm? I got a lot of strength in my arm. I make a lot of money. What you like to do?' I said, 'I like to travel when my family grow up.' Then he become champ, a big shot, and he send me to Italy."

"I remember that," I said. "You and Pop went over, and it was a great disappointment. You went to Pop's town and everybody wanted money, so you never went to your town."

"Rocky, he give me three, four thousand dollar," she said, nodding. "We should stay three month, but we stay twenty-one days. Too much sadness there. Everybody expect, expect."

"That saddened Rocky, too," I said. "A heavyweight champion is the one athlete who is known and looked up to all over the world, and in Italy, where his parents came from, they wanted money."

"Not everybody want," she said. "We got letter—I threw away now—from Japan, everywhere. They write, 'He's unusual boy. We don't write you because he big shot, but because of what he is. Some people they champ, but nothing else, but that's why we write you, the mother and the father.'"

"And I'm sure," I said, "that letters like that made you and Pop proud."

"Then everywhere he go," she said, "Rocky he leave things. I get package from Waldorf Astoria. Shoes, shirt. I used to thought it was something for me. I say to him, 'I used to teach you, you not like that.' He said, 'When I young boy you used to teach me to try this, do that. But now I got to be the real Rocky. That's why they call me that.' Some people they honest. They send you, and they say, 'Rocky was in this room.' Some people they take."

"It's so odd," Linda said, "how Rocky wanted to make it big since he was a small child. Others would dress to it, but not him."

"He was what he was," Peter said.

We talked on, and at one point Mom got up and left the room and came back with her wallet. From it she took some photographs of Rocky, in one of which he was with Muhammad Ali, and when we all got up from the table I thanked Linda and then Mom.

"So many memories, Bill," she said. "So much to talk."

"But good memories, Mom," I said, "and I shall always remember you and Pop."

"And you give my best to your wife and your daughter," she said.

Peter and I walked out to our cars. He was to lead me to the motel where I had a reservation, and we shook hands.

"I hope it was all right," I said. "I hope I didn't . . ."

"Oh, no," he said. "It's eight years now. For a time it was rough, but it's good for her to talk now. Now Mom lives for one thing, the beautiful memories of Rocky."

"And good luck with the sporting goods business," I said. "I'm really impressed by how well you're doing."

"I'm doing real well," he said. "It really surprises me how well it's going."

"And who knows?" I said. "Maybe you'll find what Rock did with his money."

"Who knows?" he said. "We've sure been giving it a try, and we'll keep on trying."

When he was champion they ran at him with all kinds of schemes. They wanted him to sign notes for them or lend them money outright or sponsor them on singing or acting careers. One of them wanted to start a band, and another he had never heard of wanted him to go halves with him in a night club in Buffalo. They tried to get him into uranium and copper and oil wells, a dairy and a home-oil route, but following the red tail lights of Peter's car I closed my mind to that. There was nothing to think about, and I was remembering Mom.

18

The Same Person Twice

At first, there is a single fertilized egg. Life then begins as it does for any ordinary child, but some time between the first and tenth day after conception and for reasons that are beyond the ken of science, the egg separates. The forty-six chromosomes perform what has been described as "the dance of life." Each divides precisely in half, and now two eggs continue to grow in the womb. In each egg all the hereditary factors—forty-six chromosomes bearing an estimated fifty thousand genes—are going to be exactly alike. The result is the same person twice.

Bard Lindeman,
The Twins Who Found Each Other

There were these twins, Castor and Pollux. They were sons of Zeus, and before my time, but the one, Pollux, was a boxer. What I know of them I got from Theocritus, who lived in the third century B.C. and is regarded as the creator of pastoral poetry, and who, in *The Dioscuri*, left a stirring account of Pollux flattening a burly giant, who, it has seemed to me, was misnamed Amycus. Today Castor and Pollux sit in the heavens as the twin stars of the constellation Gemini.

In my time, Charles Cartier, a New York advertising salesman, had three sons. The two younger are identical twins, and during the early 1950s one of them, Walter, was a ranking middleweight fighter, and the other, Vincent, was a young lawyer. Since the days of the mythologists, identical twins have fascinated their fellow man—particularly geneticists and psychologists in more recent years—and Walter and Vincent Cartier fascinated me.

I met them first in 1949. Vincent, the lawyer, was waiting to hear if he had passed the bar examination. Walter, the fighter, was waiting to fight, two nights later in New York's St. Nicholas Arena, a young puncher named Vinnie Cidone.

"Which one of you," I said to them, "was born first?"

This was in one of the dressing rooms at Stillman's Gym. They were handsome young men, with almost classic profiles, wavy brown hair, and deep blue eyes. The lawyer was wearing a sports jacket and slacks, and he was leaning against one of the wooden partitions and smoking a pipe. The fighter was lying, stripped and face down, on the rubbing table, his head turned and resting on his forearms, and an old rubber named Doc Jordan, in soiled slacks that hung loose on him, a sweater and wearing a gray skull cap, was massaging the muscles in the fighter's shoulders and back.

"We really don't know who was born first," the lawyer said. "There was a mix-up. We were mixed up right after we were born."

"And we've always looked so much alike," the fighter said, "that people have trouble telling us apart. Even our father had trouble when we were small."

He rolled over on the table and, swinging his legs over the side, he sat up. He nodded toward his brother.

"Our father used to dress him in pink," he said, "and me in blue so he could tell which was which. He used to call him Pinky and me Bluey, and every once in a while he still calls us that."

"Were you street scrappers when you were kids?" I said.

"Yes," the fighter said. "We fought all right."

"Did you ever fight each other?" I said.

"Our father used to match us," the lawyer said. "He gave us boxing gloves and taught us to fight. We used to box exhibitions. We used to box at country fairs around Connecticut."

"Didn't you ever fight each other when you meant it?" I said.

"No," the fighter said. "I've really got the greatest brother in the world. I mean that."

"Who was the better fighter when you were kids?" I said.

"Well, I was the boxer," the lawyer said. "He was the puncher."

"Did you ever want to be a professional fighter?"

"No, I wanted to be a lawyer."

"You have to take a lot of punishment to be a fighter," the fighter said. "I mean you have to punish yourself. You have to train and get up early and do road work, and it isn't easy."

"How much do you weigh now? I said.

"Sixty," the fighter said, meaning 160 pounds.

"And you?" I said to the lawyer.

"Now I weigh 152," the lawyer said.

"This interests me," I said, "because since birth you two were identical, and now because of the professions you have chosen, you have begun to alter what nature started. One of you, because he's a fighter, has developed to 160 pounds, while the other weighs less."

"And I have this," the fighter said, putting a hand to his nose where there was a small scar.

"So," I said to the lawyer, "I should think it would be a trying experience to watch your twin being hit in a fight. I should think it might be tougher than when a mother watches a son fight."

"It's not easy for a mother," the lawyer said.

"But you are identical twins," I said. "You have a relationship that, I would think, would be closer than that between mother and son."

"I'll tell you how close we are," the fighter said. "When we would go to the movies together, and if it was a double feature and one of us wanted to leave, the other would have the same thought at the same time. If he sees a good movie—say like *The Snake Pit*—I don't have to see it. If I see one, he doesn't have to see it. That's how close we are."

"So," I said to the lawyer again, "I should think it would be hard on you when you see your identical image being hit, and when you see a cut start to bleed. A face that has always been the same as yours is being hit and changed while you watch."

"It isn't," the lawyer said, shrugging but smiling, "a pleasant experience."

I talked with the fighter then about his upcoming fight, and two nights later at the St. Nick he knocked out Cidone in the first round. In fact, he was working on a string of consecutive wins that was to extend to twenty, eleven by knockout, before, one night in Madison Square Garden, I cost him his fight with Kid Gavilan.

"How do you think he's doing?" Irving Cohen said to me late in the ninth round.

Irving managed him, as he did Rocky Graziano and Billy Graham, and Charley Goldman trained him. Several years before, I had asked the Garden to move me from my permanent seat among my contemporaries in the boxing press to one adjacent to where the handlers squatted below the Ninth Avenue corner. I wanted to hear what they said during the rounds, what strategies, if any, they tried to work out, and over the years the ones I had come to know well would occasionally turn to me for my opinion.

"I have him way ahead," I said to Irving, "but you know what happened to Billy here."

Only four months had passed since that night when, in that same ring, Billy Graham had out-boxed Gavilan only to be deprived of the welterweight title when two of the three officials saw it otherwise. This one was over-the-weight, and Gavilan's title was not on the line, but I was envisioning that happening again.

"If he were my fighter," I said to Irving, "I'd tell him to go out and win the last round."

There is a basic tenet in boxing that, at the very least, you try to win the first round, not only to impress your opponent but also the officials, and you try to win the last round to reaffirm that impression. You attempt to apply this simple psychology at the opening and closing of each round, and Gavilan, with all his ability and Latin flash, was good at this and, in the last thirty seconds or so of a round, a round-stealer.

What Irving Cohen said I don't recall. At the end of the ninth round, however, after he and Charley Goldman had climbed into the ring, I could tell from his gestures, as he bent over and faced the fighter who was reclining on the stool and against the corner ropes, that he was sending him out to win that last round. Walter Cartier was a stand-up boxer-puncher with all the standard moves and a good straight right hand. He was never a runner or a spoiler, and he was pressing the fight again when, about halfway through that tenth round, Gavilan crossed him with a right and he went down. When he got up and stood, still groggy at the count of 9, and with Gavilan waiting to storm out of the neutral corner, Ruby Goldstein, the referee, searching Walter Cartier's eyes and talking to him, stopped it.

"I'm sorry," I said to Irving Cohen, as he started to follow the fighter and Charley Goldman, who was leading him back to the dressing room. "I think he had it won, and I'm sorry I gave you bad advice."

"That's all right," Irving said. He is a short, plump, pink-faced and gentle man, and I could never imagine him castigating anyone. "It's just one of those things that happen now and then."

He did have it won. When we checked the officials' cards at ringside it turned out that all three had had Walter Cartier far enough ahead so that if he had coasted the round, he would have won the fight.

I never apologized to Walter Cartier or his brother, Vincent. When I would see them at Stillman's, or up at the Long Pond Inn where, during the weeks I spent there with Billy Graham, Walter was running on the road with Billy and reading William F. Buckley's *God and Man at Yale,* I refrained. I felt that as long as the fighter was continuing to climb through the ropes to face other opponents, and as long as his brother was enduring the agonies thus imposed on him, I would avoid reminding either of them of the ending of that Gavilan fight.

"That brother, Vincent," Charley Goldman said to me one afternoon at Stillman's, watching the two walk out of the gym together. "I wish he'd leave Walter alone."

"How can he?" I said. "They're identical twins."

"I got Walter up in camp, and he's in great shape," Charley said. "Then Vincent comes up. He says, 'How do you feel, Walter?' Walter says, 'I feel fine.' And Vincent says, 'You don't look so good to me. Are you really all right?' The next thing I know, the fighter is saying he doesn't think he feels just right."

"But you have to understand, Charley," I said. "The brother takes every punch with Walter. In every one of Walter's fights he sees himself being hit. To him it's his own face and body, and he can't do anything about it but worry."

I thought of mentioning Oscar Wilde's *The Picture of Dorian Gray,* in which the subject's appearance never changes while over the years the face in his portrait grows older, but I doubt that Charley ever read anything but the boxing news and Christmas cards. I think that Charley must have sent out a hundred or more Christmas cards each year. We exchanged them, and he must have saved all of the cards he had ever received because in the furnished room he rented on the Upper West Side, and where he lived alone, he had shoe boxes full of them stored under the bed.

"I understand what's between them," Charley said, "but how can I train a fighter like that?"

Now, some quarter of a century later, I wrote to the fighter at his home in Scotch Plains, New Jersey, telling him about the book and saying that I wanted to see him and his brother again. John Condon at Madison Square Garden had supplied me with the address, and four or five nights later, at about 10:30, the phone rang and it was Walter Cartier.

"How are you?" I said.

"I'm fine," he said. "I'm in North Adams, Massachusetts."

"What are you doing there?" I said.

"I'm on the road for this company I work for," he said. "I called home and my wife read me your letter, and I'm really flattered that you want to put Vincent and me in your book. I wasn't that good a fighter."

"Of course you were," I said. "And how is Vincent?"

"Vincent is just great," he said. "He's a lawyer, you know."

"I know."

"He has two sons and a daughter, and I have two sons and a daughter. He has a very good practice, and he's a fine man and a wonderful brother. We don't see as much of each other as we'd like, but we're very, very close."

"I know," I said. "You're identical twins."

"That's right," He said, "and I often think of how lucky I am. I can actually feel sorry for people who don't have a relationship like Vincent and I have, because I don't know what I'd do without my brother."

He said, when I asked him, that the next afternoon he would be driving from North Adams to Burlington, Vermont, and when I explained to him where I lived and invited him to stop by, he said he would. The next morning I found his record in two volumes of *The Ring Record Book and Boxing Encyclopedia*. He had been inactive during 1955 and 1956, but between 1949 and 1957, when he had his last two fights, he had won forty-six of sixty, twenty-three by knockouts. He had lost three decisions, fought two draws, and been stopped nine times.

It was about four o'clock in the afternoon when I saw the car come around the turn in the road. When it turned into the driveway I went out and, as he got out of the car, he looked as I remembered him. It was late April, the day sunny and the weather warm, and he was immaculate in a lightweight dark blue blazer and light gray slacks. He had never taken that many head punches, and looking at his still handsome face, one would not know that he had once been a professional fighter.

We walked around on the property for a few minutes so that he could see the view. As I grow older it seems to me that Spring comes later each year, and as we looked across the valley the mountains were still mauve in the late afternoon sun, only here and there the distant clumps of evergreens showing life.

When we went into the house I introduced him to my wife, and then he and I sat in the living room and I asked him about his work. He said that the company he represents, Sabin Metal, reclaims precious metals—gold, silver, radium, platinum, and palladium—that would otherwise be lost in the various manufacturing processes, and that he drives more than 50,000 miles a year covering the East Coast from Delaware to Maine, persuading the manufacturers to send their scrap to Sabin, which then repays them according to the yield.

"There's silver in film," he said, "and I've gotten over a million and a half pounds of film this year from DuPont. Hospitals discard old X-rays, and I've got hospitals all over that use us. In the two-and-a-half years I've been doing it, I've got eighty-five new accounts. There's gold plating in electronic parts. When they pick up the plating from the plating tanks the gold drops off—some of it does—and they wipe them with Kleenex—Kim Wipes, they call them. They used to throw those away, and we have a company that sends us a ton of those Kim Wipes every two weeks. I got that company to use us."

"We're such a wasteful society," I said, "that I'm glad to find out you're into reclamation and seem to enjoy it."

"It's a challenge," he said, "like a fight. Am I going to be able to sell these people to use our company? Am I going to win the fight?"

"And as you go around to these companies," I said, "does anyone recognize you as Walter Cartier, the former fighter?"

"Not really," he said. "Maybe once in a while somebody will say, 'Don't I know your name from somewhere?' In selling, though, you don't talk about yourself. You talk about them."

"How did you decide to retire from boxing?" I said.

"One reason I stopped," he said, "was that my right hand wasn't flying out there any more. I'd see an opening, and I'd think, 'I should have thrown the right.' I knew I was done."

"Ray Robinson told me the same thing," I said.

"It happens to everybody," he said.

"How many fights did you have in the Garden?" I said.

"I don't know," he said. "Eight or nine."

"And main events?"

"Five or six."

"Every fighter," I said, "used to hope someday to get a main event in the Garden. Was your first one a big thrill?"

'I don't remember it as that earth-shattering," he said. "When I was a boy I wanted to get on the cover of *Ring* magazine, and I got on, and it wasn't that big a thing."

"Did you used to dream about someday being a champion?"

"I don't think I really had a great desire to be champ," he said. "I always wanted to be a fighter. I had my ten years of fighting, and I didn't become champ, but I'm not bemoaning it."

"That's good."

"I dropped out a couple of years, and then I came back," he said. "I fought somebody—in Connecticut—and I fought somebody in the St. Nick's. The Garden was closed for the circus or something, and I forget his name, but he was an up-and-coming young middleweight who didn't make it."

"I find this interesting, even amusing," I said. "As just a specta-
tor, an on-looker, I've always regarded every fight as a dramatic
event, but you don't even recall whom you fought in those last
fights."

"I really don't," he said. "The boxing is all past, and I don't live
in the past. I live in the present, what I'm doing now."

"That's fine," I said. "I think it's great the way you've been able
to adjust, but for your own information, your next to last fight
wasn't in Connecticut. It was in Holyoke, Massachusetts, and you
outpointed somebody named Eddie Andrews, and then the fighter
you fought in the St. Nick was Jackie LaBua."

"That's right," he said, smiling and nodding now. "Jackie
LaBua. I was ready to knock him out, and then I got butted and
cut my eye, and they stopped it. They let my brother work in my
corner that night, and he said, 'That's it, isn't it?' I said, 'That's it.'

"He sensed it, like the day of the fight. When the days drag on,
and you start to sweat fights out, you're in the wrong business. It's
a strain on you when you begin to think about fights. The first
fight I had was like going to take a shower, and Vincent sensed it
as soon as I did."

"I'm sure he did," I said, "because I know how he suffered right
along with you, perhaps even more than you."

"I know that," he said. "He's a wonderful brother."

He said that he had eaten a late lunch and wanted to get to
Burlington, so he would not stay for dinner. When I walked him
to his car, he showed me his business files on the back seat. The
cards were in plastic boxes, the colors of the boxes denoting the
various states.

"I make notes on them," he said. "When I go in to see someone
I know all about him, about his family, how many children he
has, if they're in school or what they're doing. I know his hobbies,
what he shoots in golf or if, like around here, he skis. Then we
have something else to talk about besides business."

He was that kind of a fighter, a thinking fighter, meticulous not
only in his training but in the fight itself. Watching him I used to
think that I could actually see him scheming his moves as he set
up his punches, and I felt that one of his problems was that he
was seldom able to relax in there or, as they say, "get loose."

Several weeks later I drove to New Jersey, and that evening he and his wife, Patricia, had dinner with me at my motel. She is slim, dark-haired and dark-eyed, and she had a golfer's tan. They have three children, a daughter, Patrice, who works for a cruise line, and two sons, Vincent, named after his uncle and a University of Florida graduate who is in management training, and Gregg, then a sophomore in high school.

When we ordered drinks his wife asked for a glass of white wine and I had my usual. Walter passed.

"You don't drink?" I said.

"I never tried it," he said. "I just don't see any reason for me to take a drink, or any reason to take a smoke."

"That's my Mister Perfect," his wife said, smiling at him. "He doesn't smoke, he doesn't drink and he doesn't chase other women."

Walter was smiling too, and he shrugged.

"You're so good," she said, looking at him and laughing, "that you're no good."

"I trained that way," he said. "When I first went into camp, Charley Goldman said, 'What time do you want me to wake you?' I said, 'You don't have to wake me.' He said, 'You want to loaf?' He thought I was trying to goof off, but I'd be in bed by 9:30 or 10 o'clock, and I had my own alarm clock."

"And Billy Graham told me," I said, "that he never liked to run on the road with you. He said you ran like a reindeer."

"Irving Cohen and Whitey Bimsteim," he said, "liked it when I was in camp with Billy, because then he'd be ashamed not to get up early in the morning."

"That's my Walter," his wife said. "Now he's an addict at work. He's a devoted worker."

Walter was shrugging again.

"You are, Walter," she said, and then to me, "He's sincere, and he can only sell what believes in. All these hot-shot kids today, they want to wine and dine them, and then little Walter comes in and he sells them."

"I was at one company recently," Walter said, "and there was another salesman there. The fella came out and he said to the salesman, 'For me to use you, I'd have to change everything in the place.' The salesman didn't know what to say. He should have said, 'Of course you do, but I'll tell you why.' You have to overcome objections, and to me that's a challenge, like a fight."

"And when he does well," his wife said, "it's like winning a fight."

"I'll tell you one fight that Walter didn't win," I said to her but to both of them, "and because of me."

"What one was that?" she said.

"The Gavilan fight," I said, and I went into it. I told them about Irving Cohen turning to me during that ninth round and what I said and why. Walter, listening, was nodding, and then he shook his head.

"You didn't lose me that fight," he said. "Walter Cartier lost it."

"How much time was left in the round?" his wife said.

"A minute, or a minute-and-a-half," he said.

"I thought it was just seconds," she said.

"No," he said. "I've seen the pictures, and I was a little groggy, and I said to Ruby Goldstein, 'Why didn't you give me another knockdown?' "

"And if it hadn't been for me," I said, "you'd have boxed that whole last round differently."

"Only Walter Cartier lost that fight," he said. "It's what I tell our sons. Our son Vincent was a miler. In high school he broke Jim Ryun's high school record for the mile. At the University of Florida he pulled his Achilles tendon as a freshman and then he had mono, but I used to tell him if something went wrong in a race, that it's no good putting the blame on other people. You have to take the responsibility yourself.

"I learned that," he said, "when I was selling real estate. We sold home sites for second homes and retirement homes in a recreational project. There were several salesmen, and we moved with groups of customers. Weekends they'd stay in hotels, and they'd have their free rooms and breakfast, and you had to sell them that day. You'd have them in your jeep because the roads were not in yet, and you had to put the pressure on, but not so they'd be offended.

"When we went through a dry spell, we'd tape the presentations, the whole tour. We'd play it, and they'd put a critique on you, and we developed a philosophy that we had to blame ourselves. The only fella who lost the Gavilan fight was Walter Cartier himself."

"That's fine," I said, "but, anyway, I'm going to straighten it out with Vincent too."

"Vincent will feel the same way," he said.

"I'm not sure," I said, and then I turned to his wife. "You see, I feel that Vincent, as an identical twin, was going through experiences during Walter's fights that were totally different from those that Walter was experiencing in the ring. Vincent was seeing his own face, in a very real way for him, being assaulted by blows while he could do nothing about it."

"After one fight," Walter said, "I had to have ninety-five stitches."

"Ninety-five stitches?" I said. "In one fight?"

"When I fought Joey Giardello in Brooklyn," he said. "In the tenth round I got cut over one eye, and in the last few seconds it was so bad that Giardello wouldn't hit me and they stopped it. They put ninety-five stitches in to close it."

"That must have been terrible," I said, "not only for you but for Vincent."

"Vincent is a wonderful person," his wife said.

"I know," I said, "but I've wondered about something else. The bond between identical twins is so strong that, it seems to me that a wife, marrying one, may find that relationship, at least at first, sometimes difficult to accept."

"Not with Vincent," she said. "As I said, he's a wonderful person, a wonderful husband, and a wonderful father. Other lawyers play golf. He's in his office working on cases."

"Like Walter," I said.

"Like Walter," she said.

The next morning he picked me up at the motel and we drove the twenty-five miles or so down to Middletown. Vincent Cartier lives in a white-shingled ranch house in a community of well-kept homes set on well-tended lawns, and in the driveway Mike, his sixteen-year-old son, was washing a car.

When Vincent came out of a back door and greeted us he looked as I had expected. From the first day that I had met them it had not been really difficult to distinguish one from the other, for by then Walter had been fighting for three years, developing his body for the demands of the ring, while over the same period, Vincent had been developing his mind for the exactions inherent in the practice of law. He still appeared the slimmer of the two, his facial features slightly less rugged, and he was wearing black-rimmed glasses.

He led us into a sun room at the rear of the house, and introduced me to his wife, Frances. In the room beyond, there was a billiard table, and two of the walls were almost covered with photographs of ballplayers and fighters of the late thirties and early forties. There were pictures of Walter, posing with some of his contemporaries, and with his opponents at weigh-ins.

"There we are up in Connecticut," Vincent said, pointing to a picture that had taken on a brown tint by now, "when we used to box each other."

In the picture there are two small boys and a referee in an outdoor ring, caught by the camera as the two were about to initiate an exchange of punches. Their boxing trunks reach to their knees, and the gloves are big on their hands.

"That's our older brother, Charley, refereeing," Vincent said, "and that's Walter on the left. You can see that he's looking to punch, and I'm just looking to jab. He was always the more aggressive."

"That's a marvelous picture," I said. "It tells so much."

"That's right," he said. "It does."

We went back to the sun room and we sat down.

"I've forgotten now," I said, "which of you was Bluey and which was Pinky."

"I was Bluey," Walter said. "It started in the hospital."

"It started with ribbons they put on us," Vincent said.

"And how old were you when the boxing started?"

"About two or three years old," Vincent said. "Our dad was a fight fan, and he'd fought as a youth. That's how we got to going to the country fairs. We were very soft-faced, angelic-looking boys. During the Depression we moved, and we'd come into a school and we looked like sissies. We were always challenged, and somehow Walter would come forth first. He'd say, 'All right, let's fight.' He seemed to have that anxiety to be a fighter, even when we boxed in New England at those country fairs, and one season we were at six or seven of them."

"And what were the fights like?" I said.

"They were fixed fights," Vincent said. "Our brother was the referee, and in the first round one would get knocked down. In the second round the other would get knocked down. The third round was a slug fest, and then Charley would call it a draw. We also boxed in the Navy. We went in together and stayed together."

"Where were you in the Navy?"

"Just in California," Walter said. "That's all."

"And when you boxed each other," I said, "didn't the exchanges of punches ever get so hot that it turned into a real fight? Didn't you ever really try to belt each other?"

"We never had a fight," Vincent said.

"Never," Walter said, shaking his head.

"I can vouch for that," Vincent said. "In the Navy there was a comment in the paper, 'Never pick on one Cartier because you're picking on two.'"

"And you never wanted to be a fighter?" I said.

"Never," Vincent said. "I was always inclined to be a professional man, and so I'm a trial lawyer."

"And I presume that in school you were in the same classes together. Did you do your homework together?"

"As I recall we did," Walter said.

"We did it together," Vincent said, nodding.

"And we got the same marks in everything," Walter said.

"I think Walter's were a little better," Vincent said.

"I don't think so," Walter said.

"In class, who would answer a question first?"

"I think he did," Vincent said. "I thought he was smarter."

"I don't think so," Walter said.

"You see," Vincent said, "when Walter wanted to be a prize fighter, nobody in the family wanted him to be. My father was opposed. He took him to Bobby Ruffin. Do you remember Bobby Ruffin?"

"Yes," I said. "The lightweight."

"I used to see him fight," Walter said. "I was a fan of his."

"My father decided to see what Bobby Ruffin could do to discourage my brother," Vincent said, "but Walter boxed with him, and it encouraged him."

We were getting now to why I was there, why I had wanted to see them both again and together.

"And every time Walter fought," I said to Vincent, "I thought of you. It's difficult for a mother when her son fights. Billy Graham's mother wouldn't watch on television or listen on the radio. She'd wait for his phone call after the fight was over. On the nights when Rocky Marciano fought, a doctor used to drive his mother around in his car. It just seems to me that, for an identical twin, the affinity would be even greater, and it would be even more difficult to watch the fight."

"It's awful," Vincent said, shaking his head at the thought of it. "It's the greatest torture you can imagine. I don't know if it's a greater affinity, but I think the world of my brother."

"I used to see Bobby Ruffin fight," Walter said, looking at Vincent, "and I was ducking punches. Imagine what you were doing for me."

"And I must confess to you," I said to Vincent, "something that I did for Walter. In the ninth round of the Gavilan fight, Irving Cohen asked me how I had it, and I said I had Walter ahead, but I thought he should go out and win the last round."

"I didn't know it was Bill," Walter said. "All I remembered was that Irving said he'd asked one of the newspaper men."

"I heard it was Bill Heinz," Vincent said, nodding.

"Walter Cartier lost it," Walter said.

"There's a sidelight to that," Vincent said. "It dates back to one time when Walter was in Stillman's Gym, and Gavilan was looking for a sparring partner and Walter was looking for someone to spar with. I guess Walter hit Gavilan with more punches in three rounds than he did in the fight, and Gavilan's trainer never let Gavilan spar in the gym with Walter or fight him.

"It came about that Gavilan needed a fight and took Walter. Walter was sick in bed in Greenwood Lake, and the Boxing Commission came up, but I only let Walter punch the bag. He went and rested, but he was not physically strong."

He paused.

"Now I knew I conveyed my nervousness to Walter," he said,

"so I tried to stay in the background. My nervousness was too visible. When he fought Gavilan I was sitting in the back, bobbing and weaving with every punch. At the start of the tenth, I was going to yell at Walter that he had the fight by a large margin."

He turned to his brother.

"You were way ahead, Walter," he said.

"But how can I blame anybody but myself?" Walter said.

"Excuse me," Vincent said, standing up, "but I've got to get a drink of water. I'm getting nervous just thinking about that fight."

"And that fight," I said to Walter, after Vincent had left, "was twenty-six years ago."

"I know," he said. "I have a wonderful brother."

"Irving and Charley," I said, "used to hate to see him come into camp."

"I know," he said.

"You were a tense fighter anyway," I said. "You didn't relax between moves."

"That could be," Walter said.

"What's that?" Vincent said, coming back into the sun room.

"I was just saying," I said, "that Walter was a tense fighter. Between moves—exchanges of punches—he didn't relax. He was never able to coast, and in the course of a fight that mounted up to a physical burden."

"That's true," Vincent said, "and I felt, in a lot of ways, responsible. The emotion and tension I felt, I probably conveyed it. If I had to go through it again, I would move to California and he'd be a better fighter."

"No you wouldn't," Walter said.

"I'm serious," Vincent said to me. "I did it out of thinking he needed me. He didn't need me, and I was harming him."

"But you weren't," Walter said.

"You feel you're losing part of yourself if you're not involved," Vincent said. "Relatives don't belong in there."

For lunch he suggested that we drive down to Sea Bright, on the Jersey shore. I got into Vincent's car, Walter following us in his, and he led us to a large, rambling restaurant with rooms on several levels, one of those establishments that has the look of having been there for many years and having a local reputation for good fare. The waitress led us to a table in the bar and Vincent and I ordered drinks.

"Nothing for me, thank you," Walter said to the waitress.

"I never drank either," Vincent said to me. "I started after he stopped fighting. You know how it was at the Long Pond at Greenwood Lake, with the bar right there. Twins try not to embarrass the other, and I never wanted to have a good time while Walter was in training, and I never had a good time."

"I can believe that," I said. "Between some identical twins there is an intuitive understanding that's almost mystic. I remember that when I first met you two, Walter explained how, when you went to the movies together and one wanted to leave, the other had the same impulse at the same moment."

"I'm not sure it's anything mystic," Vincent said. "You have a tendency to see things the same. I don't use profanity. Walter doesn't. We never used it with each other."

"That could be environmental," I said.

"I remember once when I came down to see you," Walter said. "I had just had a discussion with my children, about some problem, and you had had exactly the same thing with yours and had said the same thing."

"But when you were still very young," I said, "and growing up in the same house, didn't you ever quarrel, say about some toy?"

"We never had any jealousy," Vincent said.

"That's right," Walter said.

"If there was one apple left," Vincent said, "I'd want him to have it. He'd want me to take it."

"That would be an easy one for King Solomon," I said. "Just divide the apple in two."

"That's right," Vincent said.

While we ate we talked about fighters and fights we remembered, and we exchanged opinions of some of the better fighters of today. The movie *Rocky* had just come out, and Walter said he hadn't seen it.

"Did you see it, Vin?" he said.

"No," Vincent said. "I didn't, and I'll tell you why. He loses in the end. I've seen enough heartache and losing in the end. It happened with me."

After lunch I got into Vincent's car again, and with Walter following us once more, we drove out onto Sandy Hook, that spit of land that marks the entrance to Lower New York Bay. To protect the shoreline, huge, rough-cut blocks of granite have been deposited there, with what must have been massive machinery, in angular disarray. Standing on them, the waves slapping against them below us, we could see across the water to the north, the towers of Lower Manhattan Island gleaming in the early afternoon sun. I wondered if the blocks had come out of the bedrock of the island, perhaps even out of the excavation for the World Trade Center. The southernmost of the twin towers, shielding the other, was the only noticeable change there now from the way it looked when I had come up this bay on that troopship on that gray and fog-shrouded morning thirty-two years before.

We said good-by to Vincent there, and Walter and I drove back to Scotch Plains. He lives in a fourteen-room English Tudor house, secluded among large evergreens, oaks, and maples. His wife and their younger son were at their country club, so we drove there for dinner, and it was only after I was home again that yet another question came to mind and I phoned him. He said he was working on his expense account.

"And I'm still on the identical twin kick," I said. "When you and Vincent exchange gifts, say at Christmas or on your common birthday, do you ever find you've bought each other the same thing?"

"We don't exchange gifts," he said.

"Not even at Christmas," I said.

"We never did," he said. "We didn't have to. I've never bought him a gift, ever. You wouldn't buy yourself a gift, would you? You know?"

19

Somebody Up There Likes Him

> Hey, Ma—your bad boy done it. I told you Somebody up there likes me.
>
> Rocky Graziano, July 16, 1947

He said it into a radio microphone that had been thrust in front of his face in the ring in the Chicago Stadium. It was 120 degrees under the ring lights, and his hair hung in black streaks, soaked by his own sweat and the water they had sloshed over him between rounds. His right eye was a slit, and over his left eye there was a dark cake of dried blood. In the sixth round of the second of their three vicious fights, he had just knocked out Tony Zale. Now he was the middleweight champion of the world, and it was an event that involved me as did none other among the hundreds I covered in sports.

"You're a tough man to get hold of," I was saying now on the phone.

"Yeah, yeah," he was saying. "I get up early, and then I'm out."

"I know," I said.

I had been calling the apartment in New York for days. Several times I had talked with his wife, Norma.

"He's gone again, Bill," she would say.

"When will he be in?"

"Who knows?" she would say.

"Listen," I was saying to him now. "I'll be in New York on Friday, and I want to see you at your place about eleven in the morning."

"Yeah, yeah," he said. "Good."

"Now, I'm dragging all the way in just to see you," I said, "so you be there."

"Yeah, yeah," he said. "I'll be here, and I'll tell you anything you want to know. You always wrote good about me, Billy. You know?"

"Yes," I said. "I know."

A reporter has an obligation to objectivity, and although we had a racing handicapper who operated as a bookmaker right in the sports department of my paper, I never bet on a horse race, a ball game or a fight. In every reporter, however, the struggle against subjectivity goes on, and coming up to that second Graziano-Zale fight, I lost that struggle.

It was the night before the fight, and we had been sitting around the living room of the hotel suite in Chicago for an hour or more, listening to a Cubs' game on the radio. Rocky was lolling in an arm chair, and there were a couple of sparring partners on the sofa. Irving Cohen, who managed him, and Whitey Bimstein, who trained him, had been sitting with a card table between them, counting through batches of tickets, and I saw Whitey look at his watch. I looked at my own, and it was ten o'clock. In twenty-four hours, the fighter would have to climb into a ring once more against the man who, nine months before in Yankee Stadium, in the sixth round and after taking a frightening beating himself, had hit him a right hand in the body and a left hook on the chin to knock him out and end what those who had been around long enough called the greatest fight since Dempsey-Firpo.

"All right," Whitey said. "You better get up to bed now, Rock. It's time you were in."

He got up from the chair and stretched and started out the door. Whitey motioned over his shoulder with his head and I followed them out. Nothing had been said about it, but I knew now why Irving Cohen had asked me to come over to the hotel and why, now, I was a part of this night before this fight.

It had started five months before. In New York they had revoked his license for failing to report the offer of a bribe he had not accepted for a fight that had never been held. There were those of us who had gone to the hearings of the New York State Athletic Commission and who were certain that we could see through this to the politics behind it, and we had been appalled that such a thing could happen in this country.

An uptown Manhattan politician named Joseph Scottorigio had been murdered. Who killed Scottorigio? It is a question that still hasn't been answered, and for weeks the New York papers played it big. For weeks it confounded and plagued the Manhattan police and the District Attorney's office, until they came up with this prize fighter and the bribe offer he had ignored, and Rocky Graziano chased Joseph Scottorigio off the front pages.

As I covered the hearings, what I wrote for the front page was what transpired. What I wrote for my piece on the sports page each day was what I had come to know about this former Lower East Side hoodlum who, it turned out, had been in and out of reform school, jail, and prison, and who had found in boxing a way to make a legitimate living.

I knew it was a tough row to hoe in this garden where I was trying to plant my small seeds of reason. The paper was conservative, resolutely Republican. In my time it had opposed Franklin Delano Roosevelt and Fiorello LaGuardia. It stood firm against Harry Truman, organized labor and any social legislation that, it seemed to me, wasn't current during the administration of Calvin Coolidge. I could never have written politics for it, but it had given me my start and I felt an abiding filial affection for it, and I could write sports.

Two days before a scheduled fight with Cowboy Reuben Shank in Madison Square Garden, Graziano had pulled out, complaining of a bad back. It was the contention of the District Attorney that the problem was not with the fighter's back but with an offer of $100,000 that had been made to him by an unidentified party in Stillman's Gym to take a dive for Shank and that he had failed to report. Graziano admitted that someone had come up to him with an offer that he thought was a gag, and that was the D.A.'s case.

To anyone familiar with boxing, the proposition was absurd. Cowboy Reuben Shank was a journeyman middleweight whose best move against Graziano would have been to take the next train out of town and back to Keensburg, Colorado. Any syndicate trying to place enough money on Shank to profit from a $100,000 payoff would have signaled that a fix was in and driven the fight off the books.

I wrote that and I wrote that you had to know Graziano and you had to know Stillman's Gym to understand how he had looked upon the offer. He was the most exciting fighter, those who had seen them both wrote, since Stanley Ketchel, and Ketchel had been dead by then for thirty-seven years or since, as John Lardner put it, "he was fatally shot in the back by the commonlaw husband of the lady who was cooking his breakfast."

When Graziano fought, you could breathe the tension. When he fought in the Garden, you could feel it over on Broadway, and the night he fought Zale for the first time you could sense it two hours before the fight between the cars jammed along the Grand Concourse, half a mile from Yankee Stadium. When he trained at Stillman's, he packed that place to the walls. They would be stacked on the stairway to the balcony, and they would be packed on the balcony, too.

"I'll be glad when that Graziano stops fighting," a fight manager said to me there one day. "It's gettin' so you can't even move in here."

His dressing room would be mobbed, too, and with the characters to cast three road companies of *Dead End*. There was one there, a little guy named Barney, who always wore a dirty cap, the peak to one side, and who played the harmonica. He played it, not by blowing on it with his mouth, but through his nostrils.

"Ain't he a good musician?" Graziano would say, sitting back and listening. "Did you ever see anybody do that before? I'd like to get this poor guy a job."

This minstrel had three numbers in his repertoire—"Darktown Strutters' Ball," "Beer Barrel Polka," and "Bugle Call Rag." While he was playing "Bugle Call Rag," blowing on that harmonica through his nostrils, he would salute with his left hand.

"Ain't that great?" Graziano would say. "Why can't I get this guy a job?"

The virtuoso seemed satisfied because Graziano was staking him. He staked a lot of them. One day I saw him give the shirt he was wearing to some hapless hanger-on. The Christmas of the first year that he had made any real money he bought a six-year-old Cadillac and loaded it with $1,500 worth of toys. He drove it down to his old East Side neighborhood, and he handed out the toys to the kids and another $1,500 to their parents. He never mentioned it, but it came out because a trainer at Stillman's who lived in the neighborhood had seen it.

"Look, Rocky," Irving Cohen said to him, "it's nice to do things like that, but you haven't got that kind of money, and you've got to save money. You won't be fighting forever."

"Sure, Irving," Graziano said, "but those are poor people. They're good people. They never done no wrong. They never hurt nobody. They just never got a break."

One day in Stillman's he walked up to Irving. He asked him how much money he was carrying.

"I've got fifty bucks," Irving said.

"Give it to me," Graziano said, "and hustle up another fifty for me."

Irving circulated and borrowed fifty and gave it to him. As you came into Stillman's there were rows of chairs facing the ring, and in one of the chairs a former fighter, still young but blind, was sitting. When Graziano sat down beside him and started to talk to him, Irving sidled up behind them, and he saw Graziano lean over and slip the folded bills into the breast pocket of the other's jacket.

"There's something in your pocket," Graziano said, and he got up.

I wrote that and more, weighing it all against the absurdity of the charges, and I wondered how long I would be permitted that freedom. After all, how long could a paper, patterned to please stock brokers, corporate executives, and the ad agencies and their clients that sustained it, afford to speak for a prize fighter, an ex-convict with a fifth-grade education, against the office of the District Attorney and the undoubted integrity of Colonel Edward P. F. Eagan, Yale graduate, former Rhodes Scholar, lawyer and chairman of the New York State Athletic Commission?

Late one afternoon I found out. When I checked my mail cubi-

cle in the sports department, there was a typed note there from
Wilbur Wood.

"Mr. Speed," the note read, and Keats Speed was the managing
editor, "suggests that you write no more opinion pieces about
Graziano. WW."

I wrote one more. I knew that neither Wilbur nor Speed came
in early enough mornings to check the copy going into the first
edition that went to press at 10 A.M. After the first edition, the
piece was yanked.

"Didn't you get my note?" Wilbur said, when I saw him in the
office later that day.

"Gee, Wilbur, I didn't," I said. "I was in a hurry to write my
piece and catch my train to Connecticut, and I didn't check my
mail until this morning."

"Well, that's the end of it," he said. "No more pro-Graziano
pieces. That's an order."

"Whatever you say," I said.

"It isn't just what I say," he said. "It's what Speed says and
what a lot of other people on this paper are saying."

"You're the boss, Wilbur," I said.

The afternoon that Eagan announced that Rocky Graziano was
banned, ostensibly for life, from boxing in New York State, I covered that. In that crowded hearing room, I watched the fighter,
who had seemed to have finally found his way in this world, drop
his head into his hands, his elbows on the table as he sat there
across from Eagan, and I rushed back to the paper and wrote the
piece that ran under the eight-column headline that bannered page
one.

"Listen," Wilbur Wood said to me, coming back from the city
room after the edition had closed. "The city desk wants you to get
ahold of Graziano and find out how he's taking this. You're his
good friend, so he'll talk to you, and it should make a good piece
for tomorrow."

"Sure, Wilbur," I said, thinking that yes, I am his good friend
and now you want me to play that friendship you all found so em-
barrassing, but it is a good piece if I can find him.

With Irving Cohen and Jack Healy, who was another of his

managers, I found him. In the fighter's new buff and light blue Cadillac, with "Rocky" on the doors, with Healy at the wheel and Irving beside him, we drove into the Lower East Side. It was early February, and darkness had come by now and there was a mist in the air. At Cooper Square, Healy turned under the El and drove down a side street and parked across from a Chinese laundry on the first floor of an old tenement. Some kids had a bonfire going in the street, piling crates on it, and Healy got out and walked across the street and into the building.

In about ten minutes he came out and Graziano was with him. As they crossed the street toward the car, the wavering light from the bonfire played on them, and then they were silhouetted by the lights of a car turning around in the block.

"Hey, Rocky!" I heard the driver of the car shout, leaning out. "You're still all right!"

Graziano turned around on the wet street and waved his hand, and then he came over to the car and he opened the front door. His face was drawn and his eyes small and Irving Cohen moved over to make room for him on the front seat.

"I been sleepin'," he said. "For three hours I slept at my friend's place."

He started to slide into the front seat. Then he saw me sitting in the back.

"Oh," he said. "Hello."

"Hello, Rocky," I said. "I'm sorry to bother you at a time like this."

"That's all right," he said. "It's a job. I understand."

He was in the car now and he shut the door. Healy got in and drove to the end of the street and started uptown.

"I don't want to pester you, Rocky," I said, "but I have to ask you a couple of questions."

"That's all right," he said. "I understand."

"Were you nervous going in to hear that verdict today?"

"No," he said. "I wasn't nervous. Not nervous."

"How is that?"

"Well, I figured," he said, "I figured that the guy, that Eagan, would say, 'Dismissed.' You know, 'This case dismissed.'"

"But you could tell in the hearings, Rocky," I said, "that they were going to throw the book at you. I mean you could sense it as Eagan began to describe the findings."

"I know," Graziano said, "but I kept on thinkin' the sonofabitch was gonna say, 'But because of the contributions Graziano has made to boxing.' I figured the bastard was gonna say something like that."

"And then what?"

And then it all came out, all of the expletives, all of the vulgarities. The close air in that car was filled with the obscene oaths and the unprintable invectives. He was throwing them wildly, the way he threw punches in the ring where he had found a way to fight back against all the hurts he had invited and that society had inflicted upon him. Now, cornered and wounded again, he was seeing society as his enemy again, personified by Eagan.

"I'll kill the bastard," he was saying. "I'll get a gun. I'll kill the sonofabitch. The sonofabitch should be dead. I'll . . ."

"For Christ sake, Rock!" Healy was saying, and he had slowed the car and he had turned toward him.

"Please, Rocky!" Irving Cohen was saying. "Don't even talk like that!"

"I'll kill him," he was saying.

"Come on now, Rocky," I was saying, and I was leaning forward and I had my hands on his shoulders as he sat there between Healy and Irving. "For God's sake, stop that. You listen to me."

"You listen to Bill, Rocky," Irving was saying. "You listen to Bill. Bill knows."

What did I know? I told him it wasn't the end of his world. I told him that he could fight Zale again, maybe in New Jersey or maybe in Illinois, and that this time he would lick him. When he did, he would be the middleweight champion of the world, and public opinion would turn then on Eagan, and then he would get his license back.

We were at Union Square by now, and Healy turned the car around and drove south again and they dropped me off at my paper on lower Broadway. On the way we kept saying the same things to him over and over again, and when I wrote my piece, of course I left all of that out. They were just words, but some of those he had known had gone to the electric chair and others he had run with were in Sing Sing doing twenty to life, and his whole future was balanced on that pinnacle of public opinion. If I wrote that, there was no way he would ever get his license back, and so I wrote what I could about his hurt and that he would take his wife and Audrey, their small daughter, to Florida while Irving Cohen tried to plan something out.

So the second Zale fight was made for Chicago, and I saw the fighter in training in the East and then out there. Nothing was ever said about the ride from Cooper Square to Union Square and then downtown again, but now, five months later, I was following Whitey and him out into the hallway and up the stairs to the next floor.

They had two rooms there, with the door open between them. In one there were two beds, one for the fighter and the other for Whitey. In the other there were three cots for the sparring partners and Frank Percoco, who would work in the fighter's corner with Irving and Whitey.

"You better try these trunks on," Whitey said.

The fighter undressed. He had been training for two months and he was in great shape, and Whitey handed him the trunks, black with red stripes, first one pair and then the other, and he tried them on, squatting down and then standing up.

"The first ones are too tight," he said, handing the second pair back to Whitey. "These are best."

He got, naked, into one of the beds then, and he pulled the covers up to his chest. He had put two pillows together under his head, so he was half sitting up, and Whitey looked at me and I looked at him, and he walked into the other room.

"So, I'll go now, Rock," I said.

"Okay," he said.

"You have to lick this guy, Rock," I said, and I was standing by the bed, looking down at him. "If you ever had to win a fight, you have to win this one."

"I know," he said, nodding.

"I despise them for what they did to you," I said, "and you hate them, and there's only one way you can get even. If you lose tomorrow night, you're done, not only in New York but everywhere. You have to win, Rock."

"I know," he said.

"You have to stick to it," I said. "You have to win the title, because when you win the title it's yours, and they can't take it away from you outside the ring. You win it and they need it, and as I told you in the car that night, they'll come crawling back, begging you on their hands and knees."

"I know," he said, lying there in that bed and looking up right at me. "If I have to, I'll die in there, tryin'."

We shook hands and he snapped off the light over the bed and I left. I took an elevator down and went out and called a cab, and riding back to my hotel and thinking about it I was embarrassed. They come no more decent than Tony Zale and no tougher than he was inside the ropes, and what was I doing telling someone he would have to take those brutal shots in the belly and to the head while I would just sit there at ringside, looking up into the brutality?

They drew $422,918 for an indoor record and they had them packed to the walls again and up to the rafters. Suddenly, the hot, humid, sweat-smelling air was stilled of sound and then Al Melgard at the Stadium organ started "The Sidewalks of New York," and a roar went up in the back and down the aisle he came. He had the white satin, green-trimmed robe over his shoulders, and Whitey and Irving and Frank Percoco were behind him. The roar, and then the booing, was all over the place now, and Whitey was rubbing his back as they came. Then, two steps from the stairs, he broke from Whitey and took the three steps in one leap and vaulted through the ropes, throwing his arms out into the roar and the boos so the robe slid off.

"Yes," I said to myself, "he'll stick it all right."

He stuck it, and there were times when it looked as if he would have to die doing it. Under his right eye the flesh had swelled so that it shut the eye, and when Zale cut the left eye, the blood flowed into it so that he was stumbling around almost blind and seeing only through a red haze. Snarling, he motioned Zale to come in, and Zale threw all of his big stuff at him and he took it all. There were times in the third round when I said to myself that if this were just a fight, and not bigger than a fight, he would go down. I said to myself that he couldn't win it, and then an odd thing happened.

Between the fourth and fifth rounds, Frank Percoco took a quarter—two bits—and pressing with it between his fingers, he broke the skin of the swelling under the right eye. When the blood came out the swelling came down enough for the fighter to see. In the sixth round, with Zale helpless on the ropes, Graziano, in that frenzy that made him what only he and Dempsey and, I guess, Ketchel, were, was hitting him wherever he could find a place to hit him, and the referee stopped it.

"Well," I said to him, "the world is a big place, and how does it feel to be the middleweight champion of it?"

In that basement of the Chicago Stadium he was standing, naked once more, in the shower stall off the dressing room, his right eye shut again, a metal clip holding the other cut closed. Only a fireman in uniform was with us, guarding the door that Whitey had opened just long enough for me to get in.

"I don't know," he said. He had closed down the flow of the shower so that it barely dripped on him. Cut and bruised and hurt, and leaning back and resting one arm on the shower handles, he was trying to think and to talk. "I don't know. I mean . . . I mean as a kid . . . I mean I was no good. I mean nobody ever . . . you know what I mean?"

"I know what you mean, Rocky," the fireman said suddenly. "You're giving a talk on democracy."

"I mean, I never. . . ," the fighter said to me, and then he turned to the fireman and, sort of studying him, he said, "You're a good guy. You're all right. You know what I mean?"

The next day it started in the Chicago papers, as I had told him it would, and it was the same in the New York papers when I got back two days later. Nothing had changed, really, neither the fighter nor the charges against him by those who had called him a liar and a hoodlum, but now those who had been crying out against him where crying out for him as a citizen wronged.

"Well," Wilbur Wood said, a smile on his face and sticking out his hand, when I walked into the office, "we had it all the way."

"All the way?" I said, shaking hands. "What did we have all the way?"

"Graziano," he said, still smiling. "Haven't you seen the other papers?"

"Yes," I said. "I've seen them."

"We had him all the way," Wilbur said. "All the way."

"Good, Wilbur," I said. "I'm real glad."

My gladness was to be short-lived. Just when, it seemed, the pressure of that public opinion and the promise of a big gate for this third fight with Zale would force New York State to restore his license, someone got it out of the War Department that he had gone AWOL from the Army in 1943, had spent nine months in Leavenworth, and had a dishonorable discharge. In this game these misguided patriots were playing with the life of a hounded and tortured human being who had served his time and was trying to make an honest living, he was now back at Square One.

"How did you mess up like that?" I asked him.

"This captain," he said, "he come out from behind his desk. He said, 'You think you're so tough?' He started to take his coat off, like this. What was I supposed to do? I belted him—pow!—and flattened him, and I took off."

And I had mislead him. Bending over that bed in that hotel room in Chicago that night, I had told him that once he won the title, they could never take it from him outside the ring but, of course, they did. Because Abe J. Greene, the head of the National Boxing Association, refused to be cowed by them and stood up for him, they let him defend that title against Zale in the ball park in Newark, New Jersey, and they paid him for it, but he was no fighter then. The things they had done to him had taken out of him that which had made him the fighter he had been, and Zale knocked him out in the third round.

Trying to bring him back, Irving Cohen signed him for a fight in Oakland, California, with Fred Apostoli who, nine years before, had been middleweight champion. Ten days before the scheduled date, riding the train into town, I was checking the sports pages in the morning papers, when I saw the story out of Oakland. Rocky Graziano had disappeared, and Jimmy Murray, the promoter, was threatening to sue him and Irving Cohen. At the paper I tried to write whatever piece I had in mind, but I gave up and called Irving Cohen at his office.

"Where's the fighter?" I said.

"We don't know," he said.

"What are you going to do?"

"I don't know," he said.

"Listen, Irving," I said. "You've got to do something. You know his whole future depends on this. You've got to square this, and you've got to do something right now."

"But I don't know what to do," he said.

"Stay right where you are," I said. "I'll be up there in a half hour."

He had a small office in the Brill Building on Broadway. When I got there it was noon, and I found him with Teddy Brenner, who was making matches for a small club then and later headed boxing at Madison Square Garden.

"Have you found him?" I said to Irving.

"No," he said. "We don't know where he is. We don't know what to do."

"I'll tell you what to do," I said. "Call Terry Young and Lulu and Bozo Costantino and Al Pennino and anybody else you can think of from the old neighborhood. Tell them to form a posse and go out and find him, because he'll be hiding out somewhere in one of his old haunts. Tell them to have him call you, or come up here."

The four I had named were lightweight fighters of the time. Terry Young had brought Graziano, while he was running from the Army, to Irving, and we waited while Irving made some phone calls.

"They'll look for him," Irving said when he came off the phone, "but I don't know."

"Now call the Capitol Hotel," I said, "and reserve a suite for five o'clock. Then tell the Garden to call the news services and all the papers, and tell them that Rocky Graziano will hold a press conference at the Capitol at six o'clock."

"But what if we don't find him?" Irving said.

"Please, Irving," I said, "don't worry about that now. We've got almost six hours, and if he doesn't show, you will."

I went out and had a sandwich, and then I walked over to the boxing office at the Garden to be sure they had made the calls to the sports desks of papers and the news services. It was about three o'clock when I got back to Irving Cohen's office, and we sat around there for another hour, waiting for the phone to ring.

"What do we do now?" Irving said.

"Well, we sit and hope," I said. "We've still got two hours, but if he doesn't show, you will. You'll go over to the Capitol, and you'll speak for him. You know, as well or better than I, that he's not equipped to fight now, and you'll tell them that. You'll say that if he had hurt his hand or had some other injury, a physical examination would reveal that, and the fight would be postponed. The hurt that has been done him outside the ring, however, doesn't show up in an exam, but it has left him so emotionally and mentally disturbed that he is now as ill-equipped to fight as if he had a physical ailment. You'll say it wouldn't be fair to those who'd pay the money to see him fight Apostoli or anyone else right now. You'll say that, and you'll say you'll make whatever amends you have to make to Jimmy Murray for whatever expenses he's had setting up and promoting the fight."

"That's right," Irving said. "We will."

"Good," I said.

"But I don't think I can say all that," Irving said.

"Of course you can," I said.

"No," Irving said, shaking his head. "That's the truth. He's in no condition to fight, but I'll never be able to say it, to explain it like that. I won't get it right."

"All right," I said. "I'll write it out for you."

I sat down at a typewriter there, and I wrote five or six paragraphs and I handed the two pages to him. He read them and folded them and put them in his pocket, and at about five o'clock the phone rang, and Irving picked it up.

"Good!" I heard him say. "Where is he? Good. Now listen. Tell him to be at the Capitol Hotel by six o'clock. We have a suite there in my name. Tell him it's a press conference. Tell him to be sure to be there at six o'clock. You have that? At the Capitol Hotel, across from the Garden, at six o'clock. Good."

He put the phone back on the cradle and he looked up, smiling.

"They found him," he said. "They're going to tell him to be sure to be there. Now I just hope he shows up."

Yes, I was thinking, and he may not. With all he has gone through, and all he has taken, he may just decide that it is hopeless, and go over the hill again.

At 5:30 Irving Cohen left for the Capitol, and just before six o'clock Teddy Brenner and I followed. The suite was at the end of a floor, and they were all there waiting. At 6:30, we were still waiting.

"Come on now, Irving," one of them said, finally. "What's going on? Where the hell is he?"

"He's on his way, I'm sure," Irving said. "I'm sorry to hold you up, but I'm sure he'll be here."

"But when?" somebody else said. "You call us all in here and there's no fighter. We've got deadlines to meet, and we can't sit around here all night. What are we supposed to do now?"

"Well," Irving said, "I've got a statement here, if you'd like me to read it."

"Hell, yes," somebody else said. "Read it. At least give us something."

He took the pages out of his pocket and unfolded them and started to read. Jack Hand of the Associated Press and I were half sitting together on a radiator cover, like all the others taking notes, and he knew how close I was to the fighter and he nudged me.

"Did you write this?" he said.

"Hell no," I said, going on with my note-taking. "I'm a stranger to it too."

"It sure sounds like you," he said.

When Irving finished they started the questions. We were clustered around Irving and the door to the hall was still open, and then I heard someone say it.

"Here he comes now."

He came through the door and into the suite. He had on a beautiful camel's hair polo coat, but there was a growth of several days beard on his face and under the coat he wore an old woolen shirt and dirty slacks and there were heavy road work shoes on his feet.

"I'm with my friends," he said.

Only some of them were his friends, but he had stopped just inside the door, and now he held both hands out. You could hear every breath in the room.

"What happened, Rocky?" one of them said. "What's the matter?"

"It's like I got a scar on my face," he said, staring through them and bringing his right hand up to his right cheek. "Why don't they leave me alone, or put me in jail?"

He always spoke from where he lived, and that did it. It did it in the papers the next day. *Collier's* picked it up from the papers and ran two autobiographical pieces, and the following September, his New York State license was restored. He fought Charley Fusari in the Polo Grounds and stopped him in the tenth round while I, doing a magazine piece about what it is like to be a fighter's wife, walked the streets of Brooklyn with Norma, her mother, and a friend of theirs. On the nights he fought, she could not bear to stay in the house.

They live now in a yellow-brick high-rise apartment house on the southeast corner of Fifty-seventh Street and Second Avenue in what, with the construction that went up there right after World War II, became one of the more fashionable sections of the city. Under the canopy a slim, rather tall woman of late middle years, precise and imperious in a light tan and brown pants suit and wearing a wide-brimmed, buff take-off—maybe by Don Kline or Adolpho—of a man's fedora, was standing. At her feet were three pieces of matched tan luggage, and the uniformed doorman was walking the street toward the corner, blowing his whistle and waving his right arm and trying to flag down a cab.

I watched him, when he had finally got one, trot along beside the cab to the canopy and then help the cabbie load the luggage into the trunk. Then he ushered the woman into the back seat and shut the door, and I followed him into the lobby.

"Rocky Graziano," I said, and I gave him my name. He picked up the phone and talked into it and turned back to me.

"You can go right up," he said. "It's 16-G, like in Graziano."

Not B, like in Barbella, I was thinking, walking to the elevator. He was born Rocco Barbella, one of seven children, three of whom died in infancy, of an alcoholic, often unemployed father and a mentally and emotionally disturbed mother who was in and out of institutions. While he was running from the Army, he took the name of one of those he used to run with in the streets.

"Whatever became of the original Graziano?" I had asked him the last time I had seen him, some dozen years before now.

"In the can," he said, "doing twenty to thirty. He was like a three-time loser. You know?"

I knew that while he was fighting, Irving Cohen had made him buy annuities, and that, beyond that, he himself had been doing very well. I would catch him occasionally on TV with Martha Raye, once with Cesar Romero and Margaret Truman. His autobiography, *Somebody Up There Likes Me,* had headed the best-seller lists, and off it they had made the movie starring Paul Newman, who caught the sullen moods but not the exuberance that made the fighter exciting just walking down the street.

"I just made The Big One," he told me that day.

"The Big One?" I said. "What's that."

"A million bucks."

"You're worth a million?" I said.

"Yeah," he said. "My accountant just told me. How about that?"

When I got off the elevator now he was standing there in a black knitted, short-sleeved sports shirt, gray slacks, and black loafers. The lines in his face were deeper, the full head of hair was still black but graying at the temples. We shook hands, smiling at each other and voicing greetings. He led me down the hall to the apartment where, when he opened the door and led me in, a dog, light-brown and knee-high, came toward me, it's head going and sniffing at me and blocking my way.

"He won't hurt you," he said. "He's a Lab."

"Lab's don't hurt you?" I said, the dog still sniffing at me.

"Yeah," he said. "C'mere, Plumber! The guy who give him to me is in the plumbing business, so I named him Plumber."

He led me through the small foyer and into the living room. Sunlight was coming through sliding glass doors that open onto a terrace, and he motioned me toward the sofa with a coffee table in front of it. As he sat down in a chair across the table from me, we could hear a metallic rattling coming from beyond the dining area in what I presumed to be the kitchen.

"Excuse me," he said, getting up. "It's Plumber. He wants me to give him some water."

He got up, and I could hear him filling the pan. As he came back and sat down I could hear the dog lapping the water.

"Every morning," he said, "he gets me up six o'clock, six-thirty. He wants me to take him out, so I take him out. I go to sleep early, like nine, ten o'clock. You want a beer?"

"No," I said, "but thanks."

"I don't eat," he said, "but I'm drinkin' twenty beers a day. "No pasta, no bread, no candy, no ice cream, but I'm drinkin' beer."

"You look good," I said. "I've talked with Norma on the phone. How is she?"

"My Jew?" he said. "Good. She's fine."

"You were lucky," I said. "You married a Jew and you had a Jewish manager, and they made you save your money."

"You're right," he said. "That's right, my wife and my manager."

"How are the girls?" I said.

Audrey must have been about three when he fought Zale in Chicago. She was in a crib in one of the bedrooms of that hotel suite there, and after the fight the noise of the celebration in the sitting room awakened her and she began to cry. When he went in to her and bent over the crib, she looked up at that face with the swelling around one eye and the bandage above the other.

"Daddy, what happened?" she said.

"You see what I mean now?" he said. "Stay out of the gutter."

"Audrey's good," he said now. "Her husband manufactures watches, and they got a boy two and a half named Aaron—Aaron Weissman—and they live downstairs. Roxie's husband manufactures cloth in the garment center, and they got a boy, Allen, about ten."

The dog was at the door now, barking.

"Plumber!" he said, and then to me, "Somebody must be in the hallway. He'll stop in a minute, but you got to see this."

He got up and walked toward the glass doors. On the floor, to one side, was a bronze statuette of a boxer, poised to throw a straight right hand.

"It looks like a Joe Brown," I said, kneeling to examine it. "I don't mean the ex-lightweight champ, but the sculptor in residence at Princeton University."

"You got to write this," he said. "Muhammad Ali. They give him this, the Garden did, for somethin'. He said, 'I ain't gonna take it. That's a white man.'"

"It is," I said.

"So he don't take it, and I'm at the Garden and Teddy Brenner tells me the story and I said, 'I'll take it.' I took the plaque off, but it's a guy gettin' ready to throw a right hand, and I used to throw a right hand."

"I'll say you did," I said.

That right hand and the anger he put into it against all those opponents who, to him, personified the society against which he was making his fight made him the fighter he was. He had put it in words in his dressing room in the Chicago Stadium after he had knocked out Zale, and he was still unwinding and they had him in a corner, their pencils and papers out and making notes.

"I wanted to kill him," he said. "I got nothin' against him. He's a nice guy. I like him, but I wanted to kill him."

Sixteen months before, he had fought Marty Servo in the Garden. Servo had just knocked out Freddy "Red" Cochrane to win the welterweight title, but this was over that weight, and now in the second round Servo had already been down twice and Graziano had him against the ropes. With his open left glove under Servo's chin he was holding Servo's head up, and with his right he was clubbing him again and again until Servo went down the third time and they stopped it.

After I had written my piece and got back to the apartment, I still hadn't got rid of it. One of the reasons we write is to try to unburden ourselves of the weight of what we see and hear and feel, to get it all out, but the brutality and viciousness of that haunted me so that for hours I tossed, unable to get to sleep.

Two years later, after that press conference in the Capitol Hotel, Graziano and Irving Cohen and Teddy Brenner and I were going out to eat. The fighter was leading us down Eighth Avenue, walking with those quick, nervous, swinging strides.

"Where are we going?" I said to Irving Cohen.

"We're going to that place where Marty Servo tends bar," Irving said. "Rocky likes him, and he always tries to bring business into the place."

Servo was never a fighter again after that beating. He had to give up his welterweight title and the security it could have brought him without ever defending it, and now, when we walked into the place, he was standing behind the bar. He had on a white jacket, and when he saw us his face brightened and he leaned over the bar to shake hands. When he shook hands with Graziano he smiled and faked as if to hook with his left. Graziano leaning over the bar, stuck his left hand under Servo's chin as he had that night, and he faked to throw the right. Then the two of them dropped their hands and laughed.

"Every once in a while," I was saying to him now, and we were seated again, "I see you on a TV commercial. Do you do a lot of those?"

"Oh, jeeze," he said, "I done Coldene. I done Brioski. American Motors. Chrysler Motors. Cadillac. I do Ford Motors. What's that breakfast thing?"

"I don't know."

"Post Cereals," he said. "Lee Miles Transmissions. I do mostly television, so friggin' many. Then I just do verce-over—*voice* over —for Honeycomb Cereal."

"You must have a good agent," I said.

"I got no friggin' agent," he said. "I'm a free lance. I do the "Mike Douglas Show" twice a month. I got a contract. Let me get a friggin' cigar. You want a cigar?"

"No," I said, "but thanks anyway."

When he came back he had the cigar, lighted, in his mouth. He handed me a glossy print of a picture taken of himself with Richard Nixon in the White House and a leather-bound folio.

"That's a movie I made with Frank Sinatra in 1967," he said. "They give me the script. Then I do a lot of convention shows. Olin Mathieson. Pearl Burey . . ."

"Brewery?"

"Yeah. Country Club Malt Liquor. Commercials, and they have a convention. Then I lecture at colleges and high schools."

The last time I had seen him he had told me that, in schools, he gave talks on juvenile delinquency, and that he had just lectured on criminology at Fordham University. I asked him what he said.

"I spoke to all the kids who were graduatin'," he said, "and a lot of elderly people, like professors and priests."

"But what did you tell them?" I said.

"You know what it is," he said. "I start out, whether I'm talkin' about criminology or juvenile delinquency, and I say, 'You know, I'm so glad my father took the boat, because this is the best country in the world, and if there was another country like this one, I'd be jealous.'"

"Then what do you tell them?" I said.

"I say, 'If you're a juvenile delinquent, two things will solve your problem. All you need is a good alibi and a good lawyer.' Then I tell 'em about the guys I knew went to the chair, and I tell 'em about *Somebody Up There Likes Me,* how they made the movie and about the book."

"So these days," I was saying now, "what do you tell them when you lecture?"

"I say, 'I'm very glad to be here on this occasion. I couldn't be with nicer people.' Then I give a couple of jokes, like a comedian. I'm a comedian. I think I am."

"I'm remembering," I said, "something that Irving Cohen's wife said to me once. I've forgotten her name."

"Jean," he said. "They live in Arizona now."

"It was the night before the Zale fight in Chicago," I said. "She had stopped by the suite in that hotel, and at one point you stood up. You walked across the room to go into the next room, and she said to me, 'You know, there's something about that boy. There's an electricity, a vitality, about him, so I have the feeling that, whatever he does, he'll make a success of it.'"

"She said that?"

"Yes, and she was the first one to spot it. I used to think of that when I'd see you on TV with Martha Raye. You were lucky twice in your life and in two careers. As a fighter you came along in Tony Zale's time, and you two meshed like gears, and made great fights. Then in television, who else could you have made such a partnership with but Martha Raye?"

"Yeah," he said. "That's right."

"How did she discover you?"

"She didn't discover me," he said. "It was her writer, Nat Hiken. A guy calls my manager. I was in Stillman's, and the guy comes over. He says, 'My name is Nat Hiken. You got an agent?' I said, 'I got a friggin' manager named Irving Cohen.' He says, 'We're lookin' maybe to put you on the Martha Raye show. We're looking for a boy friend for Martha Raye.'

"What Nat Hiken told me was some guy says, 'Get some stupid guy like Rocky Graziano.' Nat says, 'Why not get Rocky Graziano?' The guy says, 'He can't talk. He can't read.' Hiken says, 'I'll go see him.'

"I go to his office. I meet Marlon Brando, and they give me a friggin' stupid script. Big words I can't pronounce. Hiken says, 'Don't worry. The public doesn't know what the script is.' I go on and the guys are sayin', 'Great! Great!' I was playin' myself."

"You always did," I said, "and I've often thought that it all goes back to Frank Percoco, and that two-bit piece. If he doesn't break that swelling under your eye, you don't see. If you don't see, you don't win the title. If you don't win the title, none of this happens."

"Yeah," he said, "and they did the identical same thing in the picture *Rocky*. Since the picture came out, kids nine or ten think I'm that Rocky."

"And I've never heard," I said, "of twenty-five cents that was parlayed into as much as that quarter Frank Percoco happened to have in his pocket. What's he doing now?"

"He's retired," he said. "He's got a little house on Staten Island he bought about thirty years ago."

"And Whitey's gone," I said, "and he saved your life that night."

"Yeah," he said.

It was after the fight, during that celebration in that hotel suite. The fighter had walked into that bedroom when he had heard the child crying, and he had bent over the crib and talked to her. Then, because it was so stifling hot and humid there, he had walked to a window to open it wider. As he tried to raise it, Whitey, walking into the room, started to do it for him. At that moment the window flew up and the fighter fell forward over the sill, and Whitey grabbed him around the thighs as he was about to plunge the ten stories to the street. Had he gone to his death, I am sure they would have surmised in the papers, the climate of public opinion being what it was at the time, that he had double-crossed the mob by beating Zale and been thrown or pushed, because another of his managers was Eddie Coco, who had a record of twelve arrests and known mob connections.

"And Eddie Coco," I said now. "The last I knew, he was doing twenty to life for killing that parking lot attendant in Miami."

"He got out," he said, "but he's back in again."

"What for this time?"

"He got caught shylocking. He was on light parole."

"I'm remembering," I said, "when you ran out on that Apostoli fight in California. No one knew where you were, and I got Irving Cohen to get Terry Lulu and Bozo Costantino and Al Pennino to find you for that press conference. What are they doing now?"

"Terry Young got shot and killed," he said. "Lulu's still got the bar at Thirteenth Street and Second Avenue, and Al Pennino is workin' on the docks."

"And you've moved about three miles north."

"But it's still the East Side," he said. "I say I had three careers. A robbin' career, a fightin' career, and an actin' career. Listen. Can we do this in a restaurant?"

"Sure," I said. "Anywhere you say."

"I got to save my table," he said, getting up.

"But before we go," I said, "can you just show me around for a minute?"

"Sure," he said, sliding open the glass door to the terrace and leading me out. "We got four-and-a-half rooms, and we got this wrap-around terrace, and we got all these plants and these trees here and . . ."

He had led me back through the living room again and into the foyer. He was starting into the bedroom.

"Wait a minute," I said. "I want to see these paintings."

On one wall of the small foyer there were a half dozen framed oils. One was a copy of Picasso's *Girl Before a Mirror* and there was another of his *Three Musicians,* and there was a French Impressionist street scene.

"Where did you get these paintings?" I said.

"I done 'em," he said, and then, indicating them, "Rocky done this one. Rocky done that one . . ."

"These two are Picasso copies," I said.

"Yeah," he said. "I copied them, when I couldn't afford to buy 'em. I like his painting."

"What about this street scene?"

"Like in Greenwich Village," he said. "My grandmother and grandfather had a place on Bleecker Street, and I done that."

"These are good, Rock," I said. "They really are."

"Yeah," he said. "I draw fairly well, like a fighter, but it comes out good."

"It does," I said, "but I didn't know you could paint."

"When I was in the reformatory," he said, "I went to art school. I learned to mix colors, and I paint friggin' good."

"I'm impressed."

"Then I got all these books," he said, sweeping an arm toward the book shelves. "I got letters from Presidents. I got more plaques than Jesus Christ. I got them all in the what-do-you-call-it —the basement?"

"Right."

"Listen," he said. "We got to go."

"Sure."

He led me out and I followed him to the elevator. He pushed the button and we waited.

"I've just been up to Brockton," I said, because I knew he and Rocky Marciano had been close friends. "I saw his mother and his brother Peter."

"Yeah," he said. "How are they doin'?"

"They're doing all right," I said, and the elevator had come and we got in and started down, "but they can't find Marciano's money."

"What money?" he said.

"All the money he made," I said. "They can't find it, and they think he may have buried it somewhere."

"There wasn't any money," he said.

He was leading me out of the elevator now, and through the

lobby and out onto the street. He gave the doorman a wave, and started toward Second Avenue.

"What do you mean, there wasn't any money?" I said.

"Hey, Rock!" someone, passing us, said.

"Hey!" he said, turning and waving, and then to me, "The guy lost his money."

"He lost his money?" I said. "How do you know he lost his money?"

At the news stand near the corner he stopped and gave the dealer a quick hand shake.

"C'mon," he said to me. "We got to make this light."

We crossed the street, hurrying, and we started south on Second Avenue. He was walking with those quick strides, and at Fifty-fifth Street we turned west. Just before we reached the corner at Third Avenue, he opened the side door of P. J. Clarke's and led me in. P. J. Clarke's is an old saloon and restaurant that has been there for ninety years and looks it, and that, for the last fifteen or so, has attracted a mix of celebrities in politics, entertainment, and the *haute monde,* and those who want to be around them.

He led me to the small table just inside the door where his friend Phil Kennedy who, Graziano was to tell me, "sells telephones for Electronics, Inc.," was sitting, and he introduced us. Kennedy's jacket was hung over the back of his chair, and he had been making a list on a yellow pad in front of him on the red and white checked tablecloth.

"This used to be Frank Costello's table," Graziano said, as we sat down. "We get it every day. I want a beer. You want a drink?"

He waved to a waiter, shirt-sleeved and in a white apron, and he gave him the order.

"Back to Marciano," I said, and then to Phil Kennedy, "We were just talking about Rocky Marciano and . . ."

"Some fighter," Kennedy said. "I'd have liked to have seen him in there with Ali."

". . . and his family," I said, "can't find his money."

"He lost it," Graziano said.

"How do you know that?" I said.

"I was with him," he said. "Out on Long Island. A real estate deal. He signed for four hundred thousand, and the deal went bust. His name was on the paper, so it was his money."

"They don't know that in Brockton," I said.

"How can they know?" he said. "I mean they're good people up there, but what do they know about things like that? It's different around here than it is in Brockton. You know?"

"But he was so close with his money," I said.

"Yeah," he said. "Listen to this. I'm goin' to California, and when I walk through the plane to the first class, he's sittin' in the coach. The guy just retired. You know? So I say hello, and when I sit down in the first class I say to the stewardess, 'Rocky Marciano is back there.' She says, 'Rocky Marciano? He is?' So I tell the stewardess to tell the captain we got plenty of seats in the first class, and he sits next to me.

"Now we get off the plane, and I get my luggage. I say to him, 'Where's yours?' He says, 'I don't have none. I don't need luggage.' So we walk to get a cab, and I say to him, 'Where are you stayin'?' He says, 'I think I'll stay with you.' I said, 'Great!' I mean, it's good for me too.

"I'm stayin' at the Beverly Hills Hotel, and the guy has just what he's wearin'. I got some nice knits, so now he's wearin' my shirts, and the guy was bigger than I was, so he stretched them so I couldn't wear them no more. He used my tooth brush."

"You're kidding," Kennedy said.

"So help me God," Graziano said, raising his hand. "Then I used to leave to go to work—I was doin' a show—and one day I come back and they call me from the desk. They say, 'You know, Mr. Graziano, your room is free here, but not the long distance phone calls. We have to pay the telephone company for those calls.' I said, 'What calls? I didn't make any long distance phone calls.' She said, 'Oh yes. There's calls to Brockton, Massachusetts, and Florida.' I said, 'Wait a minute. That's the other Rocky.' The guy must have made two hundred phone calls."

"That's almost unbelievable," Kennedy said.

"We'd make personal appearances together," Graziano said. "We'd be sittin' up there at some dinner, and he'd say to me, 'Ask if anybody's got a private plane.' He was a nervous guy. He wanted to get out. Go. Go. Half the time he didn't know where we were goin' next. It used to embarrass me, but I'd have to say, 'If anybody's got a private plane, Rocky Marciano and I want to go to our next appearance.' Then some guy would take us."

"And that's the way he went in the end," I said.

"Yeah," Graziano said. "Too friggin' bad. You want another drink."

"No, thanks," I said.

He had summoned the waiter, and he ordered another beer.

"You know," Kennedy said, nodding toward him, "this guy is very popular."

"I know," I said, "and I remember when he wasn't."

"Yeah, Bill knows me a long time," he said, "and you know somethin'? Jacqueline Kennedy was in here the other day, and she gave me three kisses and a hug. Here. Right here, in P. J. Clarke's."

"I've seen him," Kennedy said, laughing, "kiss Elizabeth Taylor, Jacqueline Kennedy. He's very hugable."

"Yeah," Graziano said. "Everybody likes me. The black people, all over the country, for some stupid reason, like me."

"He went to Astoria one night," Kennedy said, "and he stood them on their heads. Five hundred drinking Irish cops. The Irish Archie Bunkers with badges."

"All Irish cops," Graziano said, "and I'm an Italian."

"And had your troubles with cops," I said.

"There was a collegiate poll," Kennedy said. "You know who was the most popular in the country? Ralph Nader, and this guy was sixth."

"Yeah," Graziano said. "I was never in San Antonio, Texas, in my life. I get off the plane and they throw a red friggin' blanket out for me to walk on. It just amazes me. I get in a 747 plane to go to California. The captains says, 'I'm flyin' at such and such a speed, and we got Mr. Rocky Graziano aboard. Have a drink in honor of Mr. Rocky Graziano.' Yesterday I was sittin' down with the diplomat from Cuba, and I'm goin' there in three weeks. He invited me."

We talked for a while then, while he had two more beers, about fighters and fights we remember. When we were joined by a couple of others, and the conversation became provincial, revolving around their circle of acquaintances who are strangers to me, I got up and shook hands around the table and, when he stood up, with him.

"You got everything you want to know?" he said.

"Everything," I said.

"You sure?"

"I'm sure."

"If there's anything else," he said, "call me at home, but call me before eight o'clock in the morning. After that I'm not there."

"I know," I said.

Out on Third Avenue sunlight bathed the now open street that, in the old days, was roofed and darkened by the El now long gone. The sidewalk was crowded with office workers, young clerical and junior executive types, in twos and threes, gesticulating as they talked and walked down their lunches, and by secretaries hurrying to get back.

At Fifty-third Street I was one block from the four-story, walk-up apartment house on the corner of Second Avenue, its exterior bricks painted a battleship gray, where my wife and I lived when I started to write sports after I came back from the war that day and my hand shook so that I had to quiet it before I could press the button in the entry. It was there that we used to battle the mice that came up the two floors from the market on the street level, and it was there that I tossed that night, so appalled by the animalism I had seen in the fighter as he had clubbed down Marty Servo whom he liked. It was there, too, that I brought all my troubles, as I tried to be somebody by being with those who were, and found that their aspirations and their problems became mine.

How many miles I had flown by now and how many miles I had driven to see those I had wanted to see again, I don't know. I had saved Rocky Graziano for last, and I had seen them all now, and so, after all those miles, I didn't walk the last block. Are they still battling the mice? I don't know. My battle would be the same battle it has been for all the years, to try to put it all down—the way it looked and how they looked and what they said and how they said it—and to try to get it as right as I could get it in this book.